MASTERPLOTS
1964 ANNUAL

1964 ANNUAL

Essay-Reviews of 100 Outstanding Books
Published in the United States During 1963

Edited by
FRANK N. MAGILL

Associate Editor
DAYTON KOHLER

SALEM PRESS
INCORPORATED
NEW YORK

LIST OF TITLES

v

vii

PREFACE

MASTERPLOTS 1964 ANNUAL is the tenth volume to be published in the Masterplots Annual series, and it rounds out a decade of reviewing and reporting on one thousand outstanding books published in the United States since 1954. As usual, this volume deals with many subjects besides fiction. Categories covered include fiction, 54 titles; history, 13 titles; poetry, 11; biography, 9; letters, 3; literary criticism, 2; memoirs, 1; drama, 1; natural science, 1; philosophy, 1; sermons, 1; miscellaneous, 3.

An innovation that will be found for the first time in the Masterplots Annual is the identifying signature of the contributor who prepared each individual article. In last year's volume, although articles were not individually signed, the names of the contributing staff members were shown in the front section of the book—with three glaring exceptions, for which apologies are in order. Though each contributed several articles to the 1963 Annual, the names of Gordon W. Clarke of Eastern Oregon College, Willis Knapp Jones of Miami University, and William Tillson of Purdue University were inadvertently omitted from the list of contributors. What makes these omissions especially embarrassing is the fact that Drs. Clarke, Jones, and Tillson are among the oldest of all Masterplots staff members in point of service. Dr. Clarke was among the first to become associated with the Masterplots project as the result of an interview at the University of Illinois in 1948. Dr. Jones was sought out in the early 1950's to help with Latin-American drama. Dr. Tillson also joined the staff about ten years ago.

It is always a pleasure to discuss good first novels because they hold out the hope that a new talent is in the process of mastering the intricacies of the novel. Several such efforts appeared during the year, including Ask AT THE UNICORN by Norman Thomas; Susan Sontag's THE BENEFACTOR; THE COLLECTOR, a chilling horror story by John Fowles; Yves Berger's THE GARDEN, a beautiful, imaginative work by a French critic and teacher still in his twenties; THE SAND PEBBLES, an adventure story of the Yangtze area during the 1920's, and the Harper Prize Novel winner for 1963, by Richard

McKenna; Paul Brodeur's THE SICK FOX; THE TIN DRUM by the impressive young German writer Günter Grass, whose second novel, CAT AND MOUSE, also appeared in this country in 1963; and Thomas Pynchon's V., winner of the William Faulkner Foundation's award for 1963.

Other novels of note reviewed in this year's Annual include AFTERNOON MEN, Anthony Powell's first novel, originally published in 1931; Nobel Prize winner Ivo Andrić's BOSNIAN CHRONICLE; John Updike's THE CENTAUR, which won the National Book Award for fiction; Guimarães Rosa's highly praised epic of Brazilian outlaws, THE DEVIL TO PAY IN THE BACKLANDS; THE EDGE OF THE STORM by Agustín Yáñez, a story of rural Mexico first published in 1947 (Al filo del agua); Ford Madox Ford's 1908 version of Henry VIII's brief marriage to Katharine Howard, now published in this country for the first time; THE GIFT, another example of Vladimir Nabokov's keen insight and superior writing ability; THE GIRLS OF SLENDER MEANS, about which the same remark can be made for Muriel Spark; THE GROUP, wherein Mary McCarthy, stiletto dripping, moves relentlessly among seven of her pitiable creations until all motion ceases; THE UNICORN, Iris Murdoch's ambitious, nervy effort that may become a classic; and John Cheever's THE WAPSHOT SCANDAL, Dayton Kohler's essay-review of which begins on page 290 and is recommended reading.

A number of excellent short story collections appeared during the year, among them volumes by Joyce Carol Oates—her first collection—John O'Hara, Thomas Williams, Doris Lessing, Reynolds Price, Caroline Gordon, Cecil Dawkins, and Graham Greene.

Volumes of poetry that attracted attention in 1963 included, among others, collections by Vernon Watkins, Denise Levertov, E. E. Cummings, John Logan, May Swenson, first volumes by Frederick Seidel and by Martin Halpern, and a long narrative poem by Evan S. Connell, Jr. During the year other books of poetry meriting attention also appeared, notably an enlarged edition of Mark Van Doren's COLLECTED POEMS and the SELECTED POEMS of John Crowe Ransom, winner of a National Book Award. These have not been discussed in the present volume, however, because they contained no material marking a new advance in the work of either writer.

Outstanding books on history published in 1963 include F. W. Deakin's THE BRUTAL FRIENDSHIP, a careful study of the Hitler-Mussolini relationship during World War II; the second volume of Shelby Foote's trilogy on the Civil War; Edward Crankshaw's fascinating picture of the end of the Habsburg influence in Europe; Cecil Woodham-Smith's careful analysis of the great nineteenth century Irish famine; Barrie Pitt's excellent study of the final year of World War I; an exhaustive background study of the Battle of Verdun by Alastair Horne; Klaus Mehnert's analysis of the struggle between Peking and Moscow; and two quite different studies of the Cumberland area of the United States.

There were excellent biographies of Dostoevsky, Francis Bacon, General George C. Marshall, Pierre Laval, Keats, Byron's wife Annabella Milbanke, Giuseppe Verdi, and the Duchess of Suffolk. Letters of F. Scott Fitzgerald and the letters of Robert Frost to Louis Untermeyer also appeared in book form, as well as another volume of Boswell's papers.

Two superior books of literary criticism were published in 1963: THE FARAWAY COUNTRY by Louis D. Rubin, Jr., and Cleanth Brooks' astute survey of William Faulkner's works. Miscellaneous volumes of note include a revised edition of Ignazio Silone's THE SCHOOL FOR DICTATORS, Albert Camus' NOTEBOOKS: 1935-1942, a book of sermons by Paul Tillich, and a fascinating study of deep undersea life by Jacques-Yves Cousteau.

The confines of time and space limit our coverage to a fraction of the many fine books published in 1963, but we trust the thirty-three contributors to this volume have provided a body of comment and criticism that will be useful to all who are interested in examining one hundred of the most enduring works the year produced.

FRANK N. MAGILL

CONTRIBUTING REVIEWERS FOR 1964 ANNUAL

Stephen Barney

Jonathan Baumbach

Joseph L. Blotner

James Boatwright

Fred Bornhauser

Michael Campbell

Gordon W. Clarke

J. Perry Cochran

R. H. W. Dillard

Philip Evanson

George Garrett

Frank K. Gibson

Max Halperen

Robert Hazel

G. Burke Johnston

Willis Knapp Jones

John P. Kirby

A. Sidney Knowles, Jr.

Dayton Kohler

Howard Mackey

David Madden

Frank N. Magill

Donald L. Mull

Preston Newman

Robert T. Robertson

William R. Robinson

John Rodenbeck

Earl H. Rovit

Margaret Bowman Tilghman

Tench Francis Tilghman

William Tillson

Harvey Curtis Webster

Charles Workman

AFFINITIES

Author: Vernon Watkins (1906-   )
Publisher: New Directions (New York). 99 pp. $3.50
Type of work: Poetry

   A new collection of poems by a Welsh poet of solid achievement and great promise

Although Vernon Watkins has published four volumes of his own poetry, plus a translation of Heinrich Heine's *Die Nordsee,* his long association with Dylan Thomas has, quite unfairly, resulted in the overshadowing of his own reputation as a poet, so that he has been reduced almost to a footnote in the Thomas biography. The national background shared by the two men serves to intensify the tendency to bracket them as "Welsh poets" who must be compared; and in the comparison, the bravura Thomas personality and the Thomas legend, now rapidly crystallizing, give the latter a great advantage.

To venture prophecies about the future of literary reputations is a task filled with danger, for it is not given to many to have the prophet's cloak cast upon them; yet the guess might be made that, in the long pull, Watkins may emerge as the better and more enduring poet. We are still bedazzled by the impact of Thomas' personality, still under the spell of the lyric voice and the wild rush of words. Thomas has had upon many readers the same hypnotic effect that Swinburne had upon his contemporaries: they are so carried away by the verbal gymnastics that they are blinded to the fact that all this language is essentially empty, that the seemingly inspired poet is really saying little. In addition, there was Thomas' annoying, perhaps deliberate, carelessness: his refusal to write sentences that could be parsed or to insert the conventional punctuation that might have clarified his meanings.

Such comments as the foregoing serve only as a kind of negative approach to Watkins: to say what he is *not* rather than what he *is.* Watkins is not a slapdash, lazy poet overwhelmed by words and content to let words be his master. One of the first of his characteristics that the reader notices is that he has a spare, tight style, that he is a craftsman who has control of the medium by means of which he works. This statement does not mean that his poetry is "easy" in the sense that this term can be applied to many poems of the last century, for what modern poetry is easy? Perhaps it cannot be so. John Press has written an unusually interesting book on this subject, yet even he was compelled to walk a tightrope in his effort to separate "deliberate and perverse" obscurity from the obscurity that inevitably arises from the nature of the poet's experience. But at least Watkins is free from the current fashion of the esoteric image, the obscure reference, the private language.

The two "affinities" of his title would seem to be art—perhaps, more narrowly, poetry—and nature. As might be expected, the "nature" part of the volume deals with his region of England, Wales and Cornwall: the remembered valleys and waterfalls, the town of Swansea, "tossed by the wave of time to a hill," or the gray Atlantic waves breaking on the Cornish coast, the voice of a stream heard under hazel

1

trees in the autumn. One of the most beautiful poems in the volume, "Music of Colour," falls into this group. Written in Sapphics—not often a successful form in English—it is a kaleidoscope of the scents, sounds, and, above all, the colors of high summer in a wood haunted by the footsteps of Eurydice. This is summer, "this perennial wonder. . . . True for this moment, therefore never dying." It is a truly beautiful poem that catches and holds, as in a clear glass, the essence of a summer day shimmering with heat. Yet the poet knows that in autumn at Michaelmas "the stream understands the leaves/ Better than in high summer."

Watkins seems haunted by the image of autumn leaves falling upon running water—time hurrying all things away. And here, perhaps, lies a point that might be suggested in connection, not only with Watkins, but with many contemporary poets who use nature as a theme. For the Romantics of Wordsworth's time there existed an essential unity between man and nature; it was the task of man to rediscover and to establish this unity anew. But to the poet of our time, nature—no matter how deeply he may love or how beautifully he may describe her—is only a symbol, usually of the passing of time, of the inevitability of change:

A young moon hangs in space
But shines with a different meaning.

To the contemporary poet, cut off by modern civilization from any close contact with her, nature becomes so charged with symbolic meanings that he can no longer write of her in direct, simple terms. Wordsworth's primrose by a river's brim is, in very truth, far, far more to him than merely a yellow primrose. Thus it is that as we read the poems in this volume dealing with nature we often have the uneasy feeling that the poet is somehow struggling to say what he wants to say, that his lines are often clotted with meaning. Herein lies the difficulty of this kind of poetry, its effort to express the apparently simple yet very difficult paradox of man confronted by cyclical nature and fleeting time:

In the stream's watery glass
We pass, and do not pass.

It is the wheel and the stream.

To another aspect of the "affinities" suggested by the title belong the poems celebrating those poets of the past and of the present who have evidently meant much to the author: Charles Williams, T. S. Eliot, Dylan Thomas, Wordsworth, Keats, Heine, Hölderlin. These poems are exercises in "the noble art of praising," and in the verses that give the book its title the author expresses, in couplets in the style of Pope, his judgment:

In every smith whose work I come across
Tradition is the ore, fashion the dross,

a statement which places him in the great current of English poetry.

The longest of these poems, "The Childhood of Hölderlin," celebrates that strange German genius, long neglected and recently rediscovered by contemporary poets as part of the revaluation of nineteenth century literature. Hölderlin, whose closest English counterpart might be John Clare, was the archetype of the Romantic poet; following an unhappy love affair he went mad at the age of thirty-two and, after a brief period of lucidity, retired into mental darkness for the remaining thirty-seven years of his life. It is the figure of Hölderlin that draws together the two halves of the affinities: art and nature. Watkins deeply admires Hölderlin as a poet who "fashioned the shafts of the Odes/ a quiver of joy," an eccentric rejected by both Goethe and Schiller, yet a man whose "fragments outshine their accomplished works." Of Hölderlin it is usually said that he was chiefly concerned with the "polarity" of Greek epic and tragic poetry: the serene gods untroubled by fate and man inexorably bound by it. Watkins, however, places the German poet not only in the classic but also in the Christian tradition, for Hölderlin knew that

> Harmonious nature differs from exiled man.

The essential unity of man and nature, felt by the Romantics, was broken by the Fall. Yet could there be "A second genesis of the first Adam" with the primal harmony of the world restored, that unity would also be restored, and "Hölderlin's dream would live." In the figure of Hölderlin, then, Watkins seems to find a synthesis of the Greek and Christian traditions.

That Watkins is a genuinely religious poet is apparent from his earlier volume, *Cypress and Acacia*, published in 1959. In the present book there are several very beautiful religious poems: "Quem Quaeritis?" and "Five Poems of Magdalenian Darkness," for example, written in a simpler, more direct style than are the other poems in the volume and marked by deep sincerity. To most readers these will be the best-liked of the contents of *Affinities*.

This is unquestionably an outstanding collection of poems, though whether it marks an advance over *Cypress and Acacia* is open to debate. The poet's style seems to have become more involved, more closely woven; and perhaps there are too many poems in praise of other poets, generous as this praise may be. But there can be no doubt that Vernon Watkins is a very real poet who deserves to be better known.

Tench Francis Tilghman

AFTERNOON MEN

Author: Anthony Powell (1905-   )
Publisher: Little, Brown and Company (Boston). 221 pp. $4.00
Type of work: Novel
Time: Between the two World Wars, probably the 1920's
Locale: London and the country

A satiric treatment of Bohemian and semi-Bohemian painters, their mistresses, friends, and acquaintances

> Principal characters:
> WILLIAM ATWATER, a dilettante museum official
> SUSAN NUNNERY, the girl he wants
> VERELST, the man she goes off with
> RAYMOND PRINGLE, a bad painter
> HARRIET TWINING, briefly his mistress
> HECTOR BARLOW, a painter of moderate talent
> SOPHY, his mistress and model
> SCHEIGAN, an American publisher
> NAOMI RACE, a giver of dreadful parties

Wide attention and considerable acclaim have been given in recent years to Anthony Powell's series of novels called *The Music of Time*. *Afternoon Men*, published in England in 1931, will give some Americans their first opportunity to read Powell's first novel, a work in which he seems to be laying part of the groundwork for the series that followed.

As his epigraph, Powell prints part of a paragraph from Richard Burton's *The Anatomy of Melancholy* which describes "a company of giddy-heads, afternoon men. . . ." These men, and most of their companions, will seem quite familiar to readers acquainted with English fiction of the 1920's and 1930's. They will see dialogue suggesting that of the early Aldous Huxley and of Evelyn Waugh. There is even a touch of the atmosphere of Michael Arlen's *The Green Hat*, without, of course, that novel's heavy attempts at seriousness. The names of a number of characters—Susan Nunnery, Walter Brisket, Ethel Chalk, Wauchop, Un-

dershaft, Mrs. Beamish—will sound Huxleyan, although the house party which concludes the novel lacks the elegant decadence of those in early Huxley novels. The dialogue is from time to time witty, in a few places suggesting the ear for fatuous British speech displayed by E. M. Forster most strikingly in the passages of social comedy between Adela and Ronny in *A Passage to India*. This novel does not, however, pretend to the seriousness which forms the counterpoint for Forster and Huxley. Its preoccupation is the satiric depiction of the shallowness of these lives.

Through William Atwater we come to know the variegated circle. Failed twice for the Foreign Service, Atwater puts in time working at a museum and amuses himself only slightly if at all with friends such as Raymond Pringle. This young man's "early life had made him painfully inhibited and he was a naturally bad painter, but a dreadful veneer of slickness picked up in Paris made people buy his work occasionally." Powell himself works in acid: "Pringle never had much difficulty in getting shows as there was a small but obstinate public that bought his pictures, never enough to satisfy Pringle himself and only just enough to make it worth the gallery's while to give him another show, but never deserting him entirely." Hector Barlow is a more nearly successful painter who tries to exert a kind of dominance over Pringle. He is also in advance of him in that he possesses Sophy, an attractive mistress who doubles as his model, and he frequently tries to choose which of three women he should marry in order to be best supported while he paints. In the orbit of these men for longer or shorter periods are the elusive Susan Nunnery, the complaisant Harriet Twining, and an assortment of male grotesques. They include Frotheringham, the failure; Walter Brisket, the homosexual; Dr. J. Crutch, the crank; Wauchop, the successful painter-teacher, and Scheigan the American publisher, who might have come out of Nathanael West or been a cousin to Fitzgerald's Wolfsheim.

There is a certain amount of partner-changing before the principals go down to the country, near the seaside, to stay with Pringle in an uncomfortable rented house. Harriet becomes Pringle's mistress only to distress him by being caught in the act with Barlow. Pringle walks into the sea, leaving a suicide note behind on the cold beef set out for lunch. Harriet, unknowing, watches him from a distance, disparages his physique to Atwater, and then makes love with Atwater. Pringle's prolonged absence is found extremely tiresome by Mrs. Naomi Race, a giver of notoriously bad dinner parties who is distinguished by having known Rossetti. She browbeats the other guests into consuming the lunch in spite of their host's apparent demise. They have first considered the alternatives. "The table is laid," Harriet has observed. "We can eat the food now and call it lunch. Or we can eat it at half-past seven and call it supper." Finally even Atwater disapproves of Pringle. "I almost agree with Naomi Race," he remarks. "She says he's let us all down." When Pringle reappears no one is greatly surprised. There is considerable debate about the size of the gratuity to be given the man who fished him out of the water. Then later Harriet snuggles into Pringle's arm again.

By the time of their return to London, Atwater learns that Susan Nunnery, the only girl who can make him feel real emotion, has gone to America with Verelst, a man with considerable money and polish who looks—the rest assure one another—really very little like a Jew. Atwater sees ahead of him nothing but the boredom of his job, the tiresomeness of the repetitive parties, and the unchanging round of the social charade.

Powell's comedy may derive from the inane *mots* his characters deliver or from his penchant for recording their often amusingly fatuous conversation down to the last unnecessary repetition. Speaking of Sophy, Atwater confides to Pringle, "I could never be more than a friend to any fat girl." When Pringle tells Atwater that he and Harriet will probably be married, Atwater replies:

> 'Really?'
> 'Yes.'
> 'Congratulations.'
> 'Thanks,' said Pringle. 'We like each other a good deal.'
> Atwater said: 'That always makes

5

marriage more satisfactory, if you both like each other a lot.'

'We do.'

'I'm delighted to hear it.'

'I think she's lucky in a way.'

Occasionally the situations may verge on the ludicrous, but for the most part the humor is understated and brittle, like the characters themselves. To amuse himself, one suspects, Powell uses one running gag: he is Undershaft, who is now playing the piano and living with an Annamite woman in New York. The others talk about him frequently, but he neither appears nor affects the novel in any appreciable way.

This first novel was clearly the work of a professional, marked though it was by characteristics of others who had shaped much of the fiction of the period in which it appeared. Powell's admirers will not find it a vintage item, but they may see in it touches that foreshadow a sureness of style and subject to come later in *The Music of Time*.

Joseph L. Blotner

THE AGE OF LOUIS XIV

A History of European Civilization in the Period of Pascal, Molière, Cromwell, Milton, Peter the Great, Newton, and Spinoza: 1648-1715

Authors: Will (1885-   ) and Ariel Durant
Publisher: Simon and Schuster (New York). Illustrated. 802 pp. $10.00
Type of work: Cultural history
Time: 1648-1715
Locale: The continent of Europe and the British Isles

The history of European culture and the struggle between faith and reason during the reign of the Sun King of France

Principal personages:
LOUIS XIV, King of France
BLAISE PASCAL
MOLIÈRE
JEAN BAPTISTE RACINE
OLIVER CROMWELL
JOHN MILTON
JOHN DRYDEN
JONATHAN SWIFT
ISAAC NEWTON
PETER THE GREAT, Tsar of Russia
BARUCH SPINOZA

Will Durant has been writing for a long time. Early in the century, while teaching philosophy at Columbia University, he began, in a New York Presbyterian church, a program of biweekly lectures on history, philosophy, and literature that continued for thirteen years. Out of them grew a series of pamphlets published originally as "Little Blue Books" by Haldeman-Julius. Combined in one hard cover, in 1926, as *The Story of Philosophy*, the work

6

sold more than two million copies. Durant has also written an autobiographical novel, *Transition* (1927). But his chief interest has been *The Story of Civilization,* planned in ten volumes. This has been a gigantic undertaking, starting with *Our Oriental Heritage* (1935) and intended to conclude in 1968 with an account of the fall of the Bastille and the beginning of the French Revolution.

In the first six volumes, only Will Durant's name appeared as author, but with Volume VII, *The Age of Reason Begins* (1961), he acknowledged the collaboration of his wife. Volume VII embraces the eight decades between 1558 and 1642, covering the course of European civilization from Queen Elizabeth to the time of Galileo and dealing in extensive survey with such representative figures as Shakespeare, Bacon, Montaigne, and Rembrandt. The present volume continues the history of the Age of Reason as it clashes with the pursuit of faith by the Jansenists during the reign of the Sun King, Louis XIV of France. In this work, as in the earlier volumes, the reader must remember that from the first the writer is essentially a philosopher. Philosophers, along with poets and artists, are his greatest interest. Men of science also attract his admiration, but to concentrate on his idols he skimps political scientists and economists. Perhaps the best of the present volume are thirty-seven pages devoted to the reactionary Baruch Spinoza.

The Age of Louis XIV might be described as a series of loosely connected and uneven essays. The best are brilliant; some of the others are not particularly illuminating. Someone described one of his earlier volumes as a splendid superstructure on a rather shaky foundation. The description could also be applied here. Despite the ten-page bibliography of source books and the twenty-three pages of chapter notes, the wealth of scholarly research over this well-documented period has not been thoroughly utilized. However, the authors have not tried to start controversy or overturn previous concepts. The only debunking of earlier accounts occurs as the authors point out that the story of Newton and the apple does not appear in the writings of Newton or his early biographers, but only seventy years later in Voltaire's account.

History serves best to show the life of man in the period covered and to point out the forces that molded the past and brought the present into being. In the seventeenth century, when adventuring seafarers of many nations were girdling the earth, more attention might be given to a search for their impelling motives. In the chapter on Portugal there is an illuminating comment that the Iberian Peninsula was "dying of gold." The population of Madrid dropped from 400,000 to 200,000. The gold of the New World, instead of being spent to encourage industrial enterprise at home, was being lavished on manufactured articles from England and Holland. The Church in Spain, "trying to redeem the wealth and buttress the faith," financed the Baroque art and architecture interpreted by the authors as a sign of the decadence of the age.

Whatever difference of opinion may exist about some of the historical details given—and there are grounds for controversy here—readers will agree that the vivid writing makes for exciting reading, though some critics may bemoan the pulp-paper style. This form of narration, interlaced with well-turned phrases and humor, explains the popularity of all the works of Will Durant. Speaking of the artists' lack of position, for instance, the Durants write: "The aristocracy was too interested in the art of life to have time for the life of art." Discussing the plot of the first novel in French literature, *La Princesse de Clèves*, they summarize by saying that "The husband cannot believe she is faithful and worries himself to death, gored, so to speak, with his own imaginary horns." Telling how Alexander Pope blasted the writing of Richard Bentley, Durant says that "Bentley died in July, 1742, from a complication of Pope and pleurisy. He was the greatest and the most insufferable scholar that England ever produced." At the end of the section on the French period, before going on to discuss the culture in the Netherlands, the authors begin a chapter with the confession that they "exhausted, jumble together in a cowardly appendix some Immortals who are beginning to die"; then they deal briefly with minor figures.

Scholars generally hesitate to deal in superlatives, but this volume of *The History of Civilization* is full of them. Besides the estimate of Bentley already given, we find this: "Blaise Pascal was not only the greatest writer of French prose but the most brilliant defender of religion in all the Age of Reason." Again: "Louis XIV was the greatest patron of art and literature that history has ever known." And this: "Swift wrote the most famous and savage satire ever directed against mankind."

The Durants' view of Europe during the reign of Louis XIV falls into five divisions. Book I, beginning with the Peace of Westphalia in 1648, after young Louis had been on the throne for five years, narrates the clash in thinking between the Jesuits in power at court and the followers of Cornelis Jansen. Philosopher Durant provides a concise explanation of Jansenism, describing it as following St. Augustine's belief in the supremacy of predestination and divine grace rather than the free-will concept of the Jesuits. In this view, before the creation of the world God chose the men and women who were to be saved and doomed the rest to damnation. To the Jansenists, good works, no matter how good, could not earn salvation except by the aid of divine grace. Salvation through works would make superfluous the sacrifice of Christ. The Jansenists also considered unquestioning faith superior to reason. To them, therefore, science was a silly presumption, having its foundations in reason that is based on the senses which deceive human beings in a hundred ways. Reason, they insisted, cannot provide a solid base for morality, the family, the state, or the understanding of God.

In subsequent chapters, the Durants examine the thinking of the Port-Royal school. Chief object of the authors' admiration is Blaise Pascal, whose productions included the first mechanical adding machine, experiments on the height of a column of mercury at different altitudes, and the calculus of probabilities on which is founded today's insurance tables of sickness and mortality. But most of the pages devoted to this talented French predecessor of Voltaire concern his eighteen *Provincial Letters*, supposedly written by a Parisian to a friend in the provinces and influenced by Montaigne's *Persian Letters*. Later readers found their attacks on the Jesuits unfair in their use of material out of context and in their imputing to all Jesuits extravagant comments made by a single priest. In one of the many nuggets of information tucked away in the pages of this book (like the comment that George Washington's favorite poem was *The Campaign*, by Joseph Addison, dealing with Marlborough's victory at Blenheim in 1704) the Durants point out that these letters by Pascal gave to the word "casuistry" its derogatory meaning of specious subtleties defending wrong ideas or actions.

The chapters on literature in the book also contain some of the Durants' most valuable material. Their concise treatment of Restoration drama, thoughts on the *Spectator* papers, and their evaluation of Molière are exciting. Of the latter's qualities, they write: "Not only the writer who belongs to the history of France, it is the man: the harassed and faithful manager, the deceived and forgiving husband, the dramatist covering his grief with laughter, the ailing actor carrying on to the hour of his death his war against pedantry, bigotry, and superstition."

Book II, dealing with England during this same period, starts with the beheading of Charles I and the expulsion, chiefly to the United States, of the Royalists. The Durants make the comment that the American Civil War was only the continuation of this earlier civil war, with the descendents of English aristocrats in the South fighting descendents of English Puritans in the north. They also point out that

Puritanism agrees with Judaism in almost everything except the divinity of Christ.

Christopher Wren "born in religion, nurtured in science, and completed in art," comes in for the authors' enthusiastic study as the architect of "the finest church ever built by Protestants."

Book III, "The Periphery," tells the story of Scandinavia, the Jewish Enclaves, Italy, Spain, and Russia in the time of Peter the Great, while France was at her peak of glory. Book IV, "The Intellectual Adventure," looks at the scientific quest in all fields and in all countries, material revealing the encyclopedic information of the authors. Fifty pages on English philosophers are followed by a glance at the French thinkers and a longer look at Spinoza and Leibniz. The final division, Book V, deals with the weakening of France and the declining days, after seventy-two years on the throne, of the Sun King, whose life and reign are summarized in this manner:

He waged devastating wars, indulged his pride extravagantly in building and luxury, stifled philosophy and taxed his people to destitution; but he gave France an orderly government, a national unity, and a cultural splendor that won for her the unquestioned leadership of the Western World. He became the head and symbol of his country's supreme epoch, and France, which lives on glory, has learned to forgive him for almost destroying her to make her great.

Willis Knapp Jones

ASK AT THE UNICORN

Author: Norman Thomas (1926-   )
Publisher: New Directions (New York). 222 pp. $3.75
Type of work: Novel
Time: The present
Locale: The village of Dyfnaint in Wales

A Welsh-born young American returns to the land of his birth in search of his identity

Principal characters:
> MORGAN JOHNS, a young Welsh-born American
> GRANDO RHYDDERCH (TWN SHON), a blind old man, remembered friend of Morgan's early childhood
> CARADOC, the stationmaster, and
> WILL TWICE, his brother, old men of Dyfnaint
> GWYLAN, Will's daughter
> MR. PRITCHARD, landlord of the Unicorn
> MR. AND MRS. PARRY, householders of Dyfnaint
> OWEN and
> MAIR, their son and daughter

It is a fortunate year than can count among its blessings the appearance on the literary scene of a fresh and promising new talent. Such is the endowment of the Welsh-born American, Norman Thomas, as he presents this, his first novel, in which he offers to the reader a story that, in spite of the occasional awkwardness of a young writer seeking his own way, is a work of considerable originality and delicate charm. Making use of age-old themes so peculiarly the preoccupations of modern man—alienation and return, retreat from the cost of involvement, nostalgia for lost innocence—Mr. Thomas leads his hero, Morgan Johns, on a quest for the self-knowledge which the rebellious young man, ostensibly seeking an aged friend remembered from childhood, only dimly perceives as the true object of his pilgrimage.

It is night in Wales when the story begins, and a thunderstorm is raging. A train pulls into Dyfnaint, and a lone figure, Morgan Johns, gets off. As he attempts to make his way to the village, a tree, struck by lightning, carries the young man down with it as it falls. Recovering strength to stand and walk, he approaches the stationmaster's cottage, knocks, and is admitted to the light and warmth of a small room where a one-eyed old man tenderly cares for "a grey bigpregnant cat like a fur bowler . . . on a brass bed . . . and a fluffed-up-in-itself speaking-to-itself bird in a fire-corner cage. . . ."

Clean and dry again after a while, the young man sits quietly with the old.

> 'I'm looking for a man,' Morgan finally said.
> Without taking his eyes from the fire the old man said, 'Everyone comes looking for something.'
> 'His name is Rhydderch.'
> 'I do not know a Rhydderch, but you could ask at the *Unicorn.*'

After a long pause, the old man

10

speaks again, this time to tell the young stranger stories of Dyfnaint where " 'You will see things . . . that you saw years ago and new things you will see though they have been present all the time. You come back on tradition but leave tradition and the smell of brimstone comes on the wind. And always there is wind. Three hairs on the chest of a woman and she is burnt as a witch . . . There could be little people stuck with pins . . . A daughter quiet with eyes so dark and skin so white was born of father and his daughter. It was kept a creature mute by daughter's mother . . . and father was killed by daughter . . . Now the daughter lives with creatures only she can see.' "

All this, and more, is Wales, the old man says, and then wants to hear from Morgan about the cities he has never seen. Ostensibly describing the San Francisco from whence he has come, the young man tells the old of his own rootless and rebellious self as he attempts, with a kind of swaggering insouciance, to follow an uncertain path between the middle-class conventionality of his father and the beatnik revolt of his youthful sensitivity.

In this, Morgan's first encounter in Dyfnaint, the author introduces the elements that go into the making of his story: the lonely isolation evoked by the train as it discharges its single passenger into the darkness; the wild beauty of Wales suggested by the tumbling bushes and crashing trees in the storm; character, especially in its idiosyncratic and crusty manifestations; an emerging concern for the helpless, innocent, and trusting; the pervasiveness of the survivals of Wales' ancient mythic past; the protective armor of tough cynicism with which the disen-

chanted insulate themselves against the pain of caring.

During the few days of the story's duration, first as a guest, both hated and loved, at the Unicorn, the village inn, later as a roomer, both suspected and trusted, in a private household; during a fishing trip at sea and in wanderings about the town and countryside; and, finally, back at the station-master's cottage, the young man's values are tested in a variety of ways. Side by side with village suspicion and bigotry, hatred and violence, there are offered to him friendship unquestioning and freely given by two eccentric old men and an eager lad; the love of a sensitive, intelligent young woman who gives her heart without thought of self-seeking; the confidence of a guileless young girl who stirs in him a memory of his own lost innocence; the humble gratitude of a feeble-minded pensioner in whose behalf, out of a pity he thought long buried, he accepts the blame and its consequences for an act of violence he did not commit. In the blending of these encounters with the pervading beauty of mountain, sea, and sky, as well as the survivals of his ancient and remembered past, comes the awakening of love that brings Morgan to the object of his search and the willingness, at last, to pay the price of belonging and sharing.

While the author makes use of age-old and, in recent years, often well-worn themes, he does so in a manner entirely his own. In a lilting language that, even on the printed page, has about it a quality of music, he tells his story with a poetic imagination that includes the ability to set a scene with dramatic vigor and intensity, a firm hold on the life of the senses, tenderness without sentimentality, innocent

11

ribaldry, and bitter knowledge—resources that promise much for what-

ever Mr. Thomas may choose, in the
future, to do with his undoubted gifts.

Margaret Bowman Tilghman

THE BALLAD OF THE SAD CAFÉ

Author: Edward Albee (1928-   )
Publisher: Atheneum Publishers (New York). 150 pp. $1.75
Type of work: Drama
Time: The recent past
Locale: The general store in a dead and tiny town in the South

*A very long single-act play about the prospects and ravages of love, adapted for the
stage from the novella by Carson McCullers*

> Principal characters:
>   THE NARRATOR, a choric commentator
>   MISS AMELIA EVANS, a masculine, introverted young woman
>   COUSIN LYMON, her beloved hunchback cousin
>   MARVIN MACY, frustrated lover of Miss Amelia
>   HENRY MACY, his brother, a troubled observer
>   STUMPY MACPHAIL,
>   EMMA HALE,
>   MRS. PETERSON, and
>   MERLIE RYAN, chief of a number of townspeople

Those who saw the Broadway production of *The Ballad of the Sad Café*
in the fall of 1963 divided mainly into
two camps: those who found it another triumph for Edward Albee and
those who found it a disappointment
in comparison with the novella by
Carson McCullers. Occasionally, a reviewer like Howard Taubman in the
New York *Times* might say that "Edward Albee has converted Carson Mc-
Cullers' strange, tender prose poem,
The Ballad of the Sad Café, into a play
flecked with weird, halting poetry.
Their art has joined to reveal the terrible and dim face of a shattered and
unnatural love." But by and large the
response was enthusiastic to "a beautiful piece of theatre," with little or no
notice taken of its source; or it was un-
enthusiastic, with considerable attention—sometimes quarrelsome—paid to

what, given its source, it presumably
might have been.

The question of what aesthetic values are at stake in translating a work
from one genre to another, and what
degree of success is the consequence
of doing so in any particular case—
this question is complex enough and
interesting enough to fill many volumes of discourse. There is no simple
answer, but perhaps we should assume
for the moment that each version of
any myth or story, in whatever medium or genre, must first answer on its
own terms for its own qualities; and
that only after that can there be a prof-
itable comparison to ascertain such
matters as the importance of debt, innovation, transcendence, or excision.

Granting this much, the primary
consideration should be how good a
play this work is as a play. As usual,

we must be careful to distinguish between what we may have heard and seen performed by a first-rate troupe in a New York theater and what we read on the printed page in our own study. This is not to say that there is no relationship between the two, but only that we must be cautious of the professional possibility of converting a poor play into an exciting theatrical experience, or a good play into a boring evening. Actually, the more playgoing we have done, the more we have worked on stage or backstage, the more grease paint we have in our veins, the better equipped we are to read properly any play we have not seen, to visualize what it really is as play, and to judge it both ways, as a literary construction and as a vehicle for acting. It may be said that the best critique of any play is an ideal production of it; but such an ideal is attainable only through knowing first what is on paper as text, and knowing then how to play it on the stage.

Anyone who reads the printed version of *The Ballad of the Sad Café* after having seen it at the Martin Beck Theatre is not likely to quibble with the interpretation which was given it. There is an organic unity between the two. In the first place, it is a simple play and there is not much in the situation, the scene, or the relations between the characters which will leave much room for diverse interpretation. The play is not a *Hamlet* or a *Waiting for Godot*. The lines are clear and the stage directions are precise. Even the setting is carefully sketched in by the playwright. All this is not to say that the meaning is absolutely overt; there is something of the mystery of human motive which will always remain to tease us. But this kind

of psychological concern is an after-effect, a lingering desire to plumb the meaning of what we have been allowed to observe. New performances of the play will not and cannot clear this up completely. For a kind of understated rendering of a stated theme is built into the text.

The town is quiet and lonesome; "on an August afternoon, there is absolutely nothing to do." But once it was a little different; there was a café which served as a focal point of social interest for the whole community. This café was opened by Miss Amelia Evans, quite contrary to all previous expectation, when her lonely and self-centered life was revitalized by the entrance into it of her hunchback Cousin Lymon, only too quickly to be spoiled by her indulgence of his every whim. From a pathetic dependent he turns into a confident clown, then into an arrogant trouble-maker and finally into a heart-breaking deserter.

There is one thing which Miss Amelia will not allow him—knowledge of her weird and short-lived marriage to Marvin Macy some ten years before; but Cousin Lymon obtains this knowledge on his own, and therein lies the crux of this dramatic situation. Marvin Macy had been a bad egg, always on the brink of criminality, but once attracted to Miss Amelia, he quickly reformed—took a job, acquired property, became a responsible citizen. In one of the funniest courting scenes in drama, Marvin wins her hand. But after the marriage there is no consummation, nor is one devoutly to be wished by Miss Amelia. Frustrated, Marvin goes to all lengths to gain his marital rights, even signing over his acreage to her, but at last he reverts to his wickedness, takes to

13

the road, and ends up in the penitentiary.

Some four years since Cousin Lymon's advent have elapsed when Marvin returns to invade the hitherto sociable café. Miss Amelia loves Cousin Lymon, but she will not allow him to love her, or at any rate to say he does. He stops saying he does, and indeed soon proves he does not love her. Now he is fascinated by Marvin, hovers on his every word, becomes his very shadow. The triangle is tightly closed: Miss Amelia loves Cousin Lymon; Cousin Lymon loves the worldly Marvin; and Marvin loves (or has loved) Miss Amelia. The community waits breathlessly, some with trepidation, some with malevolence. The climax approaches. It takes the form of a fight, physical combat between Miss Amelia and Marvin. They rest up, grease up, and haul off. Miss Amelia, always strong and mannish, all but vanquishes her foe before Cousin Lymon intervenes and in attacking Miss Amelia allows Marvin to take the advantage. He has his revenge at last. Miss Amelia, sobbing and panting, sees Marvin and Cousin Lymon lay the café in waste and disappear together down the road. Now once again the town is quiet and lonesome; "on an August afternoon, there is absolutely nothing to do."

The play, then, is about love and its consequences, including its loss. "But what sort of thing is love?" the Narrator asks.

"First of all, it is a joint experience between two persons, but that fact does not mean that it is a similar experience to the two people involved. There are the lover and the beloved, but these two come from different countries. Often the beloved is only the stimulus for all the stored-up love which has lain quiet within the lover for a long time hitherto. And somehow every lover knows this. He feels in his soul that his love is a solitary thing. He comes to know a new, strange loneliness. . . . The quality and value of love is determined solely by the lover himself.

"It is for this reason that most of us would rather love than be loved; and the curt truth is that, in a deep secret way, the state of being beloved is intolerable to many; for the lover craves any possible relation with the beloved, even if this experience can cause them both only pain."

Marvin Macy's love for Miss Amelia is fairly normal, though obsessive; he feels unworthy, makes himself worthy, is rejected by the woman who marries him, and reverts to unworthiness. Cousin Lymon's love for Marvin is easy to understand; he has the same will toward evil, finds in Marvin's raunchiness and lechery all that he would like to be and do if he were physically able, and besides all this recognizes in him the malignant enemy of the kinswoman he might have loved but who will not be loved. Miss Amelia's love for Cousin Lymon is a natural phenomenon (though subject to the label of unnatural in kind); as kin he substitutes for her late father, as dwarf he becomes her child and care, and as man he poses no threat to her deeply frozen virginity. But why does she marry Marvin? She certainly suffers no delusions of a new way of life. Rather —and this occurs before the coming of Cousin Lymon—she can *use* his companionship, his help around the place, and, not least of all for a profit-motivated woman, his worldly goods. Perhaps in some subconscious way as well she is preparing masochistically

14

for the ultimate climax which is to determine her life as a recluse.

All this is in the play, or readily suggested by it. The rendering of its subject and the interest of its theme are sufficient to justify the play with regard to content. Its form and structure are something else. Here there are three controversial elements to be considered, elements which might explain the dissatisfaction on the part of some critics, but which on the other hand might be constructively defended.

The first is the use of a flashback to represent the time of Miss Amelia's marriage; this flashback, which occurs in the middle of a present starting four years and some months back, is a narrative or cinematic rather than a dramatic device, and therefore it makes abnormal demands on an audience. This element combines with the second, the use of a narrator, to effect a ritualistic note in the play. If a modern audience can accept a narrator functioning as a kind of synthesizer of cause and effect, an explicator of time sequence, as well as a traditional chorus, this element is a strong virtue of the play; if an audience cannot, it will have to be called a defect. Perhaps a modern audience could be persuaded that the introduction of a choric narrator amounts to the introduction of point of view in the drama, which is of course usually conceived as existing without it.

The third element under consideration is the least defensible; it is Albee's use of subjunctive-colloquial-elliptical forms of the verb *to be*. His motive seems to have been half a matter of dramatic ritual, half a matter of realism. Neither explanation seems to justify the license.

In the original novella, Carson McCullers has of course a narrator, and easily manages the flashback. Nothing could be more normal for fiction. Albee adapts these elements satisfactorily in the stage version. But Mrs. McCullers puts into the mouth of her characters standard English usage, and nothing is lost thereby. It is difficult to see why Albee, who follows his original so closely in so many ways, should have felt any desire to effect this innovation. No purpose is really served. It is at this point that we might really prefer the fiction rather than the drama. Otherwise the adaptation is so close (in sequence of events, physical detail, statement of idea, and diction) that the authorship really is as dual as the attribution on the cover and title page suggests.

In conclusion, we can say that what Albee has brought to the story is his experience in writing dialogue and shaping action for the stage. The theme happens to coincide with his outlook, but he has not made it his own. It is still the impact of Carson McCullers that we feel (as Albee intended we should), though we may miss the firm and evocative style which she employs to *tell* rather than to render her story.

Fred Bornhauser

15

THE BENEFACTOR

Author: Susan Sontag (1933-   )
Publisher: Farrar, Straus and Company (New York). 273 pp. $4.50
Type of work: Novel
Time: From some time in the 1920's to the present
Locale: An unnamed European capital

The strange story of a young man's quixotic journey over the dreamscape of his own mind and his attempt to make his life interpret his dreams as a way to complete self-realization

> Principal characters:
> HIPPOLYTE, the narrator
> FRAU ANDERS, his mistress
> JEAN-JACQUES, a writer, Hippolyte's friend
> MONIQUE, Hippolyte's second mistress
> LUCREZIA, Frau Ander's daughter, Hippolyte's third mistress
> HIPPOLYTE'S WIFE, unnamed, a girl from the provinces
> PROFESSOR BALGARAUX, the elderly leader of an exotic cult
> FATHER TRISSOTIN, a priest

The Benefactor, thirty-year-old Susan Sontag's first novel, is an exceptionally good philosophical comedy, but it is not as successful as Yves Berger's *The Garden,* which it in many ways resembles. While Berger, a Frenchman, assimilates beautifully certain American literary and raw material elements, Miss Sontag has less control over European elements. However, intellectually, and perhaps imaginatively, Miss Sontag attempts much more. Sometimes as strange and as perverse as Djuna Barnes' *Nightwood, The Benefactor* fits into no American tradition; it is much closer to *The Garden* than to *The Tenants of Moonbloom.* The author explores a contemporary theme with an ironic, classical style, reminiscent sometimes of Thomas Mann's. Some reviewers have charged that her style sounds like a bad translation from a European language. "But then my felicity was brought to a swift and cruel end" is a fair example of what they had in mind. But high moments in the novel justify stylistic or thematic comparisons with Pirandello, Gide, Camus, and Kafka.

This novel is probably one of the most cerebral ever written by an American woman. Miss Sontag studied at the University of Chicago and in the Harvard Graduate School, lived a year and a half in England and France, and now teaches philosophy at Columbia University and reviews weighty books for *The New York Review of Books.* From start to finish, the hero of her novel is certainly addicted to philosophical reflections. But although the novel is a profound intellectual construct, the illustrative episodes are dramatic, the dreams have a poetic immediacy, and the characters are never mere exotics or symbols. At its best, *The Benefactor* is a fine blend of narrative, scene, and commentary.

Miss Sontag spawns another of those anti-heroes with whom the twentieth century literary world is becoming over-populated. Although he decries exhibitionistic unconventionality, Hippolyte (the last name is withheld) will strike

16

many readers as bizarre indeed. At sixty-one, a recluse, he tells his story as he ponders the meaning of his youthful adventures, many of which occur in dreams whose significance is sexual and religious. Whether as activator, onlooker, or as participant in the life into which he has immersed himself, Hippolyte is complex and comically real. Friend, patron, lover, member of an occult sect, film actor, husband of a docile provincial girl, spectator of the homosexual underworld at salons and cafés, white slaver, would-be murderer, he chronicles his real and unreal life with an engrossing verbosity that is odd for one who once desired to explore "the various styles of silence." But as a young man he has a compulsion to contradict, and irony has seized him by the throat.

His friend, Jean-Jacques, tells him that he is "a character without a story. . . . You are your own idea, thought up by yourself." He has "taken a vow to be absurd." Consequently, Hippolyte becomes "a great comic fragment." Someone else notes his resemblance to "the knight of the sad countenance"; appropriately for the age of anxiety, he is a Don Quixote who ventures upon his own dreamscape. Embarked upon a resolution to see and feel his own life completely, he builds a bridge between his dream and his daytime occupations; as the-man-who-dreams, he attempts to give his dreams the quality of acts. He "grooms" his life for the "judgment" of his dreams, with the intention of ridding his private life of his public self. In this most important of his many projects, he is warned against his dreams, admonished to confess and rid himself of them, encouraged to submit to them, and exhorted to be proud of them by various friends.

As he becomes involved in this process, Hippolyte superimposes dream personages upon real people and vice versa; some people become accomplices while others become mentors of his dreams. Out of this strange involvement, he emerges as a "guilty benefactor." Jean-Jacques claims that Hippolyte does not suffer because he assumes everybody else is like the self in which he is so subjectively immersed; but Hippolyte argues that he wants people to be what they want to be—the very wish he has for himself.

As the author's ally, the reader's interpreter (also, the anti-hero's double?), Jean-Jacques raises many of the reader's own questions concerning Hippolyte's "religion." A writer and a former boxer, he pursues in the nocturnal streets what he calls "the homosexual parody"; in exotic costumes, he earns a modest living as a prostitute and petty thief. He believes that people should occasionally exchange their various masks. In a life as surrealistic as a dream, he seeks the pleasures of disguises, secrecy, entrapments, and being-what-one-is-not. He is Hippolyte's confidant and opposite. "You wish to unify," says Jean-Jacques. "I practice the arts of dissociation." Monomaniacal Hippolyte later confirms Jean-Jacques's observation: "I think best when I think one thing, feel most deeply when I feel one thing." Together they exemplify two aspects of what may very well prove to be a single state of mind.

Two other male influences in Hippolyte's life are Father Trissotin and Professor Balgaraux. While Hippolyte enters one phase in his development in which he believes that it is "not in the communion of bodies, but in the exaltations of the spirit" that one achieves complete self-knowledge, he rejects the

17

priest's injunction that he "confess rather than express." Much more acceptable is the professor's philosophy that "men cannot be saved until they have gone through all kinds of experience." As the leader of a sect of Autogenists, he teaches "liberation through contradiction of one's settled life and the unleashing of one's deepest fantasies"—an enterprise upon which Hippolyte is already embarked.

Hippolyte's women are intriguing. With Monique, a sensual little causemonger, he enacts the idea that the sexual act is a way of experiencing the loss of self. With Lucrezia, he experiences disinterestedness in sex and learns something about appearances: once, he saw her only through the eyes of her mother, Frau Anders, and her lecherous old lover, the Maestro, and thought her to be the victim of both. But as her new lover, he learns that it was she who corrupted her own mother.

Another of Hippolyte's women is the unnamed provincial girl whom he sets out systematically to marry. One of Miss Sontag's techniques is the suddenness with which she introduces a new turn in the narrative: Hippolyte decides to end his apathetic bachelorhood, seeks a woman, and marries her in several pages; just as suddenly, she dies. Hippolyte is both husband and benefactor; he allows his wife to be what she likes most, a housewife who makes fine jams, and he leaves her virginity intact. Reflecting on the subject of self-love he decides that the "better solution is detachment—neither loving nor hating others, neither assuming burdens nor laying them down. The only proper object of both love and hate is oneself." In self-love one reconciles love and separateness. His wife's faithfulness tempts him to test his disinterested attitude to-

ward her by creating opportunities for her to be unfaithful, but she remains Penelope. Her sudden death occasions reflections of another sort: "Death is the most interesting event in life." It is comparable only to dreams, for in neither is revision possible. "Life is a movie. Death is a photograph."

The most important person in Hippolyte's life and dreams is Frau Anders, a wealthy Jewish dilettante of thirty when she becomes his mistress. She is the embodiment of his passionate relationship to his dreams, "the vessel in which I deposited the substance of my dreams." On her body he solves the puzzles of erotic technique. He becomes her lover, benefactor, shadow, judge, accomplice, master of ceremonies, and victim. He is attracted to her because for her the arbitrary is the norm, and only consistency appalls her; thus, when they run away together to North Africa, he discovers her "unlimited capacity for boredom," her insatiable appetite for the exotic. He tells her that she exists only for his dreams; she consciously coöperates by playing all the personages in his sleeplife. Loved not as a person but as a persona, she suffers; he finds the acting out of *her* dreams impossible. But with the intention of helping her realize her true, dream self, he sells her to an Arab merchant—his first altruistic act, for which he suffers twinges of guilt. She appears, a disfigured, diseased old woman, in the midst of his affair with Monique; deciding she is too sad to live, he commits his second altruistic act by burning the shack in which she is sleeping. Later, when he is married, she reappears, now fleeing the Nazis, and he hides her in an immense old house. Years later she reappears again, once more a beautiful woman. "Why

18

should you be afraid of me?" she asks. "Because you are there," he replies; like a dream she is persistent and indestructible. Frau Anders seems to collaborate with Hippolyte in transforming herself into a dadaistic dream creature. The circumstantial transmutations of Frau Anders parallel the ontological transmutations of Hippolyte.

Hippolyte's grandest gesture of benefaction is the renovation of the gigantic old house for Frau Anders. The atmosphere of each bizarre room is designed to induce the acting out of a particular dream wish. In one room she may enact again her captivity with the Arab; another contains mirrors that reflect the ruins of her beauty; another is a chapel; another provides means for expressing strong emotions; another is for sexual purposes. The house is a museum of her past and a brothel "from which she could select the pleasures of her future." It is Hippolyte's most deliberate attempt to erect a physical objectification of his dreams; this project contrasts with a younger notion when he once stripped his room to bare essentials and slept on a pallet on the floor. Although the purpose of the house is to cause a transformation in Frau Anders by enabling her to enact her secret fantasies, her response raises the question: does the "fulfillment of a powerful fantasy" ever bring happiness? Frau Anders ends by desiring the unsubmitting Hippolyte more than the house. When she leaves, he moves in. Years later she returns. With self-love and love for Hippolyte as her professed motives, she evicts him.

Hippolyte's "outer involvement" and his "inner experiences" become enmeshed in response to the dictates of his dreams. Although he is mixed up with many people, his own life is blank, so that Jean-Jacques explains Hippolyte's obsession with a young chess player as the attraction of one blank soul to another: "a mirror of your own blankness." Hippolyte's real life is in his dreams and in his waking contemplation of them. The reader haltingly follows the evolution of his attitude toward them. His dreams direct his life; his life directs his dreams. They haunt him; then he haunts them. They are parasites upon his life; then his life is a parasite upon them. His life is made to interpret his dreams. The dialogue between his waking and his sleeping life becomes a dialogue among the dreams as they come to have a life of their own.

Jean-Jacques warns him that he must "outbid" his dreams. Since he has always regarded them not as a gift but as a task, he becomes his own benefactor as he fervently strives to achieve a perfect union between his most private self and his dreams. He believes that in the responsibility of one's dreams lies the energy of one's true self, as De Quincey suggests in the epigraph of the novel: "The Dream knows best; and the Dream, I say again, is the responsible party." Hippolyte's concept of freedom is reconciliation to oneself, oneself as one really is, the self of one's dreams. "Dreams, like smiles, fade rapidly," he says. "But what if the face faded away, and the smile remained? What if the life on which the dreams fed withered, and the dreams flourished?" The most lucid expression of Hippolyte's narcissism is the statement that "Dreams are the onanism of the spirit."

It is always a difficult task to describe a dream in a compelling manner, but Miss Sontag makes Hippolyte's vivid and intriguing, even though some go on for pages. There are the dreams of the two rooms, of the unconventional party, of piercing the roof of the cathedral, of the elderly patron, of the piano lesson, of the mirror, of the arena, and of the puppets. Miss Sontag convinces her readers that "all events in dreams are extraordinary, and banal, at the same time." The emotions which recur in the dreams—surprise, humiliation, and a desire to please—suggest that the narrator has been confined in some institution. They all seem to be dreams of shame. Indeed, Hippolyte's aim in acting out the dreams is to purge himself of some impurity. While religion urges him to feel guilt for his desires, the Autogenists encourage him to feel proud of his creative energies, to regard the self as the well-spring of all well-being.

Whether they constitute a coherent view or not, the author presents many interesting observations about dreams. "The temple of public dreams" is the cinema. Like an actor in films, Hippolyte sees a profound analogue between his acting and his behavior in dreams; he even tries to reshape the scripts in the langorous style of his dreams. It is much more difficult to manipulate life, for in striving to live by one's dreams one must depend on the collaboration of others, who have dreams of their own; the result is a hopeless situation, an impossible aspiration. Instead of contemplating his navel, Hippolyte contemplates his dreams in an effort to produce "an alertness without content, a state of shimmering weightlessness." His acts in his dreams are characteristically ritualistic: "outward agitation contradicted by inner trance." In his dreams gestures gain the status of ritual: "I welcome gestures which are repeated." In the huge house, he attempts to remove his dreams by integrating

them fully into his life through a supreme act of ritualistic concentration, "to dissolve the means, now that they had brought me to the end." So his emergence from the house is both "a rescue and a cruel eviction"; a new man, he is "cleansed and purged" of his dreams. But without them he ceases to interest himself; he interests only other people, to whom he is an ordinary benefactor.

Last Year at Marienbad is one of the few movies which may legitimately claim a second viewing for the sake of fundamental comprehension, and *The Benefactor* makes such a claim as a novel. The final chapter seems completely to contradict everything preceding it. Hippolyte discusses and gives excerpts from an autobiographical novel which he has recently uncovered. He appears to have written it as a young man, but because it contradicts everything he has just told us, he regards it with suspicion. It omits his life, being a description of his dreams presented as though they were real episodes. In turn, a letter, which appears to have been written to some person in authority, contradicts the autobiographical novel.

A review of *The Benefactor* could be written in the form of questions alone without detracting much from the novel's stature. How can the reader believe a word said by a character so ironic, ambiguous, and paradoxical (the easiest kind of character to get going, but the most difficult for a reader to accept)? Is the narrator really an old man when he tells the story? Is he now or has he ever been in an insane asylum? How sincere or true are the death of Hippolyte's wife and the drastic change in Jean-Jacques? Indeed, is Jean-Jacques really Hippolyte himself? Was

20

the woman who evicted Hippolyte actually Frau Anders? Is the reader's confusion meant to be a contributing factor in the picture of human life that emerges from that confusion? Does the author wish to demonstrate the fact that life is a mixture of dream and reality by deceiving the reader? Is this novel mainly a philosophical exploration, or a parody of similar novels, or simply a joke on the reader of such novels? Is this book meant to be exhibit A of the novel as conundrum?

An early hint to the reader that he should weigh the degree of authority with which this most biased of narrators is to speak comes in the statement that "When we write the truth, we should address ourselves." Perhaps the author's most blatant note to the reader appears in Hippolyte's own notebook near the end: "Don't Believe Everything You Read." When he comes to the line, "The reader knows that I do not subscribe to the version of my life presented in the letter," the reader knows only that he had better read again. Hippolyte writes a note to himself regarding his task as a young autobiographer: "make clear the separation of dream from waking life." But this becomes the reader's task. At sixty-one Hippolyte concludes: "And now the past as a whole, dreams and waking life alike, presents itself to me as fantasy."

This novel may strive, in its implications, to be both comic and terrifying, but it is too seldom either. There are arid stretches of prose, for the book is much too long. The development of the premise (dangerously close to being both a fictive and a philosophical *notion* rather than a genuine conception) is labored. But *The Benefactor* remains one of the year's most original and stimulating books, giving one every reason to expect that Miss Sontag's second novel will be brilliant.

David Madden

21

THE BIRTHDAY KING

Author: Gabriel Fielding (Alan Gabriel Barnsley, 1916-   )
Publisher: William Morrow and Company (New York). 383 pp. $5.95
Type of work: Novel
Time: 1939-1945
Locale: Germany

An examination of the World War II German consciousness in terms of a mercantile family and its associates

Principal characters:

> FRAU WILHELMINA WEIDMANN, head of the Weidmann Group, a large German industrial firm
> ALFRIED, her elder son
> RUPRECHT, her younger son
> BARON NICHOLAS VON HOFFBACH, a partner in the Weidmann Group
> BARONIN CARIN VON HOFFBACH, his wife
> LEO, their son
> ALEXANDRA VON BOEHLING, the youthful friend of the von Hoffbachs, later Ruprecht's wife
> FELIX GRUNWALD, Kommandant of the Albrechtstrasse Prison
> GUDRUN GRUNWALD, his wife
> HUBURTUS GRUNWALD, their son

The German novel is in essence open-ended and metaphysically oriented, an orientation in which lies its distinctive difference, and a difference which the American novel shares with it, from the British tradition of fiction. The English novel may be introspective, but it is almost never speculative, whereas introspection in the German novel is necessarily of itself at the same time speculation. The English novelist, through an examination of external behavior in relation to fixed social forms, points to character; the German novelist, through an examination of character, points to regulative principle, a universal dialectic of which character is but the type. The world of *Middlemarch* is the semi-determinative context in which Dorothea, Rosamund, and Lydgate reveal themselves; while the social scene of *Buddenbrooks,* as thickly-textured and

thoroughly drawn, is but the local manifestation of a Schopenhauerian-Wagnerian drama of Will and Idea working itself out in the decline of the Buddenbrooks family. Even the vast historical and intellectual processes symbolized by the *portmanteau* characters in *The Magic Mountain* are but externalized potentialities of the consciousness of Hans Castorp, the German Everyman as philosopher. Whether such differences are traceable to those between the empirical and the idealistic philosophical traditions, or whether both are merely reflections of nationalistic temperamental bias is moot. But if the causes are remote, the effects are none the less evident, and nowhere more so than in one tradition's apprehension of the other.

Gabriel Fielding's *The Birthday King* is an English novel with a German subject, an attempt, with the means of the British tradition of the novel, to grasp those characteristics of the German mind which permitted the enormities and atrocities of World War II, to plumb, in short, those proclivities alien to the mode in which it works; and the representation of the German mind achieved is all the more remarkable for the non-Germanicism of its form. In three of his four previous novels, *In the Time of Greenbloom, Through Streets Broad and Narrow,* and *Brotherly Love,* Fielding has traced the life of John Blaydon, the last examining the effects upon him of a family situation centering around his older brother. In *The Birthday King,* a family situation, in which a young man's attitude toward his elder brother is paramount, becomes endemic of the plight and the susceptibility of the German mind during World War II. Thus the pattern of his "English" fiction serves Fielding, in the novel which he has himself termed the result of a "long obsession with the innocent malevolence of the Nordic mind," as the condition for revealing the guilt implicit in innocence, the concrete fruits of German abstractionism.

The Birthday King himself is Ruprecht Weidmann, "life's delicate child" whose delicacy is attuned to what life can bestow upon him, the eternal infant at his own birthday party, awaiting the world which he has been led to expect as his due, selfish only in that the innocent's consciousness does not extend beyond the self. Ruprecht is the creature of the luxuriously comfortable, civilized middle-class world from which he springs. Younger son of a wealthy Jewish-Catholic mercantile family, he is cynical about his Christianity in the light of prevailing political realities, almost unembarrassedly derogatory about his non-professed Jewish heritage in the light of prevailing anti-Semitism. But his dedication is not so much to the cause of the Führer, whose title slips a commonplace deification from his mouth, as to that of his emerging as easily, as successfully, even as profitably as possible from what at the beginning hardly even looms as a coming ordeal. The novel opens with Ruprecht, the young apprentice scientist home for the weekend, involved in a family conference to determine the control of the Weidmann industrial interests. Also participating is Baron von Hoffbach, whose aristocratic motive for mingling with the middle class is in large part the desire of participating in their wealth. The leadership of the Group, given the blindness and advancing age of the Frau Kommerzienrat, naturally falls to the elder son Alfried. But Alfried, torn between his desire to enter the priesthood and his love for a young nun, resists the pressures of his younger brother, for whom the former choice would naturally mean control of the Group, and postpones the decision of his vocation for two years.

Shortly thereafter Ruprecht meets at the baron's estate, Schönform (the name suggesting the beautiful forms of a nearly lost aristocratic way of life in memories of which the baron attempts to immerse himself as protection against the increasingly hideous realities in which he is all too thoroughly involved), Alexandra von Boehling, with whom he falls in love. When he returns to the Berlin Institute eighteen months later, in 1941, he is able to resume his pursuit of Alexandra, who is staying in the Berlin residence of Carin, Baronin von Hoffbach.

23

Carin, infatuated with Ruprecht, has decided to add him to her evidently infinite list of lovers. When she becomes infuriated with him for his conduct at an official dinner party, she gives to an S.S. officer information, revealed to her by Ruprecht, which suggests, in the distortion of her passion, that Alfried, whose mysticism dates from a childhood vision of an angel and whose criticism of the regime from a visit to America, is both a lunatic and a traitor. Later that night Ruprecht becomes her lover.

The following chapter opens with Alfried in prison, the victim of his brother's apparently accidental and innocent betrayal. Because Alfried is the scion of a financially important family, and because such a significant personage as the baron is feebly and futilely manipulating for his release, his imprisonment is regarded as an unfortunate political mistake, and he is relegated to the comparatively soft job of handyman at the Kommandant's house, where he is thrown into unwilling association with Frau Grunwald and her son Huburtus, who attempt to involve Alfried in their neurotic mystique of Christianity, aestheticism, and National Socialism. When Alfried resists what he feels is the test they are trying to impose upon him, his treachery, a treachery for them traceable to his Jewish blood, is confirmed, and he is subjected to torture and mutilation for secret information which he does not possess.

In the latter stages of the novel, as Hitler's regime approaches its inevitable dissolution, Carin betrays in bed to Huburtus, who has become her latest lover, in a perverse gesture of self-degradation—perverse especially in that she has just come to feel absolute contempt for him—the fact of her husband's complicity in a plot to assassinate Hitler. Her betrayal leads to the Baron's strangulation by the S.S. The Grunwalds fulfill their religio-political vision by committing suicide together upon the death of Hitler. Huburtus, during his parents' death throes, terrified at the prospect of death, spits out a capsule of poison, strips his parents' bodies of valuables, sets fire to the house, and slinks away into the darkness, itself the apotheosis of his reality. Ruprecht, by now the established head of the Weidmann Group, experiences slight qualms in anticipating the return of that brother whom he inadvertently sent to imprisonment and torture.

Fielding does not attempt to trace the ultimate causes of the terror which was Nazi Germany, but his delineation of the German mind suggests those attributes which permitted it insidiously to grow and flourish: a self-interest all unenlightened, an idealism which, in its mistaking the self for the world, inevitably blinds itself to the being of anyone other, inevitably leads to that innocent betrayal of one's brother—the indifference, the acquiescence themselves the conditions of the terror—which figures the betrayal of man. Even Alfried comes to realize that his vacillation was little more than desire for the money. And if the baron finally knows his guilt, he is left with only the self-gratification of dying well, an act which is something, but too late, and not enough.

Donald L. Mull

24

BLACK CLOUD, WHITE CLOUD

Author: Ellen Douglas
Publisher: Houghton Mifflin Company (Boston). 232 pp. $4.00
Type of work: Two novellas and two short stories
Time: From the 1920's to the present
Locale: The towns of Homochitto and Philippi, Mississippi

Colored-white relations in particular and the texture of experience in general are presented as they impinge on the consciousness of sensitive girls and women

As epigraph for her book Ellen Douglas uses William Blake's poem, "The Little Black Boy." Her title is drawn from the same source. Thus we can more clearly see one of her principal concerns in these stories: to penetrate beneath the black and white clouds which clothe the souls of men. But here—unlike Blake's poem where the black and white pigments supply protection from the hot beams of God's love—the black and white skins tend to keep God's children apart. Each unit in this book explores black-white relationships, all of them those of master and servant, but intimate relationships compounded of the sense of the past, of shared experience, and occasionally of love.

The four parts of the book are set alternately in Homochitto, on bluffs three hundred feet above the Mississippi across from the Louisiana side, and in Philippi, near Lake Okatukla and the Arkansas side. Several characters appear in two or three of the sections. Only one, "I Just Love Carrie Lee," bears little relationship to the others except for theme and place. Set in Homochitto, it is a short story told in the first person by a white woman raised by Carrie Lee, as were her children after her. Carrie Lee has been in the family for fifty years—rescued by it, sheltered by it, trained by it, and (despite her husband and children) chattel to it. The nameless narrator insists that she just loves Carrie Lee— and she does—but much of what she says is full of the amusement of a master chuckling at a quaint, lovable, and superstitious servant. She has more of a debt to Carrie Lee than she knows, despite her frequent avowals, and the need of her grows greater as time passes. She prefers Carrie Lee's company to that of most white people: "She understands me. When I think about it, it sometimes seems to me, with Bill and Mama dead and the children grown and gone, that Carrie Lee is all I have left of my own." Of these two old women, Carrie Lee (whose guide has been "Trust in the Lord and love little children") is by far the richer, one suspects.

The other short story, "Jesse," is set in Philippi. It is narrated by Anna Glover, a young matron who chauffeurs an old Negro, Jesse Daniels, back and forth to her house so that he can give her son guitar lessons. The lessons are of small value, but little by little, casually, Jesse tells Anna Glover something of the heartbreaking tragedies of his childhood and youth. The story ends with a Dostoevskian touch. In the middle of the night Anna writes down two sentences to exorcise the mood his stories have created. She goes back to sleep. In the morning she discovers that she has written: "There are those of us who are willing to say, 'I am guilty,' but who is to absolve us? And do we expect by our confession miraculously to relieve the suffering of the innocent?" Then she sees that, for the word, "relieve," she had first written, "escape."

Anna appears in both novellas. In the first, "The House on the Bluff," young Anna McGovern is seen in the Homochitto home of her closest friend, Caroline Baird. The narrative gives glimpses of the Bairds in affluence, in genteel poverty, and then in solid retrenchment. The two families "are joined by all the complicated strands of kinship, love, and enmity that bind together families who have lived cheek by jowl in a small town for five or six generations." Anna's brilliant and attractive playmates have two mothers: widowed Margaret Baird and the old Negro woman Tété, an iron disciplinarian. Young Keith Baird remains handsome as he grows, but he becomes more and more difficult in the years that follow, until his recklessness cripples him in an automobile accident. When he dies not long after, he is not yet out of his teens. Looking back later, Anna feels that Keith's problems should have been recognized: "not one mother but two, each peculiarly unfitted for any category he might try to put her in; not a living, loving father, but a dead one, embalmed forever in his successful gregarious youth; not a family united in comfortable likeness and stability, but one split, yes . . . *split*, in time between feckless wealth and hard-working poverty, and in status between black and white."

Anna and Caroline return to Homochitto with husbands and babies. They sit outdoors in the gathering evening with their children, and there is a sense of the continuity of the generations, even though the loss of Keith still obtrudes itself. The neighborhood has depreciated further, but it is hard to sell the old house. "Margaret says they'll probably stay on," writes Mrs. Douglas in the novella's last lines, "at least as long as Caroline and Thomas are willing."

Although the focus of this story is sometimes blurred (Is it Keith's problem? Children's growing awareness? White-black relationship?), the portrait of Tété is strongly drawn. She is likely to remind the reader—for all her insistence on up-to-the-mark decorum —of William Faulkner's Dilsey in *The Sound and the Fury*. This fiction, like that of many of Mrs. Douglas's contemporaries, is work of which one may say, Faulkner was there first. The insights in this book are often keen and of a feminine sensitivity, but the direction in which this work goes is not that of Ellen Glasgow but rather of the creator of Yoknapatawpha County.

The last novella concludes the book. Set in Philippi, it takes its title from the refrain of a spiritual serving as epigraph: "Hold On." Whether this functions symbolically is difficult to say. It is clear, however, that it functions literally, for this is what Anna Glover does. She holds on to the belt of Estella's dress to keep the huge and beautiful colored woman from drowning when their small boat is swamped on Lake Okatukla. Estella is the former maid of Anna, who is the happily married mother of three small boys. She has invited Estella on the fishing party to try to establish once more the old friendship the two had tentatively, carefully, and painstakingly established. The near drowning becomes a nightmare she cannot shake. When her husband will not help her talk it out, she turns to the shy white man who

26

helped in the rescue. He in turn (like Jesse) tells her of the hardships of his early life, particularly of the old Negro woman who saved his life, and of her death, one which "makes you feel to the very bone of your soul the mystery and heroism of a human life." By the end, Anna has begun to recover, to lose her feelings of guilt for having pushed Estella away with her foot

when she appeared about to drown them both.

All four stories deal with the interdependence of white and black, and the best of them make the reader feel something of "the mystery and heroism of a human life"—something that Blake, for all his concern with another life, could not but have found estimable.

Joseph L. Blotner

BOSNIAN CHRONICLE

Author: Ivo Andrić (1892-   )
Translated from the Serbo-Croatian by Joseph Hitrec
Publisher: Alfred A. Knopf (New York). 429 pp. $6.95
Type of work: Novel
Time: 1807-1814
Locale: Travnik, a city in Bosnia

An epic tale of a people and a region during Napoleon's rise and fall

> *Principal characters:*
> M. JEAN DAVILLE, the French Consul-General
> MADAME DAVILLE, his wife
> HUSREF MEHMED PASHA, the Turkish Vizier, 1807-1808
> CESAR D'AVENANT, the Vizier's personal physician and interpreter, later assigned to the French Consulate
> SELIM III, Sultan of Turkey, deposed by revolt in 1808
> MUSTAPHA, Selim's successor
> AMEDEE CHAUMETTE DESFOSSES, Daville's assistant
> FRA IVO YANKOVICH, a parish priest in Bosnia
> COLONEL JOSEPH VON MITTERER, the Austrian Consul-General
> IBRAHIM HALILI PASHA, the successor to Husref Mehmed
> LIEUTENANT-COLONEL VON PAULICH, von Mitterer's successor as Austrian Consul-General

In 1961, Ivo Andrić was awarded the Nobel Prize for Literature as a result of what the Swedish Academy called "the epic force with which he has depicted themes and human destinies from the history of his country." The Academy made special mention of Andrić's Bosnian trilogy of which *Bosnian Chronicle* is the longest if not the best. The other two works in the trilogy are *The Bridge on the River Drina*, the

subject of almost universally excellent reviews in this country, and *Miss.*

All three parts of the trilogy were written during World War II while the Nazis occupied Yugoslavia. Andrić, who had participated in a Bosnian revolutionary youth movement dedicated to freeing the Slavs from Austrian rule before World War I, was serving as the Yugoslavian Minister to Germany when the Nazis invaded his homeland.

27

He returned to Belgrade and spent the entire war as a virtual recluse studying and writing in his apartment. The trilogy, published in 1945, made Andrić a dominant figure in Yugoslavian letters almost overnight. Since 1945 he has held that dominance almost unchallenged except for the efforts of Milovan Djilas.

Two main characteristics distinguish all of Andrić's works: his ability to capture the spirit of his country and its people—obviously a labor of love—and his use of a point-counterpoint relationship between two characters. His word pictures of the Bosnian countryside shine through even the obvious difficulties of translating those pictures from Serbo-Croatian into English. His characters are never introduced singly, but always in pairs and are always totally dissimilar. The principal thrust of all of Andrić's plots deals with the transitory nature of men and events coupled with a degree of what must be termed fatalism for want of a better word.

Bosnian Chronicle is laid in the city of Travnik in Bosnia, a territory roughly the size of West Virginia, during the period from 1807 to 1814. By this time the wave of the Ottoman invasion had crested in Europe and was washing slowly back through the Balkans. The Turks, however, still retained control of the area through the offices of the viziers' residences in all the major cities and in provincial capitals. Napoleon was already reaching forward in his attempts to conquer all of the European continent. The Austrian emperor, afraid of internal difficulties and weaknesses, was striving to maintain peaceful relations with the French.

In the small province of Bosnia rumors ran riot of the forthcoming installation of two consulates, one French and the other Austrian. While the townspeople argued as to what the consequences would be, one of the elders quieted them with a statement that in large measure becomes a recurrent theme of this book:

"As for these consuls, who knows what's what? Maybe they'll come, maybe they won't. And even if they come, the Lashva won't turn around and flow backwards—it will run the same as now. We're here on our own ground, anyone else who may come will be on strange ground and he won't tarry long. Armies have gone through here before and they never could hold out for long. Many have come back here to stay, but so far we've always managed to see the back of them, just as we will see the back of these consuls too, even supposing they come."

Seven years later this same elder in commenting on the closing of the consulates states:

"Travnik is sweeping out the consuls. The people will talk about them another year or two. The children will play at consuls and kavasses down by the river, riding on wooden sticks, and afterwards they too will forget about them as if they had never existed. And everything will be the same again, just as, by the will of Allah, it has always been."

This spirit of fatalism, of the fact that men and events come and go but the Bosnian way of life will continue almost uninterrupted, echoes again and again through this novel. The Bosnians themselves are described as being and believing "that they were somehow different from the rest of the world, and that they would conquer or absorb all the foreigners who had invaded their land."

Resident in Travnik when the story opens are three diverse groups of citizens. The largest consists of Turks and local Moslems who want only to get rid of all the rest who are not of the soil of Bosnia. The second largest group in terms of numbers is made up of Christians, of whom the Catholics are in the majority. The Catholics look forward to the opening of the Austrian consulate as a means of bringing to them the protection of the mighty Catholic emperor in Vienna. The third is the community of Jews, friendless and persecuted, longing for the opening of the French Consulate because to them Napoleon is a friend to the Jew. Over this mélange presides Husref Mehmed Pasha, the vizier, personal representative of the Turkish sultan.

To this strange land in February of 1807 comes first the French consul-general, Jean-Baptiste-Etienne Daville. Daville is a weak man who longs only for a peaceful position in which he will be forced to make no decisions but can spend his time writing rather dull, insipid poetry. On his first visit to the vizier, Daville meets the hostility of the Turkish population and of the Catholic population that is to continue for his entire tenure in Travnik. When he protests to the vizier over his treatment, he is told that such things are to be expected from the people of Bosnia, as they are boors, louts, and stupid peasants.

The arrival of the Austrian consul-general, Colonel Joseph von Mitterer, brings to the story the first of the many instances in which Andrić sets two characters in opposition to each other. Daville wants only quietness and tranquillity, while von Mitterer burns with ambition; where Daville longs for peace in Europe, von Mitterer has the soldier's desire for war. Daville wants to leave Bosnia only because he hates the country and people; von Mitterer wants to leave only because he believes that Bosnia represents the backwash of more important events. The two consuls spend their days trying to convince the vizier that Turkey's future is tied to the fortunes of their respective emperors. Each uses the numerous spies available to secure information that they believe will be helpful and which will be praised "back home," but neither succeeds in doing anything more than amusing the local population.

As the years pass, Napoleon extends his dominance over more and more of Europe. Intrigue and palace revolts in Istanbul cause sultans and viziers to come and go. Von Mitterer, at best a failure, is succeeded by another Austrian soldier, Lieutenant-Colonel von Taulich, who, while more efficient, does little to aid his country. And Daville suffers as winters succeed summers and the years move forward. The winters, in particular, are painful.

As early as the month of November the winter bore down hard on all life and changed the face of the earth and the appearance of the people. It killed and flattened the valley, hardening and settling the fatal desolation and leaving no hope of change. It emptied the granaries and shut off the roads. Birds fell dead from the air, like phantom fruit from invisible branches. Wild animals came down from the high mountains and wandered into town, their fear of winter stronger than their fear of man. In the eyes of the poor and homeless one could see terror of a defenseless death. People froze on the roads, for there was no medicine against winter.

Napoleon's invasion of Russia and his first great successes, followed by his doom as winter descends, bring the story to a close. With the defeat of Napoleon, Daville arranges for the closing of the consulate. Looking back over his seven years, he realizes the futility and the waste of the time spent among the Slavs—in fact, the futility of his entire career. For twenty-five years he had blundered, groping and finding, losing and regaining, swinging from one enthusiasm to another, and now, tired, spent, inwardly run dry, he has arrived at the point from which he had started when he was eighteen years of age. Then he realizes that there is no road leading to peace and the good life. Instead, men have "simply groped around and around, always along the same path that led them up the garden path eventually . . . or just traveled on, spent themselves, and grew weary."

As in most of the other novels by Andrić, nothing really happens in *Bosnian Chronicle*. One completes the book with a deep sense of the beauty and the harshness of that region that was to become Yugoslavia; of the capacity of the Slavs to endure the pains and perils of the present with stolidness based on the knowledge that this too would pass; of the pettiness of most humans; and of the desire of men to be free of foreign dominance.

Most of all, the reader is aware of the impermanence of man and his puny activities. In Andrić's words, ". . . everything must come down, even one's friends and supporters. And the man who got up in arms and tried to save himself or the others, achieved nothing in the end."

Frank K. Gibson

BOSWELL:
The Ominous Years
1774-1776

Author: James Boswell (1740-1795)
Edited by Charles Ryskamp and Frederick A. Pottle
Publisher: The McGraw-Hill Book Company (New York). Illustrated. 427 pp. $8.50
Type of work: Journal and letters
Time: September 24, 1774-May 16, 1776
Locale: Edinburgh and London

The account of two years in the life of a man who said, "My avidity to put as much as possible into a day makes me fill it till it is like to burst."

Principal personages:

JAMES BOSWELL
SAMUEL JOHNSON, Boswell's friend and mentor
MARGARET MONTGOMERIE BOSWELL, James Boswell's wife
VERONICA,
EUPHEMIA, and
ALEXANDER, their children
ALEXANDER BOSWELL, Lord Auchinleck, Boswell's father
THOMAS MILLER, Lord Justice-Clerk of the Scottish Higher Court of Justiciary
WILLIAM MILLER, his son, who challenged Boswell to a duel
HENRY DUNDAS, the Solicitor-General, whom Boswell considered challenging to a duel
GENERAL PASQUALE DE PAOLI, a Corsican patriot and Boswell's friend
SIR JOHN PRINGLE,
JOHN STUART, Lord Mountstuart,
LADY CHARLOTTE MOUNTSTUART, his wife, and
ALEXANDER MONTGOMERIE, Earl of Eglinton, Boswell's fashionable London friends
HENRY THRALE, a wealthy brewer, and
HESTER LYNCH THRALE, his wife, Johnson's friends
WILLIAM JOHNSON TEMPLE, a clergyman, Boswell's friend and confessor
EDWARD DILLY, a London bookseller
JOHN WILKES, a member of Parliament
MRS. MARGARET RUDD, an adventuress and courtesan

It is interesting to speculate on what the consequences might have been, in the judgment of posterity and in their private lives, if Boswell and Johnson had never met, or if their chance encounter in Tom Davies' back parlor on May 16, 1763, had not developed into a sincere friendship between the grand cham of English letters and the doltish young Scotsman thirty-one years his junior. Boswell had hoped to make Johnson's acquaintance in London but that first meeting was not particularly auspicious. Twice the young man was roundly snubbed to teach him proper conduct in the

31

company of his betters, and he went home to write in his journal that scrofula-marked Johnson, in spite of his great humor and worth, was a man of dreadful appearance and disagreeable manners. In fact, each possessed more traits of temperament and background likely to keep them apart than common tastes to bring them together. Johnson was awkward, gloomy, sternly moralistic, dogmatic. He was also a man of reputation in the world: the great lexicographer, the arbiter of literary taste, master of the Augustan style. Boswell was a mere hobbledehoy of uncertain prospects, the citizen of a nation that Johnson professed to dislike and a bundle of contradictions constantly veering between melancholia and high spirits, lechery and remorse, folly and prudence, drunkenness and vows of sobriety. A contemporary called him "a tom-tit twitt'ring on an eagle's back" and Macaulay pronounced him a fool. He was neither, though he often appeared so to the world's eyes. Johnson responded to those qualities in Boswell that interest us today—his generosity, unabashed candor, lively sensibilities, good humor, and innocent desire to know, to be known, to please. Boswell found in Johnson the true mentor of his life, the source of authority and wisdom that his own austere father could not provide. So the two became friends and passed together, as Samuel Collings showed them in his satirical drawing, into literary legend.

The nineteenth century accepted uncritically the image of Boswell as a busybody who pursued Johnson with notebook in hand, a sycophant mounting into immortality by clutching at the great man's coattails. This view made it possible to see Johnson without Boswell, but not the other way

around. Today, with the publication of Boswell's journals and private papers, we are in a position to see the two men in different perspectives of personality, activity, and influence. We know, for example, how much of Boswell's life and art stand apart from Johnson's as well as the compensatory nature of their friendship. Certainly English literature would be the poorer without *The Life of Samuel Johnson* and *The Journal of a Tour to the Hebrides,* works to which the interplay of writer and subject gives the force of life and the force of art. The *Life* is still our portrait of the man; from its pages Johnson comes at us massive and head-on, shaggy in his rusty brown coat and black worsted stockings, rolling his head, blinking, gulping oceans of tea, discoursing eloquently, and handing down opinions on every subject under the sun. The man is Boswell's great and unique creation; he continues to exist for us in all the vigor and idiosyncrasy of his physical presence. It is otherwise with Johnson the writer. Nothing Boswell has to say can add to or detract from a reputation now preserved on library shelves and well documented by research and criticism. The writer, so noble in thought, so rigorous in his expression of the vanity of human wishes, so stately in the rolling sentences and rounded periods of his style, has receded into the literary history of his century. But with Boswell the situation is different. Nimble-minded, absurd, fallible, disarmingly honest, he comes closer to being our true contemporary. Like the characters in much modern fiction, he was a man in search of identity and his place in the continuity of things. He desired, more than anything else, a fixed and consistent character, but he was such a mixture of parts that for him the problem of human behavior became a lifelong matter of inward confusion and a source of speculation. He kept a journal because he needed some kind of record to assure himself that he was real. In the process of reporting on his day-by-day activities he also reported on the stir and bustle of the world around him. We read him now for the unsparing story of his life and for the social picture he drew. His journals contain our liveliest and most revealing account of eighteenth century social life. Among the writers of diaries and journals only Pepys surpassed him in the ability to involve the reader in the world's business or to offer himself, naked and defenceless, to the inspection of a later generation.

Boswell: The Ominous Years, 1774-1776, ninth in the series of the Boswell journals, opens on this note of candid revelation. Boswell had just emerged from a morbidly disturbing episode in his legal practice, as set forth in *Boswell for the Defence*. John Reid, charged with sheep-stealing, had been his first criminal client in 1766. Boswell won him an acquittal. But in 1774 Reid was again arrested on the same charge and once more Boswell was called to defend him. The case was hopeless from the start, but before its end the figure of the sheep-stealer confined in the Tolbooth came to dominate Boswell's energies and his imagination. The result on his part was an almost Dostoevskian searching into the nature of guilt and the order of justice, and the execution of the condemned man on September 21 left Boswell almost in a state of shock. But the trial led to a more serious threat to his peace of mind. In a desperate attempt to get his man off, he had written to *The London Chronicle* a letter casting reflections on the impartiality of Thomas Miller, the Lord Justice-Clerk who presided over Reid's trial; Boswell's foolish hope was that the letter might reach the eye of the king and that a pardon might be forthcoming at the last minute. Publication of the letter produced an unforeseen result: William Miller, son of the Lord Justice-Clerk, challenged Boswell to a duel. In this situation Boswell behaved with a mixture of timidity and brashness. He and his wife waited with trepidation while the affair was being aired. Relatives and men of influence were consulted; Johnson's advice was asked. But in the end reason prevailed and Boswell's apology was accepted, but not before he had registered in his journal a full account of his disturbed emotional state at the time. The irony of this story is that Boswell learned nothing from this experience. In 1776 we find him considering calling out the Lord Advocate after that official had criticized Lord Auchinleck. Fortunately, his departure on his annual visit to London kept him from carrying into execution his quixotic determination to defend the family honor.

At the same time he was in bitter dispute with his father over the entail of the Auchinleck estate. Dismayed by his son's profligacy, Lord Auchinleck had entailed his estate to prevent its being sold by his improvident heir or attached for debt at some future date. His lordship's intention was to give heirship to "males and females indiscriminately" of his own body, but Boswell, buoyed up by feudal sentiment, insisted that the right of inheritance should be vested in male heirs only. ("I swore to my father that if the estate was fixed on heirs whatsoever I would cut my throat," he recollects, and remembers another oath "when, with a piece of the Old Castle in my hand, I knelt upon the ruins and swore that if any man had the estate in exclusion to the rightful heir this stone should swim in his heart's blood. . . .") This quarrel, with all its clashing of strong personalities, came at a time when Boswell's creditors were pressing him and he was suing his father for payment of his debts. There is little wonder that Lord Auchinleck considered disinheriting his oldest son.

Another cause of Boswell's distress is typically Boswellian. His wife, we are told, was "averse to much dalliance." His predisposition to lust asserting itself, he meditated more and more on the idea of concubinage: "Suppose a man is *too many* for one woman, to use a common phrase, may he not be allowed to have more?" When he discussed the matter with his wife, she told him he might go to whom he pleased. He wrote in his journal: "I was unsettled."

That word describes with fair accuracy Boswell's account of his life in Edinburgh. In this respect the title given by the editors to this section of the journals is misleading, for at this time his conduct appears no better and no worse than it had been in earlier years or in those that immediately followed. To him Edinburgh was never the Athens of the North; it was a place of family responsibilities and professional drudgery, burdens lifted only by his annual excursions to London and the light of Johnson's presence. "His mind is at once a magnifying glass and a prism," he writes. "It enlarges and brightens, separates and colours objects." Boswell finds little brightness or

relief in his Edinburgh environment. Instead, violence breaks in. He keeps his wife awake and almost sick with worry while he sits all night at the gaming table. He resolves to stay temperate, but after drinking five bottles of claret with a friend he falls down a steep flight of stairs "with a good deal of violence, which sobered me much. It was amazing that I was not killed or very much hurt." On another occasion he tells how "when I got home I was shockingly affected, being so furious that I took up the chairs in the dining-room and threw them about and broke some of them, and beat about with my walking-stick till I had it in pieces, and then put it into the fire and burnt it. I have scarcely any recollection of this horrid scene, but my wife informed me of it. She was in great danger, for it seems I had aimed at her both with chairs and stick. What a monstrous account of a man!" At another time, being in "a fit of gloomy passion," he throws a guinea note into the fire, but in typical Boswellian fashion he rescues it with the tongs and later has it redeemed at full value at the Royal Bank.

If Edinburgh is on the rim of Boswell's world, London is its hub. The book contains two accounts of his expeditions to the metropolis. In these we sometimes have the impression that we are reading the *Life* over again, for Johnson is always in the foreground or lurking just around the corner while Boswell attends Mass, pursues wenches, or hobnobs with the fashionable or the wealthy. During the second of these visits Johnson and Boswell visit Oxford and Lichfield and after their return Boswell finally brings Johnson and John Wilkes face to face at Mr. Dilly's dinner table. Because much of this material is already familiar, it invites comparison with the accounts given in the *Life*. Sometimes the biography contains the expansions or additions that Boswell made later; at times we find suppression of personal feeling or comment in the transfer. For instance, the *Life* reports Johnson's injunction that Boswell should try to "divert melancholy by every means but drinking." The passage in the journal contains this added reflection: "I thought then of women, but no doubt he no more thought of my indulging in licentious copulation than of my stealing." Another episode in which the journal version is more sharply rendered is the report on Johnson's exchange with Strahan's apprentice boy. Here is the scene from the *Life*:

Mr. Strahan had taken a poor boy from the country as an apprentice, upon Johnson's recommendation. Johnson having enquired after him, said, "Mr. Strahan, let me have five guineas on account, and I'll give this boy one. Nay, if a man recommends a boy, and does nothing for him, it is sad work. Call him down."

I followed him into the court-yard, behind Mr. Strahan's house; and there I had a proof of what I had heard him profess, that he talked alike to all. "Some people tell you that they let themselves down to the capacity of their hearers. I never do that. I speak uniformly, in as intelligible a manner as I can."

"Well, my boy, how do you go on?" —"Pretty well, Sir; but they are afraid I ain't strong enough for some parts of the business." Johnson. "Why I shall be sorry for it; for when you consider with how little mental power and corporeal labour a printer can get a guinea a week, it is a very desirable occupation for you. Do you hear,—take all the pains

you can; and if this does not do, we must think of some other way of life for you. There's a guinea."

Here was one of the many, many instances of his active benevolence. At the same time, the slow and sonorous solemnity with which, while he bent himself down, he addressed a little thick short-legged boy, contrasted with the boy's awkwardness and awe, could not but excite some ludicrous emotions.

The version in the journal is as follows:

Strahan had taken a poor boy from the country as an apprentice on his recommendation. He asked five guineas from Strahan, I suppose to account of his literary rents and profits, and, speaking of the boy, said, "I'll give him one. Nay, if one recommends a boy, and does nothing for him, it is not well" (or some such phrase). "Call him down to me." I went after him into Strahan's back yard, and there I had an example of what I have heard Mr. Johnson profess, that he talks alike to all. "Some people," said he, "tell you that they let themselves down to the capacity of their hearers. I never do that, Sir. Let a man speak intelligibly and uniformly." (Of the last words I am not quite certain, as the observation was made to me at Harwich in the year 1763, and my journal at that period has been lost.) "Well, my boy," said he, "how do you go on?" "Pretty well, Sir. But they are afraid I ain't strong enough for some parts of the work." Johnson. "Why, I shall be sorry for it; for when you consider with how little mental power and corporeal labour a printer can get a guinea a week, it is a very desirable business for you." (The words were pretty exactly these; and the little, short thick-legged, sniveling urchin, as one may say, was shaking himself and rubbing his pockets, while Johnson rolled superb.) "Do you hear—take all the pains you can; and if this does not do, we must think of some other way of life for you. There's a guinea." The creature thanked him, and had not parts enough to do it well.

The effect of immediacy in this scene is in its visual detail and phrasing, especially in the typically Boswellian picture, "Johnson rolled superb."

The present volume begins in a period of unrest and gloom. It ends on a note of comedy. During his London visit Boswell's curiosity was aroused by the notorious Mrs. Margaret Caroline Rudd, a woman recently freed after a trial involving forgery, for which her paramour and his brother had been hanged. A letter addressed to his wife —but never sent—tells how he went to call on the lady uninvited, found her not at home, and decided to await her return. Then follows an account of the interview between the adventuress and the rake. Boswell finds her charming because she "perfectly concealed her power to charm." He seizes her hand and kisses it; she shows the "compliance" of a lady of fashion. He sings a song for her, "The Snake." Although he never hints at an intrigue, he wonders what she thought of him. By indirection we know what he thought of

her. "I would not for a good deal have missed this scene," Boswell writes— and neither would the reader. In the letter the story is smoothly told in the light of retrospect. The notes in the journal are disconnected but more revealing:

> For [the] first [time] delirium [seized me. I. "Is a] pretty ankle one of your perfections?" [She.] "Yes." [I. Your] eyes—" [She.] "Poets and painters have told me enough of them." [When I took a] kiss, [she said, "I have] heard I had [a] fine mouth." [Snatched] several, [with] passion. Twice [I said] "Adieu"; at last. "God bless you."

Boswell: The Ominous Years is in several ways the best volume to appear since the first, *Boswell's London Journal*. It is sharp in portraiture and beautifully structured in its unfolding progression from its overcast beginning to its brightening tone and tempo in the London sections. Boswell hobnobs with the great, the notorious, the sordid with casual familiarity. Best of all, he never pretends to be anyone or anything other than himself. For most readers this picture of a sincere but weak and bedeviled man will be as much as honesty can give or art reveal.

Dayton Kohler

THE BRUTAL FRIENDSHIP
Mussolini, Hitler and the Fall of Italian Fascism

Author: F. W. Deakin (1913-   )
Publisher: Harper & Row (New York). 896 pp. $10.95
Type of work: History
Time: 1942-1945
Locale: Italy

A study of Mussolini and the last three years of his regime

Principal personages:
BENITO MUSSOLINI
ADOLF HITLER
COUNT CIANO, Mussolini's son-in-law
VICTOR EMMANUEL, King of Italy
DINO ALBERTINI, the Italian Ambassador in Berlin
MARSHAL PIETRO BADOGLIO
COUNT DINO GRANDI
BARON HANS MACKENSEN, the German Ambassador in Rome
DR. RUDOLF RAHN, German Ambassador in Rome

F. W. Deakin, of Oxford University, who was a library assistant to Sir Winston Churchill for many years, has written a book which is probably as thoroughly documented and authoritative as one can be at the present time on the subject of German-Italian relationships during World War II. In his own words, Deakin has tried "to marshal and select the massive, and at the same time fragmentary, unpublished evidence, which might throw new and detailed light on the collapse of Italian Fascism under the impact of military disaster." To accomplish his purpose, Deakin consulted all the records he reasonably could, including the Italian material collected by the Allied forces at the end of the Italian campaign, now at St. Antony's College, Oxford, and other Italian material once held by the Allies but since returned to Italian authorities. On the German side, Deakin consulted the unpublished records deposited on microfilm in the British Public Records Office, the materials of the German War Office Archives now

in the United States, and other records. He also consulted a large number of printed sources, including those published in England, the United States, Germany, and Italy. Further, he discussed the events with many persons still alive who had first-hand knowledge of them.

Some readers may wish for more commentary than the author has written, even though Deakin warns in his preface that "apocalyptic commentary" will be held to a minimum in his book. The reader simply must learn to be patient with the abundance of detailed material, the basic record of the events, which the author has assembled in his lengthy work. If there is a fault in the presentation of this wealth of material in *The Brutal Friendship,* it is not that there is too little information. Rather, any fault will be in the manner of presentation of the material. The reader must be alert at all times to the identity of the source of the material presented; the sources are not always made clear, and a wool-gathering reader can easily

37

be misled. It is important, for example, to have in mind always whether comments given about Italians were made by Italians or by Germans.

Deakin sees the Axis relationship between Italy and Germany as primarily the result of mutual admiration and friendship between Adolf Hitler and Benito Mussolini, two strong men who envisioned themselves, among other things, as the saviors of Europe from communism. The very title of the book, *The Brutal Friendship*, comes from a statement credited to Adolf Hitler in his final days: "My attachment to the person of the Duce has not changed . . . but I regret not having listened to reason which imposed on me a brutal friendship in regard to Italy." About the same time, however, Hitler revealed that his friendship for Mussolini and Italy had been, in his judgment, one of his mistakes. Deakin notes that Hitler commented, "It is visible that the Italian alliance rendered more service to the enemy than to ourselves. . . . Our Italian ally has embarrassed us everywhere. . . . It will have contributed, if we do not win in spite of everything, to making us lose the war." Despite his feelings about the alliance between Nazi Germany and Fascist Italy, Hitler always thought of Mussolini the man as a dear and admired friend. Even as late as July, 1944, at the leave-taking between the two dictators which was to be their last sight of each other, Hitler is reported to have said that Mussolini was his best, possibly his only friend in the world.

Such personal friendship was to continue. Even after Mussolini had been deposed as the political leader of Italy and taken into custody by the Badoglio government, which succeeded the Duce's Fascist regime with the help of the Italian king, Hitler's friendship was an active relationship. The German operation named "Eiche" was personally ordered by Hitler to effect Mussolini's release from Italian custody. After considerable intelligence efforts, necessary to learn Mussolini's place of captivity, which changed several times, a German force using gliders liberated the Fascist Duce from his imprisonment at Gran Sasso.

The epigraph to the last chapter of *The Brutal Friendship* is a statement made by the Duce on March 3, 1945, "Tutto cio che è entrato nella storia non si cancella." ("All that has entered history cannot be erased.") Mussolini recognized that his time had about run out. After resigning all allegiance due him before leaving the headquarters of his supposed government at Milan, which was really a puppet regime operated by German military forces, Mussolini seemed to have no purpose. Deakin suggests that the once proud and posturing dictator of Italy was consciously discarding all the relics and tokens of his power, purposely breaking the image of the Duce he had worked so hard to construct during almost two decades of control in Italy. Apparently the iconoclastic purposes were not recognized by the people who still surrounded the fallen dictator. Yet what a change they could have seen from the proud figure of Benito Mussolini, Il Duce, gesticulating and shouting to crowds of thousands of Italians from his balcony in Rome, to the huddled figure, garbed in a German enlisted man's overcoat and steel helmet, in the back of a truck—a German vehicle—when partisans captured their victim on April 27, 1945, the day before his new captors shot him down at the gates of a villa near Mezzagra.

The story told in *The Brutal Friendship* is not a biography, not the personal story of Mussolini. It is the story of the dissolution of a relationship between two countries, a relationship which perhaps began in distrust and certainly ended in Italy's becoming the scorned subject nation of Germany. This is a chapter in Italian history which presumably Mussolini's countrymen will be slow to forget.

Gordon W. Clarke

A BURIED LAND

Author: Madison Jones (1925-   )
Publisher: The Viking Press (New York). 295 pp. $4.95
Type of work: Novel
Time: 1939-1940; 1947
Locale: Warrington, Tennessee

A multiple-murder story, in which the hero eventually admits his implicated guilt, serving as a vehicle to carry a particular point of view identifiable in the title

Principal characters:
>PERCY YOUNGBLOOD, a clerk in the TVA and later a lawyer
>TRACY YOUNGBLOOD, his father
>RACHEL YOUNGBLOOD, his mother
>CORA KINKAID, seduced by Percy
>FOWLER KINKAID, her brother
>UNCLE KISHE BAKER, kin to the Kinkaids
>DORCAS BAKER, kin to Uncle Kishe
>JESSE HOOD, Percy's accomplice
>EDGAR CADENHEAD, Percy's senior partner and mentor
>ABBY DELOACH, Percy's girl friend
>LONNIE WASHINGTON, a boy who shot his father
>MRS. WASHINGTON, his mother
>MAGRUDER, the district attorney
>JUDSON DUKE, a storekeeper
>JUDGE BUCK

Madison Jones's third novel is carefully constructed to argue a familiar philosophy from a murder for which the blame is not resolved until three more murders have been precipitated by the first. The dedication of the novel to Donald Davidson, like that to Andrew Lytle in Mr. Jones's second novel (*Forest Of The Night,* 1960), is useful and necessary in identifying the point of view, for the novelist has taken such pains to convert a *roman à thèse* into a story of remorse that the novel ends up uneasily balanced between two moralities, almost between a code and an ethic. The reader is supposed to mourn the passing of the values represented by the hillbilly in what is now the depths of Appalachia —or the new "South" in fiction; but the direction of the story makes the hero's predicament one of greater pathos: Percy Youngblood is a willing but not wholly conscious traitor to the code of his locality, and the greater subject of the novel, not permitted to dominate the action, is the tragedy of youth which somehow or other is seduced from the beliefs of its fathers until it comes to see too late that old saws are truer to life than modern instances.

This collapse of communication between father and son may equally be the fault of the older generation, but that possibility is not admitted in *A Buried Land*: Percy is the villain of the region and the awful example of the sermon preached from the text of the epigraph from Aeschylus's *The Eumenides*: "Woe on you, woe, ye younger gods!" That the novelist's parents share the dedication with Donald Davidson may be an indication that the work as a whole is an act of affection or of expiation by one who has come through, in less obviously violent a manner, the same crisis as Percy Youngblood, a crisis many now in their forties must have shared.

The novel is almost wholly set in Warrington, Tennessee, beginning in 1939 or 1940 when the little country town is in turmoil with the last clearances of people, trees, and houses from the valleys which the newly completed nearby dam will now begin to flood, turning it into "a buried land." "This is a dramatic place. . . . We've got the Stone Age and the twentieth century bumping into each other here . . . you brush elbows with Neanderthals every day," says Percy later in the novel; and, looking back at 1940, he adds, "I thought we had drowned most of it, but there's still a lot. You can hear the tribes chanting on Sunday morning." And better for Percy if he had hearkened to the hymn he heard when he went to pick up Cora Kinkaid from a meeting and thus initiate the tragedy:

". . . where I first saw the light
And the burden of my heart rolled away."

Among the loot the social turmoil of 1939 offers is young Cora, already seduced by Percy's friend, Jesse Hood (the "hood"); she is alone in town now that her mother has died from the eviction from the family farm and her brother Fowler is working nights at the dam. Fowler is "a tough one to get tangled with," thinks Percy, but he accepts Jesse's reply—"a dumb bumpkin" —and Jesse's casual gift of Cora because Percy is also alone in town now that he has broken with his father over working for the TVA.

Given this situation, two violent acts initiate the plot of the novel—one the literal murder of Cora, the other the metaphorical murder of Tracy Youngblood and all he stands for; both are committed in circumstantial fashion by Percy, and the greater of these is parricide. Percy would not have seduced Cora had he not previously revolted from his father's hillbilly ways and followed the "younger god," here represented as the TVA; and Tracy Youngblood metaphorically bleeds to death from the wound of his firstborn's revolt and desertion. The latter defiance is completed by Percy's absence from the gathering which witnesses the disinterring of the family graves, a scene that must have happened often throughout the hill country in those prewar years and to which the author does full justice.

This second chapter is largely narrated by Percy's mother, Rachel, as she reviews the argument between father and son; to Tracy's terse, concrete, and

40

limited objections to being evicted by a dam Percy can counter only with the large and as yet unrealized objectives of the TVA—in the setting of the doomed family kitchen he sounds as if he were suffering from dropsy of the imagination. The agrarian theme is nicely summed up in the disinterring with the discovery of Tracy's grandmother's copper coffin; through its glass plate Tracy sees for the first time the sleeping face of the old pioneer. For a haunting moment time reels back, only to be accelerated violently when the glass breaks and the face instantly crumbles to dust as the twentieth century breaks in.

Some few months later Cora, after suffering the ministrations of an abortionist, bleeds to death on the back seat of Percy's car; he and Jesse drop her body in one of the abandoned graves, secure in the knowledge that this land will soon be buried under water behind the dam. For these "young bloods" the episode is dead and buried.

Not so the older order: Fowler Kincaid begins the search for his sister and by the end of the first part he has rejected two explanations for her sudden disappearance. The preacher offers him the comfort of "the Lord giveth and taketh away. . . . He can give it back." Fowler sneers, "What about that valley down there? He going to give that back?" The preacher says, "If it's His will. Or else give you something in place of it." "They ain't a thing I want in place of it," Fowler answers, and he speaks for a whole order of existence.

The murder of Cora and the drowning of the valley are thus related and conflated so that a familiar small-town tragedy assumes universal proportions. With Fowler's murder of an "oily,"

"swarthy" man (possibly the brother of Jesse's "little wop woman") who offers the other explanation for Cora's disappearance—that she has run off with a man—the first part of the novel ends and the elements of the drama are visible. The other three parts of the novel bring Percy to realize that he cannot make peace with the old gods until he confesses to Cora's murder, reveals her burial place, and admits his violation of his father's code.

Bringing Percy's parricide home to him is accomplished by forces outside him, as is appropriate for a follower of the new materialism: when he returns eight years later to his home town and the cozy nook prepared for him by the arch-villain, lawyer Edgar Cadenhead, the presence of Jesse and the return of Fowler from prison exert pressures not on his conscience (for Cora's death is of secondary importance in the novel's scale of values) but on his ambition, the primal evil on this scale. As Cora's death is an outward and visible sign of the inward and spiritual disgrace of Percy's killing of his father, so the events of latter parts of the novel repeat and reverse the action of the first part. A number of new characters are introduced for this purpose but those who represent the old order remain: Rachel, the mysterious Judson Duke who with the felt presence of Judge Buck represents the Furies, and Fowler Kinkaid, who is largely responsible for Percy's salvation.

As a representative of "the younger gods" Percy is, of course, a hard nut to crack, and a number of complementary actions are necessary to create inner turmoil in his shallow breast. Dorcas Baker, Fowler's cousin, takes the place of Cora and acts out a latter-day solution to the mystery of Cora's disappear-

41

ance of leaving town for the big city, but not before she has told Fowler Percy's odd story about a fellow "up north" who got a girl in trouble and got rid of her. Percy's girl friend, Abby, turns on him and reminds him that "We are bumpkins, we came from bumpkins." Acting on Dorcas' hint, Fowler murders Jesse, and Magruder, the district attorney, begins casting a net which Percy feels is slowly and surely implicating him; in desperation he kills Fowler.

This detection of Cora's mysterious death is complicated by a new murder. Lonnie Washington murders his father, one of "the stamp . . . that nature would not yield to change," or, as the doctor expresses it, "the primitive patriarch." In spite of lawyer Cadenhead's cool advice to leave the case alone, Percy leaps to Lonnie's defense "trying to keep a boy from getting ruined for something he probably couldn't help." But Lonnie's case makes him aware of his own parricide and incapable of conducting the boy's defense, circumstances brought home to him on the eve of the trial when he fails to persuade Mrs. Washington to act as a witness for Lonnie—"he kilt his own pa. It ain't a easy thing to forgive." The wheel has come full circle: "For an instant—so familiar everything seemed —he had the clear impression that this was his mother . . . seated at the table with him." The impression is confirmed that night when Uncle Kishe Baker summons up in memory the ghost of Tracy, "fine a man as ever was."

One jump ahead of Magruder, Percy takes his mother to visit the site of the old homestead and the grave of Cora; to her he confesses his sin and turns

himself over to the forces of law. The "younger gods" have been humbled by the old order's reassertion of power deep in the most unlikely prospect. No man, it seems, can escape his county affiliations provided only that he return to the scene of the crime. This is an awkward resolution which the carefully parallelled plots, the pace of the action, the symbolic tinct of many of the details (such as the hymns mentioned earlier and the Biblical allusions in the name of Rachel), and the decided power of the writing do not wholly overcome.

But Mr. Jones has within his grasp a problem as central to our life today as any one cares to name. The heroes of his three novels have all been educated out of an ostensibly uneducated environment, most obviously Jonathan in *Forest of the Night*. In coping with this environment, education is found wanting, as Duncan in Mr. Jones's first novel, *The Innocent* (1957), freely acknowledges by his return to the home farm and his immersion in its affairs and as Percy is eventually forced to recognize. The central problem is this: "Where on earth is the educated man now at home?" The Latin root implies, for Mr. Jones, that such a man is led out of his home region, and few would contest the fact. The problem will not be solved by the novelist's taking his hero by the nose and firmly leading him back to the farm, but on Mr. Jones's own showing his work offers grounds for hope that he is one of the writers today who is in a position honestly to reconcile the life of the region and the life of the intellect.

Robert T. Robertson

42

BY THE NORTH GATE

Author: Joyce Carol Oates (1938-   )
Publisher: The Vanguard Press (New York). 253 pp. $4.50
Type of work: Short stories
Time: The present
Locale: Rural upstate New York

A first collection of fourteen stories by an extremely talented, uneven, but promising writer who specializes in an evocation of the Gothic with Northern exposure

It is unusual enough in itself for a contemporary publisher to take a chance on a collection of short stories by an unknown writer. Miss Oates' collection, *By the North Gate,* not only merited that privilege soundly, but rewarded the publisher's courage and acumen by being richly praised by the reviewers and by causing a small commercial stir. Reviewers, impressed perhaps by the wholesale quantity and cold-blooded quality of gratuitous horror in the fourteen stories, invoked Faulkner and occasionally Kafka in their evaluations. *By the North Gate* is an impressive achievement, and even more impressive considering the relative youth of the author, but it does her work no service to associate it with either of these giants with whom her affinities are, after all, rather slight. There is little that is large in Miss Oates' stories—either metaphysically or thematically large. She has had the sense, rare for a young writer, to distance herself within the limits of her reach, restricting her focus to a kind of landscape and perspective that is deliberately small and yet capable of a variety of treatment.

Her most successful and characteristic setting is in a rural, vaguely marginal, upper New York State area (roughly between the great industrial centers and the Lake). However, her farmlands are rarely in fruition; they

are typically frozen over by a weedy winter frost; the farmhouse kitchens are overheated against the outside cold and they smell of worn linoleum. And here she will usually place a large family, three generations deep, flinted, crusty people whose capacities for communication, for love and hate, are buried so deep within them that when they are evoked they tend to manifest themselves in some violent eruption. The surfaces of her stories are as deceptively placid as rutted fields, but the terrible groundswell culminates in sudden fissures of emotion, cries of anguished frustration, sporadic outbursts of mindless violence. Miss Oates usually avoids the device of first-person narration ("Images" is an unsuccessful exception), presenting her stories from a position of laconic understated impersonality which at its best intensifies the horror by the flat banality of the telling. Among contemporaries, her tone and style remind one most of James Purdy (ruralized and stripped of his conscious artistry) and Flannery O'Connor (without her occasional sense of lyric beauty). Unlike both, however, she is innocent of a sense of humor, mordant or religious.

Her stories tend to cluster in a mythical "Eden County" where the inhabitants have long ago fallen from grace and where the mortal condition of futility has become a prison of custom.

There her characters accept the wheel of iron without protest and without search for escape save in the sudden flurries of ferocity to which they are as much spectators as actors. Her most persuasive characterizations are with the very youthful and the very elderly. In the solid Romantic tradition she sees a link between age and childhood, finding in both a perverse proximity to the deep springs of unawareness where an Eden County might be truly Edenic. Thus her children and old people have a special capacity for suffering their exclusion from the Garden, and their suffering is particularly poignant because it is soundless, wretched, and normatively insane. For her world receives its norms of behavior from the people who are neither very young nor very old—the real slaves to spiritual poverty, the genuine nomads of the barbarous land that the author surveys from the North Gate. The direct knowledge of the children in "The Census Taker" and the tormented grief of the old men in "Swamps" and "By the North Gate" provide the compassionate displaced center of Miss Oates' theme. Measured by the standards of Eden County, their outraged protest is disproportionate, a sickness that is ignored with only the minimal sympathies of conventional decency. Measured by the outrage, however, the others are pitilessly condemned as hopeless—as in utter irrevocable despair. From behind her impersonal narrative point of view, Miss Oates shatters the imperturbable lens and becomes inexorable judge. It is an indication of her youth, however, that her judgment is not wholly free from a kind of sentimental *Weltschmerz* which perjures the sentence and turns the horror of the vision against the sen-

sibilities with which she responds to it. There can be a posturing even in agony.

Thematically Miss Oates seems to be concerned with the incessant ephemerality of life, the inexhaustible Heracleitian monster which destroys each moment in its passing and floods the agonized consciousness with overwhelming incertitude. Everything changes; nothing can be seized upon and held fast. Nothing can be known with certainty as truth; no form of beauty or virtue remains constant in the steady flow of existence ("Sweet Love Remembered"). Change is seen in Miss Oates' world as the vital enemy which saps the strength of ideals, which sullies goodness and beauty, which erodes the tenuous bonds of human contact. And memory is seen as a pathetic human artifice, distorting, helpless, and unreliable, a jerrybuilt bridge across the flux tottering on illusory piers in nothingness. This is surely a terrifying perception ("The Census Taker"), but Miss Oates contradicts it with an opposing interest. Although she projects the terror in the vision of the existential slide into the abyss, she is also arrogantly contemptuous of the human strategies which men have fashioned to ward off the terror—the strategies of tradition, categories, conventions, law. Her sympathies are quite patently on the side of the revolt against the flimsy abstractions which civilization has erected.

And yet perhaps there is an important confusion in this ambivalence which Miss Oates has not yet mastered. As she projects the two positions, the terror of the flux and the pomposities of the human conventions against it, she fails to find a viable third position on which she can safely stand. In the metaphysical grammar of her fictions, she leaves herself without a choice. She is philosophically incapable of embracing the Heracleitian flow with exhilaration, and she seems temperamentally too ascetic to accept the human constructs of a prudential coexistence. There are faint intimations in her work of a possible religious position, one which can combat the flux as the major enemy, even while it enjoys the luxury of despising mere human conventions from an exaltation of superior grace or faith or supernal surety. But these intimations are almost vestigial in her bleak sermons in frozen stones. If she does launch her metaphors from a religious point of view, it is a religion of Good Friday, and the sky is darkened in the height of the afternoon. The effects of this moral confusion are to force her dramas into sensationalism, to make her individual actions grotesque rather than symptomatic.

In the stories which depart from the marginal rural characters (especially seen in the figure of Grace in "Pastoral Blood"), Miss Oates betrays a youthful clumsiness. She has little imaginative understanding (as does Purdy) for the middle-class horrors of well-fed and well-bred people. Similarly, her story which leaves Eden County entirely for the world of collegiate bohemia ("The Expense of Spirit") demonstrates that her range at the moment is seriously limited. But she is a very young writer, and if one has a sense of *déjà vu* in reading stories like "An Encounter with the Blind" or "Boys at a Picnic," she does exhibit a voice and metier of her own in "Sweet Love Remembered" and "The Fine White Mist." In what direction her talent will grow, whether it will contract and intensify as Miss O'Connor's has done, or whether it will broaden into wider human range, it is impossible to predict. But this first collection brings the most fashionable of Gothic horrors to the unlikely rural areas of New York State and displays a considerable talent in the doing.

Earl H. Rovit

CAT AND MOUSE

Author: Günter Grass (1927-   )
Translated from the German by Ralph Manheim
Publisher: Harcourt, Brace and World (New York). 189 pp. $3.95
Type of work: Novel
Time: World War II
Locale: Danzig, Germany

A novel telling of a young Catholic fanatically devoted to the Virgin Mother but thwarted in his desire to perform heroic service for his idol and humanity

Principal characters:
PILENZ, the narrator and an admirer of Mahlke
JOACHIM MAHLKE, a frail boy with a large and active Adam's apple
TULLA POKRIEFKE, a skinny girl
FATHER GUSEWSKI, a practical-minded priest
WALDEMAR KLOHSE, a severe school principal

The spiritual recovery of Germany has lagged far behind its economic recovery, and nowhere has this lag been more apparent than in the failure of German literature to regain the eminence it had attained before World War II in the work of Thomas Mann, Franz Kafka, and Herman Hesse. All of these writers diagnosed the malady then festering in the German soul, a spiritual malaise to be seen in the horrors of the Nazi regime. That malady and its effects have been long in healing, but the recent emergence of several writers of the first rank suggests that the new Germany is finding its voice and being spiritually reborn. Perhaps the most notable among them, certainly the most heralded, is Günter Grass, whose first novel, *The Tin Drum*, established him as a major figure in the postwar reconstruction of German literature. With *Cat and Mouse*, his second novel, he reinforces his claim to that status by perceptively probing into what continues to ail the German spirit.

Though narrated in 1961 by an adult named Pilenz, who works as a secretary for a Parish Settlement House, *Cat and Mouse* is set in the years of World War II, when Pilenz was a teenager and schoolboy. Caught up in the dull round of secular life in a socialist state and poignantly aware of a great spiritual emptiness in his world (he is a Catholic who lost his belief in God in his youth), Pilenz feels compelled to tell the story of his boyhood friend, Joachim Mahlke, who disappeared, after deserting the army, by diving into a sunken minesweeper where they played as boys and Mahlke had a secret retreat. Though fifteen years have elapsed since then and the time of writing, Pilenz has anxiously sought out Mahlke on every occasion and in every place where he could possibly appear; he has never given up hope that his friend will "resurface." Thus *Cat and Mouse* is dedicated, as it were, to resuscitating the spirit of Mahlke, to rediscovering a spiritual basis for German life and art.

The resuscitation, or the writing of the novel by Pilenz, is a complicated matter. Time has dimmed and confused his memory, so that his story is as much a reconstruction of the past as a recollection of it, as much the re-

46

creation of Mahlke, and of that part of himself Mahlke represents, as memory. A self-conscious artist, Pilenz realizes that his story, written out of inner necessity, is like all art a fusion of reality and the imagination. What he remembers most vividly, and provides him with a grip on the past and himself, is a boyhood scene in which he or one of his friends—he remembers it differently each time he returns to it —encouraged a black cat to pounce on Mahlke's mouse, that is, his Adam's apple, while he lay asleep. About this fable-like incident Pilenz constructs his tale of how the beast of death eventually kills Mahlke's mouse. Ultimately a novel about writing a novel, *Cat and Mouse* is a definition and revival of those spiritual qualities lost with Mahlke's disappearance, the dialogue of recollection being a way of making him reappear in the consciousness of the narrator and his public.

Endowed with an abnormally large and active Adam's apple and lacking in physical grace and beauty, Joachim Mahlke was an unnoticed figure among the neighborhood children until he learned to swim at the age of fourteen. Thereafter he was a moral force—in leading them in the swim to the sunken boat, in diving into dangerous depths and staying beneath the surface for long periods while collecting trophies, and in being modest and considerate. He was not, however, nature's darling: besides lacking physical grace and beauty, he never tanned and the cold water chilled him blue and coarsened his skin. Furthermore, he had no interest in girls or in displays of virility. Rather, he was driven by self-consciousness to use the power he was blessed with to hide his Adam's apple, to redeem his natural being and

shortcomings. For that purpose he devoted himself to self-transcending ideals, represented alternately by the Virgin Mother and military heroes. These provided him with religious idols before which he could kneel in purifying devotion.

Always audience conscious, Mahlke originally wanted to be a clown so that he could make people laugh and help them be happy, but the Catholic Church, the German state, through its heroes and schools, and the war sapped his faith and channeled his power toward destructive ends. Eventually, he who had been called the Redeemer by a classmate caricaturist, is refused recognition for his military exploits by the school that had taught him that heroes are made by slaughter in the name of the state, and is led to betray his initial religious and humanistic impulses by the pressure of social and political circumstances. Frustrated in his aspiration to reveal the truth to school children, he is left with nothing to believe in, with no honorable task to perform. His disappearance into the minesweeper comes as a final gesture of knowledge and repudiation, perhaps an awareness of his inability to hide his Adam's apple, certainly a recognition of the inability of his society to harbor his spiritual talents and aspirations or acknowledge their source. Thus his was the hero's dilemma: he was the victim of the contradictions between his inordinate desire to serve and the refusal of the common order to tolerate him and his idol.

The disappearance and absence of the heroic, then, is what ails Germany in Günter Grass' diagnosis. But the traditional heroes are not those whose loss he laments, not the supermen of the Nibelung championed by Nietzsche and Wagner. What Grass resuscitates, replacing them with the Virgin Mother, is the Christian-chivalric vision in which masculine power is bound in service to feminine tenderness, in which nature is tamed and saved from its inherent evil through devotion to purifying spiritual values, in which the magnetism of love replaces domination by tyrannical force.

Mahlke's ultimate defeat hinges on the triviality of a medal stolen from a war hero at school, a circumstance which seems at first glance a narrative weakness; but it is actually the novel's strength. Though it is in places reminescent of Kafka's allegory and Mann's irony, conspicuously absent from *Cat and Mouse* are the demonic powers that haunted and doomed the characters in their works. Pilenz, though he cannot be sure he incited the cat to pounce on Mahlke's mouse, knows he is implicated in his disappearance and so writes out of guilt, using art as a vehicle to redeem his sin. Recognition of what he has lost, of how far he has fallen, implies a spiritual awakening sufficient for the first steps toward freedom from necessity, the bondage of the past. Correspondingly, Grass' fable-like story, blending symbolism and irony with realism, expresses the power of the imagination to transform the "real," to forget enough of the past to entertain ideals again, to believe enough in its spiritual origins and power, as Mahlke did in the Virgin Mother, to make genuine art again possible.

Lyric and comic as well as tragic, the final import of the novel, then, is that the German spirit can face its past with history, avoid possession by its demons, and be aware of the spiritual power and transcendent values necessary for a truly new and healthy life.

William R. Robinson

CAUSE FOR WONDER

Author: Wright Morris (1910-   )
Publisher: Atheneum Publishers (New York). 272 pp. $4.50
Type of work: Novel
Time: The present and thirty years ago
Locale: Los Angeles and Schloss Riva, a castle in Austria

The story of a man who in his confrontation of the past with the present finds a meaning to the continuum of his life

Principal characters:
>WARREN HOWE, the narrator
>FREMONT OSBORN, his uncle
>ETIENNE DULAC, the owner of Schloss Riva
>FRAU DULAC, his wife
>SOL SPIEGEL, a dealer in salvaged goods
>SEYMOUR GATZ, an agent
>CHARLES HORNEY, an educator
>WOLFGANG PRUTSCHER, an Austrian scholar
>KATHERINE BROWNELL MORLEY, a society matron and old flame of Howe's
>BRIAN CAFFREY, her grandson
>GEORGE, a fairly harmless lunatic who haunts the Schloss

Wright Morris has long been a master of the sleight-of-hand. His fifteen books are marked by the brilliance of his skill but some, as might be expected, are rather less successful than others. Where his most recent work has been a savage and sardonic picture of contemporary American life, *Cause for Wonder,* although the *Angst* remains, is finally merely an amusing and ingenious pastiche—a literary *tour de force.*

The cards Morris holds in the complex game he plays with the reader are those of time, past, present, and future. We travel with the narrator Warren Howe, an unachieved writer (". . . if you could tell the difference between what happened, and what you wanted to happen, you would write a great book") and quester for self-identity back and forth through time and space, redefining and rediscovering experience.

The occasion of the novel is an announcement of the death of Etienne Dulac, an audacious eccentric who is master of Schloss Riva, a magnificent memory-haunted ruin of a castle near Vienna. A group of people, all influenced in one way or another by Dulac's example, gather at Riva to attend his funeral and to uncover the mystery of the castle (the mystery of the past) which has given Howe, and hopefully the reader, cause for wonder.

The black-rimmed announcement leads Howe not only to Riva but to other voyages as he tries to raise someone from the depths of his past to help him exorcise the ghost of Dulac. His agent, Seymour Gatz, who having read *The Great Gatsby,* goes around calling everyone "Old Sport," offers to pay his way to Riva to investigate the property; Gatz has a client who is eager to buy a "place to hide." Howe first approaches his uncle, Fremont Osborn. Fremont, by plowing fifteen hundred acres in an arid section of Texas which he continued to work through desolation and ruin with a kind of deliberate passion, is a child of his time—the first to plow the dustbowl, the first to buy a car worth more than his home. Time has brought Fremont at last to a trailer court as a handyman where, as he sits in his hook-and-eye shoes, he warns Warren, "You can't live in the past, boy. Can't even die in it." The ironic flood has left him, shored, not believing in the past, but yet a perversely heroic embodiment of it.

Fremont had visited Warren at Riva thirty years before when an avalanche had literally forced the latter to spend the winter in the castle licking his physical and spiritual wounds; so had Katherine Brownell and Sol Spiegel. Charles Horney, however, Howe's boyhood pal, the fellow whose life is ultimately a reaction to his, had not been invited. Charles has since constructed a famous school for the present, all of its buildings underground ("As he says, if you live in the present you can't help but be ahead of your time"). Would he, had he had the chance thirty years before, have uprooted that career which was to lead to fortune and *Time* magazine cover fame? Yes, says Horney, for "Just a postcard, Warren —saying how much you missed me." The invitation now, of course, comes too late.

At last Howe finds a cohort in his plot to recapture the past—Sol Spiegel, enterprising head of Spiegel's Salvage. Spiegel collects everything; there is no flotsam he cannot mark up and make a profit on. He had shared Riva with Warren and is eager to salvage what he can of the past.

So the group forms at the castle: Howe, Spiegel, Dulac's wife (a former opera singer with the voice of an angel but the body of an unfortunately large toad—a fitting memorial to the perversity of Dulac's vision), Wolfgang Prutscher, and finally Katherine Brownell Morley with her young, egg-shaped grandson, Brian Caffrey. Three decades before, Prutscher had been a friend to Howe and tutor not only to Katherine, an art history major from Buffalo, but also to the sons of the slightly *Dada* Monsieur Etienne Dulac, who lived in a medieval castle, filled with several centuries of debris, on one of the lower Alps. So Howe came to Riva and Katherine, whom he once perhaps had loved and who had once perhaps loved Prutscher, all now middle-aged, to gather at Dulac's funeral. Dulac defeats expectation, however. He is, on the arrival of his guests, still technically alive though senile, or, as one of the characters guesses, pretending to be senile. But despite debility, his stature is revealed. Dulac, who in his castle, his domain, had evaded modern time, the draft, plumbing, and central heating, could not evade Hitler. The castle had become a refuge for Jews; when the oppressors came for their victims Dulac was taken too on a stretcher with the others. The Germans, not wishing to destroy the castle, had laid siege to it and starved Dulac's army out in classic fashion. After the war his wife was able to find him and nurse him to a small health and a rather diminished sovereignty (the castle is available for guided tours).

The relationship between Dulac and Howe's Uncle Fremont is inescapable. Both through audacity, a kind of heroic madness, attempt to escape the restrictions of the conventional world, attempt to re-create the terms of existence to suit the needs of identity. Both are ultimate pioneers.

Who has sent the obituary notices? Dulac himself, with the aid of Prutscher—to Katherine whom, of the three men during that long-ago winter, only he was man enough to bed; and to Howe of whom Katherine says, "Warren hasn't changed. He came along to take notes. It helps him believe it." With his reality established, Dulac can at last die in a room full of "the scent of apples, firm and rotten, and smell of compost in the dark corners . . . like a storm cave, a burial site strangely appropriate to the remains, such as they were of Monsieur Etienne Dulac." And time itself becomes meaningful.

Skull time—wouldn't that do for all of them? A form of daylight time salvage, a deep-freeze where time was stored like the mammoth in the Siberian cake of ice. In his stomach green grass, on his flanks red flesh on which time had left no marking. But even that was less timeless than Howe's non-melting pond of ice. No thaw would reach it. In the round of his skull that time had stopped.

To bear in mind—what was that but the gift of life? The sane man and the madman had it, the junkman's yen for salvage. A lock of hair, a ring, a looted ruin. What could possibly be more commonplace, or more miraculous? Monsieur Etienne Dulac, the madman who had put time in its place. What place? The madcap round of his skull. Ridiculous to waste sad time on the clock's face, on the rock's face, on the Moon's face, or the timeless face of Dulac. What time was it? At any moment such time as there was was present. It came and went unbidden, as Brian Caffrey had come to Riva, and would take away with him his own time-less report.

Howe would never know, nor if he knew would recognize, the image that would one day emerge, like the mammoth, from the deep-freeze between his ears. Was that why it seemed a good place to hide? What, after all, was this Riva, this apple-scented bier for a madman, but a symbol, suitably haunted, of the mind? A looted ruin crowded with ghosts. That time-cheat, Monsieur Dulac, no longer truly lay on his bier of apples, but had been borne away in Brian Caffrey's block of ice.

This passage achieves a kind of epiphany which almost justifies this allusive and elliptical work. Wright Morris is an important American novelist and the pleasures of his fiction are extensive. Like Ring Lardner before him, Morris is a deadly serious comic writer with a fierce eye for the grotesque distortions of our nightmare time. At his best, while showing us the moral erosions of our culture, he is devastatingly funny and deeply compassionate. In *Cause for Wonder* the wit remains, but not the compassion. Despite the book's inventiveness and brilliances (the style in its quirky way is almost flawless) it is hard to care about the desires and pratfalls of the characters; nothing real seems to be at stake, and one cannot, as one must, take seriously the comic acrobatics of the plot. Morris knows as well as anyone how to make prose do what he wants it to do. Perhaps this is the reason for the disappointment of this new novel—he knows now too well. Where Morris' best novels have been created out of love, *Cause for Wonder* has been willed through technique out of bemusement. Bemusement is not enough.

Jonathan Baumbach

51

THE CENTAUR

Author: John Updike (1932-   )
Publisher: Alfred A. Knopf (New York). 303 pp. $4.00
Type of work: Novel
Time: 1947
Locale: Olinger, Pennsylvania

A novel that utilizes mythology, real life, and theology to dramatize a contemporary situation comparable to that of Chiron and Prometheus

> Principal characters:
> GEORGE CALDWELL (CHIRON), a general science teacher at Olinger High School
> PETER CALDWELL (PROMETHEUS), his fifteen-year-old son, later "an authentic second-rate abstract expressionist" painter
> CASSIE CALDWELL (CHARICLO/CERES), George Caldwell's wife and mother of Peter
> MRS. VERA HUMMEL (APHRODITE), a high-school gym teacher
> AL HUMMEL (HEPHAESTUS), her husband, a lame garage owner
> PENNY FOGLEMAN (PANDORA), a ninth-grade student and Peter's first love
> LOUIS M. ZIMMERMAN (ZEUS), the supervising principal at Olinger High School

Read the first time with no thought of writing about it, *The Centaur*, John Updike's third novel, and winner of the 1964 National Book Award for fiction, is nearly unmitigated delight. The style hurries the reader without harrying him. There are quickly occurring unusual incidents—like George Caldwell's coming upon Vera Hummel in the shower room, the Bacchanalian basketball game, the hilariously serious class in which Caldwell tells the story of the universe from chaos to man—that seem to have deeper significance, but which you let lie lightly in the back of your mind. Though the surface plot is no more full of extraordinary action than that of *The Poorhouse Fair* or *Rabbit, Run,* it engages thoroughly. It is not the sex, of which there is less than in *Rabbit, Run* and which is handled with functional naturalness, that keeps the reader involved. It is not the depth of characterization either, for even at a first reading the characters seem to stand for mythological characters as well as for themselves and one feels that the fusion is imperfect.

The characters are adequately believable, as is the action as a whole, only because Mr. Updike's skill compels one to accept his mythical real universe and the people necessary to its rowdy movement that hurries ahead in at least a simulation of order. Of course, in a first reading part of the delight comes from the realization that John Updike is writing interestingly about the human condition—something like that of Chiron and Prometheus whom one readily identifies as Caldwell and his son Peter; characters somewhere between angel and beast too often striving hubristically to become like gods; people good and bad, miserable and ecstatic, sometimes accepting limits with good humor and good sense, alive and nearly cheerful even when the worst occurs.

This is the reaction of the reader as he reads for the first time. Reading more critically a second time, he becomes aware of both glaring defects and greater significances. He sees, for example, that the mythological index (which is inaccurate sometimes and often a source of distraction) points up the failure of Mr. Updike to fuse altogether satisfactorily myth and reality; indeed, once one becomes seriously aware of the myth behind the reality, confusion begins to destroy partially the novel's effectiveness. Caldwell changes so swiftly back and forth from Chiron, the noblest and wisest of the centaurs, to his everyday self as a high-school science teacher that we are annoyed even as we admire Mr. Updike's dexterity. (Indeed, one sometimes wishes that Mr. Updike's pyrotechnical dexterity would change into simple ponderousness.) With Peter/Prometheus the novelist succeeds better, perhaps because he starts with the ordinary Peter as a realistic boy instead of starting, as he does with Caldwell, by letting us see him first as though he were in fact a centaur. But the greater significance comes through despite distraction. Aware as one was only in part at first, he is able on a second reading to survive by-the-way annoyances sufficiently to make him think again of man's condition as it is expressed in the quotation from Barth that ends by describing man as "the creature on the boundary between heaven and earth."

The greater significance one discovers on a second reading involves itself with a spectacular unevenness that almost "outmuscles time and tide" as it conveys both the feeling of ecstasy and the fear of doom the injured father and his Promethean son feel fre-quently. The ordinary events which Mr. Updike's skill suspend into the extraordinary dramatize both the apocalyptic vision of a civilization about to burn out and the counterpointing hope of joyous redemption. Whether the father gets to school on time or gets his old car to start, partly because of and partly in spite of the mythological parallels Mr. Updike intends, takes on the importance of Columbus' search for a Western passage or a mystic's search for God. Although The Centaur is marred seriously by an ambitiousness that veers toward pretensiveness, it survives all of its equatings of Caldwell with Chiron, of his wife with Ceres, of Zimmerman with Zeus, of countless other characters with innumerable mythological figures, because Mr. Updike cannot escape his real commitment, the question of how Man, modern American man, and America can endure. And, of course, Mr. Updike does command his difficult substance enough of the time to make one want to praise more than he blames a novel that makes one hope Mr. Updike's future work will really assume major proportion. At the same time he must admit that The Centaur is ungainly when set beside the neat perfection of most of his short fiction and the more controlled novels, Rabbit, Run and The Poorhouse Fair, which preceded it.

The greater significance, awkwardly intertwined with the progression of the "real" story, is religious here as it always has been in John Updike's fiction, a point made by C. Fitzsimmons Allison in his discussion of Updike in the June, 1963, issue of The Episcopalian. In The Poorhouse Fair, his first novel, a sympathetic humanist, Conner, who believes the day will come when suffering will be abolished, is in conflict with a horribly believable present reality that forebodes a future when the nation has become populated by pleasure-seekers who "live as cells of a body do in the coffin." In *Rabbit, Run*, Harry Angstrom is the eternal seeker (again sympathetically portrayed) of heaven on earth, subtly countered by Father Eccles, who hopes and works for the salvation of all those he can, despite his awareness of the difficulties the author points out following the title page in a quotation from Pascal: "The motions of grace, the hardness of the heart; eternal circumstances." Since *Rabbit, Run* poses rather than attempts to solve the problem Pascal's *pensée* suggests, probably it is his best novel; but one must recognize that this novel's relative failure is caused by commendable ambition. Overtly, the simple story of three days in the life of Caldwell and his son Peter, ambiguously complex with its mythological cohesions and puzzles, it is also the story of any man who perpetually faces the depravity and beauty of the real world represented by the high school in which Caldwell teaches. Caldwell is defeated, but he does not retire and he *does* pass on the potential of limited victory to his son Peter, just as Chiron did to Prometheus and as Christ did to members of the churches according to Christian theologians. Despite all the ineptitudes *The Centaur* contains, it is Updike's most interesting novel because of what it attempts to show: man's limited condition which must be faced in the hope that "the love within which all other love finds speech" will prevail and alleviate the tragedy inevitable in man's fate.

It is impossible to avoid pointing out some of the flaws that make *The Centaur* imperfect despite its immense interest. One cannot avoid wondering why the skillful, almost too neat, writer of short stories collected in *The Same Door* and *Pigeon Feathers* insistently mixes up naturalistic and poetic techniques, unnecessarily clogs the book with similes that point up the animal part of man's nature (usually too obviously inserted comparisons to horses), and uses, though infrequently, slick and awkward sentences side by side with the felicitous, painterly sentences that make one think of Mr. Updike as one of our best stylists. Yes, one knows that all of this is to be found in Joyce from *Ulysses* onward and in other books of importance, but Mr. Updike does not yet show enough mastery of matter to justify the pyrotechnics that deflect attention. Despite one's overall admiration, there are times when one feels that *The Centaur* is either a huge joke underscored by the inclusion of a mythological index or a common reader's *Finnegans Wake*.

This judgment is unfair, however, because Mr. Updike proves, even in his slightest stories, that he is as much a novelist in quest as Caldwell/Chiron, his protagonist, or any serious, unsolemn novelist one can think of. He has been compared with Saul Bellow, whom perhaps he resembles most, but Mr. Bellow has more to say and more rarely commits ineptitudes. In some ways, notably in his sense of humor and exercise of proportion, Mr. Updike is better than J. D. Salinger, William Golding, and Patrick White, with whom he has been compared often. If one must make comparisons—and how else can one give those unfamiliar with Updike's work a just notion of his merits?—he resembles most J. F.

Powers in *Morte D'Urban,* though Powers fuses myth and reality better, and Iris Murdoch, particularly in her first gay novels, *The Flight from the Enchanter, Under the Net,* and in her current *The Unicorn.*

Perhaps it is no accident that both Miss Murdoch and Mr. Updike used beasts like gods or vice versa as characters and titled their novels with mythological man-animal words which suggest the ambiguous status of man in the universe. Indeed, it is the great virtue of both writers that novel-writing is also a search for a satisfactory metaphysic and/or theology, just as it is hopeful that they still have many years to write novels more thoroughly satisfactory than those that they have completed. One hopes they will fuse successfully myth and reality and embody their metaphysical quest with total aesthetic propriety by inventing a kind of novel that is an artistically satisfying embodiment of the perpetual quest in which all who exist are engaged.

Harvey Curtis Webster

THE CIVIL WAR: A NARRATIVE
Fredericksburg to Meridian

Author: Shelby Foote (1917-   )
Publisher: Random House (New York). 988 pp. $12.50
Type of work: Military history
Time: December, 1862-February, 1864
Locale: The United States of America and The Confederate States of America

A novelist's gracefully written secondary story of the military campaigns of the Civil War, the second volume of a three-volume study

When Shelby Foote began this massive study of the Civil War, he had a considerable reputation as a rising young novelist whose interest in history had manifested itself in a well-received short novel, *Shiloh.* After that book he turned from fiction, at least temporarily, and embarked upon the seemingly unlikely project of writing serious history on the scale of such specialists as Allan Nevins and Bruce Catton. He had not only his career as creative writer and the absence of degrees and reputation working against him, but also the simple fact that as the hundredth anniversary of the Civil War approached writers on all aspects of the subject were suddenly as thick as thieves. The first volume, telling the story of the conflict from Fort Sumter to Perryville, surprised, if it did not silence the skeptics. It was, as might be expected, beautifully written. It was obviously the product of sound, impeccable research. It was objective and fair to a fault. Clearly the writer knew his subject as well as the professional historians and just as evidently he passed all the basic tests. The book was well received, yet there was still a wait-and-see attitude: the second volume would tell the story.

With the publication of this second volume Mr. Foote has more than consolidated his gains. In the learned journals his reputation has justly soared, and at this stage the real advantages of having a history written by a good novelist are undeniable. Dealing with the crucial middle years of the war, he offers the reader things that the professional historian so seldom can offer —a deep imaginative feeling for and re-creation of place, and an ability to suspend both disbelief and judgment in dealing with the *characters* of those men on both sides who led the war, paradoxically creating more rounded, dimensional portraits of the great and lesser known principals precisely because of the kind of ambivalence found in good fiction. The objectivity of the novelist proves to be more strict than the conventional rigor of the historian.

Not without modesty, Mr. Foote is aware of his achievement and the tradition he is working in. In the "Bibliographical Note" he writes: "Richmond Lattimore's translation of the *Iliad* put a Greekless author in close touch with his model. Indeed, to be complete, the list of my debts would have to be practically endless. Proust I believe has taught me more about the organization of material than even Gibbon has done, and Gibbon taught me much; Mark Twain and Faulkner would also have to be included, for they left their sign on all they touched, and in the course of this exploration of the American scene I often found that they had been there before me." Out of context there is a certain arrogance here, the swagger of the johnny-come-lately who not only chooses to move into the restricted neighborhood of the specialists, but also chooses to tell them how to keep their lawns and tend their gardens. However, within the context of his remarkable achievement, Mr. Foote's confidence in its value seems no more than the honest self-appraisal of a master craftsman in a job well done.

At no point has Shelby Foote tried to invade the precincts of primary research. He has done what can be done and what should be done; he has brought together in sensible structure and in polished, readable detail a distillation of the fruits of many vineyards and many laborers, early and late. Yet there is much that is original in his method. Of all the secondary historians he has best understood the importance of the neglected West. With the exception of certain foreign students of military history most of the historians have accepted at face value the point of view of the participants: that the War was settled in the East because both sides intended it that way. As a novelist Mr. Foote knows more about point of view than to accept without serious question the protestations of antagonists and eye witnesses. He has carefully assembled the little-known details of the brutal campaigns of the vast, sprawling Trans-Mississippi area. Similarly he is aware of the importance of the whole complex of naval warfare, and his history offers the first coherent account of the ships and the men who sailed on them, died in them. Thus his history already stands as the most complete narrative of the War available.

There are some limitations, the deliberate limitations which make the book manageable. Mr. Foote has limited himself to the military history, only by implication and suggestion touching on the total (and impossibly complex) world of issues, of cause and effect. Much is suggested, but always without the inevitable weakness of insoluble argument.

The reader can no longer hide behind the comfortable reticence of wait and see. All blurb writing aside, we are now in possession of two thirds of the finest narrative account of the war which ripped the viscera of our nation and whose scars are still evident and ugly to behold. Shelby Foote's epic is relevant and timely, yet, like all good history, it is for all time. Now we can only wait, perhaps a little impatiently, for the final somber chapters to be written.

George Garrett

THE COLLECTED STORIES OF ELLEN GLASGOW

Author: Ellen Glasgow (1874-1945)
Edited, with an Introduction and notes, by Richard K. Meeker
Publisher: Louisiana State University Press (Baton Rouge). 254 pp. $5.00
Type of work: Short stories
Time: 1897-1925
Locale: Virginia

Stories of ghosts, courtship, and marriage in Virginia

Richard K. Meeker has here collected all twelve stories from the pen of the noted Virginia novelist, Ellen Glasgow. Seven of them first appeared in 1923 in the volume titled *The Shadowy Third and Other Stories.* Four of the stories in the new volume were published in magazines between 1899 and 1934. The last story in the collection—never given its final revision by the author—remained unpublished until 1962, seventeen years after her death and at least thirty-five years after it was written.

Most of Miss Glasgow's literary drive obviously went into the writing of her eighteen novels. That there were so few short stories seems due to two factors. For one, she preferred to study the slow working out of cause and effect, and for this the novel form was better suited. Also, she was advised by a literary friend she trusted to eschew the shorter form in order fully to realize her literary talent in the longer one. That she wrote short stories at all, Professor Meeker suggests, was due to two factors: she needed money, and the aftermath of the war so disrupted her sense of social evolution in a world she now thought mad that she found herself for a time unable to use the large canvas needed for her cause-effect studies.

Ellen Glasgow's stories have been out of print and untreated by critics for more than thirty-five years. Having collected the stories, the editor poses the question of whether this neglect has been justified. The thorough and careful introduction, together with the editorial notes appended to each story, will help the reader to give his own answer.

Four of the stories in this volume, those which dominated *The Shadowy Third* when they appeared in it, are ghost stories. They suggest Henry James of "The Jolly Corner" or "The Turn of the Screw," but, unlike his work, they insist on the literal reality of the ghosts without creating the sense of horror and engaging in the deep psychological exploration James did. These stories, like most of the others in the new volume, drew upon autobiographical materials. Frail, misfit children suggest the author as a child.

A character like the Mammy of her own childhood dominates "Whispering Leaves," a story in which, says her editor, she is "reliving her childhood at Jerdone Castle." The subject is often nervous illness, which Miss Glasgow knew in her family and in herself. Interesting overtones reflect a kind of primitivism combined with post-Darwinian romanticism. And here, as in other groups of stories, the villain is likely to be a man—dominant, repressive, and selfish. In an obvious psychological mechanism, these men are in several instances psychiatric practitioners who hurt where they should heal.

Professor Meeker points out some of the factors operative in these stories. The strength and persistence of ideas —as real as solid objects—is one. Another is the clearly apparent borrowing from Edgar Allan Poe. From him Miss Glasgow learned a good deal about the use of environment, particularly in old, run-down dwellings, to suggest and symbolize human decay. "The Fall of the House of Usher" influenced all four of these stories, most particularly "Jordan's End." Her link with twentieth century Southern literature is demonstrated, however, by her using decadence to suggest a generalized social phenomenon rather than treating only a single blighted family.

The stories dealing with marriage and courtship reveal clearly Miss Glasgow's feelings that marriage more often than not constitutes a kind of bondage for women. A persistent pattern of antagonism toward men runs through these tales of unhappiness. Their composition, just after an unsatisfactory engagement, emphasizes the use of autobiography again. One of them, "Thinking Makes It So," seems an exercise in romantic wish-fulfillment, but the others are more like the previously unpublished "The Professional Instinct," in which woman appears as passionate and noble while man appears calculating and ignoble. Here romantic love is a curse rather than a blessing. These women learn from hard experience that men are not to be trusted. The escape from love, whether through the passage of time or stoic resignation, is something to be welcomed, even at the cost of a broken heart.

Two stories in the collection consider the moral aspects of mercy killing as Miss Glasgow once more imbues her fiction with images of decline, failure, and death. It is this vision which links these stories with others, such as "Jordan's End," in which former Southern grandeur has declined finally into decadence and disaster.

Stylistically, these stories are marked by Miss Glasgow's familiar ironic commentary on character and incident. She makes use too of full description, often rather heavily symbolic. At times these characteristics are mixed incongruously with the twittering of young Southern women—belles and near-wallflowers— and with diction which suggests the romantic magazine fiction of the early years of this century. In answering the question he poses at the beginning of his introduction, Professor Meeker notes that Ellen Glasgow was at bottom more a moralist than a historian. Fond as she was of epigram, irony, and paradox, she had, he writes, all the elements necessary in a great short story writer except that of "a respect for the form." Devotees of Ellen Glasgow's work may well agree with him. Others may feel that both she and her public benefited from the fact that she followed her inclination to explore cause and effect on the large canvases which gave her talent as well as her subject the room it needed to be seen at its best.

Joseph L. Blotner

THE COLLECTOR

Author: John Fowles (1926-   )
Publisher: Little, Brown and Company (Boston). 305 pp. $4.95
Type of work: Novel
Time: The present
Locale: London; and a cottage on the outskirts, in Sussex

A chilling novel of a nondescript man's kidnaping and imprisonment of a girl to whom he is attracted

> Principal characters:
> FREDERICK CLEGG, a clerk
> MIRANDA GREY, an art student
> GEORGE PAXTON, a painter, Miranda's friend

John Fowles' first novel, *The Collector*, is notable less for the scope of what it attempts than for the scrupulous and convincing fidelity (and in this case fidelity is of necessity imaginative) which it renders. Mr. Fowles is a miniaturist—in fact, the plot of the novel in skeleton seems capable of sustaining hardly more than the substance of a short story—but it is a tribute to his skill and perception that he sustains throughout the length of the novel not only the suspense which the nature of the plot renders almost inevitable but also the full revelation of character which allows the miniature to capsule both the human heart's capacity for life and its potentiality for unconscious evil.

Fowles, like John Hawkes, deals with the grotesque and the horrible, and his horror takes its edge from his ability to make it appear almost ordinary. In *The Collector* abnormality is not so much a distortion of the ordinary as a failure of humanity which is itself almost an apotheosis of the ordinary and the drab against which the

extension of the imagination constituting humanity is defined. The action is extremely simple: a colorless, stupid young clerk—the quintessence of all lonely, unimaginative, anonymous little men—named Frederick Clegg (the ugly little monosyllable recalling Matthew Arnold's Wragg and all her implications) becomes fascinated with an attractive twenty-year-old art student named Miranda Grey, makes her the partner of his curiously non-erotic marriage fantasies, and devotes all his time to observing her when he can and discovering what he is able to learn about her life. When he wins a huge sum in a football pool, Clegg, whose only pleasure in life is his butterfly collection, decides to add Miranda to his collection: he will kidnap her and keep her prisoner until she learns to love him. Accordingly he buys a house in a secluded district one hour from London, prepares a basement room for the comfort, but also the absolutely secure detention, of his "guest," and carries through his kidnaping plan. The larger part of the novel

59

simply follows the life of prisoner and warden to the inevitable, given the mind of Clegg, but nonetheless ghastly conclusion.

The technique of *The Collector* is essentially the juxtaposition of two orders of mind: Clegg's pathetic but terrifying self-enclosure and deadness, and Miranda's youthful, sometimes banal, but always vital and imaginative love of life. The first section is Clegg's account of his obsession, his plan, and his forced imprisonment of Miranda; the second is Miranda's secret diary written during her incarceration. The grisly two-part coda is, of course, again Clegg's.

Clegg's style is the image of his mind: flat, cliché-ridden, impervious to the rhythms and nuances of anything beyond itself. In it he haltingly gropes his way through the tangled history of his uncomprehended impulses and their fulfillment: his capture of Miranda and his efforts to win her love, her repeated attempts to escape and the eventual resisted seduction of her captor, his vengeful photographing of her nude and bound, and, ultimately, the unexpected "something" which he never, he thinks, intended but around which his thoughts continually hover in the first section. The horror of Clegg's monologue is that he takes perfectly for granted the entirety of his mad scheme, never questioning that the pain which he inflicts upon another human being is other than entirely justified. That Miranda will finally come to love him he never doubts, so that he puts her off from moment to moment, promising her that he will release her shortly if only she will accept her condition peacefully, while all the time he intends to make her imprisonment one for life. Clegg is

incapable of comprehending the existence of another human being, and hence of even comprehending the confused drives which move him. But in his character there is pathos, mixed with horror, which springs from the longing he feels for that which he does not understand, the yearning toward the beauty and spontaneity of life from which he is forever cut off, and which he must render inert and lifeless, a butterfly in a collection, to call his own.

Miranda's diary is the breath of life in the suffocating atmosphere of Clegg's claustrophobic mind which the basement prison, completely closed to fresh air and sunlight, symbolizes. Covering the same span of time as Clegg's narrative, it records her fright and frantic desire eventually to escape, feelings mingled with a curious fascination at a mind so utterly alien. Clegg is for Miranda a new world, if not a brave one, and he becomes at first jocularly her Ferdinand, and then her Caliban, for whom she tries to open the possibilities of art and life, but a Caliban nearly deaf to the island's music, and one who meets her attempts with learned-by-rote clichés, misanthropic and self-interested because that is what he expects of the world, which constitute the fabric of his consciousness. Intermixed with her account of her predicament are Miranda's reflections on her past life, particularly her relation with the older painter, George Paxton, and out of the analysis of her life submitted to the cruel test of the present experience comes a new sense of her identity, an awareness of her flaws of character and a readiness, forged in the suffering of her ordeal and despair, for that future which will be so cruelly snuffed out.

Part of Fowles' great success lies in

making no extraordinary figure out of Miranda—she is bright, artistic, sensitive, but there is nothing original or dazzling in her self-discovery—and yet conveying, in the bleak context of Clegg, the enormous value of those virtues which she does possess, value which shines the brighter, if more pathetically, in the fact of its final extinction. For *The Collector* is the world of *The Tempest* debased and inverted, with no Prospero to hold what are here not even bestial forces in check, with

the human imagination succumbing before its absence. And Clegg's is the Gilbert Osmond syndrome on the lowest frequency—the desire for the other as possession, the inability to grant the autonomy of another human being. Yet the strength of the novel comes in large measure from the writer's ability to make Clegg's subhumanity humanly believable and even moving. It is by means of that subhumanity which destroys it that Miranda's humanity remains indelible.

Donald L. Mull

A DAY IN LATE SEPTEMBER

Author: Merle Miller (1919-   )
Publisher: William Sloane Associates (New York). 343 pp. $4.50
Type of work: Novel
Time: September, 1960
Locale: New England

A carefully patterned novel that is in part a satire of man's ability to see the world as he wishes to see it and in part a vitriolic attack on the present scene

Principal characters:
MAC, a writer who exiled himself during the McCarthy era and who has just returned to the United States
PHOEBE SHEPLEY, a woman who has promised to leave her husband and return with Mac to Spain
GORDON SHEPLEY, Phoebe's husband, a thoroughly unscrupulous person who has discovered that culture can be made to pay
JANICE CARVER, Phoebe's rich friend
EVERARD CARVER III, a politician, dependent on Janice's money
ABEL SORENSON, a radical of the old school
CLAY SORENSON, Abel's son, a doctor
IDA SORENSON, Clay's wife
CONSTANT HAZELTON, Mac's ex-wife, who refused to follow him to Europe and later remarried
GEORGE HAZELTON, Constant's husband
JONT, Mac's son, whose custody was retained by Constant, but who is about to join his father in Spain

The lines by Marcel Proust that prefix *A Day in Late September* supply one of the keys to the novel:

The bonds that unite another person to ourself exist only in our mind. Memory

as it grows fainter relaxes them, and notwithstanding the illusion by which we would fain be cheated and with which, out of love, friendship, politeness, deference, duty, we cheat other people, we exist alone. Man is the crea-

61

ture that cannot emerge from himself, that knows his fellows only in himself; when he asserts the contrary, he is lying.

The key lets us into a familiar literary room, that in which reality faces illusion, in which maturity lies in recognizing the truth about oneself—and acting upon it. More than one character in Merle Miller's novel seems capable of stripping away his illusions, but only one takes action. He can, as he puts it at the end of the novel, "get up and walk." The others are engaged in fun and games—vicious games that hurt themselves and others, but no less childish for all that. Both the general theme of the novel and the viciousness with which its characters strike at one another are more than a little reminiscent of Edward Albee's *Who's Afraid of Virginia Woolf?* The parallelism extends even to the novel's hectic, semi-surrealistic climax that recalls the harrowing close of the Albee play.

The form of the novel is also a fairly familiar one. It is broken into short sections, the point of view shifting from section to section, as eight characters tell the story of one crucial day in their lives and, by means of looping flashbacks, of their entire past. None of them, as it proves, really knows how others see him, or understands what drives anyone else. And each of them re-creates his past and present to suit himself; memory proves a cheat. Dr. Clay Sorenson, thinking of his unmarried daughter who is now two-months pregnant, remembers the day when their intimacy disappeared:

One July evening two years ago after a day of disheartening heat, dazzling brilliance, and one diagnosed malignant tumor, Clay had come home feeling, as usual, defeated and hopeful, happy and sad. He had kissed [his wife] Ida, who was surprised and flustered. He had spent half an hour with his father, who had made him laugh twice. . . .

Clyte, who had just turned fourteen, was in the living room, which was pink and bright and cheerful. . . .

Clay, feeling like an entire ocean of love, invaded her pink and emerald isle to kiss her on the cheek. She looked up from her book and to his amazement was annoyed.

"Oh, Dad, stop pawing me," she said, her voice at that moment reminiscent of her grandmother's.

From that time on whatever there had been between Clay and Clyte was irretrievably, no doubt inevitably, gone.

In the closing pages of the novel, Clyte remembers the episode differently; she had been repeating algebra in summer school and was feeling sorry for herself:

"One day you came home and first you gave Mother a bad time because supper wasn't ready and you were going to some meeting of some kind, and . . . then you came in and I was feeling miserable because Chris was away being counselor at a camp. You asked me how I was, and I said I was okay, which was a lie, and then you asked how I was doing—I remember just how you said it. 'How are you doing with algebra the second time around?' Which if you ask me was a cruddy way to ask the question. I said fine, also a lie, and then you said you'd a letter from my smart kid brother, J. P., who was out in New Mexico . . . and I thought, What's that got to do with me? We are two different people, and you are always bringing up how much smarter he is. You started to kiss me, and I said, 'Oh, Dad, stop pawing me,' and then I went upstairs and cried."

62

Is Clyte telling the truth? We have no reason to suppose that she is.

But Miller is not simply reworking a tired theme and form. His novel does "get up and walk" in its own right. For one thing, his net catches a number of fish. The same ability to reshape the past exhibited by Dr. Sorenson—so that one can never learn from experience because the experience itself changes—applies to the social and political scene. This is something that Mac, the central character of the novel insofar as there is one, has good reason to know. He had joined a number of organizations later tagged red or pink. "But he became increasingly unhappy with his comrades. *Those* people were going to make a better society? Why, there wasn't one who was able to make a decent marriage. And there wasn't a nonhater in the lot." By the time of the McCarthy era, Mac had long since grown politically conventional, but as a TV writer he was listed in *Red Channels,* cut off from his job, and about to be subpoenaed by a Congressional committee. None of his friends, even those he walked with in the picketlines, now recognized him. His wife, Constant, had been among the most fiery: she had circulated petitions, marched in May Day parades, spoken at rallies, derided liberals as weak; but now that Mac had been blacklisted, she struck out at him: "You'll notice *I'm* not in any trouble because of playing footsie with the Reds. *I* knew from the beginning. . . ." Refusing to submit to the indignity and indecency of a public recantation in Washington, Mac fled to Europe; Constant, having refused to follow him, later remarried and retained custody of their son. As the novel opens, Mac has returned in the midst of the Nixon-Kennedy campaign.

He has grown distinctly apolitical. But his attempt to suggest that he sees no great difference between the two candidates is met by the same stupid fanaticism that had existed when he left. If there is no integrity in one's memory of the past, there can be little in the present.

A Day in Late September begins and ends with Mac, a moderately successful writer who has learned that salvation on any level can come only from oneself, that it is therefore necessary to face life as honestly as possible, and that the only values worth having are those which the individual can express —dignity, loyalty, courtesy, discipline, self-respect. But he sees precious little of these around him as he surveys the American scene. Unfortunately, as Miller's spokesman, Mac is the weakest point in the novel. Too often he is encountered saying the right things, or thinking them:

> I must teach my son many things, thought Mac. I must teach him not to rail against circumstances that cannot be changed; I must teach him . . . that we make decisions at our peril but that once we've made them we're committed. I must teach him to be kind.

Again:

> This country is beautiful. I am fond of this country. I wasn't always, but I have —I hope—learned to put up with its inperfections just as I have learned to be forgiving of my own.

But Miller does try to make the character breathe. Mac achieves his present state of poise only after considerable struggle, and he must struggle continually to maintain it. Many of his judgments of other people are much too hasty and superficial—designedly so. And he has certainly been wrong about Phoebe Shepley, one of his two reasons for returning home; the other is his son, Jont, whom his ex-wife now seems willing to release into his custody.

The extent of Mac's mistake is not, however, immediately clear when we meet Phoebe in the second episode of the novel. She exemplifies perfectly the mind's ability to reshape both present and past. Married to Gordon Shepley, she had met Mac in Spain and she has promised to leave her husband. Lying in bed, she thinks of her husband, Gordon, as childish and insignificant, "a small, incomplete child of forty-one"; Mac is a superb specimen of a man. Her love for Mac is enduring. Her life with her husband will end that day when she tells him of her affair with Mac. We do not, at this point in the novel, have any reason to doubt the general drift of what she has been thinking. But as the novel proceeds, we learn that nothing of what she has been thinking can be trusted. Her husband is scarcely very lovable, but he is not insignificant. A firm believer in the value of private detectives, he has known of her affair for some time, and he is murderously certain that he can fend off Mac. Furthermore, Mac is only the latest of a long series of affairs; Gordon possesses tapes and intimate pictures of some of these and he is perfectly willing to produce them. Thoroughly unscrupulous, he sees the world as a jungle where one never takes off one's combat boots, "not even at night. You are never safe in the jungle." Nor is Phoebe's image of Mac correct; he is scarcely an Apollo. And her comment that she intends to tell her husband about Mac represents an unspoken lie, for she has told Mac that her husband already knows and that her departure has been arranged. When, at the end of the novel, Mac realizes her basically destructive nature, he turns her away, at the same time commenting on the weakness in himself that made him refuse to see her clearly up to that point: "I'm afraid it's not so much that I love Phoebe; I'm afraid it's more that I wanted Phoebe to love me." From some inner reserve he summons up the strength to leave without her.

In and around this central movement, the other characters and monologues are woven: lying on his deathbed is Abel Sorenson, crusty, honest, outspoken, whose integrity may be passed on to a few like Mac, who may in turn pass it on to his son; going through a crisis is Abel's son, Dr. Clay Sorenson, who realizes too late that he is the indifferent rock on which his wife's sanity has splintered; passing into the darkness of insanity is Clay's wife, Ida, who is no more able to know what her husband is made of than he is to know her (actually, he is, for all his faults, a perfectly capable, honest, hard-working doctor who has some reason to be proud of his professional achievement); standing just where he wants to be, at a rich house party, is Gordon Shepley, whose jungle manners are hidden under smiling suavity, who hates culture but edits a cultural magazine, who despises his readers but loves their money, who loathes his host and hostess but basks in the need they have of him; loathing each other and everyone about them are the host and hostess, Everard Carver III, who is running for Congress, and Janice Carver, who owns the money. Gordon, Everard, Janice, and, at the end, even Phoebe are grotesque examples of people who possess some degree of self-knowledge but who are unwilling or unable to act upon it. They cannot "get up and walk."

Max Halperen

THE DEVIL TO PAY IN THE BACKLANDS

Author: João Guimarães Rosa (1908-   )
Translated from the Portuguese by James L. Taylor and Harriet de Onís
Publisher: Alfred A. Knopf (New York). 492 pp. $5.95
Type of work: Novel
Time: Early twentieth century
Locale: The backlands of Bahía and Minas Gerais

An epic in prose based upon the exploits and adventures of the outlaw bands who conducted war in the backlands of Brazil

Principal characters:
RIOBALDO, an old outlaw, the narrator
DIODORIM, alias Reinaldo
HERMÓGENES, Riobaldo's one-time ally, later an enemy

In an admiring essay which acts as a preface to the American edition of *The Devil to Pay in the Backlands,* Jorge Amado, author of *Gabriela: Clove and Cinnamon,* who is often thought of as Brazil's foremost contemporary writer, calls Guimarães Rosa "our master novelist," "the great writer to whose formation my generation, which immediately preceded his, contributed and for whom we cleared the way." Amado describes *The Devil to Pay in the Backlands* as "brutal, tender, cordial, savage, vast as Brazil itself, the image of Brazil drawn by a writer with a consummate mastery of his craft."

João Guimarães Rosa was born in Minas Gerais in 1908, studied medicine, practiced as a country doctor in the backlands, and took part in the civil war of 1932. Entering the Brazilian diplomatic service in 1934, he has served as a consul, as the secretary of the Brazilian embassy in Bogotá, as embassy counselor in Paris, and as an ambassador. Thus, like so many Latin American writers, he has included in his life a vast range of experiences, particularly in the service of his country.

Rosa first made himself felt on the Brazilian literary scene with *Sagana,* a collection of short stories published in 1946; he has subsequently had an impact, says Amado, that is second only to that produced by the publication of Gilberto Freyre's *Casa-Grande e Sensala* in 1933, an American edition of which appeared in the same year as the Brazilian publication of *Sagana.* Since 1963 has seen the publication in the United States of both Freyre's sequel to *Casa-Grande* (*Sobrados e Mucambos,* translated as *The Mansions and the Shanties: The Making of Modern Brazil,* by Harriet de Onís) and Rosa's greatest work, it is something of an *annus mirabilis* for the cause of Brazilian literature in North America. It is also noteworthy that both of these books were published by Alfred A. Knopf, whom Amado calls with justice "a friend of literature and a friend of Brazil."

The goal of his generation, as Amado sees it, has been to transform

65

the literary language of Brazil into something closer to the vernacular, to make the vernacular, in turn, capable of literature. In *The Devil to Pay in the Backlands*, a product of the generation that followed, one not only sees this goal triumphantly achieved but achieved in that literary form most magnificently suited to the vernacular —the epic. Narrated through a single voice and without a break in its nearly five hundred pages, Rosa's fine novel reminds one, "brutal, tender, cordial, savage, vast" as it is, of nothing so much as Homer. It is obvious that Rosa had the *Iliad* and the *Odyssey* in mind as he wrote. Even more obviously, however, he has deliberately rejected all the merely literary accretions that have gathered around Homer in the course of the past three thousand years and restored the epic vision to its authentic source in the folk.

The narrator is the Achilles of Rosa's tale, but an Achilles nearly anonymous beneath the overpowering scope of his own adventures, humbled and humanized by what he has been through, like the aged Beowulf. In his youth Riobaldo had run away to join one of the bands of outlaws in the backlands, men who made war, for reasons often lost in the violence and suffering of their struggles, against the government in power, whatever it might be, and against each other. Becoming, like Achilles, a great leader reluctantly, Riobaldo even acquires a Patroclus, in the person of Reinaldo, who confides in him, secretly, as an ancient Greek might have done for fear of magical misdealings, the fact that his real name is Diadorim. It is this act more than any other that reveals Diadorim's love for and faith in Riobaldo. When Diadorim dies after

taking Riobaldo's place in a battle with his arch-enemy Hermógenes, and when Riobaldo discovers that his Patroclus is really a girl who had been in love with him and with war, his career is broken; all his self-doubts come to a head, to be assuaged only in the consciousness, which he shares with the reader, that he has taken part in a kind of vision, the peculiar transcendental vision of the epic. As the narrator of his own story he becomes purified himself and at the same time creates in the reader the catharsis that is the appropriate effect of epic.

All of the epic conventions become utterly natural in *The Devil to Pay*. With the catalogue, for example, which in other literary epics so often becomes a mere sterility, we find our sense of event undergoing the true Homeric expansion:

Among so many, I fraternized with only a few of those jagunços, trusting to my guardian angels. But only the fairly decent ones. These were: Capixúm, an even-keeled backwoodsman, from the plains of São Felipe, who had moved around a lot; Fonfrêdo, who could chant all the priest's prayers, ate no meat of any kind, and who never said who he was or where he was from; the one whose name rhymed with his, Sesfrêdo, I have already told you about; Testa-em-Pé, a crafty Bahían who drank a lot; Paspé, a herdsman from Jaiba, the handiest and most obliging fellow I ever ran across; good-hearted Dadá Santa-Cruz, nicknamed Caridoso . . . Carro-de-Boi . . . Catôcho . . . Lindorífico . . . Diolo . . . Juvento, Adalgizo, Sangue-de-Outro . . . Dagobé, Eleuterio, Pescoço-Prêto, José Amigo . . .

A passage like this one demonstrates the magnificent way in which Rosa has attained to a Homericism without strain, a vernacular grandeur. The

66

names themselves, with their mixture of outlandish nomen (outlandish even in Brazilian Portuguese) and mysterious cognomen, are representative of the true epic tone and the vision behind it, the union of natural and supernatural in the horrid game of war. Riobaldo's own attitudes, moreover, are those of a real Achilles—his faith in his luck, his self-respect, his love of handiness, even a kind of snobbery. Such passages are a testimony as well to the extraordinary skill of the book's two translators and to the sensitivity with which they have rendered and maintained not only Riobaldo's narrative voice but all of Rosa's epic nuances as well.

It is obvious that although some critics will doubtless feel called upon to read *The Devil to Pay* as a species of social history, Rosa has done far more than that. The book is almost dateless; the places it takes the reader have changed their names and become different. Its action, thus, is without time or place, occurring on a stage that we recognize as related to that upon which we live but only remotely, a stage where life is more barbarous, certainly, than our own, but also a good deal more noble. The characters of *The Devil to Pay* are therefore ourselves magnified, ourselves at our worst and at our best. Rosa has given them, as Amado says, "the immortality that art alone can give," demonstrating, given the very unsuitable conditions for the genuine epic in the twentieth century, a kind of heroic courage himself, for which all his readers can be grateful.

John Rodenbeck

DOSTOEVSKY

Author: David Magarshack (1899-   )
Publisher: Harcourt, Brace and World (New York). Illustrated. 399 pp. $8.75
Type of work: Biography
Time: 1819-1881
Locale: Russia and Europe

The life of the great Russian novelist in its many aspects: personal, artistic, political, and journalistic

Principal personages:
    FYODOR MIKHAILOVICH DOSTOEVSKY
    MIKHAIL, his oldest brother and business partner
    EMILIA, his first wife
    PASHA, her son
    APOLLINARIA SUSLOV, his mistress
    ANNA, his second wife
    MIKHAIL KATKOV, one of his publisher-creditors
    IVAN TURGENEV, his great literary rival

David Magarshack brings to this work his experience as biographer of three other members of the Russian literary pantheon: Chekhov, Turgenev, and Gogol. He also has the advantage of much new material recently published in Russia—a dozen books within the five years preceding the publication of this study, and a thirteenth being the fourth and final volume of Dostoevsky's letters. A further indication of the amount of work Mr. Magarshack has done is the fact that all the translations from the Russian in the book—and they total a great many pages—were done by himself. He had, of course, previously translated novels of the author whose life he now treats.

This biography is a full and painstaking job. It throws new light on problems in Dostoevskian literary studies (such as the basis for the suppressed child-rape scene in *The Devils*), further documents well-known events in the writer's life (his conviction for treason and transportation to Siberia), and helps to make more understandable his psychological complexities (the radical-reactionary dichotomy in his nature).

The facts of Dostoevsky's life, from his birth on October 30, 1821, are given in generous detail and set in their proper milieu. There is the profound and unhappy impression made by the father upon the son. Although Dostoevsky tried late in life to say a good word for his father, he found few to utter about the army doctor whose failure was capped by his murder at the hands of the peasants on his estate who could bear his brutality no longer. Magarshack traces the son's unhappy years as a cadet in a military engineering school—unhappy because both he and his brother had decided long before that the only career they cared about was literature. Dostoevsky's success with his novel *Poor People*, at the age of twenty-three, was followed by successive disappointments in the critical coolness that greeted the next half-dozen works he published. But this misfortune was capped by disaster when Dostoevsky was arrested by the Tsarist police on April 23, 1849, as a member of the radical Petrashevsky Circle. The facts of the false execution contrived as a lesson by the Tsar and the four years of dreadful privation in a Siberian prison which followed are well known. Using letters of Dostoevsky and additional materials from works such as *A Writer's Diary*, Magarshack vividly renders the horrors of that exile and the four years' military service in Siberia which completed the sentence, then shows how these hardships astonishingly helped to make Dostoevsky a fanatical supporter of Tsarist autocracy and a writer who placed his faith in the innate wisdom of the lowly Russian peasant. The years of magazine journalism, of emergence as a national figure, and literary success capped with the triumph of *The Brothers Karamazov* make fascinating, if less dramatic, reading.

With the additional information at his disposal not available to earlier biographers, Magarshack is able better to analyze the factors which made Dostoevsky the strange and difficult man he was. If he was moody and bad-tempered, jealous and spiteful, there were obvious predisposing causes. There was the epilepsy which depleted his strength and so shocked his first bride on their wedding night that she never got over the experience. Failure and unhappiness dogged him in love, in and out of marriage. And the humiliation he endured at the hands of Emilia, his first wife, and Apollinaria Suslov, his sometime mistress, was due in part at least to a clear streak of masochism. When good fortune brought him a young wife who cared for him (even if her devotion was more to the literary figure than the man), his happiness was mitigated by the neurotic, self-destructive streak in a new form: compulsive gambling. Scarcely ever free of debt in normal circumstances, Dostoevsky fanatically played his absurd system and lost thousands of borrowed rubles at the tables of Baden-Baden, Homburg, and other casinos. A temporary émigré to escape creditors and to write (his wife extended the exile to break his ties with demanding in-laws), he became more and more anti-Western and pro-Slavophile. When he returned to Russia this fierce chauvinism combined with jealousy to provoke bitter quarrels with Turgenev. It emerged, too, in his fiction, finding its strongest embodiment in *The Brothers Karamazov,* the great novel which began to appear serially only a comparatively short time before his death on January 28, 1881, from the emphysema which plagued him during the last fifth of his life.

Magarshack provides insights which help to explain the behavior of this tormented genius. These are extremely important, for if there is anything here that will dismay the nonspecialist, it is likely to be the discrepancy between the effect of reading the great novels themselves and reading about the often petty, often distraught artist who produced them. As a criminal still under sentence, he had written extravagant and sycophantic odes to the monarch who might pardon him. The biographer comments that the novelist was later aware that his vicious fulminations "were caused by some deep-seated irritant, the consciousness that, having compromised once by writing those fulsome 'odes' to the Tsarist family, he had been driven from one extreme to another till he found himself propagating policies that seemed to run counter to the humanitarian ideas he had believed and still believed in at heart." Another manifestation of psychological complexity was the Pan-Slavism of this Christian who had to force himself to believe yet who advocated in his fiction "the Russian idea," the idea that Russia, at the head of all the Slav peoples, and acting as the physical vehicle for the Orthodox Church, would save mankind.

If Magarshack's necessary commitment to the life rather than the works makes it no easier for us wholly to understand "The dichotomy in his nature, the cleavage between the creative artist and the embittered conservative politician," this signifies not so much a deficiency in the work as the inevitable dividing line between biography and literary criticism. Be that as it may, any critic writing about Dostoevsky's work will now, like any ordinary reader who picks up this book, find himself indebted to David Magarshack for this comprehensive study of the great Russian writer.

Joseph L. Blotner

THE EDGE OF THE STORM

Author: Agustín Yáñez (1904-   )
Translated from the Spanish by Ethel Brinton, with illustrations by Julio Prieto
Publisher: University of Texas Press (Austin). 332 pp. $6.50
Type of work: Novel
Time: 1909-1910
Locale: A village in the Archdiocese of Guadalajara, Mexico

A *poetic novel about the heart and mind of Mexico during the last days of the Díaz era*

Principal characters:
MICAELA RODRÍGUEZ, a girl of the village
VICTORIA, a visitor from the city
MARÍA, the niece of the Parish Priest
MARTA, Maria's sister
FATHER MARTÍNEZ, the Parish Priest
GABRIEL, his ward
DAMIÁN LIMÓN, Micaela's lover, a young rebel
LUIS GONZAGA PÉREZ, an ex-seminarist

Whatever the cause, real novels are rather rare occurrences in Mexican literature, a literature otherwise rich indeed, both in prose fiction and poetry. Haunted of late by the Revolution, Mexican writers have been unable, by and large, to grasp the significance of their great national struggle for self-realization in terms of any deep artistic vision or in terms of the psychological insights which are necessary for novels. One exception has been Octavio Paz, the poet, whose *Labyrinth of Solitude*, a meditation on the Mexican character, has opened up with passionate and well-reasoned prose vast areas of potentiality for both artists and thinkers; another exception is Agustín Yáñez, the author of *The Edge of the Storm* (*Al Filo del Agua*), a book which is not only a real novel but which comes to wonderful grips with the whole psychological background of the Revolution, giving us through a panoramic view of life in a provincial village a profound and artistically valid vision of the reasons why the Mexican

Revolution could be described as the most therapeutic in history.

Like so many Latin American writers, Yáñez has been a leader in both the culture and politics of his native country. He is a member of the Academia de la Lengua and the Colegio Nacional, has taught in several schools and held several public offices, including the governship of the State of Jalisco, where *The Edge of the Storm* has its setting. The village about which Yáñez writes, he tells us, represents "any village of the Archdiocese of Guadalajara." In the light of what Octavio Paz has written in *The Labyrinth of Solitude*, however, we can see this village as a microcosm of the Mexican provinces.

In an image which sums up strikingly its puritanical hermeticism, its airless repression, Yáñez describes it as "a village of black-robed women." They are black-robed because no decent woman would be seen wearing colors, because black is the uniform of the Daughters of Mary, to which every respectable girl in the village belongs, because black is prescribed by the priests of the Church as suitable to clothe a people conceived and nurtured in sin. The villagers live thus in a perpetual Lent, on a perpetual Good Friday; there are no informal relations whatsoever allowed between the sexes and even marriage is frowned on. Of all the women in the village, only a few refuse to wear the prescribed color or to submit to the repression that black implies: one is Micaela Rodríguez, who turns coquette after tasting the freedom of Guadalajara; another is Victoria, a visitor from the city who lives abroad and who unconsciously disturbs the thoughts of every man in the village; a third, at the end of the book, is María, the niece of Father Martínez, the parish priest, who runs away to join the revolutionaries.

These three women represent three different ways of escaping from the closed world of the village, from the flagellation and self-condemnation of the Church, from the hypocritical Comtism of the Porfirists who seek to use the Church to keep the world of the village closed. In the case of Micaela, the way is open rebellion against the unspoken sexual regulations that surround her; her rebellion, half understood and futile because of her inability to comprehend either the village itself or the damage it has done both to her and to the young men she maliciously tries to attract, leads only to violence and death, an outburst which Octavio Paz would describe as "a fiesta of bullets" in which she dies and in which her lover, Damián Limón, lately returned from the United States, equally rebellious and driven beyond endurance by her desperate coquetry, is her murderer.

This violence is only the prelude to a larger violence, however, for Damián escapes imprisonment and becomes a part of the Revolution, where he will fight, as the book closes, for a freedom that will put an end to the tragedy of Mexico's Micaelas.

The second way is Victoria's. Unlike Micaela and María, Victoria is not a part of the village. To most of the men, she represents a sexual liberty they have never known, despite the fact that she does not encourage them in the least; it is simply the fact that she comes from far away, from somewhere outside the cycle of repression, that makes her stand in their minds for all their erotic aspirations. However, to Gabriel, the ward of Father Martínez, who rings the bells of the church with the hands of a great musician, she holds out escape in the form of art, loving him for his mastery of sound and wresting him from the grip of the village to study music abroad. Victoria's rebellion, therefore, unconscious, centered upon Gabriel, operates like the serenity of a muse. She stands for art alone; and the fact that the other men of the village see her as a symbol of their own lust merely demonstrates again the extent to which they are trapped in the bonds of their repressed desires. It is significant that she drives Luis Gonzaga Pérez, an ex-seminarist with whose parents she lives in the village, quite mad, and that his delirium takes the form of mingled rites and crude obscenities.

But it is the escape of María, the niece of Father Martínez, that spells the collapse of the village's ways in their hermetical purity. Unlike her sister Marta, who finds self-realization in submission and the duties of foster motherhood, María yearns for foreign

71

places and her joining the Revolution marks in her the discovery that these foreign places are within herself—are, indeed, within all the people of the village or of Mexico. When she goes, however, she leaves behind a population not exultant over freedom to come but demoralized by the harsh, unreal, and crippling way of life they seem about to lose. It is the threat of loss that bothers them, the loss of the past, not the promise and the challenge of the future. Father Martínez prays for himself and for the people, only barely conscious of what he and they together have jointly suffered and of what Gabriel and María have run away from. Even this consciousness, however, is enough to make him dizzy, and his dizziness is the dizziness of a whole world about to roll out of its accustomed orbit.

It is more than possible that *The* *Edge of the Storm* is not merely a good book but a great book. Beautifully written and well translated here by Ethel Brinton, it realizes completely the meaning of the Revolution as that meaning becomes increasingly clear to us. Most great novels, however, have something of the nature of definitive statements; they leave nothing further to be said in the particular direction they take. One hopes that *The Edge of the Storm*, to the contrary, will provide Mexican writers in the future with inspiration to continue to explore their heritage by means of the novel. Those of us outside the Republic meanwhile will compare this book with other novels, with the works of Turgenev, for example, particularly *On the Eve*, and will not discover that *The Edge of the Storm* is in any respect wanting. Yáñez is obviously one of the modern masters.

John Rodenbeck

THE ETERNAL NOW

Author: Paul Tillich (1886-   )
Publisher: Charles Scribner's Sons (New York). 185 pp. $2.95
Type of work: Sermons

A Protestant theologian discusses the human predicament, the divine reality, and the challenge to man

To his two previous volumes of sermons, *The Shaking of the Foundations* and *The New Being*, Paul Tillich, eminent Protestant theologian, adds this third collection. These books, he states in a preface to the present volume, should demonstrate "that the Christian message is relevant for our time if it uses the language of our time." As a form of literature sermons were obsolete a long time ago, so that considerable courage has been required on the part of both author and publisher to risk printing them for the general public. Their boldness has been abundantly justified, however, for Mr. Tillich has succeeded in reviving the sermon as literature by discovering how this traditional genre with a narrowly prescribed form and function can illuminate the experience of modern man. And he has done so in the only way possible, by concentrating on style, which in its outward appearance is a quality of language but in essence is power of thought.

72

As Christianity has waned, unable to keep abreast of intellectual progress in the West, as its churches have lagged behind the social evolution toward democracy and industrialization, its traditional language and literary forms have become increasingly archaic and irrelevant. Mr. Tillich is saved from the inertia of Christianity by his sense of history. Based on a passage of scripture, the sermon is an instrument of religious instruction whereby the universal but obscure truths of the Bible are explained to contemporary audiences. By nature, therefore, it is always an adaptation of historical revelation to the unique circumstances of a specific moment at some remove in time from the original religious experience. The temptation to make the past the measure of the present is obviously great, and seldom has it been resisted. But Mr. Tillich, adopting the existential bias granting ultimate authority to experience, resists that temptation and requires the past to justify itself to the present. Doctrine is put on the defensive, therefore; existential fact has priority over revelation; Christianity assumes the burden of continuously proving anew its power to elucidate contemporary reality. Mr. Tillich's sense of history is not unique but is characteristic of our time. The theories of evolution and relativity have established that reality is process, and so every moment has become a novel epiphany of energy or life. Power precedes form, and man, immersed in a stream of consciousness, knows for certain only the empirical and existential content of concrete experience. All art and thought, including religion, have drawn new life from these truths and have been radically transformed in character. Mr. Tillich's contribution—

though, of course, only one among many of his—has been to pour this new wine into the sermon.

The first sign of his success in doing so is his remarkable talent for selecting uncommon Biblical passages and getting slight turns of phrase or a single word to yield subtle insight into man's spiritual life. In effect, he argues the relevance of the Christian message by making Christianity appear an inexhaustible reservoir of truth in which every profound experience, providing the mind is subtle enough, can find its voice. But the true test of relevance, for both Christianity and the sermon, lies in whether they can arouse modern men to religious awareness by convincingly reminding them of their fallen state. To accomplish that task, sufficient moral passion must be aroused to prove beyond a doubt that the sense of sin or evil has a basis in fact. The problem, given Mr. Tillich's perspective on history, is to conceive of the present as deficient or imperfect.

Because the existentialist view emphasizes religious and metaphysical awareness of life as haunted by absurdity and nothingness, the sermon is a natural means of dramatizing the spiritual plight of modern man. Here Mr. Tillich is at his best. Typically Protestant, he makes the soul identical with conscience and envisages life as a moral trial in which self-scrutiny, alienation, and anxiety are man's normal lot. He not only sees it as such but lives it that way, his sermons deriving most of their effectiveness from his self-dramatization, from his portrayal of himself and of the Church, too, as implicated in the perpetual assessment of spiritual authenticity. His familiarity with modern literature and philosophy, which he takes seriously as expressing

73

modern man's spiritual being, equips Mr. Tillich with a graphic image of the human condition in the twentieth century, and he is able to use Christianity and the sermon, traditionally dedicated to the notion of this world as damned, to clarify our emptiness. Instead of seeming forced upon the subject and distorting it, both appear to emerge from its deeper recesses and reveal its innermost being.

But the sermon must do more than simply remind one of his sinfulness through inciting moral passion; it must also intellectually convince. Mr. Tillich's theology does not rise to the heights of his literary achievements. We may feel our estrangement and unworthiness as we read his sermons, but they fade away once the drama is ended; we are entertained but not changed. This effect results because Mr. Tillich assumes an immanent relation between man and God, so that the moral awareness aroused turns out to be an illusion. Sin and evil are states of mind, real, to be sure, for anyone experiencing them, so that man is not fallen in time or space but is in error about his own being. In other words, the theology contradicts the dramatization; the latter requires that sin be the definitive religious element and that moral pain and self-censure provide the essential evidence of spiritual being, whereas the former implies that the divine resides in freedom from arbitrary limitations and in joy. A sermon, a religion as a whole, must hold out the promise of redemption by setting forth an ideal of moral perfection and suggesting the existence or presence of a God who can incite a desire to live a more perfect life. It must lift up. Constant moral uncertainty casts a dark cloud of self-consciousness over whatever assurances exist that God is in his heaven. And God as law giver and judge discourages joy in the present, demands sacrifices of immediate pleasure for future rewards.

These sermons, then, strong on conscience but weak on joy, prove that Christianity is partially relevant to our time. It can help to illuminate modern man's predicament in an absurd world but it cannot articulate, at least through Mr. Tillich's style, modern man's capacity for freedom and exaltation. Mr. Tillich writes in what can be called a modern plain style. He avoids impassioned rhetoric; all appeals to passion, except for moral passion, are shunned for sober, systematic intellectual analysis intended to convince a mature and intelligent audience. His attention is on a clear comprehension of the facts of life, not on the inspiring passions or liberating release that abet religious excitement, exuberance, or joyousness. He is too wary of man's capacity to slip into pride, self-righteousness, and intolerance to rejoice in the God of love. Nevertheless the limitations of his sermons are their strength—they testify that Mr. Tillich forthrightly confronts his task by refusing to cut modern experience to fit the Procrustean bed of traditional Christian doctrine. The sermon comes alive in his hands because he finds in it a vehicle for thinking profoundly about modern man's religious predicament.

William R. Robinson

THE FAIR SISTER

Author: William Goyen (1918-   )
Publisher: Doubleday and Company (Garden City, New York). 104 pp. $3.50
Type of work: Novel
Time: A few years ago
Locale: St. Louis, Philadelphia, and Brooklyn

A recounting of the brief but dazzling career of Savata, former star of the Sepia Club, as Bishop of the Light of the World Holiness Church in Brooklyn

> Principal characters:
> SAVATA, The Fair Sister
> RUBY DREW, her devout, dark sister, "God's Scout"
> PRINCE O' LIGHT, head of the Light of the World Holiness Church
> CANAAN JOHNSON, Savata's business manager
> CUBSY HALL, a seven-year-old preacher and healer
> ORONDO MCCABE, his manager

The fiction of false prophets and religious leaders is a familiar sub-genre, as is demonstrated by Sinclair Lewis' *Elmer Gantry*. But this short novel is a remarkable *tour de force*: the first-person narrative of a colored woman in early middle age written by a white man from Texas. The texture of the language is doubly important, for just as Ruby Drew's soul is occupied with religion, so her mind and senses are intoxicated with words. This obsession combines with that over her sister's soul and God's work to form the main threads of this amusing and often compassionate story.

Ruby Drew is "God's Scout doing God's Work" as one of the Bishops of the Light of the World Holiness Church, which is based in Philadelphia. Here, in the House of Trainees, the Prince o' Light prepares new Bishops who will be sent to found mission churches, chiefly in New York, New Jersey, and Pennsylvania. As a member of The Church Zealous, Ruby is moved to track down Savata, her young, fair sister. The child of a different father, Savata had chosen a different way. In St. Louis, dressed in feathers, spangles, and little else, she highlights the Sepia Revue with such dance numbers as "If You Like It Thataway, Then You Can Have It Thataway." But Ruby Drew—diabetic, rheumatic, overweight—a permanent ugly duckling, turns loose her gift of eloquence to touch the heart of her errant sister and bring her back to the fold. There, Ruby Drew is convinced, she can put her gifts of beauty and song to greater service. "So," confides Ruby Drew to the reader, "in her fairness, and on my arm like a dove, come Savata to Philadelphia to lend her talent to Prince o' Light."

Although this Prince of the Church is slightly cockeyed (the smaller eye sees the evil of life, he tells Ruby Drew), he has both purity and magnetism—"a tall pretty-faced man with a thigh like a strong column." Having known the ways of sin himself, he is magnanimous as well as gentle with sinners. But Savata's period of training is nearly as difficult for him and Ruby as it is for Savata. She flees the House of Trainees only to be found and led back through the doggedness of Ruby Drew. Even though seduced into an

75

abandoned moment of solitary sinful dancing by Savata's spangles, the dark sister sees the long-awaited day of Savata's ordination, herself acclaimed by the Prince—for her trials—as "Saint Sister Ruby Drew." In this touching ceremony, the white-clad Prince "emceed the whole proceedings without one hitch." To the accompaniment of a chorus of hundreds, the Prince "anointed her, he blessed her, he kissed her, he prayed over her, he crowned her a Bishop. Some said it was like a wedding—of Savata and Prince o' Light; and oh maybe that would have been better than all what happened."

"All what happened" involves the effect of the serpent in the unique garden formed by the Light of the World Holiness Church founded by Ruby Drew and her fair sister in the borough of Brooklyn. With Ruby Drew as business manager and Savata as presiding Bishop, the church grows. Savata's theory is that "the Church is theater and ought to give its worshippers a chance to spiritualize out their mental emotions—the Church Modern." A refurbished dance from the old Sepia Revue days aids in the process, and religion booms. But Savata does not wholly neglect doctrine. Since they are "the Black Jews by our ancestry," Savata hires Canaan Johnson to tutor the congregation in Hebrew at a dollar and a quarter an hour. His gift of eloquence leads to seduction and discord. "He did have a lip for the word," Ruby Drew declares; "words just slipped forth from those thick lips like half sucked gum drops."

Canaan Johnson's usurpation drives Ruby Drew from the Church. In one counterattack Ruby attempts to bargain the services of a small rock-and-roll guitar player for the return of her rightful position. When she brings this prodigy to the Church he tells Savata, "My name is Cubsy Hall, I am seven years old, and I am a boy preacher in the service of his Name. I have appeared all over the U.S.A. and have just finished an engagement at the Old Stone Church and am on my way to a nationwide tour of forty-one cities in this great nation of ours. Sometimes I lay on hands and heal." But British-accented Orondo McCabe, Cubsy's manager, together with the young healer's aunt, frustrates this plan by construing Ruby Drew's long baby-sitting as attempted kidnaping.

Ruby's ultimate effort is the summoning of Prince o' Light from Philadelphia for a "trial" before the Congregation meant to oust Johnson and return Ruby Drew for once and all to her rightful place. But both she and Prince o' Light are repudiated. He wanders off, ultimately to relapse into sin. Ruby Drew tries to help Savata on the inevitable day when Canaan Johnson absconds with the Church money. But Savata's ecclesiastical career is over, and after months of drudgery in atonement, she vanishes. Ruby Drew holds together the shell of the Church, but she has not the zeal to hang on to Savata. "Well, thank you for listening to my story," she tells the reader, adding, "And, thank you, Jesus."

The book is full of praise and thanks, sometimes uttered when Ruby Drew is flexing her vocabulary, as "Thank you, Jesú." Unfulfilled in marriage, she is fulfilled at times as she uses her linguistic gift on the errant. And she does all she can to enhance it: "For you see I was building up me a vocabulary to ram like a log against the barred door of iniquity." Her unwittingly sensuous pleasure in words is almost of the same intensity as the feeling she sometimes gets from Prince o' Light, of whom she steadfastly refuses to believe the nasty rumors born of "pure trash of gossip and envy." Ruby Drew's style is a consciously literary one, and some of the book's best comic touches derive from her vocabulary. She is a connoisseur of words, and her sensibilities are on the alert. When Cubsy Hall apostrophizes Savata as "some fabled Priestess of Eros, some houri . . . ?" Ruby Drew cannot restrain herself:

"What's that word houri?" I asked.

"Look it up, Ruby," castigated Canaan Johnson.
"I don't like the sound of it," I objected.
"Look it up and don't distract Cubsy Hall's beautiful elegy to Savata."
"Elegy?" I says. "What's that?"

Ruby Drew lacks the beauty, the fire, the flair of her fair sister, but William Goyen shows us through her words and thoughts that the treasures she has piled up—drudging in ramshackle churches, weeping on the crosstown bus—are richer than those of words alone.

Joseph L. Blotner

THE FALL OF THE HOUSE OF HABSBURG

Author: Edward Crankshaw (1909-   )
Publisher: The Viking Press (New York). Illustrated. 459 pp. $7.50
Type of work: History
Time: 1848-1916
Locale: The Austro-Hungarian Empire

   A history of the collapse of the House of Habsburg, with special attention paid to the life and reign of Emperor Franz Joseph I

Principal personages:
EMPEROR FRANZ JOSEPH I
ELIZABETH, Empress of Austria and Queen of Hungary
ARCHDUKE RUDOLF OF HABSBURG, Crown Prince of Austria-Hungary
FRANZ FERDINAND, Archduke of Austria, assassinated at Sarajevo
COUNT GYULA ANDRÁSSY, Hungarian statesman and diplomat who helped to establish the Dual Monarchy
COUNT EDUARD VON TAFFE, Austrian statesman and premier of Austria, 1879-1893
COUNT ABIS VON AEHRENTHAL, Austro-Hungarian foreign minister, 1906-1912

   The Fall of the House of Habsburg is, in reality, two stories in one: the long, eventful, and tragic life of Franz Joseph of Habsburg-Lorraine, inextricably intertwined with the equally eventful story of the progress of a large section of Central Europe from backward absolutism to bloodthirsty nationalism. Both stories possess unlikely casts of characters with totally impossible aspirations. Franz Joseph sought love in his personal life, authority in his public life, and security in both. He tried to preserve the Dual Monarchy and his own absolute power, and the two were identical in his mind, in a European age which challenged and destroyed all absolute rulers and multinational states. Never a tyrant, he sought only peace and stability, but he found his portion to be war and shattering change.

The picture of Franz Joseph presented by Edward Crankshaw is well drawn and eloquent. The agony of the monarch's personal life is described in detail from his reluctant and unwanted accession to the throne in the midst of the Revolution of 1848 through his death in 1916, midway in a war he knew his empire could neither win nor survive. Reared in the age of Metternich and inheritor of his system, he never fully outgrew it. Absolutely unbending in his refusal to part with a scrap of his patrimony with good grace, he rejected both the cession of independence to his Italian provinces and the recognition of Prussian preëminence in Germany, only to lose on both counts when his army suffered an unnecessarily humiliating defeat in 1859 at the hands of Franco-Piedmontese forces and a crushing defeat in 1866 by Prussian arms. The fault, in both cases, was his own. His concept of the monarchy was one in which the emperor exercised absolute power for the good of the people.

Franz Joseph flatly refused to recognize nationalism, the most important force of the nineteenth century, and that non-recognition, plus the fact of the genuine tyranny practiced by the Hungarians in relation to their minorities after 1867, and by his own officials to a lesser extent, conspired to produce an empire not entirely erroneously referred to as the "prison-house of nations."

As Mr. Crankshaw observes, the Habsburg Empire was most certainly not a prison-house of nations, but its population, the twelve usually denominated ethnic groups, consisted of twelve minorities in search of a majority. Of the twelve—German, Magyars, Czechs, Poles, Slovenes, Ruthenians, Rumanians, Croats, Serbs, Slovaks, Italians, and Muslim Slavs—only three, the Germans, Magyars, and Poles, were fully content with their lot. The Germans around Vienna were content to dominate the army, the bureaucracy, and the cultural life in the western half of the empire. The Magyars, dashing and arrogant and living in a sea of what they considered to be inferior peoples, demanded and received in the famous *Ausgleich* of 1867 virtual internal independence and the right to "Magyarize" the minorities that collectively outnumbered them. Similarly, the Poles were satisfied only because Vienna gave them a free hand to lord over the Ruthenians and to make Cracow the center of Polish culture. The remaining nine nationalities had, or came to have, real grievances against Habsburg rule. The Turkish threat had dissipated, relaxing the bond that held the South Slavs to the Habsburgs, and the "threat" of Romanov Russia appeared to be more of a promise to the Slavs who had only recently rediscovered their nationality. Even more important, the Kingdom of Serbia, independent since 1878, attracted the South Slavs who knew Franz Joseph and his empire only through Magyarization policies. It was this Austro-Serbian friction that ultimately resulted in the destruction of the Habsburg Empire and which brought on what the British historian Cyril Falls, writing after World War II, advisedly referred to as the "Great War."

It was Franz Joseph's dynastic appetite, sharpened by the loss of his Italian provinces, that demanded the territories of Bosnia and Herzegovina in return for his support of the western position at the Congress of Berlin. Thus Franz Joseph acquired, at one stroke, two restive provinces, the active hostility of Russia, and a latent problem with Serbia. Even after 1878, peace might have been guaranteed had his foreign policy been oriented toward anything other than the mere preservation of his remaining frontiers. He and a succession of foreign ministers, none of whom after the great Count Andrássy showed any great ability, associated the empire with German diplomacy and its perils. After 1890 any Austrian *rapprochement* with France and Russia was all but impossible and friendship with England scarcely considered. Indeed, Franz Joseph and his diplomatic corps showed greater concern for relations with Rumania and Bulgaria than for the great powers. Count von Aehrenthal's high-handed annexation of Bosnia-Herzegovina in 1908—the provinces had remained legally Turkish since 1878—could have resulted in the outbreak of a general war. As it was, it resulted in a crisis that left Russia bitter, Serbia openly hostile, and the population of Bosnia-Herzegovina (which were very well administered by the Austrians) even more Pan-Slav in sentiment. The outbreak of World War I was to stem from these causes and to result directly from the assassination of Archduke Franz Ferdinand, heir apparent to the Habsburg Empire.

As Mr. Crankshaw points out, Franz Joseph's devotion to his authority and his domains after 1900 reflects the failure and tragedy of his personal life. His wife, the exquisite Empress Elizabeth, was possibly the most beautiful woman in Europe and easily the most impossible. Empress at sixteen, she spent the first years of her reign quarreling with her domineering mother-in-law and divided her later years among horses, travel, and hypochondria, at the same time avoiding throughout any sense of responsibility toward her position or her imperial husband. She bore him a son and daughters, but the emperor, who loved and humored her, never understood his children, especially moody and unpredictable Archduke Rudolf, his only son and heir apparent. Mr. Crankshaw relates the story of a suicide pact between Rudolf and Maria Vetsera at Mayerling in detail, drawing in some instances on hitherto unpublished sources. The manner of Rudolf's death added to Franz Joseph's agony, which was compounded by the later assassination of Elizabeth. Finally, the assassination of Franz Ferdinand, even though he was personally repugnant to the emperor, completed the tragedy of his personal life and opened the last chapter in the history of the Habsburgs.

The Fall of the House of Habsburg is an excellent book, readable, and well written. It is basically sound history, even if Mr. Crankshaw exhibits certain anti-Magyar and pro-Habsburg prejudices. There are a few elementary errors that should have been corrected by alert proofreading: the *Dreikaiserbund* is listed as having been consummated in 1875 when it had already been in existence for three years, and the author frequently refers to Prussia

79

after 1871 when he really means Germany. These are, of course, minor details which do not detract from the value of the work.

Howard Mackey

THE FARAWAY COUNTRY
Writers of the Modern South

Author: Louis D. Rubin, Jr. (1923-   )
Publisher: The University of Washington Press (Seattle). 256 pp. $4.95
Type of work: Literary criticism

Eight essays on the relationship between the South and some of its most representative and important writers

The Southern Literary Renascence is a phenomenon that has attracted many commentators and critics who have attempted to define its origins and to explain what it is. This book is a valuable addition to the growing library of definition and explanation of one of the most fecund and vital literary chapters in the history of the United States.

Mr. Rubin states the thesis and purpose of the book in the preface: he hopes to demonstrate "that Southern literature is of a culture, and that a culture exists in time, and that changes in that culture are mirrored in its literature." The first chapter, "The South and the Faraway Country," is an exercise in limiting and clarifying what his subject will be. This is followed by examination of specific writers and works: "The Road to Yoknapatawpha: George W. Cable and *John March, Southerner*," "Chronicles of Yoknapatawpha: The Dynasties of William Faulkner," "Thomas Wolfe: Time and the South," "Burden's Landing: *All the King's Men* and the Modern South," "The Golden Apples of the Sun" (an essay on Eudora Welty's novels), "The Poetry of Agrarianism" (specifically, the poetry of Donald Davidson, John Crowe Ransom, Allen Tate, and Robert Penn Warren), and "William Styron: Notes on a Southern Writer in Our Time." These are followed by a summary chapter, "Postscript: A Look Backward and Ahead."

The first chapter is a closely argued account of the true relationship that exists between the modern Southern writer and the country that has borne him. Mr. Rubin sees Mark Twain as the prototype of the modern Southern writer, and an image from *The Adventures of Tom Sawyer* as the central illuminating image for all the important Southern poets and novelists who were to come. Cardiff Hill is "beyond the village and above it . . . just far away enough to seem a Delectable Land, dreamy, reposeful, inviting." What distinguishes the *modern* Southern writer from his nineteenth century counterpart (excepting Twain, who, like most twentieth century writers, left the South) is his alienation from the community. To the romancer of the nineteenth century, reality was what he saw around him. History, change, violence—these did not divorce dream and reality, as they do for the later writers. Every important modern Southern writer (and Rubin includes Cable in this group) must recognize that he is *from* the South but not *of* it; that

80

his ability to render truth as an artist depends on his detachment from his own community. What the reader must recognize about the South that is described in fiction and poetry is not actuality, not the "real-life" geographical area in which people go about their business, unconscious of the forces of history, legend, and dream which move them. The writers of the modern South, in Rubin's words,

> live in another country. It is not the country in which they were born, nor the country to which they once fled, nor yet the South to which they came back. Like Mark Twain's Mississippi River community, it is the country of fiction. There they may see the meaning of things in time, for as they write they step outside of every day life toward a timeless perspective in which a fountain splashing in the town square becomes a sign of change, a Confederate cemetery a symbol of man caught in time, a rotting mansion in the Mississippi wilderness the emblem of what human beings in a time and place aspired to be, and what they became.

Mr. Rubin rejects the conventional view of Cable, promulgated by Richard Watson Gilder and Edmund Wilson, as a propagandist, a preacher, in *John March, Southerner*. In Mr. Rubin's view, Cable is the transitional figure between the genteel Southern romancer and the realistic novelist like Faulkner. Cable was the first Southerner to write about Southern character and circumstance as they really were, and he was rejected and attacked for his labor. The love plot of the novel attaches him firmly to the past tradition, but his "subject matter, his attitude, and his method look forward to the literary renascence of the twentieth century." He was kin to "members of the generation of the 1920's and 1930's, those who saw the South not in slavish worship but appalled fascination." He was, then, the first of the alienated Southern writers, bound to and repulsed by their regional heritage.

The chapter on Faulkner covers what will be pretty familiar ground for most readers. It should come as no surprise that the editor of a newspaper published in Jackson, Mississippi, would say that Faulkner belongs to the privy school of literature, while the rest of the world sees him as a great tragic novelist. Mr. Rubin stresses Faulkner's central role as moralist, with love as the nucleus of his moral vision. More interestingly, Mr. Rubin emphasizes the number of writers Mississippi has produced and tries to explain it. How did this region produce Faulkner, Welty, Stark Young, Shelby Foote, Elizabeth Spencer, Tennessee Williams, Hubert Creekmore, and many others? His answer isn't cheering for the liberal, for the meliorist. Mr. Rubin points out "that nowhere else in the South has the tension between tradition and change, between moral precept and animal instinct, between wealth and poverty, between order and disorder, between black and white, between aristocracy and redneck, been so sharply drawn, and so dramatically revelatory." The implications of this account of the relation between culture and art are disturbing indeed.

Thomas Wolfe is the only important modern Southern writer who does not come from the "Southern squirearchy, with its antebellum roots," and this fact, Mr. Rubin says, explains much about the difference between him and the other writers. He is the complete Romantic, who sees the world in purely egocentric terms. The tension that exists in the personalities of the other writers is not present in Wolfe's novels. There is an objectivity in Faulkner, Warren, Welty, a detachment, that is completely foreign to Wolfe's method and attitudes. Mr. Rubin argues that the literary and cultural tradition which serves as the first ˈstep in a process of identification, rejection, detachment was missing in Wolfe, and he was forced to *create* value out of himself, his feelings, his individual sense of truth. That time of his life when his sense of himself was strongest, his feelings most intense, his sense of truth most sure, was his youth. And it was his youthful romantic view that he celebrated. It is really his only subject.

Warren's *All the King's Men* and Eudora Welty's *The Golden Apples*, for all their differences, both have central characters who are detached from the community. Jack Burden rejects Burden's Landing, which seems to him to symbolize outmoded values, and embraces the world of action and expediency, as symbolized by Willie Stark. Mr. Rubin describes the action of the novel as Burden's eventual realization that the values he has rejected are viable, even if not in the form which Burden's Landing conceives of them. Virgie Rainey, in *The Golden Apples*, becomes painfully aware that the limited, protected world she has known will not allow knowledge of time and the "real world"; to move outside the little Mississippi community through art is to move into isolation, loneliness, separation. Mr. Rubin illuminates both novels and both writers, in two of the best studies in the book.

"The Poetry of Agrarianism" is the least impressive essay in the collection, mainly because the thesis becomes too demanding and the poetry is wrenched into shapes it cannot comfortably take. But Mr. Rubin does point out telling differences between the attitudes of two generations, that of Davidson and Ransom, and of Tate and Warren. All four men "use" the Southern past in varying ways and look to the past with varying degrees of longing.

The Faraway Country is organized chronologically, and the last chapter, which deals with William Styron, is a kind of valedictory to the Southern Renascence. The conditions that produced the writers of the first three decades of the century, the conflicts of past and a rapidly changing present, have been radically modified. The Southern writer of today will still be "Southern," but the situation is different. No longer will the past that Faulkner knew so intimately be available. No longer will the conflicts and injustice be so brilliantly lighted. Mr. Rubin sees the direction of the future symbolized in the career of Styron. His first book, *Lie Down in Darkness*, was praised, Mr. Rubin thinks, not because it was a good novel (which he believes it is), but because it seemed to be *Southern*, in the Faulknerian manner. That this was not so was demonstrated by the reception which the second novel, *Set This House on Fire*, received. It was not Southern in setting, the characters were not Faulknerian, there were no Civil War reminiscences—and the novel was universally damned. But Mr. Rubin defends it, convincingly, on the grounds that Styron is writing the only kind of Southern novel possible for him, a novel in which the protagonist can return home only after he has worked out his destiny in isolation and aloneness. The "faraway country" of Cardiff Hill has been destroyed completely by time and no longer can be looked to as an ideal. This is a provoca-

tive conclusion to a coherent and convincing argument.

James Boatwright

THE FIFTH QUEEN

Author: Ford Madox Ford (1873-1939)
Publisher: The Vanguard Press (New York). 592 pp. $6.50
Type of work: Novel
Time: 1539-1542
Locale: England and France

A trilogy, first published in England 1906-08 but not previously printed in this country, dealing with the brief, tragic marriage of Katharine Howard, Henry VIII's fifth Queen

Principal characters:
HENRY VIII, King of England
PRINCESS MARY (later Mary I), his daughter
ANNE OF CLEVES, his fourth wife
KATHARINE HOWARD, his fifth wife
THE DUKE OF NORFOLK, her uncle
THOMAS CROMWELL, Lord Privy Seal
THOMAS CULPEPPER, Katharine Howard's cousin
STEPHEN GARDINER, Bishop of Winchester
THROCKMORTON, one of Cromwell's spies
NICHOLAS UDAL, Latin tutor to the Princess Mary
THOMAS CRANMER, Archbishop of Canterbury
LASCALLES, Cranmer's spy

Here is a full-bodied historical novel, written in the grand Victorian manner, of the brief and tragic marriage of Katharine Howard to Henry VIII. Many of us remember Henry's first wife, Katharine of Aragon, because of Shakespeare, and Anne Boleyn, his second, because she was the mother of Queen Elizabeth I. But the others— Jane Seymour, Anne of Cleves, Katharine Howard, and Katharine Parr— are only dim ghosts flickering through the twilight of history. Moreover, the reign of Henry VIII has not been a favorite with historical novelists, for it is overshadowed by the greater age of Elizabeth which offers so much more to an imaginative writer. And the period of Henry is much more difficult

for a modern reader to understand; it was not the high Renaissance of Elizabeth's time but, again, a twilight between the Middle Ages that were dying and the new age that was struggling to be born.

The story opens in the bitter winter of 1539, as the barges of the great officers of the Crown sweep up the river toward Greenwich in the wake of the king's barge. The new queen, Anne of Cleves, has landed in England, and already the rumor is that the king has said she resembles "a pig stuck with cloves" and that her body stinks so vilely that no man can endure it. The inoffensive Jane Seymour had died two years before, having given Henry his long-desired son, the sickly Prince Ed-

83

ward; and the Cleves alliance was the next move in the complicated political chess game. It would present a strong Protestant front against France and the Empire. On the success of this alliance the Protestant faction at Court had staked their political futures—and their heads; and now the whole scheme was about to be wrecked upon the king's dislike for his new queen. It was no wonder that the Chancellor of the Augmentations, standing in the stern of Cromwell's barge, shivered with more than the winter wind.

To the court, as it lay in the palace at Greenwich, comes the heroine of the novel, Katharine Howard, in the charge of her cousin, Thomas Culpepper, to seek the protection of her uncle, the Duke of Norfolk, Earl Marshal of England and the victor of Flodden Field. She is the daughter of poverty-stricken Lord Edmund Howard, a younger son of the ducal family, whose house, far in the north in Lincolnshire, had been burned in one of the all too frequent local uprisings. By chance she is injured in a riot, outside of the palace, between Lutherans and Catholics; by chance she meets the king and attracts his attention. She is appointed one of the ladies in waiting to Princess Mary, an appointment that will inevitably bring her into further contact with Henry. From that moment her life becomes a part of English history, with the headsman's block on Tower Hill standing grimly only two short years away.

As Graham Greene points out in his introduction to this edition of the novel, the book is in the tradition of Shakespeare's historical plays. In most novels of this type, the main characters are the author's inventions, while the figures from actual history appear in the background to give color and verisimilitude. But in *The Fifth Queen* all the characters are real figures from history, even down to the Magister Nicholas Udal, author of the long-forgotten play, *Ralph Roister Doister*. So it is with Shakespeare's histories. Hence, a reader familiar with the history of the period is aware of much dramatic irony as the story moves along: Bishop Latimer, for instance, exhorting to repentance a friar who is to be burned for heresy. When the sinister figure of Cromwell appears, we know that the axe is waiting even for him.

Thomas Cromwell, the Lord Privy Seal, dominates the larger part of the book as he had dominated Henry for years. Hated by the old nobility because of his low birth—he was the son of a brewer—and by the Catholics because of his destruction of the monasteries, he represents the "new men" whom the Tudors brought forward to do their work for them. The few noble families that had survived the Wars of the Roses could not be trusted; they looked back to a feudal past wherein their ancestors had set up and pulled down kings. But Cromwell, who had risen to power through his betrayal of Wolsey, looked to the future: to an absolute monarchy in which the king's word would be supreme. With his treachery, his network of spies throughout England, he is a revolting figure; yet the reader cannot but admire his vision of a realm set free from a renewal of the anarchy of the Wars of the Roses. He favors the Protestant cause less from doctrinal than from political reasons; he is politically astute enough to sense that the new Protestantism will offer a firmer base for an absolute monarchy than the old Catholicism. He served Henry by treachery and cruelty, but he served him well. Yet so horrifying a man is he that the reader rejoices in his downfall.

Among the characters of the second rank there stands out the figure of Princess Mary—the future "Bloody Mary" of history books. Ford gives an unusually brilliant picture of her: a girl so bitten to the soul by her mother's divorce and her own subsequent proclamation as a bastard that she is now only a rigid figure of hate. To good Catholics, she is almost a saint; to her father, she is a frozen block against which even his imperious will is shattered. And to any reader who may be interested in her reign, little more than a decade in the future, this portrait gives an illuminating psychological insight into the causes that made her the ruler that she was to become.

But above all, there is the figure of Henry VIII, this giant of a man whose vast shadow stretches over the whole story. As depicted by Ford, he resembles nothing so much as a half-tamed wild animal, at one moment pathetically docile, at the next, tearing into pieces those whom he had seemed to love. He is haunted by the fear of damnation for his persecution of the old faith, yet he cannot return to it. In the final dramatic scene between him and his fifth wife, she tells him what he is: a man who blows hot in the morning and cold at night, a straw tossed by every conflicting wind. For all his absolute power and his cruelty, he is a pathetic and tragic man.

And there is Katharine. In her recent book, *The Queens and the Hive,* Dame Edith Sitwell calls Ford's heroine "the lewd, sly, pitiable little ghost" who, to use another of Dame Edith's favorite phrases, "rose like a wind, died like a wind." In truth, she had only a brief summer on the sea of glory; and historians seem to agree that she was "probably" guilty of the crimes of unchastity charged against her. Ford gives us a very different interpretation. His Katharine Howard is a girl too honest, too deeply religious, for the world in which she had to live. She sees men as only all white or all black; she sincerely believes that the old faith can be restored. Indeed, her brief reign did mark the return to power of the reactionary group, a momentary reversal of the triumphant march of Protestantism. But she is betrayed by everyone; even her uncle Norfolk, a hater of the new age, betrays her. And so Henry, who deeply loved her but who could never stay of one mind, sent her to the block on Tower Hill.

The real protagonists of this novel are, however, not Henry VIII and his queen; they are the old Catholicism of the Middle Ages and the new Protestantism of the Renaissance. The novel is set on one of those great dividing lines of history; and Henry himself has a foot, in its great square-toed shoe, on either side of it. He was half Catholic, half Protestant; he turned away from Latin because it reminded him of the old language of the Mass that he had destroyed, yet he wanted to be head of the English Church. The hands of the clock could be briefly stopped, but they could not be turned back. As Katharine is bluntly told, there is the unescapable fact that there are too many in England who have grown rich from the spoils of the Church and that these men will never give up the lands and goods that they have obtained. Even her uncle, the Duke of Norfolk, head of the Catholic party and of the old nobility, wears in his hat a jewel taken from a chalice in the Abbey of Risings. The

85

"new nobility," come up under the Tudors, is founded on wealth stolen from the Church. Here is a hard economic fact, against which theology and even Katharine's faith will be shattered.

Katharine, "mazed," as she says, by the reading of old books, moves toward her tragic end because she expects men to be better than they can be. Her world is not peopled by heroic figures from classical antiquity. Yet in the end it is she who triumphs, and Henry, who sends her to execution, who is defeated.

As was said earlier, this is a long, elaborate historical novel in the good old Victorian tradition. It has an immensely complicated plot—intrigue is piled upon intrigue, incident upon incident, for hardly a character in the story can be trusted. Each is utterly

false, thinking only of himself, endlessly shifting sides, betraying and being betrayed. But at least these are full-blooded people, not the hollow men who flit, twittering like bats, through most contemporary novels—"these unfortunates," as Dante calls them, "who never were alive." The style fits the book. We are at one moment in the glare of torches and in the presence of the enormous scarlet king; at the next, plunged into the darkness of a corridor of one of these vast palaces. The warhorses, sheathed in iron, solemnly prance; the state barges slide up and down the Thames; Norfolk's tucket is blown in a "triple convolution" of sound. It was a magnificent and a terrible world, and Ford makes it live again in all of its terror and splendor.

Tench Francis Tilghman

FINAL SOLUTIONS

Author: Frederick Seidel (1936-   )
Publisher: Random House (New York). 50 pp. $3.75
Type of work: Poetry

A first book of dramatic monologues by a young Harvard graduate, born in St. Louis, about whom Robert Lowell has said: "Seidel . . . keeps up a dense, all-out eloquence. He explores subjects that are sometimes shocking in the Roman manner of Suetonius and Juvenal. . . . Here is power that strikes."

At the outset one is struck by this new poet's strange and adventurous blend of polished academic form with a ragged content usually left to less disciplined writers. The juxtaposition produces interesting tensions. The first poem in the volume, "Wanting to Live in Harlem," is a recall of sexual desire and search, aroused by his mother's colored maid. He shifts between boyhood dreams in St. Louis and adolescent experience in Boston and New York. The verse is strongly influenced by

Robert Lowell's early work. In fact, the following passage could have come from *Lord Weary's Castle* or *The Mills of the Cavanaughs:*

And run to grab her beads and crucifix
and missal,
I to find my violin and tuning whistle
To practice my lessons. Mendelssohn.
Or Bach,
Whose Lutheran fingering had helped
pluck
The tonsured monks like toadstools
from their lawns,

And now riddled the armor I would
have to shuck . . .

"A Widower" is a grimly pathetic portrait of an old man whose life has become centered on his bathroom. It is deliberately ugly in subject, deliberately beautiful in style. It is as if one placed a chamberpot in a gilded frame and called it a nineteenth century portrait. In fact, quite often Seidel's purpose seems to be to shock, or at least to startle, as in this description of the Seine:

Itching from Kotex pads, from green,
polluted perch,
The Seine scratches itself lovingly along
the quais—

Possibly he is adjusting his academic mode to include a poetic territory just short of the badlands of total exhibition where the Beats dwell.

Quickly, though, one sees in "The Coalman" some cogent reasons for the just attention which Seidel has received. In this very firm poem he has conjured a stark but sympathetic imagery. It is a zero winter night; the coal trucks go by; and

The Mine Workers' huge Santa Claus
Made of coal derivatives beams
His head-lamp on their new all-glass
office . . .

With the following passage,

When the small streets crack like sticks,
If they snap a gas pipe . . .

the reader is prepared for a powerful concluding movement in which the very grotesqueness of the final image is inspiredly appropriate:

The ice wind has flattened the river.
It tears the skin from my lips like Bible
paper.

I see me and the miners, the drivers,
And some poor nigger customers
Who can't buy the smokeless fuel
Eating our soft coal whole,
And vomiting and vomiting slick eels
Of blackness. I can see this.

It requires quite a sturdy talent to pull off a sound-jammed phrase such as "soft coal whole" and a strong imagination to bind together in one cultural symbol a group of people who still live on soft coal in an age of oil. The stubborn insistence of "I can see this" is so successful as to become more than a bitter addendum to the statement of the poem; it indicates even the silent, laconic gestures of head and hand characteristic of the poor.

Only a few dull poems are included in *Final Solutions*. "The Heart Attack" is one such, with its echoes of Browning, Robinson, and Lowell: its conventional scene-setting, its unflagging and exhausting procession of ironies in the voice of a mistress haranguing an old man, its smooth-sifted rhymes and perfunctory stanzas. But it must be remembered that this is a first book and unavoidably exhibits traces of the university student trailing clouds of the library masters of monologue.

Seidel's verse relies upon a keen sense of rhythmic phrasing and a clear eye for images imbedded with the salt-crystals of irony. He has learned well Eliot's technique of juxtaposing the trivial and the weighty, the tawdry and the comely. For example, he speaks of lamé slippers and Belsem in almost the same breath, with jolting effect; and a callous rabbit hunter is made very plausibly to stand for all human cruelty. In "A Year Abroad," Seidel mixes, in the Eliot-Lowell manner, a stew of contrasts, displaying an intellectualized approach in a dryly urbane quotation concerning a first century Roman defeat in the Teutoburg Forest, then plunging immediately into present-day Europe and America. He alternates between eras in a survey of the history of military violence. A short passage serves to display the almost Brechtian irony in verse of flawless velvet:

> Though it was Varus who when Herod died
> Crunched up Judaea, from Teutoburg Forest he
> Would bear the Eagles of Varus back to Rome:
> History's straight-man, ambushed by his aide,
> His trusted German, into suicide,
> Bald, civilized, delicious—never praised,
> But chosen by Augustus. Rome gawked, amazed . . .
> The NATO General salutes the prizes.
> His Holiness stops at *et credo*, and rises
> To touch the braid and tatters. Washington

And Bonn have flown the long-lost Eagles home.

It would be not only unfair but also senseless to speak of Seidel as "promising"—that limbo into which critics toss nine out of ten young poets. The plain fact is that, in reading poem after accomplished poem, the reader is apt to feel that some miracle has occurred and that Seidel was *born* fully equipped to write. Even though quite young and at times frankly imitative, he is already a mature poet technically, with a great deal of polish, and at times an emotionally deep man with words. The central device of his idiom is the tension he creates by giving such a lustrous surface to materials one would not customarily expect to see so well dressed. No mistake about it, Seidel sees, hears, and feels richly, and he moves gracefully among his world's objects.

Robert Hazel

THE FIRE NEXT TIME

Author: James Baldwin (1924-   )
Publisher: The Dial Press (New York). 120 pp. $3.50
Type of work: Essays
Two essays showing that the plight of the Negro in America is the white man's plight as well

James Baldwin is the most important Negro novelist now writing in the United States, but his importance springs from something other than the quality of his fiction, undeniable though the latter may be. The author of three novels, *Go Tell It on the Mountain, Giovanni's Room,* and *Another Country,* which range from the highly praised to the wildly controversial, Baldwin is most significant for his gradually assumed role as the central spokesman for the American Negro. From television interviews to a highly publicized conversation with Robert Kennedy, Baldwin's voice and his intense and informed opinions on the present racial situation have become familiar to the American public as the soundest articulations of what the Negro feels the dilemma of contemporary society to be. In a symposium on the modern novel several years ago at Yale, Baldwin made it abundantly clear, in contrast to his fellow Negro novelist Ralph Ellison, who spoke in far more general and technical terms, that to him the central issue on the American scene, an issue which any discussion, social, political, or aesthetic, was bound to come to terms with, was the problem of the Negro. That problem has been central to Baldwin's previous non-fictional writings. *Notes of a Native Son,* his first collection of essays, is Baldwin's autobiographical record of growing up to the consciousness of being a Negro, a consciousness of alienation and otherness forced upon him not only by the white world but also by his very environment, a black world hyper-aware of its subjugation and those lines of demarcation drawn by the white. In his second collection of essays, *Nobody Knows My Name,* Baldwin presents his adult consciousness of the racial problem, one, as he shows, hardly restricted to the South in that the Northern white is no more capable than the Southerner, though his incapability may take subtler forms, of granting the Negro his individual humanity, of granting, one might say by extension, the autonomy and individuality of any man. As the title of that collection indicates, the fate which the Negro suffers at the hand of the white man is that of anonymity, of being converted (if one can speak of conversion when the original entity is not even perceived) from a human being into an abstraction of blackness carrying those normative overtones traditional in the Western bifurcative symbolology of whiteness and blackness. Thus, for Baldwin, the Negro's problem of identity is at the same time the white man's problem of identity, the latter dependent, in its insecurity, on dehumanizing and emblemizing the Negro, and the total problem is less a racial than an American one, a function of the American mind's abstracting tendency, an aspect of the Jamesian "complex fate."

In "My Dungeon Shook," the brief first essay of the two comprising *The Fire Next Time,* Baldwin reiterates material familiar from his two earlier collections. Taking the form of a "Letter to My Nephew on the One Hundredth Anniversary of the Emancipation," the essay spells out the inevitable pain of the conditions which the young Negro must face for no reason other than that he is black, conditions fixed by the white's belief in the Negro's inferiority (or, what is just as bad, his inability to act on the knowledge of that belief's falsity) and his maintenance of his own identity in the belief's maintenance. The writer states that "the danger, in the case of most white Americans, is the loss of their identity. . . . Any upheaval in the universe is terrifying because it so profoundly attacks one's sense of one's own reality. Well, the black man has functioned in the white man's world as a fixed star, as an immovable pillar: and as he moves out of his place, heaven and earth are shaken to their foundations." It is the task of the black man to show the white his own reality, to make him see as fallacious the insecure identity which rests on a series of rigid misconceptions about the nature of man and to accept the fluidity of identity and the possibility of each human being.

The second and major essay of the volume, "Down at the Cross," which appeared originally in *The New Yorker* under the title "Letter from a Region in My Mind," treats the problem of identity from an opposite, and for the white man frankly frightening, standpoint, that of the Black Muslim, for whom the white is just that pernicious abstraction which the black is, in Baldwin's terms, for the white. It begins with an agonized descent into Baldwin's past, his discovery in his fourteenth year of the evil in himself and the world without, his turning to an almost fanatical religiosity for refuge, the only other alternative offered him being a life of crime and violence, and his pained discovery that the Christianity offered him in the Negro church he attended did not extend to all men: "When we were told to love everybody, I had thought that that meant *everybody*. But no. It applied only to those who believed as we did, and it did not apply to white people at all." But this consideration of racial consciousness' religious manifestation serves basically only as a prologue to the heart of the essay, a conversation between Baldwin and Elijah Muhammad, leader and prophet of the Black Muslims. Baldwin details the tension and apprehension he felt upon being, in effect, summoned into the presence of Elijah, the struggle in his mind between his rejection of Black Muslim beliefs and his sense of the Negro's plight. Preconceptions about the man, however, vanished in Elijah Muhammad's presence, a presence majestically calm which communicated to his followers a worshipful obeisance which had nothing of frenzy in it, but the serenity which comes from absolute certainty of rectitude. And the beliefs which produced that calm certainty—that the black race is the chosen of Allah, that the white race is the manifestation of demonic powers, that when the black race is returned to the true faith of Islam the deliverance will come and the doomed race of white men will be annihilated. "There is nothing new," as Baldwin observes, "in this merciless formulation except the explicitness of its symbols and the candor of its hatred. Its emotional tone is as familiar to me as my own skin; it is but another way of saying that *sinners shall be bound in Hell a thousand years.* That sinners have always, for American Negroes, been white is a truth we needn't labor, and every American Negro, therefore, risks having the gates of paranoia close on him." This formulation is only the explicit converse of the white man's belief, perhaps submerged, but the one on which his sense of identity rests, in the Negro's inferiority.

Baldwin's plea is that the American Negro realize that he "has been formed by this nation, for better or for worse, and does not belong to any other—not to Africa, and certainly not to Islam," that he come to terms with the reality of his past and shape his future out of it. But such a realization cannot come about unless the white man also can take stock of his heritage and, in recognition of that which he has bequeathed the Negro, open the way for the discovery of the true American identity, regardless of race. Else the blinding abstractionism of the white may generate an even fiercer antithesis which will finally prove the annihilation of both: "If we do not now dare everything, the fulfillment of that prophecy, re-created from the Bible in song by a slave, is upon us: *God gave Noah the rainbow sign, No more water, the fire next time!*

Donald L. Mull

THE FIRST DAY OF FRIDAY

Author: Honor Tracy (1915-   )
Publisher: Random House (New York). 246 pp. $4.95
Type of work: Novel
Time: The present
Locale: Rural Ireland

A wryly comic novel dealing with the predicament of a young Irish landowner who cannot leave home but must preserve Anglo-Irish dissent and save the lovely country from the Irish

> *Principal characters:*
> MICHAEL DUFF, an Irish squire whose peaceful inheritance becomes a maddening cross to bear
> MRS. DUFF, his mother, devoted to television and the vaporous past
> ATRACTA MOIN SMITH, the incompetent housekeeper who leaves her mistress apoplectic and her master a slave
> DULCINEA BROWNING, Michael Duff's fiancée
> FATHER BEHAN, the parish priest who battles daily with devils not altogether of his own making
> KILRANY, an Anglo-Irish peer and a self-declared keeper of the Protestant faith
> ALFRED SMITH, the housekeeper's husband, also a jailbird

Honor Tracy has answered Sean O'Casey in his own terms. He suggests in *Purple Dust* that the English will never understand the Irish, that Irish mansions cannot be preserved out of sentiment for the past, that only the Irish can inherit the Irish earth. In *The First Day of Friday,* Honor Tracy in her own "wayward comedy" knows that the Irish must have the Anglicans; that the mansions will fall to ruin anyhow, particularly when the Church and outsiders buy them up and impoverish the old gentry; that only the hold of the past on the present can preserve a land so lovely "that Michael constantly wonders how the Creator has come to give such a land to such a people." This book is the third lambasting of love Miss Tracy has aimed at the land of her own ancestry if not her native country.

The first day of a series of sacred Fridays is the beginning of the end.

Young Michael Duff has discharged Atracta Moin Smith, his inherited housekeeper and cook, for the nineteenth time; by the time this domestic ritual act reaches into the twenties he is undone, a victim of the relationship between master and servant. On the nine Fridays he experiences defeats of life and death, bureaucracy, peasantry, love, despair, exhilaration, exhaustion, and resolution. Brooding over all his land is the Church, not his Church of England, but the ancient power of Catholicism embodied microcosmically in the person of the housekeeper, whose right to the name of Smith is sanctioned only by courtesy.

Along with his crumbling manor, the debilitated but beautiful land, and an ancient title, Michael Duff has been willed Atracta Moin Smith and her triplet brood, the latter from some source never referred to. Being taxed to death, killed slowly by inefficiency

91

of workers on his estate, and desperately in love with Dulcinea Browning, the daughter of a neighboring landowner, the young squire must put up with the private moronics and the public disgrace of Atracta Smith. Her ignorance has a kind of epic quality: she gives her mistress sixpence to take instead of pills after hearing the dying woman say that medicine costs so much that it was as expensive as taking sixpence. From her first whining "Master Michael, Honey," to her last grotesquerie, the slatternly servant broods over Georgetown and extends her image into Michael Duff's future. He cannot escape from her because she is too much for him. She is Ireland.

For a so-short moment sanity falls on the ancestral acres in the person of Alfred Smith, her "husband," a man of many aliases; he asserts the ancient wisdom of the belt and whips his wife and the triplets into order and politeness. After police officers haul Smith away on a charge of bigamy, Michael begins in earnest his attempt to escape his destiny. He plans to sell his land, release Dulcinea from her father's scholarly clutches, and elope to the world. But he cannot. His mother, who has never done anything positive in her life, has the bad grace to choke to death, laughing at Atracta Smith, who claims she is worth more than Mrs. Duff's beloved and deceased dog. When the clan meets in mock grief, a cousin from England who has turned Catholic stays on as Michael's nemesis and the housekeeper's protector. He stoutly maintains and hires a lawyer to prove that the servant must not be fired —in fact, cannot be. The lawyer makes a case that only Atracta herself could break, and so she does. Then to her rescue comes Father Behan. Gaelic and transfixed, this priest has inspired Michael himself in former times with his erudition and eccentricities (he exhorts his private demons publicly). Father Behan has Atracta drop the suit, fall on her knees to ask forgiveness, and pledge not only her allegiance but her confidence to master. (A wonderful subject is discovered but never dwelt upon; Atracta in her low cunning knows that now is not the time to disclose to Michael Duff the facts of his father's death, a terrible mistake of identity.) In a flash of revelation, a horrible moment of useless truth, Michael understands that he cannot escape this maudlin fury, that he is not Orestes but Telemachus fated to stay and defend.

Kilrany, the local Anglo-Irish peer, joins the ranks of the obsessed when he takes over the ministrations of the Anglican priest. In his first—and funny —sermon he summarizes the servitude of the Anglican communicants who are the victims rather than the masters in the Irish landlord system: ". . . But we do not have to try and obliterate our past. On the contrary, we should cling to it, head high, for we are not ashamed of it and it is all we shall ever have. . . . Dearly beloved brethren, the time is up. To God the Father, God the Son and God the Holy Ghost, amen. And now, The Queen."

William Tillson

FLOWERING OF THE CUMBERLAND

Author: Harriette Simpson Arnow (1908-   )
Publisher: The Macmillan Company (New York). Illustrated. 441 pp. $6.95
Type of work: Regional and social history
Time: 1780-1803
Locale: Kentucky and Middle Tennessee

A descriptive study of life on the frontier, chronicling the actions and attitudes of the early settlers in the Cumberland region

Flowering of the Cumberland is a companion volume to *Seedtime on the Cumberland,* published by Mrs. Arnow in 1960. This study, like the earlier work, is a labor of love. The author knows the region well because she was born in the area and has spent much of her life there. She writes of the past history of the Cumberland with pride and with great respect for the achievements of the early settlers. *Flowering of the Cumberland* is a work of arduous and meticulous research, including old documents, memoirs, wills, diaries, account books, newspapers, and she has utilized the writings of the outstanding authorities on such specialized subjects as agriculture, religion, and industry in America.

When the earliest settlers arrived in the Cumberland region in the 1780's, the most serious obstacle barring their advance was hostile Indians. Such tribes as the Cherokees, Chickasaws, and Creeks sought to exterminate the invaders and destroy their fortifications. Until the power of the Indians had been destroyed, the settlers were forced to live in stockades. Those few who chose privacy over security paid the high price of death and loss of scalp.

Life inside the stockade was far from pleasant because it was crowded, unsanitary, noisy, and uncomfortable; however, it provided safety from the savages. The Indians were so numerous that a planting or hunting party had to

include a number of guards to prevent a surprise attack. Although the woods were full of game and the streams abounded in fish, the settlers knew hunger because of the Indians who were lurking nearby. The dog was truly man's best friend on the frontier because he could give the alarm and alert settlers to the danger of an Indian raid.

The last large-scale attack on the Cumberland frontier occurred shortly before midnight on September 30, 1792, when four hundred Indians converged on Buchanan's Station. The Indians atempted to breach the barricades time after time, but each attack was broken. Sally Buchanan, the wife of Buchanan's son, was credited with saving the fort by distributing bullets and whiskey to the defenders. Sally, with complete disregard for her personal safety, made trip after trip to the storehouse all night long. When one realizes that she was in the eighth month of pregnancy, the story of her devotion and heroism becomes even more astonishing. The man who broke the attack had never fired a gun before. He was Jimmy O'Connor, a recent arrival from Ireland. O'Connor was given a blunderbuss to shoot, and because he put too much powder in the weapon it flashed like a cannon. It is believed that after the tremendous flash and explosion the Indians gave up the attack. After this date Indian raiding parties were much smaller.

The frontier family was an extremely close-knit unit. They worked together, prayed together, and almost always stayed together. Divorce, according to Mrs. Arnow, was almost completely unknown. The selection of a wife was the most important decision a man would make. He looked for a partner—the one person whom he could trust above all others, one who could manage things and make the correct decisions. The author cites Andrew Jackson as an example. After his wife died Jackson's plantation began to fail because he did not have a person who could watch and direct the actions of the overseer.

Mrs. Arnow's research indicates that the children of all families were wanted and usually spoiled because parents were pleased with strong individuals who exhibited their independence. The author writes:

> In spite of the disinclination of parents, to follow the rule beloved by the Puritans—"Spare the rod and spoil the child" —and in its place put the old saying, "You can't spoil a baby", the spoiled babies often grew up and showed an ability to take responsibility at an early age. Twelve-year-old boys manned port holes and when even younger took long trips alone to mill; young girls milked cows and sometimes managed households when mother—usually Ma or Mama—was sick or dead; at times both sexes had to perform when scarcely in their teens an adult's work in house or field.

Again,

> . . . a young Cumberland mother wrote her husband of their eighteen-month-old, a sturdy, nimble-footed child, able to climb the parlor table, "I have at length weaned Mary; it would have amused you to see how she would fight it; she would get tired of crying and stop and then give me a slap and then spit in my face. I can't think where she learnt it from. . . ."

All children began their education in the home under the supervision of the mother. At the proper age, boys as well as girls were sent to school. Far more emphasis was placed upon reading, spelling, and arithmetic than at present. The males of the family often did chores and other tasks which today would be labeled as "woman's work" without feeling that it made them less manly. On the other hand, seldom did the husband permit his wife to toil in the field; this work was considered degrading.

The horse was considered a man's most important possession after his family and his land. Although the horse was not the only form of transportation, it was the most important. Horses were expensive and, like a present-day automobile, they were status symbols. Furnishings which included bridle, blanket, and saddle were an additional expense. A horse thief could expect no mercy on the frontier. The cost of maintaining a horse while traveling was most expensive because the horse was the first concern of the traveler.

In the early days dogs of all types were necessary. Some were utilized as watchdogs and others were trained as hunters. Mrs. Arnow states that in the early days every family had about a dozen dogs. Later one newspaper complained that there were too many dogs in the area. In addition to dogs the farmer kept cattle, hogs, sheep, and chickens. These animals served to produce food for the family and products for the market. The livestock was a necessity but produced problems because animals had to be fenced out of garden areas.

The author has given an excellent description of how a field was prepared for planting and of how crops were tended once the seed had been put into the ground. In Tennessee the farmer depended far more upon the hoe than the plow. The principal crops were corn and other cereals, cotton, and tobacco. The growing season for cotton was too short to insure success, and a spring freeze or a fall frost could bring disaster. On the other hand, the soil and climate proved to be perfect for growing corn. Because it could be used as the basis of the diet, sold as meal, converted into whiskey, or used to fatten hogs, corn soon became the staple crop in the Cumberland region. Tobacco was grown on a small scale as a cash crop.

During the early years the professional soldier and the clergyman were missing from the frontier, but as the Cumberland area became more densely settled they began to appear. The most lucrative profession on the frontier was law, as there was need for lawyers, judges, and politicians. Andrew Jackson, Felix Grundy, and many others achieved fame and wealth in the legal profession. Trained physicians were few and far between. Engineers were nonexistent, and surveyors were usually poorly trained. Any person who desired could open a school without having any training. The people in the Cumberland were religious, but few belonged to churches. The few church buildings which were found were small and rarely displayed a cross; it was believed that a cross suggested Catholicism. Bishop James Asbury brought Methodism into the region quite early; however, he usually preached in private homes.

Although the frontier was a violent place with many acts of murder and lesser violence recorded, according to Mrs. Arnow, not one case of suicide has been uncovered. The people constantly used alcohol, but only two alcoholics have been mentioned in the records. Whiskey served as an internal and external medication. It was consumed to break chills and fevers, rubbed on the body to end aches and pains. The consumption of a "toddy" was almost universal. The first thing the new-born babe was given was a "toddy" and the last days of an elderly person were eased by "toddies." The frontiersman enjoyed singing and his favorite type of song appears to have been religious in nature. As in other sections, he was a social and coöperative being, for he could always be counted on to be present at a house-raising or a shelling bee. He enjoyed the simple pleasures of dancing and was probably known for his ability to execute the proper steps.

Mrs. Arnow has drawn a clear, concise picture of America in an earlier day. This volume should be required reading for all students in American history. It will be appreciated by all who read it. After enough of these regional studies have appeared, we will begin to change many of the theories of American history prevalent today. This is a study recommended to all persons interested in American history.

J. Perry Cochran

FORD: DECLINE AND REBIRTH, 1933-1962

Author: Allan Nevins (1890-   ) and Frank Ernest Hill (1888-   )
Publisher: Charles Scribner's Sons (New York). Illustrated. 442 pp. $8.95
Type of work: Corporate history
Time: 1933-1962
Locale: Detroit, Dearborn, the United States, Europe

The history of the Ford Motor Company from 1933 through 1962 with emphasis on the change in policy from one-man rule to corporate management

> Principal personages:
> HENRY FORD
> CLARA, his wife
> EDSEL, their son
> HENRY FORD II, Edsel's son and postwar president of the Company
> CHARLES E. SORENSEN, production manager under Henry and Edsel
> HARRY BENNETT, Ford personnel director and Henry's confidant
> SIR PERCIVAL PERRY, Ford's British manager
> ERNEST R. BREECH, Henry II's chief assistant

If there is a single individual in America's history responsible for the American way of life as we know it today, surely his name is Henry Ford. It was Mr. Ford who "put America on wheels," as he expressed it, and in so doing became responsible for the ribbons of superhighways that now crisscross the United States, for the corner gasoline station, the tire shop, the drive-in restaurant and theater, the motel, even the "motion-picture culture" that infuses most farm families from coast to coast.

With the publication of *Ford: Decline and Rebirth, 1933-1962,* Allan Nevins and Frank Ernest Hill, with the assistance of three research associates, have completed the final volume of a three-part work on the history of the Ford Motor Company which includes *Ford: The Times, the Man, the Company, 1863-1915* (1954), written by Mr. Nevins, and *Ford: Expansion and Challenge, 1915-1933* (1957), written by Mr. Nevins and Mr. Hill.

Decline and Rebirth is replete with figures, statistics, notes, and footnotes,

and there is an admirable number of direct quotations from participants in or witnesses to events being described. The authors reveal that they had full access to Ford Archives records and this fact lends authority to what they have written.

Like the earlier volumes in the Ford series, this one was prepared under the auspices of Columbia University, and the university is to be commended for this contribution to the field of corporate literature. Corporate history makes interesting reading for many Americans because it is in America that the most dramatic developments of modern industrialism have taken place. A major difficulty in developing a satisfactory body of corporate literature, however, is the scarcity of qualified chroniclers who can present a true and rounded picture of the situation. When such books are written by academics or by theoretical economists, often much stress is placed on sociology and human relations but hardly any on the day to day problems that must be met by the businessman in order to achieve a suitable end result—problems such as production schedules, competition, advertising, research and product improvement, distribution, financing, and, justly, profits. The theoretical economist has probably never had to worry about whether he can meet the payroll at the end of the week. But at one time or another most businessmen, even including Mr. Ford, have had to face such a problem. In fact, Ford once found himself in the precarious position of owing fifty million dollars more than he could pay at the moment. He cleverly overcame his predicament by cutting prices and liquidating his huge inventory, thus raising the necessary cash while avoiding risky borrowing.

Decline and Rebirth opens with a review of the early days of the New Deal and dwells at length on Henry Ford's refusal to sign an NRA compliance certificate (although he complied fully with code requirements). The second chapter takes up the labor problem, to which much of the first half of the book is devoted. Communists had become extremely active in the labor-union movement, and the head of the American Communist Party later reported that "for a long time party officers had received urgent cables from the Comintern—hundreds in the aggregate—urging unionization of the industry and special efforts to attack Ford." *Decline and Rebirth* repeatedly criticizes Mr. Ford in the harshest tones for his refusal to recognize the labor unions; but an individualist and a believer in property rights, such as Mr. Ford was, could hardly be expected to roll over and play dead for unionists led by Communists and Socialists who were bent on destroying his life's work, and whose rank and file mem-

bers forcibly seized the Ford plants by means of destructive sit-ins—seemingly immune from prosecution by Federal, State, or local authorities, all of whom refused to perform their sworn constitutional duty of protecting the rights and property of private citizens from forcible seizure by others. It is little wonder that Mr. Ford did not respond to such treatment with admiration and affection for the unions, though the authors of this book seem to think that he should have. Eventually, Mr. Ford did recognize the unions, and he gave them a far better contract than they expected, apparently in response to the wishes of his wife rather than because of government or union pressure.

This volume covers all phases of the Ford Motor Company. For example, many readers may be surprised at the extent of the Ford overseas domain. In the late 1930's more than half a million vehicles were produced overseas in a four-year period. As World War II approached, these foreign production figures naturally declined but all during the war Ford plants in England and on the Continent, having been taken over by both combatants, turned out war equipment in huge quantities. The enormous contributions of Ford productive capabilities to our own war effort are recounted in a highly interesting manner. As was the case during World War I, Henry Ford opposed our involvement in a foreign war; but once we actually were involved, he placed his entire resources at the disposal of the government.

The latter half of *Decline and Rebirth* deals with the fortunes of the Ford empire after World War II. With the death of Edsel Ford and the withdrawal of Henry from absolute control of the company, a struggle for power

97

developed involving Harry Bennett, Charles E. Sorensen, Henry Ford II, and others. With a grudging nod from his grandfather, Henry II won out, and his first official act was to dispose of Harry Bennett. Sorensen had already been eased out of the picture.

With the help of one of the largest industrial plants in the world, more than six hundred million dollars in cash, a name almost magic in the automotive industry, and a number of brilliant and experienced automotive executives whom he had the good sense to seek out and hire, twenty-eight-year-old Henry Ford II undertook the job of rebuilding the Ford Motor Company at the end of World War II. The record of his success is well documented in this volume, which gives a vivid report of his progress and finds young Henry's enlightened business philosophy in large measure responsible for the emergence of the company from its moribundity.

Some readers will find this closing volume of the Ford story romantic in its portrayal of the lone-wolf leader fighting to protect his empire from government interference and labor-leader dominance. Others will be inspired by the way the youthful Henry II rescued a sinking ship and made it whole again. Still others may feel that in its treatment of Henry Ford, the man, *Decline and Rebirth* falls short of the mark in objectivity. Such readers will hope that someday the inventor of mass production, the originator of high wages for labor, the supplier of more than four billion dollars to a foundation for the public benefit will come under the hand of one who will assay his achievements and shortcomings not with the hindsight of the 1960's as a criterion, but in the light of the values and conditions, the times and the stresses, under which the actual events occurred. Even Mr. Ford might have acted differently in the 1960's.

Frank N. Magill

FRANCIS BACON
The Temper of a Man

Author: Catherine Drinker Bowen (1897-   )
Publisher: Atlantic-Little, Brown and Company (Boston). 245 pp. $6.00
Type of work: Biography
Time: 1561-1625
Locale: England

A popular biography of the enigmatic and incomparably influential Elizabethan whose scope of accomplishments was so broad that he has been identified both as "the father of modern science" (which he was not) and the author of Shakespeare's plays (which he was also not)

Principal personages:
FRANCIS BACON, Baron Verulam and Viscount St. Alban
ANTHONY BACON, his brother
QUEEN ELIZABETH I
WILLIAM CECIL, Baron Burghley
ROBERT DEVEREUX, Earl of Essex
LADY ALICE BACON, his wife
SIR EDWARD COKE
JAMES I, King of England and Scotland

Catherine Drinker Bowen italicizes her ambitious intentions in this biography of Francis Bacon by prefacing her book with a Plutarchian epigraph: "Authority and place demonstrate and try the tempers of men, by moving every passion and discovering every frailty." Since a phrase from this quotation is picked up in the subtitle, the reader may well expect a fully human portrait of Bacon as a private individual whose particular shape (a shape possessing both passion and frailty) is an understandable consequence of his times and circumstances. The reader is led to expect that Bacon's personality will be revealed in depth and that the peculiar breadth and intensity of his thought will be related to the "authority and place" of the turbulent English Renaissance through which he lived. This is an ambitious aim to focus on any complicated personage, but particularly so for a man like Bacon, who seems to have lived at least two distinct

lives on the principle of the extended parallel lines that never intersect.

Mrs. Bowen demonstrates that Bacon the politician seems hardly to be reconciled with Bacon the speculative thinker. As she presents the politician in his successive obeisances to power, he seems always caught up within the exigencies of the quotidian, responding like a well-trained radar set to the pips and bleeps of courtly favor and political advancement. Bacon the politician is embarrassingly like a wind-up toy which has been pre-set to become Lord Chancellor of England, Lord Keeper of the Royal Seal. Except for his one inexplicable lapse from opportunism when, as a young Member from Middlesex, he blatantly challenged Elizabeth's triple subsidy and fell from royal favor, his public life reads like a precisioned quest after the main chance. And if he ultimately lost out through an unprecedented Parliamentary impeachment, his fall from office was not at all a failure in his own calculations. Mrs. Bowen persuades us that he was an effective enough public servant, but his career as Solicitor General and, later, Attorney General, does not seem especially remarkable in an age which was, after all, rather exemplary for its remarkable men of affairs.

This quondam barrister, Francis Bacon, was also the author of the *Advancement of Learning*, the *Instauratio Magna*, and the *Novum Organum*, as well as numerous sophisticated disquisitions in the areas of legal theory, history, theology, and the natural sciences. This Lord Chancellor, perhaps taking his cue from an earlier incumbent of that high office, is the framer of the utopian fantasy, the *New Atlantis*, which eloquently concretizes some of the floating abstractions of the *Instauratio*. Bacon the speculative thinker is as broad and unmindful of barriers as his cautious *alter ego*, the politician, is narrow and concerned lest he brush too roughly against the severe limits upon his freedom. A Prometheus of the imagination, Bacon established radical colonies of thought in wilderness which his contemporaries had not even dreamed of as yet. Some of his colonies, in fact, are still beyond our own settlement. And yet as a public person he seems to have had the supple flexibility of an Osric, the malleable posture of the courtier at his toadiest. Mrs. Bowen adequately depicts these two aspects of Bacon's character, but a biography which aims at revealing the temper of such a "double" man ought to do more than merely point to the raging dichotomies. One would think that it is the responsibility of the biographer to suggest the possibilities of unity from which Bacon himself remained sundered.

But Bacon offers a more serious problem for the interpretative biographer. Outstanding in thought and action as history has proven him to be, Bacon must necessarily have been the outgrowth of some private *un*historical human being, some Ur-Bacon with real passions and frailties, a man of flesh-and-bone whose broadcast publicity is delicately prefigured in the domestic seizures of his unpublic life. We read biographies in part because we are interested in capturing the elusive man beneath (or sometimes in spite of) the personage. Because, among other reasons, we believe that we will have a richer understanding of the movement of historical forces and the internal rhythms of impersonal achievements if we can effect some sense of communion with that brother-man who acted in history and shaped the impersonal construct. We are interested in biographies because we recognize our own passions and frailties and we desire to sight on the successes and dramas of our own kind writ large. And it is this *human* view of Bacon which is most lacking in Mrs. Bowen's portrait. She seeks it, she surrounds it, and she finally pretends that she has given it, but its deficiency deprives the book of resonance and human echo.

Bacon's life was peculiarly undramatic. He was at the center of many important happenings—events intrinsically exciting and yet, in his case, strangely dull. He was an intimate of that Elizabethan dramatis personae which included Essex, Ben Jonson, and Queen Elizabeth herself, but somehow the glitter of this extraordinary group fails to encompass his personality. He occupied one of the highest positions in the London of King James I, but we receive no real sense of pomp in his glory, nor pathos in his fall into the Tower of London. His friendship with and subsequent betrayal of Essex is narrated in full keeping with the known facts, and yet such a dramatic interplay of motives and passions as must have determined the vicissitudes of their relationship is scarcely evoked. Bacon's final will and testament revoked all previous bequests to his wife, Lady Alice, for "just and great causes," but what kind of scorpion union existed between them we do not know. The human portrait of Francis Bacon which Mrs. Bowen promises us never emerges from the chronicle of events and accomplishments; the shellac and varnish of time seem to have obscured the revealing lines and effaced the inimitable expression. The politician-statesman we can know exhaustively through the records of the state; the speculative thinker we can follow along the daring arcs of his thought; the man would seem to be beyond Mrs. Bowen's capacities for portraiture.

It seems fairly obvious that Mrs. Bowen capitulates too easily before the challenge of characterological excavation which she herself has set. Granted the paucity of documentary materials bearing on Bacon's psychic life, there is yet a grand vein of rich implication which she hardly scratches. Bacon was an incomparable stylist, one of the indisputable masters of prose style in all English writing. His style was British, Elizabethan, and, beyond these cate-gories, indubitably Baconian. He could no more be *un*-himself when he wrote than he could be un-himself in his human loneliness. And this unique style extends itself to the sweep of his imaginative speculations and the postures of his political life. It is possible that a serious investigation of Bacon's *style*—the single achievement for which he is cherished in history—might yield answers which Mrs. Bowen despairs of finding. If the style is the man, then an interpretative study of the style might bring us more intimately into a contact with the personage whose face is hidden in the shadows of history.

Mrs. Bowen's capacities as a superb biographer need no endorsement. Her own style is as fluent and eloquent as ever, and her intellectual rigor is as tenacious as ever. But Bacon fails to be illuminated in his most significant reaches and one may be forgiven the speculation that the failure is in the author's lack of empathy with that strange, vaguely unattractive lawyer-courtier who happened to create continents of thought which he expressed in a prose that has enriched even as it has altered the sweep of the English language. There is an old rule which suggests that the best biográphies are written by those who hate or love their subjects. One suspects that Mrs. Bowen is respectful, slightly revulsed, and generally indifferent.

Earl H. Rovit

THE GARDEN

Author: Yves Berger (1936-   )
Translated from the French by Robert Baldick
Publisher: George Braziller (New York), 226 pp. $4.00
Type of work: Novel
Time: 1956-1958
Locale: A French village near Avignon; Montpellier

The life of the imagination and the life of action conflict in the strange relationship of a boy to his father and to his sister

Principal characters:

THE NARRATOR, unnamed, a boy of eighteen

THE FATHER, unnamed, the mayor of a small village near Avignon

VIRGINIE, the sister, four years older than her brother

Although Wright Morris' *Cause for Wonder* and Susan Sontag's *The Benefactor* explored similar themes, *The Garden* was one of the most unusual novels of 1963. The first novel of twenty-seven-year-old Yves Berger, a teacher, a critic for the Paris weekly *l'Express*, and an editor at Bernard Grasset Publishers, *The Garden* (*Le Sud*) sold 130,000 copies within weeks and was awarded the *prix femina*.

Berger has two stories to tell, the one enhancing the other, and together they constitute a composite, highly expressive poetic image. Both are paradoxical, for the first conveys the extensive reality of the subjective imagination, and the second projects the intensive exoticism of objective reality itself. Berger limits his characters, action, and locale, shutting out all else, to focus intensely on the eternal values embodied in these abstracted elements. *The Garden* is virtually barren of social and historical details; for instance, World War II is merely a background disturbance.

The narrator opens and closes with brief descriptions of his immediate situation, thus setting the novel in a time-present frame. Two years after the major events in his story occurred, he lives in solitude on his deceased father's estate. As mayor, his father fought the technological progress which the town desired; he strove to cleanse his children "of school, of the age, of time," so that they might "grow up together in Virginia about 1842." In the Virginia estates man achieved "the small amount of civilization which we need." In a single year "the dreams of mankind during a million years were consummated and consumed." The father reads to the boy and his sister, Virginie (an ironically symbolic name), about the Golden Age from historical documents, travel books, the writings of Tocqueville, Crèvecœur, Lewis and Clark, Parkman, and a legion of obscure commentators. Describing the Garden of Eden in America, his father's sentences soar: "Once the monologue was interrupted, we were a long time coming back to earth." But Virginie, with her fervor for practical learning and immediate experience, rejects the garden of images; only the self-effacing narrator is seduced by the father's sensuous words. Having lost Virginie, the father sees his "immortality" in the boy. The external conflict between Virginie and her father, between two ways of living in time and space, is internalized in the boy.

102

The father and the sister initiate the boy into the life of the imagination and the life of action. First, he achieves complete felicity with his father in the garden of innocence. The father had inherited the house from his own father and transformed it into a facsimile of the Virginian estates, but now he feels he has made "an error of principle and of method." He should have been satisfied with "an inner Virginia," resurrected within his imagination rather than reconstructed with "the expedient of things." Thus, he tells the boy: "I can never warn you sufficiently against the things which can be seen," heard, touched. "Nobody ever dreams enough." To the learning of languages there is no end; he teaches the boy the languages of the Hebrew and Hellenic cultures and the dialects of Indians now extinct. In the past "words—inhabited things," enabling men to "steep themselves at the same time in the vision and the meaning of things." In the modern age, however, words have departed from things and chaos reigns.

If man's enduring obsession is to cheat time, it is only in his imagination, the boy's father persuades him, that he can achieve temporal immortality. They take long drives after midnight, pretending to move through Virginia estates, seeming often to be one with the ground as the earth turns. Lying on a hill, they conjure up sounds and images out of eternity. Phrases from books, chanted ritualistically, give impetus to their visions of the sublime: "They hoisted me with halters up an otter path." Together, they reach Virginia about 1842, "time and evil overwhelmed." They experience again the expulsions of the Acadians from Nova Scotia and the long march of the Cher-

okees; the invasion of Virginia by the Burnt Woods half-breeds; the fall of the Golden estates; the extermination of the teeming bison. The Indians and the Virginians almost prevented "time from undoing its tapestry." After their failure, "men ought to have been created all over again." Whatever lives at the foot of the hill where they dream, deaf to "time's winged chariot hurrying near," has "its roots and strength in putrefaction," as the maggot in the grave testifies. Down there, "because of the passing of time, mankind lost its memory." As they emerge from Berger's splendid conception, the vivid dream details of American history before 1864 seem exotic and evoke an aura of surrealistic nostalgia. The father's indoctrination culminates in the boy's withdrawal from the actual estate and his addiction to the images which books provide. The only disruptions in this dream world are Virginie's visits home from the lycée in Avignon.

Certain poetic techniques enhance the novel's intuitive insights. For instance, one day, when he returns to the room he shares with his sister in Montpellier, the boy senses that his father has been there, has seen their things "mixed up together," and has perceived that they are having an incestuous affair. Immediately, the boy is inside his suffering father, and the narrator becomes a "we" as the discovery is re-experienced: himself and his father, discovering himself and his sister. "He shakes pensively the head which I hang in despair."

The novel's poetic rhythm and its time concept forbid chapter breaks. The first seventy pages are especially poetic; the image montages create impressions similar to the movies of Renais, *Last Year at Marienbad* and *Hiroshima, Mon Amour*. For instance, the boy experiences a presentiment of the future when he discovers his sister sitting in the grass, her thighs and bloomers exposed; Berger's description of the grass springing back up with phallic vigor is one of the novel's most vivid symbolic images. In these first pages, the novel moves from image to image, rather than from motive to act. While the style is fragile and lyrical in the first part and relatively tough and explicit in the second, Berger manages to create the impression of even texture for the whole novel.

The boy achieves an equally complete felicity with his sister in the garden of experience. When the mother, a mere shadow on the estate, dies, Virginie, seeing her chance to rescue her brother, persuades her father that the boy, with no one to tend to him at home, should go to school in Montpellier and take a room next to hers while she attends medical school. Appropriately, from this point on the novel has a more dramatic or narrative structure. The style, too, changes. In the first part, under his father's influence, the boy writes in long, flowing sentences, strung together with commas, for the father's Faulknerian style is appropriate to a rendering of the past; but under Virginie's spell in the immediate present, the boy obeys her command to use short, Hemingwayesque sentences. Into the best of all possible worlds Virginie endeavors to introduce various other possibilities. She urges the boy to make friends and allows him to witness the passions and erratic behavior of her own student acquaintances as they come and go constantly. "She revealed in surprises, impulsive actions, whims, caprices

. . . time with her was always trembling at the end of the line." The boy detests his sister's use of obscenity, and his adamant solitude enrages her. But slowly she comes between father and son; for example, she convinces her father that his frequent visits, during which the exchange of images continues, distract the boy from his studies. The boy becomes aware of his sister's body; during a vacation he misses his life with her in Montpellier. Thus Berger enables us to witness the assault of the life of action upon the imaginative life.

In the first phase of their Montpellier relationship Virginie tells the boy, with a gentle anxiety, her own view of life: all men die; one must live in harmony with time; the boy must grow up and grow old. " 'You must live your life' and I translated 'You must die your death.' " Virginie announces that he should write a book. Instantly, the boy imagines his father reveling in the "long, endless sentences in which the commas were hooks on which to strangle time." But Virginie insists that he include memories of childhood which she will recognize; as they recall the past he discovers he has led an earthbound existence on the fringe of his life in Virginia about 1842: "I could feel that my memory was heavily laden, unknown to me and at my cost the treacherous mechanism was recording life as it is, aging and mortal." Virginie hopes the book will uncover secrets, mysteries, adventures, vices about the boy. Above all, it should ridicule his past life with "your father," as she calls their father; it should be a means of breaking away, of changing. He insists on writing the book alone. His father, when he hears of the project, declares his trust in the boy to fill it with experiences they shared from other books.

But Virginie has deeply immersed the boy in "time-passing"; for instance, his life now follows a timetable: homework, the book, the languages. Eventually he discovers that in his creative fervor he has forgotten his father. Each of his attempts to assert the supremacy of the imagination is met by her lively response to the immediate present: his sister offers him liquor, lends him pornographic novels, allows him to stroke her body, takes him to nightclubs, to movies, and into Nature. She loves only what exists, sees everything, retains very little: "She liked for a few hours what she had promised to like for eternity." If he sees imperfectly the almond trees that thrill Virginie, "she does not possess within her the most beautiful trees, whose roots are in Virginia and whose branches are in me." However, she forces him to face the fact that Indians, contrary to his idyllic version of them as eternal creatures, were filthy, stupid, greedy people who loved death.

Immersed in the life of action, Virginie's body represents time, love, and death; luxuriating in the imagination's light, the father's garden is eternity: solitude, and cyclical recurrence. One night Virginie runs her hands over the boy's body and he discovers that "there are dreams in the tips of Virginie's fingernails." In their flow of words, the imaginations of father and son mingled incestuously; the affair between the boy and his sister begins wordlessly and moves into erotic lethargy and comas of bliss. Until Virginie revealed it to him, he hated his body. Just as he once wanted all the words associated with the permanent past, he now wants to know all the names of the parts of the perishable body; he finds it a "wonderful vocabulary." Just as the father tried to reproduce the Virginia estates, they furnish the room with "objective correlatives" of their inner passions and appetites. The boy tries to surrender to Virginie's concept of life as separate little moments, as "time passing at breakneck speed." His mortal embrace with her releases Time from its captivity in him, and him from his captivity in Time. In their languorous conversations Virginie teaches the boy the meaning of mortality. He will love her less one day, and she will love him not at all. That is life. No, he replies, that is death. "Exactly, exactly," she answers. Threatened by death, one must seize life as it flies. "Living is taking life against the current. . . . And if you are to keep me, I shall have to feel that you know me to be mortal," for it is death that makes her young and beautiful, it is the awareness that each moment is irrecoverable that gives urgency and fulfillment to their desires.

Berger demonstrates the power of the imagination to thwart the assaults of reality. At first, the boy transforms Virginie's earthy body into the mythical garden: "On Virginie's shoulders I stroke the wheels of the wagons, the runaway mules, the fur of the guzzling bears, I stroke the bumps of the bisons and the bears." Although to combat her father's warning against the things of the senses she makes herself more tantalizing and available, she spurns the boy if he has not first worked on the book. For the boy, the book is a means of making words once again contain things. Berger's implementation of the concept of the mythic, and therefore poetic, origins of language suggests that he has absorbed the ideas of Ernst Cassierer.

105

In the sexual embrace man seeks and finds mortality at its swiftest. As the boy wonders about Virginie's previous affairs, she encourages his jealousy as being a living emotion, and he is fascinated by the infernal word "jealous," in which nothing dwells. They begin to use foul language while making love, each word a maggot which affirms the intransience of the instant. Unlike mythic words which are immortal, coarse words live only by the grace of bodies, "and when the lovemaking is over, they make hideous corpses." He imagines Virginie gone and the return of his passion for words. One night she encourages him to talk lyrically of "the garden" so that she can reply: "Words, and when you have said them, when you have wallowed in them, on them, when you have made yourself drunk with words, then you open your eyes, they fall on me who am waiting . . . a real Virginia, of flesh and blood. . . ." He begins to detect the odor of death in their insular room.

Finally demanding to see the book, Virginie reads the first sixty pages of what we have been reading—an interesting, though not original, device. Horrified to find "visions conjured out of nothing," her advice about short sentences wasted, she ridicules him. In all his talk of Virginia, for instance, there is not a single mention of the slaves; there are no objects, no precise descriptions. He describes his book as one in which "there are no people and nothing happens." What his father failed to do, he has achieved: he has put the visions into words. In anger and despair, Virginie, who hoped to rescue him, now rejects him because he will never know anything: "you will fall like an overripe fruit, without having

prepared yourself to receive the earth." For him, she has wasted her time and sacrificed her body in vain. In darkness and slavery, he will become his father; he does not deserve to live. She abandons him. Thus, at their most intense, imagination and action both fail because the boy's response can be only an extreme one.

Berger brings the imagination-action development full circle. Upon his return to the estate, the boy is informed that his father has taken a trip. Half-breeds are invading this region of large estates, as they invaded Virginia about 1842, bringing an "excess of civilization which makes time pass, men wear away." He imagines that his father is looking in the mountains for men "for whom words are pictures, almost things." Doubtlessly, he found only a "people without words." But ironically the boy, now a man, repeats the process. Every night he sits in the garden holding his book (the one he has written? the one we now read?). He hears the voices of Virginie (alive yet dead) and his father (dead yet alive), who "put forward words, raise pictures. . . . I can no longer distinguish my father's voice from Virginie's." But the boy thinks that it is his father who "has the words, the pictures, in the darkness which falls and hides my book from me."

The author's own ambiguous position allows readers of each general inclination (imagination-action) to interpret the novel for themselves. But most men are composites of Don Quixote and Sancho Panza. Berger suggests that the ambiguity of reality and illusion is perpetual. Writing with equal conviction and perception about the two worlds, Berger suggests that the ambiguity of reality and illusion is perpetual. Between the polarities of time and eternity, he creates a field of tension where the two mingle imperceptibly. This ambiguity saves the novel from being esoteric, for it allows ramifications of interpretation which transcend the preciousness of a purely subjective vision.

Although this novel reminds one of the witty and lyrical comedy of Giraudoux (whether some of the ludicrous moments are intentional is not clear), it is Faulkner who haunts *The Garden*.

The style of the first seventy pages, on which Berger spent three of the five years that went into the novel, is somewhat like Faulkner's *Absalom, Absalom!* but without the American writer's convoluted sentences; and the themes of the persistence of the past and of incest suggest Quentin and Caddy Compson and their father, Jason, Sr. But in its own right *The Garden* is the creation of an original, and well-seeded, imagination.

David Madden

GEORGE C. MARSHALL
Education of a General

Author: Forrest C. Pogue (1912-   ), with the editorial assistance of Gordon Harrison
With a Foreword by General Omar N. Bradley
Publisher: The Viking Press (New York). Portrait and maps. 421 pp. $7.50
Type of work: Biography
Time: 1880-1939
Locale: The United States, the Far East, Europe, and Brazil

The first volume of the official biography of George C. Marshall, dealing with his boyhood, youth, and career as soldier and citizen down to the beginning of World War II

Principal personages:
> GEORGE CATLETT MARSHALL, SR., prominent citizen of Uniontown, Pennsylvania
> LAURA EMILY BRADFORD MARSHALL, his wife
> GEORGE CATLETT MARSHALL, JR., their fourth and youngest child
> ELIZABETH CARTER COLES ("LILY"), George Marshall's sweetheart during his cadet days at the Virginia Military Institute, later his wife
> JOHN J. PERSHING, Commander of the American Expeditionary Forces, Marshall's superior officer and long-time friend
> KATHERINE TUPPER BROWN, the charming and talented widow who became the second Mrs. Marshall

In times of crisis, by chance or providence, history has a way of producing heroes to lead their people out of grim shadows. George Catlett Marshall, a man of supreme ability and integrity, was such a figure. Sir Winston Churchill, a skillful and meticulous wielder

of words, called him a man of "singular eminence"; General Omar N. Bradley, in his Foreword to *George C. Marshall: Education of a General*, states: "I consider him the man who contributed more to our efforts from 1939 to 1951 than any other individual." Forrest C.

107

Pogue's monumental biography, of which this is the first of three projected volumes, has value for more than one reason: it is an interesting, thorough, and sound portrait of a man of towering stature, and it is a thoughtful study of the times and circumstances which prepared Marshall for his Atlantean responsibilities.

Pogue is a diligent and competent historian who fulfills his assignment (for which he was chosen by the George C. Marshall Research Foundation) without engaging in personal posturing and gesticulating. His book is objective in the best sense of the term. He is able to deliver subjective value-judgments and to take an interest in the characters whom he portrays, and yet he can treat controversial subjects dispassionately. The intensely personal element of Boswell's unique touchstone of biography is lacking; but the central figure of Pogue's work has a dignity and strength reminiscent of Samuel Johnson. There is, however, considerable difference between the men: George Marshall avoided any appearance of eccentricity, but the venerable man of letters wore his singularities with sublime indifference. Both men had integrity and unshakable steadfastness. Pogue's straightforward book breathes the flavor of these qualities.

The first version of *Education of a General* was far too lengthy for the publisher's approved scale; hence, Gordon Harrison was called in to render valuable editorial assistance in condensing and polishing the work. The volume gives promise that the finished portrait may be worthy to be viewed beside the more colorful painting of Boswell's hero.

Although records of George Marshall's childhood are not numerous, Pogue has reconstructed a quite credible boy: serious but not humorless, stubborn, and ambitious. Resenting the family's constant harping on their eminent relative, Chief Justice John Marshall, he was determined that there should be another Marshall worthy to be named with him. In late years the general recalled his family life, his playmates, and his home town with deep affection and a sorrowful sense of a vanished past. From him and from others who knew him in his boyhood the author gleaned amusing and telling anecdotes; but the chief emphasis is placed on the shaping of the boy's character and the foundation of his religious faith, which he retained through the adversities and complexies of his world and times.

The Virginia Military Institute had its share in shaping the general's character and career. Although he came from a family with a Virginia background, his Northern accent added to his trials as a V.M.I. "rat"; however, he took the hazing, often severe, with "a characteristically stoic attitude." In his own words: "I think I was more philosophical about this sort of thing than a great many boys. It was part of the business and the only thing to do was to accept it as best you could." He overcame many obstacles, including a mediocre academic record, to be named first captain of the cadet corps. While he was a cadet, he met and fell in love with Lily Coles, a Lexington belle. Like many cadets with less impressive military records, he risked suspension by slipping out to see his girl. Soon after graduation he married her, and they shared twenty-five years of happy married life in spite of her frail health and the lengthy separations required

108

by his military assignments. Her untimely death was a severe blow to him.

Pogue's account of Marshall's varied duties and experiences is a valuable picture of the career of the professional soldier of the United States. The constant uprooting and the plunging into weird crises in all parts of the world prepare an officer for diplomacy in peace and for the complicated problems of logistics, strategy, and tactics in war. Not least important in Pogue's narrative is the weaving in of Marshall's elders, contemporaries, and juniors whose names are set in history along with his. Few if any men were closer to the austere and aloof Pershing, whose likeness is vividly drawn in this volume. The delays, frustrations, and disappointments in Marshall's hopes for promotion led him almost to the brink of resignation from the service. Pogue points out the irony that Marshall was not given promotion because he was too valuable in a staff position for his commanders to release him to field duty.

The account of Marshall's second wooing and remarriage is handled with deft human interest. Katherine Tupper Brown, a talented actress, the widowed mother of three children, gave the lonely, middle-aged officer not only her charming self but her "complete family." All his life Marshall demonstrated a fondness for children and an ability to earn their friendship. He accepted the Brown children as his own, and they apparently accepted him as a father.

Pogue's principal themes may be summarized briefly as follows: George Marshall's family training established his integrity and religious faith, which were unshaken through all crises; his formal education and his duty with troops taught him valuable lessons in human relations; his teaching in the service schools prepared students who would become his trusted lieutenants in later days; his tours of duty in the Philippine Islands and China and his service during World War I gave him perspective for the global war and the equally difficult global peace which followed. The first volume ends with the beginning of that war. It is a worthy accomplishment in itself, and it is a promising prologue for things to come.

G. Burke Johnston

109

THE GIFT

Author: Vladimir Nabokov (1899-   )
Translated from the Russian by Michael Scammell
Publisher: G. P. Putnam's Sons (New York). 378 pp. $5.95
Type of work: Novel
Time: The 1920's
Locale: Berlin

A novel about the development of an artist and, at the same time, about the history of Russian literature and the nature of art itself

Principal characters:
> FYODOR GODUNOV-CHERDYNTSEV, a young writer and Russian émigré
> ZINA MERTZ, the young woman whom Fyodor loves
> KONCHEYEV, a poet and critic
> BORIS SHCHYOGOLEV, Zina's stepfather

Finished by Nabokov in Berlin in 1937, published in part at that time and completely in 1952, *The Gift* (in Russian, *Dar*) is Nabokov's last Russian novel and one which already has come to be considered one of the major Russian novels of the twentieth century, just as his *Pale Fire* is certainly one of the major modern American novels. Now that *The Gift* has been translated, under the supervision of Nabokov, it is clearly apparent that its reputation is deserved. One can mention Faulkner's novels as equivalents to *Pale Fire,* but in modern Russian literature only Pasternak's *Doctor Zhivago* can approach the brilliance and artistic skill of *The Gift.*

"The most enchanting things in nature and art are based on deception," says Fyodor Godunov-Cherdyntsev, the young poet-hero of *The Gift,* condensing there many of Nabokov's artistic theories—theories which are as Russian in regard to fate as they are universal in regard to imagination. The narrator of this novel is Fyodor's imagination, that part of him which is writing the novel over the three and a half years of its happening, so that the end of the novel is Fyodor's conscious decision to write the novel that his imagination has just completed. The gift, then, is the novel, a gift to Fyodor from his imagination. Confusing as such a method of narration may be to the unwary critic (for many American critics have mistaken the first person narrator for Nabokov himself), it is surely part of that ultimately enlightening deception of art itself, a deception designed to reveal the world as a pattern of fate quite as involved and intricately designed as the cleverest of literary artifacts.

The Russian novel is traditionally a product of Russian fatalism; thus Dostoevski's novels are considered by Russians to be Christian mystical documents and not literary novels. From Pushkin to Abram Tertz, Russian writers have written of a world in which a coincidence is a controlled event and in which the freedom of man is involved in finding his destiny rather than shaping it. Russian literature, then, depends primarily upon texture, not text. Pasternak's *Doctor Zhivago* is an elaborate pattern of "coincidence" designed by fate; Nabokov's novels are also concerned with the pattern of fate, but of a more human and whimsical fate. As he showed in *Invitation to a Beheading* (1935), one need not be a prisoner of other people's designs if one is aware of the form of one's own destiny. *The Gift* is the story of a young man who discovers the pattern of his fate, both in regard to his relationship with Russian literature and with a young woman, Zina Mertz, whom he loves, but not without his having to suffer one last joke from fate after the end of the novel ("the chords of fate itself continue to vibrate; and no obstruction for the sage exists where I have put The End . . ."), for Nabokov's fate is akin to Faulkner's "visible nature" and not above a disciplinary jest at a time when a character thinks he has all the keys to his destiny.

The plot of the novel is as involved with the history of Russian literature, to which Nabokov was bidding his artistic farewell, as it is with the characters' lives. The first chapter is involved with Fyodor's youthful poems, the juvenilia of literature; the second is romantic in the tone of Pushkin; the third is grotesque and darkly comic in the manner of Gogol; the fourth is a brilliantly witty biography (by Fyodor) of N. G. Chernyshevsky, the nineteenth century Russian novelist most revered by Marx and Lenin; and the fifth recounts Fyodor's development to an artistic stature of his own. The biography of Chernyshevsky, author of *What Is to Be Done?* (or, as Fyodor has it, *What to Do?*), has long puzzled critics who have failed to note its relevance to Fyodor's growth as an artist, to his relationship with the development of Russian literature, or to the pattern of the novel itself (Nabokov calls it "a spiral within a sonnet").

Aware that this confusion would exist, Nabokov supplied in Chapter Five a series of reviews that the biography received; these parody most typical magazine critics. One recent critic of *The Gift*, Hilary Corke, did in fact make the same foolish errors about Chernyshevsky that one of Nabokov's fictional critics did and thus supplied us with another example of life copying art, without doubt much to Nabokov's delight. Chernyshevsky, the darling of Soviet critics despite his artistic clumsiness, comes, then, to represent the man who fails art and whom life fails, and the biography, which would be brilliant apart from the novel, offers Fyodor the necessary understanding to grow past the betraying dullness of realistic art to a richer art, "a classical novel, with 'types,' love, fate, conversations . . . and with descriptions of nature." Fyodor's narrating imagination describes his (and Nabokov's) attitude toward realism and the literature of "significance" by reflecting on the story of a young poet and kinsman of N.G. Chernyshevsky who committed suicide:

Any corny man of ideas, any "serious" novelist in horn-rimmed glasses—the family doctor of Europe and the seismographer of its social tremors—would no doubt have found in this story something highly characteristic of the "frame of mind of young people in the postwar years"—a combination of words which in itself (even apart from the "general idea" it conveyed) made me speechless with scorn. I used to feel a cloying nausea when I heard or read the latest drivel, vulgar and humorless drivel, about the "symptoms of the age" and the "tragedy of youth."

This scorn for the didacticism of realistic literature has kept Nabokov's

111

genius from achieving its proper recognition at a time when such writing, which should properly be called sociology or even propaganda, is honored in the groves of academe, but it has also placed him in the front ranks of the writers who have produced and are producing today's real literature, among them Jorge Louis Borges, William Faulkner, Henry Green, Alain Robbe-Grillet, Tommaso Londolfi, Günter Grass, and Friedrich Dürrenmatt. Certainly *The Gift* is a gift to literature, and Vladimir Nabokov is just as certainly one of the few literary men of our time who can be known with assurance to be a true writer, an artist of the beautiful.

R. H. W. Dillard

THE GIRLS OF SLENDER MEANS

Author: Muriel Spark (1918-   )
Publisher: Alfred A. Knopf (New York). 176 pp. $3.95
Type of work: Novel
Time: 1945 and the present
Locale: London

A witty, unsentimental account of the lives of a group of bachelor girls living in a London club during the last months of World War II

> Principal characters:
> JANE WRIGHT, a publisher's assistant
> JOANNA CHILDE, an elocution teacher
> SELINA REDWOOD, a secretary
> DOROTHY MARKHAM, a debutante
> PAULINE FOX, a "mad girl"
> ANNE BABERTON, the owner of a highly-prized Schiaparelli evening dress
> JUDY REDWOOD, a typist
> NANCY RIDDLE, daughter of a midlands clergyman
> MISS COLEMAN,
> MISS MACGREGOR, and
> MISS JARMAN, aging spinsters
> NICHOLAS FARRINGTON, a poet and anarchist, later a missionary in Haiti
> GEORGE JOHNSON, alias HUY THROVIS-MEW, a corrupt publisher
> TILLY JOHNSON, his wife
> RUDI BITTESCH, a Rumanian and a collector of literary autographs
> COLONEL G. FELIX DOBELL, an American officer

Muriel Spark's ninth book raises questions: to what extent can a novelist pare away her materials, reducing the story almost to a series of symbolic gestures, and still be said to have written a novel? Is *The Girls of Slender Means* a novel or an anecdote? Can it stand on its own, or does it take on real meaning only when it is woven by the knowing reader into some corner of that great, gaudy tapestry being continually created in the school of English satire?

These are unanswerable questions. On first reading, the novel seems far too slight; on the second, one begins

112

to suspect that Miss Spark is up to something, after all. By the third reading, one might find himself preparing a sober article on "The Schiaparelli Dress as a Symbol in Muriel Spark's Modern *Inferno*." It is, in short, a novel that depends to a great extent on what the reader chooses to make of it.

But no matter, for few readers, in any event, are going to find *The Girls of Slender Means* without interest on any level. There is, if nothing else, Muriel Spark's brilliant style. The reader is captured by the first paragraph:

> Long ago in 1945 all the nice people in England were poor, allowing for exceptions. The streets of the cities were lined with buildings in bad repair or in no repair at all, bomb-sites piled with stony rubble, houses like giant teeth in which decay had been drilled out, leaving only the cavity. Some bomb-ripped buildings looked like the ruins of ancient castles until, at a closer view, the wallpapers of various quite normal rooms would be visible, room above room, exposed, as on a stage, with one wall missing; sometimes a lavatory chain would dangle over nothing from a fourth- or fifth-floor ceiling; most of all the staircases survived, like a new art-form, leading up and up to an unspecified destination that made unusual demands on the mind's eye. All the nice people were poor; at least that was a general axiom, the best of the rich being poor in spirit.

It is a perfect opening for a fable: simple, graphic, deceptively innocent until one stumbles over that hint of irony in the last sentence. Indeed, style is triumphant throughout. In Muriel Spark's cool sentences there is a sense of perfectly controlled critical detachment that no other current writer quite conveys.

Miss Spark's fable, as her opening paragraph makes clear, is set in the surrealist landscape of London in the last months of World War II. Her characters are chiefly the inmates of the May of Teck Club, a bachelor girls' refuge founded in the Edwardian era and given the maiden name of dowager Queen Mary. The euphemisms of its constitution evoke the moral rectitude of another time:

> The May of Teck Club exists for the Pecuniary Convenience and Social Protection of Ladies of Slender Means below the age of Thirty Years, who are obliged to reside apart from their Families in order to follow an Occupation in London.

But Miss Spark makes it abundantly clear that her young ladies have severed any ethical ties with their innocent predecessors. It is not they who need protection; it is, perhaps, we that need to be protected from them. "Love and money" are their "vital themes" today, and their instincts predatory: "As they themselves realized in varying degrees, few people at the time were more delightful, more ingenious, more movingly lovely, and, as it might happen, more savage, than the girls of slender means."

The era of these savage girls is brought back into focus by the recent death of Nicholas Farrington, a religious missionary martyred in Haiti. In 1945 he had been a poet and composer of anarchist *pensées,* and a hanger-on at the May of Teck. His martyrdom is an unexpected turn of events, and Jane Wright, once a May of Teck girl, spreads the news among her former acquaintances in a series of telephone conversations that punctuate the narrative of the old days. Thus Miss Spark's novel develops three objec-

113

tives: to lay bare the character of the girls of slender means, to ask why Nicholas should have undergone this transformation from political radical to religious missionary, and to relate the one to the other.

As for the girls of 1945, they exhibit a remarkable variety of minor aberrations. Jane Wright is a publisher's assistant who divides her time between helping her employer swindle his writers and composing meretricious letters to famous authors so that their autographed replies may be sold by the Rumanian Rudi Bittesch. Dorothy Markham is an empty-headed debutante who is careless about her lovemaking. ("Filthy luck. I'm preggers. Come to the wedding.") Pauline Fox imagines that she has dates with the musical comedy star, Jack Buchanan. Selina Redwood sleeps on an adjacent roof with Nicholas Farrington. Anne Baberton wields power through a coveted Schiaparelli gown that she lends to the girls. And behind all this there is the incessant, empty chatter of young ladies on the make. It is all a matter of girlish peccadilloes, rather than major sins, but an atmosphere of carelessness and selfishness is created in which something evil can happen.

In the group there is a girl of somewhat different proportions. Joanna Childe the "spiritually maimed" daughter of a clergyman, teaches elocution. Throughout the reminiscence, she is heard coaching her pupils in a variety of poetry that contrasts, in its emotional depth, with the superficiality of life at the May of Teck. Particularly ironic is her frequent use of Hopkins' "The Wreck of the Deutschland," with its impassioned celebration of martyrdom. Acting as a sort of *leitmotif*, the fragments of Hopkins' poem fore-

shadow not only Nicholas' martyrdom, but Joanna's as well.

It is Joanna's death, the climax of a brilliantly managed scene that begins in low comedy and ends in tragedy, that ties together the present question of Nicholas' demise in Haiti and the enigmatic relationship of his death with the May of Teck era. An unexploded bomb goes off in the garden behind the club. Joanna and several of the girls are caught in a top-floor bathroom, from which there is no escape except through a narrow window looking out on a nearby roof. Those whose hips are narrow enough can wriggle through the window; the rest must wait until firemen hack a hole through the roof. All escape except Joanna, who is buried when the building collapses. Just before the end, surrounded by those who have yet to escape, she recites passages from the Anglican liturgy.

During this episode, with its overtones of sacrifice and redemptive suffering, the evil that has been lurking in the halls of the May of Teck reveals itself. Selina, having escaped through the narrow window eludes Nicholas' grasp and returns. But she is not going back to help the others; she is returning to rescue the Schiaparelli gown. In this one act, the carelessness, the selfishness, the childish savagery of the girls is compressed into a moment of monstrousness. And we are led to believe that the religious conversion of Nicholas is also settled in this moment, for "a vision of evil may be as effective to conversion as a vision of good." Thus the threads are tied together, the objectives of the story realized. To emphasize the burgeoning of evil, we are given two postscripts. In the first, Joanna's clergyman father is shown to

114

be utterly unable to feel the import of her death. Told that his daughter had a "sense of Hell," he replies, "Really? I didn't know that. I've never heard her speak morbidly. It must have been the influence of London." In the second, a woman is stabbed by a sailor in the crowds celebrating V-J night before Buckingham Palace. Nicholas, experiencing another "vision of evil," sees the knifing but is unable to get anyone to pay attention to what has happened.

But again we wonder: can such a fragile novel support all this significance? Can greed for a pretty dress stand, not merely for moral weakness, but for incarnate evil? Is debutante nonsense appropriate in a landscape of hell? Can a novel afford only one developed narrative sequence (the bomb, the dress, and the death of Joanna)?

Again, these are unanswerable questions. We can only note how apt the title is. If ever a novel was developed with the most slender of means, this is it. But we cannot deny Miss Spark's supremacy as a stylist, nor should the reader of Waugh, Powell, Huxley, and Green fail to recognize that Miss Spark occupies an honorable place in their peculiarly English serio-comic tradition.

A. Sidney Knowles, Jr.

THE GREAT HUNGER
Ireland, 1845-1849

Author: Cecil Woodham-Smith (1896-   )
Publisher: Harper and Row (New York). Illustrated. 510 pp. $6.95
Type of work: History
Time: 1845-1849
Locale: Ireland

A history of the infamous Irish potato famine, with observations on its social, political, economic, and medical effects in Ireland, Britain, Canada, and the United States

Principal personages:
SIR ROBERT PEEL
LORD JOHN RUSSELL
CHARLES EDWARD TREVELYAN
SIR RANDOLPH ROUTH
SIR CHARLES WOOD
DANIEL O'CONNELL
WILLIAM SMITH O'BRIEN
GEORGE WILLIAM FREDERICK VILLIERS, Earl of Clarendon

One of the factors most frequently overlooked in the population explosion of the Western world over the past three hundred or so years has been the relative absence of famine. Ireland, alone among Western areas, suffered a general famine from 1846 through 1849. The results, even today, are not fully calculable. The Irish population immediately dropped nearly two million as a result of starvation, disease resulting from starvation, emigration,

115

and a probable drop in the birth rate. The Irish system of landholding was ultimately overturned, along with the final expulsion of British control over all but the northern part of the island. Bitter anti-English feelings still linger among Irish-hyphenates throughout the world. In the United States the swarm of ignorant, often disease-ridden Irish refugees aroused a storm of anti-foreign, Know-Nothing Party sentiment, which often took the form of anti-Catholicism, from which the nation has not yet fully recovered. It is interesting to observe both that secure Catholic minorities existed in most of the American states at the time of the Potato Famine and that the American public exhibited a great deal of sympathy for the Irish *in Ireland* through generous contributions for relief. As Mrs. Woodham-Smith notes, however, many, if not most, of the Irish immigrants to the United States lacked any skill other than that of spade cultivation of the potato; a great number scarcely spoke English, and most, but not all, chose to remain among other Irish in the large cities rather than to return to the soil. There, in the large cities, they were relegated to the most menial forms of labor, but even there they threatened the wages of American labor. The fact that slaveholders in the Southern states hired Irish laborers to perform tasks to which they hesitated to assign valuable slave labor hardly needs to be mentioned. The Irish contributed heavily through their labor to the building of the United States, and their descendants continue today to contribute to American culture. The population of Ireland itself, in the meantime, has declined from a peak of nine million at the beginning of the famine to its present low of around four and a half million. Perhaps those figures, applied to a people of notorious proliferousness and during a time of general population growth throughout the world, are the best measure of the effect of the "Great Hunger" of which Mrs. Woodham-Smith writes so eloquently.

Textbooks of British history generally list three great causes for the "Irish Problem" of the nineteenth century: nationalism, landlordism, and overpopulation; and Mrs. Woodham-Smith does more than justice to each of these. Because of nationalism the Irish hated the English as foreign despots, while the English hated and distrusted the Irish as inferior foreigners. The religious differences between the countries accentuated the political and national differences and made them all but insoluble. The Irish landlord system derived from the many revolts, after which the properties of the rebels had been confiscated and distributed to loyal English or Scottish followers of the crown. This situation meant that by the mid-nineteenth century virtually all of the land was owned by landlords who were not of Irish extraction, many of whom had no interest in their estates other than the regular receipt of rents from agents who were hired to wring the last farthing of rent from the peasants. Many of the Irish landlords were absentees, living in the more congenial social climate of England or the Continent, but, as Mrs. Woodham-Smith points out, absentee landlords were not necessarily hard-hearted, nor were resident landlords necessarily benevolent.

The remarkable division and subdivision of Irish properties, however, almost certainly was the result of absentee landlords and the desire to extract

116

the highest possible rent from the land. Population was increasing explosively, and as tenants divided their holdings with their children their farms became progressively smaller. Ireland, remaining almost exclusively agricultural, was almost completely dependent upon the potato to feed its population. Introduced from America, it alone may be the best explanation of the 172 percent increase in Irish population from 1779 to 1841, for the potato allowed most laborers to devote much of their land to the production of grain or other crops with which to pay the rent and to utilize the remainder for the raising of potatoes, which were practically the sole source of sustenance for the laborer and his family. Before the Potato Famine the poverty of many of the Irish was such that many of them were only barely cognizant of a money economy. Particularly in the south and west of Ireland stores in which food and clothing could be purchased hardly existed, and many of the women had lost all of the culinary skills other than the boiling of the potato. To the twentieth century mind such poverty seems hardly conducive to the rapid growth of population, but our thinking takes the principles of Thomas Robert Malthus too seriously and the practical examples of India and China not seriously enough. The plain fact of Ireland was that the poverty-stricken laborer, provided he could secure a small tenancy, had no way to go except up. He had known nothing but poverty, no diet other than potatoes. By marrying he secured a wife and probably children, both of whom would be a joy and a comfort to him and his only security in his old age. If he were no better off economically after his marriage, he was certainly no worse off, as long as his potatoes prospered.

Irish "prosperity," i.e., permanent poverty or at best extremely depressed living standards, might have cotinued for quite some time had not the potato blight, *Phytophthora infestans,* intervened As *The Great Hunger* mentions, the blight was not unknown, either in Ireland, Europe, or America. The spore of the blight is airborne but requires a great deal of moisture to survive. Once it settles on a moist potato plant it attacks the plant and multiplies at an astonishing rate. Additional moisture aids its growth, and the growing seasons of 1846 and 1848 were very wet. Although efforts were made to control it, an imperfect understanding of the nature of the blight made those attempts ineffectual.

Certainly the most controversial aspect of the Potato Famine, once the reality of a general potato blight had been ascertained, was the action, or lack of action, taken by the British government to alleviate the "distress" in Ireland. Heroic measures were called for and, surprisingly enough, as Mrs. Woodham-Smith points out, were carried into action. Sir Robert Peel the Younger not only initiated a relief program, but also led the repeal of the Corn Laws, measures which he had been elected to protect. The repeal of the Corn Laws was political suicide for himself, as he well knew, and it led in the long run to the destruction of much of British agriculture. More important, the repeal of the Corn Laws did little or nothing to alleviate starvation conditions in Ireland. Peel stood for, or by his action on the repeal came to stand for, unfettered *laissez-faire,* free enterprise. According to the principles of the political econo-

117

mists, free trade in grain would throw Irish markets open to cheap American grain, competition would drive prices down, and the distress would be mitigated. His relief program was minimal, intended only to aid the utterly destitute, and consisted of the distribution of corn meal. Again, following the dictates of political economy, corn meal was distributed because it was completely unknown in Ireland; hence, it would not be a case of governmental interference with the free market. Unfortunately, Peel erred in two respects: the extent of distress in Ireland and the fact that most of the Irish could not afford to buy grain or grain products at any price. It cannot be said that Peel did not try to aid the Irish. Rather, it should be said that his measures, which were genuinely heroic considering the time and place, were not enough.

A point emphasized in *The Great Hunger* is the influence of *laissez-faire* economics in the determination of British governmental policy. Lord John Russell, who succeeded Sir Robert Peel as Prime Minister, was a determined advocate of free trade and free enterprise, as was Charles Edward Trevelyan who, as permanent head of the Treasury, exercised more influence than any other individual in the making of Irish policy. The government uniformly attempted to do as little as possible, assuming that poverty was voluntary and that "a little suffering" would force the poor to provide for themselves. In addition, at least two and a half million Irish suffered from "normal" seasonal starvation, and the government feared assisting those who would not normally have been aided. It tried to place the burden of Irish relief on Irish landlords who, culpable as

they may have been, could not bear the weight.

The government was further hampered in the formulation of policy by suspicion and ignorance of Ireland. Murders, rural outrages, and one pathetic rebellion did actually occur, to say nothing of flamboyant newspaper articles, until to the British public it appeared that Ireland was attempting to secure both famine relief and independence from Britain. Reports from Ireland had often been exaggerated in the past, and many leaders continued to regard them as such, even at the height of the famine. It was said at the time, and with a great deal of justice, that England knew more about India than she did of Ireland. Throughout the famine the British government, consistent with the principles of political economy, concerned itself far more with the preservation of order in Ireland than with the relief of starvation. The government never seriously considered an attempt to feed any sizable portion of the population, the remedy which was really required. Instead, it followed basically a "hands-off" policy, with a minimum of aid to the most depressed, and asked only that the Irish prosper or starve in an orderly fashion.

The Great Hunger is an excellent book and well-written, as are all of Mrs. Woodham-Smith's works. She has used her sources well, and has drawn a highly readable picture, if not an entertaining one. She might have leaned a little more heavily on the Parliamentary debates of the period, but her narrative does not suffer for this lack. Her descriptions of the life of the Irish in New York and Boston are perhaps not necessary to the story, and her chapter on William Smith O'Brien's affecting little insurrection may be too long; but on the whole the work is well balanced. Anyone who believes that history is dull needs only to read *The Great Hunger* in order to be enlightened.

Howard Mackey

THE GROUP

Author: Mary McCarthy (1912-   )
Publisher: Harcourt, Brace and World (New York). 378 pp. $5.95
Type of work: Novel
Time: 1933-1940
Locale: New York City

A comedy of manners which deals with the lives of eight Vassar graduates, class of 1933

Principal characters:
KAY STRONG
LIBBY MACAUSLAND
POLLY ANDREWS
PRISS HARTSHORN
POKEY PROTHERO
HELENA DAVISON
ELINOR EASTLAKE, and
DOTTIE RENFREW, the eight
NORINE BLAKE, a classmate

Mary McCarthy has said, in an interview, how she came to write fiction. Her then husband, the eminent critic Edmund Wilson, put her into a room and *told* her to write. She followed his directions, and out of this surprising docility—surprising in the sharp-tongued and very independent Miss McCarthy we now know—came novels, stories, and the present work. Before she turned to fiction Miss McCarthy was a drama critic, and the critical impulse informs every word she has published. The title of one of her books, *Cast a Cold Eye*, could and does serve as her watchword, as the credo that stands behind the fiction, the dramatic criticism, and the studies of Florence and Venice. She is intellectual, unusual in itself in an imaginative writer, and practically unheard of in a woman writer. Bluestockings have never really caught on

in the United States, and for that reason Miss McCarthy's chilling eye is all the more striking. Add to the intellectual power a positively venomous satiric gift, a faculty for describing sexual detail that would arouse the envy of a professional pornographer, and you have some notion of what to expect in *The Group*.

The way had already been prepared in the *Paris Review* interview. Miss McCarthy was still at work on the book when the interview took place, and this is how she described it:

. . . It's about eight Vassar girls. It starts with the inauguration of Roosevelt, and—well, at first it was going to carry them up to the present time, but then I decided to stop at the inauguration of Eisenhower. It was conceived as a kind of mock-chronicle novel. It's a novel about the idea of progress,

119

really. The idea of progress seen in the female sphere, the feminine sphere. You know, home economics, architecture, domestic technology, contraception, child-bearing; the study of technology in the home, in the play-pen, in the bed. It's supposed to be the history of the loss of faith in progress, in the idea of progress. . . .

The major difference between the novel and its planned form is the limiting of action to seven years, the years of the New Deal. The story ends in 1940 in New York, during the Battle of Britain. Other more important differences exist between what Miss McCarthy says the novel is to be about and what it actually *is* about. But first, what happens, what is the story?

The story is neatly told. The opening scene is a description of the wedding of Kay Strong, one of the eight girls who roomed together at Vassar. The rest are in the church. Seven years and fourteen chapters later, the girls gather again, for Kay's funeral. Much has happened to the Group in the intervening years, and this is the subject of Miss McCarthy's fiction. What was life like for eight well-to-do girls, graduates of the country's most celebrated women's college, during the 1930's? In some ways, these chapters provide the answer, at least superficially. The marriages, careers, affairs, husbands, lovers, babies overwhelm us in endless and telling detail. In carefully chosen episodes, Miss McCarthy dissects the lives of seven of these women, as they march proudly forth into a brave new world. Scornful of the values of their parents, they will now try to apply their New Learning. And most of them are miserable failures whom Miss McCarthy murders (joyfully) while dissecting. Kay kills

herself, Pokey remains the same Very Rich slob, Libby becomes, in Lakey's words, a *mauvaise fille* (i.e., a successful career woman and wife). The attempts of Dottie and Priss to deal with sex and child-rearing in the *modern* way are hilarious and pathetic. Perhaps Polly and Helena are less spectacular failures, but never are they more than nominal successes as human beings; Miss McCarthy's tone tells us what they really are, even if the objective evidence does not.

The only remaining member of the group is Elinor Eastlake, superior, cold, haughty, inscrutable, the "Madonna of the Smoking Room"; her life remains a mystery until the last chapter because she lives abroad and does not share the lot of her former roommates. Norman Mailer, in an acute review of *The Group*, made the important point that Lakey, as she is called, is the only really interesting member of the group. The others are ignorant and basically unchanged—in other words, comic. Lakey is aware, conscious, capable of development and change, and it is she whose presence hovers and lasts.

What *The Group* is really about, surprisingly, is not what Miss McCarthy says it is about. All of that is there; the demolition of the myth of progress is dramatized in every scene. But the conservative satirist (and satire is always conservative) must mount his attacking guns from a strong and secure base of belief in the old order, or common sense, or an ideal of human behavior. What is most shocking about *The Group* is not the detailed sexual description; the really shocking fact is the implied belief, the background to the comedy. What Miss McCarthy seems to be saying is that the education of women is mostly farcical, that the relations between the sexes have become hopelessly complicated, that what is really left and worth holding onto is a view of life that few satirists in the past would have regarded with anything but horror. This view of life is presented in stunning candor in the closing chapter. For once Miss McCarthy drops the cliché-ridden and purposely corny style ("Rich and supple prose," one reviewer called it!) she has used to demonstrate the inferior minds and personalities of her characters. For once a character is allowed to speak without the ironic rug-pulling of the author. And who is this character? Lakey, a lesbian, the only one of the group not involved in the ludicrous round of courtship, marriage, child-rearing, radical politics, culture-mongering, busi-

ness. Ironically, the group thinks that "what had happened to Lakey was a tragedy," poor Lakey, with her Baroness, her years in Italy and Spain, the conversations with Berenson, the Schiaparelli clothes. Clearly she is the only character with purpose and depth, with any true self-knowledge. The Baroness had already pointed out the real tragedy, the lives led by the group who stayed at home:

"My friend, the Baroness d'Estienne, is enchanted with them. She loves American women" . . . said Lakey. "She says American women are a fourth sex."

In this *bon mot* lies what must be Miss McCarthy's judgment; this fact must contain the nettle that stung the satirist into action.

James Boatwright

THE HAT ON THE BED

Author: John O'Hara (1905-   )
Publisher: Random House (New York). 405 pp. $5.95
Type of work: Short stories
Time: The present
Locale: The American scene—mostly Suburbia
   Twenty-four varied and inventive stories by a master of verisimilitude

John O'Hara is an amazingly prolific writer. In recent years two novels and three collections of long and short stories (including the fine *Sermons and Soda-Water: A Trilogy*) have appeared. More recently a selection of *49 Stories* was published, and now *The Hat on the Bed*. How does this twentieth century Trollope do it?

He is first and foremost a professional story-writer, successful, worldly, uninvolved in theoretical argument, in the aesthetic debate carried on at colleges and universities and conducted by so many less affluent practitioners.

After a long absence, he turns up regularly in *The New Yorker;* the slicks continue to welcome him with open arms. Most important, he has an audience, and he knows it—an unusual phenomenon in American letters. (Serious writers are notoriously unread, generally.) O'Hara's audience puts his books on the best-seller lists, causes movie people to buy and use his work.

The reason why O'Hara has an audience explains, in large part, both his excellence and his defects. His appealing excellence arises from the fact that he is not "modern" in the conventional sense. His art is expansive, accessible. (And it is generous and real art). In the grand old-fashioned manner, he will write about *anybody* because he is expert about *everything*. No contemporary writer circulates as effortlessly as O'Hara or speaks with his assurance. A variety of places is equally familiar: his own well-marked precincts, "Gibbsville" and Philadelphia, the Los Angeles of beauty-parlor receptionists and blue-haired widows, Florida on the retirement plan. ("We live on $330 a month!") Ocean liners and commuter specials are like home. His characters carry Vuitton luggage, or they lunch at a luau palace. O'Hara can tell you if they have Mary Cassatt or Picasso on the wall, or if their cultural pursuits are limited to skin shows. The exterior and the interior lives of hard newspaper people, the squalid and pathetic fantasies of actors and directors, the suicidal desperation of automobile salesmen, the sadistic cruelty of a chauffeur—O'Hara's description of it all is sure, authoritative.

What his large audience does not realize, probably, is that O'Hara, the O'Hara of the stories anyway, describes a world which, although it is easily recognized, my world and yours, is nonetheless doom-ridden, mean, hopelessly corrupt. The abundance of authentic detail, of acutely observed conversations, disguises, temporarily, the horror that lurks behind and below. At his best O'Hara is a writer of terror stories, in which the terror is the yawning abyss of actuality itself. The best example in the present collection is the masterful "Saturday Lunch." Shortly before the suburban couple's guests arrive for lunch, the wife drives the real estate agent, who has come to show them his brochure, back to his office. He makes a pass at her, and she orders him from the car. On her return the conversation centers on the agent, and the guest discloses that the agent was responsible for the attempted rape and permanent crippling of a town woman known to them all. But his family was an important one and the woman thought that perhaps she *had* unconsciously flirted with him; no charges were pressed. He has continued to work. The intrusion of this almost metaphysical horror into the cozy lunch-table atmosphere is shocking enough; what makes it more shocking is the wives' air of secrecy, of their division from their husbands. It is unlikely now that Carol will ever tell her husband of the incident, and the story ends with a sense of total isolation, of imminent violence; no one understands the fragility of his hold on things.

O'Hara's most impressive stories are all informed by this despairing, nihilistic vision. The motiveless dejection of the automobile salesman in "How Can I Tell You" leads him to contemplate suicide, and both pity and terror are aroused by his wife's knowledge and understanding.

> The shotgun rested with the butt on the floor, the barrel lying against his thigh, and he held the barrel loosely with the fingers of his left hand as he smoked. The cigarette was now down to an inch in length, and he crushed it carefully.
> Her voice came softly. "Mark," she said.
> He looked at the carpet. "What?" he said.
> "Don't. Please?"
> "I won't," he said.

Occasionally his characters can and

122

do escape, as in "The Friends of Miss Julia," a savagely deadpan story about the death of a "beautician" and the response of one of her customers, Mrs. Davis, a widow from the East. She is possessed now by her own son, forced to live in California because it is "natural" for her to be with the family. The influence of the dead Miss Julia and the receptionist convinces her to save herself, to go back East. But what she leaves behind is a dismal prospect indeed.

Although it is a fair generalization that the longer the work, the less O'Hara is able to control the material or to avoid sentimental responses, in at least one of the longer stories here that generalization will not hold true. "Yucca Knolls" shows why O'Hara is frequently regarded as a social commentator, a novelist of manners. Class distinctions in Hollywood are not like those in Gibbsville and Philadelphia, but there are distinctions nevertheless, and important ones. O'Hara describes effortlessly and with unlimited expertise the changing lives of actors and directors, their movements up and down the social scale. In this community, as in any other, true human value is both rare and difficult to deal with, and it is more often than not defeated and wasted. The central figure in this story is Earl Fenway Evans, a brilliant, dissolute director who heads for inevitable self-destruction and destruction by others. Those who succeed move out of Hollywood altogether; they save themselves by settling in Yucca Knolls, by erecting barriers to keep out glamorous people, people with divorces. The Kansas of childhood is re-created in the California desert, and these exiles attempt to deny the existence of Hollywood, the site of their corruption and success.

In this story and several others O'Hara's success is complete. The dialogue is as economical and as functional as any contemporary American fiction offers. He controls rigidly the tone of these stories; he shows admirable restraint and stops when he should. This excellence is unfortunately not pure. Just as his excellence as an artist arises from his professionalism, his knowledge of an audience, so does his weakness. Too frequently in these stories (and more frequently in the novels) O'Hara writes mechanically, as if on order, or he goes on too long, and too often slips into the easy formula, the movie hero's cynical shrug. It appears that O'Hara is not a good judge of his own fiction, because when he is bad he is boring and trite—sententious, merely clever, endlessly repetitive—and the bad stories stand unblushingly by and between the ones in this collection that are pure gold.

James Boatwright

123

HE WHO FLEES THE LION

Author: J. Klein-Haparash (1897-   )
Translated from the German by Richard and Clara Winston
Publisher: Atheneum Publishers (New York). 650 pp. $7.95
Type of work: Novel
Time: November, 1939-April, 1940
Locale: Rumania and Polish Bukovina

A big novel about people trapped between the machinery of two totalitarian powers in conflict

> *Principal characters:*
> LUDOVIC (LUTZ) ALDA, a boyar landowner in Rumanian Bukovina
> KARL RUNDBERG, Alda's friend, the son of a Jewish tenant
> MIRA LINKHAND, a female financier

A best-seller in Europe, where it was published in German in 1961, *He Who Flees the Lion* has reputedly been a disappointment to its American publishers. Indeed, it is a little depressing even to someone who is not an American publisher to think of stack upon stack of such a fat expensive book in remainder. On the whole, however, it is perhaps easier to account for the book's American failure than for its European success. Despite many enthusiastic readers in the United States, *He Who Flees the Lion* has been obscured by other books with similar themes written by men who are much better known to the public. Its importance must rest chiefly on the fact that it has shown itself capable of inspiring a large amount of devotion abroad, on its size and scope of action.

In no sense but the physical can *He Who Flees the Lion* be called a great book. Compared with the work of Petru Dumitriu, for example, who writes and has written much around much the same subject, it must appear a rather amateurish production. Likewise a Rumanian by birth, an exile in France as Jacob Klein-Haparash is in Israel, Dumitriu was entrusted with

the leadership of the Rumanian State Publishing House while still in his early thirties; he has the distinct advantage over Klein-Haparash, therefore, of having remained in close contact with those circles which exercised power in Eastern Europe at a time that was crucial not only in his own life but also in the life of his country. Though written in French, furthermore, his books have appeared in translation in this country with fair regularity within a year or two after their publication in Paris, and *Meeting at the Last Judgment* has been recognized as a work of considerable genius. To put *He Who Flees the Lion* in competition with such a book and with such an author is perhaps unfair, but it is also inevitable.

Klein-Haparash has further been victimized by his translators, who seem to share the usual Western translators' almost total indifference to the not very mysterious intricacies of Eastern European spelling. One of the first tasks for a translator is to persuade his audience of his fidelity to the original, even in the absence of an original text. Orthography in Eastern Europe is the ultimate and definite register of political, economic, social, and even

124

spiritual realities—Czernowice in the Polish Bukovina, Czernowitz in Austrian Bukovina, Cernauti in Rumanian Bukovina, and Chernovtsy in the Western Ukraine, for example, are all the same Ruthenian city—and in their carelessness of that orthography the translators of He Who Flees the Lion undermine whatever confidence an English-speaking reader might place in them by intimating that they are likewise careless of those realities. It is not unusual for the name of a major character in He Who Flees the Lion to appear in three different spellings or for the name of a city to appear in two, neither one correct.

Nevertheless, in spite of such superficial defects, the book has a good deal to offer, its great virtues being the eternal virtues of the adventure story, excitement and suspense. Its hero, Ludovic Alda, is a boyar; he leads a more than double life as a conscientious landowner who dabbles in smuggling watches through a kind of Jewish underground and in spying for his country against the Russians. Sent from his native Rumania across the Ceremus into Soviet-occupied Poland during the months when that unhappy country suffered as the sole simultaneous victim of both Russia and Germany under the terms of the Hitler-Stalin Pact, Alda finds that his Jewish connections enable him to perform his job of espionage with cleverness beyond that of ordinary men. Alda does everything, in fact, with greater ease than that of other men, from dancing the hora in a Bucharest salon and making love to a Magyar baroness to shoeing horses and directing the operation of a stable on a newly established Polish collective. His talents soon carry him, in the disguise he has assumed to conceal his

role as a spy, to as close to the top of the heap as it is possible for a "native" to be on a farm run by the Russian conquerors: Alda becomes the director of the collective. And he meets Mira Linkhand.

Mira is the heroine of the book, a woman whose brains and ambitions have carried her from a Galician ghetto to a position of acknowledged supremacy at the head of a family, the Linkhands, that in the scope of its financial interests seems to surpass the Rothschilds. Trapped by her loyalty to her husband and an accident that happens to him as they try to escape the Russo-German invasion, Mira finds herself on Alda's farm. Here her personal resources come into play as she tries to make the best of her situation, meanwhile hoping and scheming somehow to escape to the American refuge which she had so foresightedly prepared for the rest of the Linkhands. Prudence tells her to keep her identity a secret and she and Alda join forces without either knowing who the other really is.

Alda and Mira represent, of course, Klein-Haparash's two main interests in He Who Flees the Lion—aristocrats and Jews, the former destined to be the victims by the thousands of the Soviets, the latter the victims by the millions of the Nazis. Nor, in terms of the life to which either the aristocrat or Jew has been used, is there momentarily any alternative. In 1939 and 1940, escape from Poland was a virtual impossibility. Here, then, is the theme of the book: that for these people, in those times, and in those places, there was no way out, no end to life's confusion but in death. It is as if the Day of Jehovah described by Amos, whom Klein-Haparash quotes as his

125

epigraph, had arrived with a vengeance, "as if a man fled from a lion, and a bear met him; or went into the house and leaned his hand against the wall and a serpent bit him."

Ludovic Alda as a stablehand with administrative ability impresses his superiors so much that the Soviets decide to send him into Moldavia as a spy and he therefore returns to his native country by the same route over which he had come. The final irony of the book, a dramatic irony, an irony of history, lies in the fact that Moldavia was invaded six weeks later, its Rumanian defenders being forced to sustain the simultaneous attacks of Hungary in Transylvania and of Bulgaria in Wallachia and Dobruja, and that it was this three-pronged assault that drove Rumania into the arms of Hitler. The plight of Mira Linkhand and Ludovic Alda therefore summarizes the plight not only of a race and a class but of a nation and even of the larger part of the continent of Europe.

John Rodenbeck

HEROD'S CHILDREN

Author: Ilse Aichinger (1921-   )
Translated from the German by Cornelia Schaeffer
Publisher: Atheneum Publishers (New York). 238 pp. $4.50
Type of work: Novel
Time: World War II
Locale: Vienna

A child's spiritual struggle for meaning and values in a hostile environment

Principal characters:
ELLEN, the child
THE CHILDREN, Ellen's playmates
THE GRANDMOTHER, Ellen's closest loved one

Herod's Children, the story of Jewish children in a Nazi world, is recognized as a postwar classic in Germany, the country of its writer. Its great appeal for that country can partially be explained by the fact that it deals with a painfully unforgettable event of German history and, though it brings back the pain, it brings also a kind of philosophical balm to redeem a nation from individual guilt by tracing the inhumanity of the twentieth century to its fundamental source. It deals with basic evils, expressed in Nazism, and with ultimate hope, an existential outlook on life. Its appeal, therefore, is more than national in scope; it is personal and universal at the same time.

The war as a setting serves as a springboard for getting into the well of human actions and to the depth of undercurrent emotions and fantasies. Certainly few stories recently told sound so thoroughly the soul of an age or ring as deeply with the purifying beauty of unyielding humanity in the face of tragedy and with the beauty of dreams and the insights of children. On the surface level it is the story of Ellen, a little Jewish girl in Vienna during the war, but essentially it is about every childlike soul that has ever waged internal battles.

Because it looks beyond the event into the dynamics and forces behind it, the theme of the book presents a com-

126

mentary on the twentieth century. The searching, the denial, the negation of values, such as seem associated with the unrest of today, are seen to have been at the roots of the appeal of Nazism and to be at the roots of all social and political fanaticism. The novel appraises, through the simplicity and warmth of a child, the cold complexities of a society that can persecute and wage war and forget its basic values. Nevertheless, it is only incidentally a work of social criticism. Its foremost concern is its statement of positive values as depicted in the growth of Ellen.

The child is essence of the man in almost all literature that relies on a child to depict its theme. The openness, inquisitiveness, susceptibility, and intuitive wisdom of the child afford a pure and fundamental exposition of humanity. Just as Huckleberry Finn, ragged on the Mississippi, shreds the garments of conventionality with his simple truth, or as Alice in a fanciful land gives an original coloring to reality, so in a different way Holden Caulfield, though hardly a child, a wanderer from that realm trying to find the settled adult world, for many readers depicts the spirit of this age. More recently the boys in Lord of the Flies seem to satisfy the reader with their portrayal of man's basic instincts unconcealed by gracious deception. So it is with this child, Ellen. She is the fundamental being who has seen into the nature of things, and what she feels and does discloses a state of humanity.

Out of place in her world, she is subject to the persecution of an incomprehensible foe. And yet she lives more deeply and surely in a world of her own than those who belong in step with the dull, empty, mechanical tramp of the many. She is empowered by her visions, made invulnerable in the fortress of her mind, and she finds a level of living exempt from the fears and cruelties of her physical environment. But her world is not that of the senseless dream. Her dreams are those of one who is searching for identity, purpose, and meaning. With her playmates —in games, childish prattle, and wishing—or alone in fear and flight and tragedy, Ellen makes a spiritual pilgrimage through a deep emotional forest in discovery of the essential self and the ideal world. She discovers the beauty of pain and sorrow. In the wind and the wild birds she learns of a new home and of the land beyond the dead. Waiting for tomorrow, she lives beyond today. She comes to believe in a humanity more real and, at the same time, more noble than the blind humanity around her.

Since the intensity of its drama takes place in the deep recesses of the mind, Ellen's story is a subject for poetry. And it is exactly in this area that Miss Aichinger's talents lie. While the plot construction of the novel is nothing exceptional, the resourceful poetic rendering of the language and the inspired portrayal of human passions achieve a sustained height of creative power. Vivid and challenging, hers is the romantic, mystical poetry that exposes the world of a child's soul. The most poetic passages render manifold beauties and moods. At times these passages are ungovernably ecstatic; at times, grave and mournful. In a stream of consciousness all experiences and reactions are transformed into a highly symbolic, poignantly personal creation. The juxtaposition of this new and purer world of the child's imagination upon the world as it is affords a contrast that demands judgment, gives intellectual weight to the poetry, and magnifies the pain and beauty of Ellen's growth.

Her growth demands her realization of and adjustment to three worlds. The most apparent world, the world of her physical environment, is the world which has disregarded Ellen's needs and rights. She must come to terms with this world on an intellectual level and, while submitting to its greater power, find a world more worthy of her unreserved allegiance. The second world, the land across the ocean, though slightly distorted by illusions, is real enough and promises a new home and happiness. This world, however, as unattainable as happiness in the first, must be rejected in every way except in its symbolic function as a place of liberty and hope. The third world is that of dreams, the New Jerusalem. It promises happiness, love, and meaning in a soul-world. This world is attainable and is worthy of a child's consecrated devotion.

Ellen's first step in her growth toward victory over life, toward her rightful place in her worlds, is a discovery of her own identity. Realizing her hopelessness in her present world and eager to cross the blue ocean to a new, peaceful, comprehensible land, but with no one to authorize her visa, she is forced to vouch for herself. She draws her own credentials, writes the word *visa* in the clumsy scrawl of a child, and signs her own signature at the bottom. By so doing, the world "over there" is displaced by a world within. She is on her way to a new world. But one must keep in mind that her trip is not merely the fanciful withdrawal of a distraught child. It furnishes a dramatic description of man's accumulative experiences in living.

After Ellen has come to recognize her own existential nature, she must then rightly relate herself to others like her. She meets several children, with whom she is later to form a strong attachment, who at first resent her. Though she is never to escape her loneliness and feelings of isolation completely, she overcomes their refusal to let her play with them by her apparent interest in them. In joining them a unity of strength and purpose is realized. She finds her own nature, purpose, and will complemented and empowered in the common interests and needs of others. When a near tragedy demands her heroic efforts, she experiences an ultimate fulfillment known only in unselfish sacrifice. From this experience and similar ones, she learns that her relation to others is reciprocal in nature, that all men must grow together. Realizing that Ellen's goodness is great enough to bless them too, the children learn from her the basis of charitable action. To Ellen the group experience is essential. Only when she properly relates herself to others and entrusts her growth to interpersonal forces, which unite the children by common bonds, is she able to begin to answer the questions that make up the great distance between her and her new home. A meaningful relation to others precedes an adequate philosophy of life.

A philosophical extension of herself comes next. Frustrated by her confrontation with the disunity of men and the mystery of time, she wrestles with a question: what is existence? Since the answer is not merely intellectual but life-consuming, her quest, which involves every aspect of her being, is depicted in the vividness and drama of allegory. With her playmates she rides in a coach of death, or of Time, toward the border separating earth and heaven. The answers to her question come from voices out of the past. Columbus tells her: "But those who are, are everywhere—and those who are not, are nowhere. Stay and listen; love and light the way. Be despised and bathe in tears—tears clear the eyes. Break through the fog and discover the world! Be—that's the passport to eternity." A declaration and projection of one's own personality was exactly wherein the uniformed Nazi failed, Ellen was later to conclude. His stifling conformity was his crime against himself and resulted in his crime against others. He was more to be pitied than hated. One's hope is in the distinctness of his past, the past being itself a kind of immortality. Time preserves what one has been. To have lived in time, individually and deliberately, impresses one's countenance upon the great frieze of eternity.

Ellen is brought not only to a conviction of the permanency of the past but also to a realization of the harmony of all events. The sea-wonders of Columbus, the chants of David, the rollickings of the resigned brave meet before her in complementary concordance, and she concludes: "It was all apparently for the glory of God, and everything done for the glory of God is harmonious." Finally the line between heaven and earth disappears. One is to be a human being; God is known through humanity and his scheme of things; the past, present, and future are only different viewpoints of eternity. With this fortifying realization Ellen is prepared to face her real world, to interpret it in the light of her spiritual insight, and to suffer the indignities and terrors of its insanity.

What follows is a story of courageous living, at times intensely moving by its solemn and overwhelming depth of feeling, at times captivating with its tumultuous action. But always underlying the story is the illuminating contrast of different levels of reality. Ellen's real self is safe from harm because it is where her interest is, in a world of individual and eternal values. She comes to rely upon the strength that comes from conviction. She comes to see her inevitable destruction as her delivery, for she does not wish to be spared for mediocrity. Yet her journey is never easy, never wholly ascertained, in spite of her sustaining philosophy. She continues to suffer the truth of wretched humanity as long as that truth is revealed to her in its greed, blindness, and agony. Her final glory, like her first, is her reaffirmation of her own independent responsibility to catch the spark within her. And she comes to realize that everyone is alone and must resolve his own basic yearnings and needs through his own resources. She comes to accept what she is and what life offers; even death is meaningful because it is part of existence.

Ellen's experiences form a dramatic illustration of the existential description of man's responses to the demands of life, as outlined by many of the modern theologians. Following the pattern of responsiveness usually found in existential description, Ellen's quest for meaning begins in despair, makes a discovery of self, faces up to life—especially in Ellen's recognizing the role of others in her life—and resolves the imponderable by living and in death. What it means to exist is her basic question, and in her own moods and imagination she develops a reliable index to reality.

The plea of Heidegger, first expressed in Sein und Zeit (Being and Time), that man must learn what Being means and develop from within his spiritual forces, is a fundamental theme of the novel. Evident also is the influence of Marcel, Berdyaev, and Tillich.

Therefore, *Herod's Children* deals essentially with a religious search and an experience of existence. The answers to life, posed by its spiritual drama, are derived from an existential approach to life, a movement especially associated with twentieth century German thinkers. In a way, then, the book demonstrates the superiority of Existentialism over Nazism, the victory of the new Germany over the old.

Charles Workman

A HIGH NEW HOUSE

Author: Thomas Williams (1926-   )
Publisher: The Dial Press (New York). 249 pp. $4.95
Type of work: Short stories
Time: From early Thirties to late Fifties
Locale: New Hampshire and other parts of New England

Stories in which adolescents, young college professors, and old men strive to achieve balance between sensitive and violent impulses

"Haven't you ever had a few experiences all at once that seemed to add up to the whole world?" Robert Stiles asks in Thomas Williams' novella "A High New House." "One day you're fairly well organized, and the next you might as well be on the moon." Since each of Williams' eight stories is a profoundly unsettling experience, at the end of the book the reader is likely to answer the above question in the affirmative.

The stories follow a similar pattern. Williams creates a commonplace situation in which something is slightly wrong in the relationships between the main character and his family or friends. Then, an entirely different, but parallel, character and situation intrude momentarily, thus upsetting the precarious balance between unease and crisis. The separate situations impinge upon the character and, with him, the

reader feels the impact and tries to make sense of the experience. While this technique is probably not original, Williams conveys many fine insights within it. His style is not impressively unique; nor is his recurrent theme original: the unresolvable conflict in man "between his violence and his gentleness." But because Williams' control over style, theme, and structure permits the fullest expression of character in action, these stories are excellent.

Williams' shivering but likable characters move in a bleak, painfully human world, and into a novella of less than seventy pages he has crammed an unbearable amount of humanity. "A High New House," the finest piece in the volume, best illustrates the substance and the virtues of the other stories.

One example of the sureness of Williams' craft is the leisurely way in

130

which he manages to involve the reader in a story that becomes increasingly vibrant with tension. Robert and Alice Stiles, in their early thirties, transform an old house near the university into a haven. Sitting at his eighteenth century desk in his brown and gold study, Robert, a professor of English about to achieve tenure, writes scholarly notes on obscure points, reveling in the care, accuracy, patience, and cleanliness such tasks require. Still strongly attracted to each other after ten years but unable to have children, Robert and Alice plan someday to adopt a European orphan. A year after moving into the high new house, their contentment harmonizes with the serenity of a September evening in New England. Thus, calmly, Williams places his hero in a position to be assaulted with the extraordinary.

Upon Robert's calm, five separate elements intrude.

A young, bearded, idealistic instructor named Lubie is the first of these elements. He awakens in Robert a strange nostalgia for the person he once was, but he also makes Robert feel like one of those "cold monsters of intellect that are the real villains of the mystic's perfectible universe." Lubie, his pale, thin wife, and his two pallid, "holy" children all love one another with a quivering intensity. When Lubie's five-year-old son attempts suicide, Robert is asked to teach Lubie's extension class at the air base. Playing the he-man, Robert is cynically witty about the suicide attempt, while Alice responds with maternal solicitousness. At this point, the reader's interest is aroused, but he is no more aware than Robert is that a process of unease has gotten firmly under way.

Robert's carefully nurtured tranquil-lity receives its second shock at the Strategic Air Command base, which appears to have been planned by an IBM Dedalus. The passing of its bombers over the university always induces a moment of ironic silence, as though in reverence to the concentrated forms of violence which are unleashed gradually in the story from episode to episode. The extension class that Lubie loves depresses Robert. He goes to a bar on the base where he meets a young major whose demeanor seems to declare: "I'm lonesome but it's just temporary; I'm really quite well adjusted, normal, happy and successful." But he is haunted by the suicide of Ernest Hemingway. How could a man so rich and famous, the writer who helped project the American image of manly behavior, kill himself? If he had been there, he would have convinced Hemingway of the meaningfulness of his life. "I guess a lot of us would have, if we'd been there," Robert replies, unable himself to assuage the major's own anxiety. But driving home that night with Alice, "suddenly an involuntary darkness came down like a shutter over his eyes, and it was an idiotic fit of compassion for Lubie and his child." Feeling unmanly, Robert hides his tears from his wife. This is Williams' characteristic way of revealing a symptom of a deep-level lack of control in his main characters.

The third shock to Robert's peace of mind comes closer home in the person of a man with a strangely symbolic name, Forrest Sleeper, who owns the property across the road and who now moves a huge house trailer onto the lot. A pile of old tires, a baby-blue Buick without front wheels, and a mattress slung over the limb of a tree, its center absolutely black, appear in the yard.

131

(Ironically, Robert thinks his own car is too ugly to park beside his house.) He finds a dirty pregnant woman, supposedly Forrest's daughter-in-law whose husband is in the army, sitting in his own kitchen, holding a dirt-encrusted baby. Williams balances this disruption with the quiet and subtle shifting of Alice's sympathies. Having come to the aid of the distressed Lubie family, she now attempts to attend to their indifferent neighbors. While Alice bathes the baby, Robert, "guilty, full of real horror," quietly takes refuge in his study, in "the good place."

A "terrible, frigid carefulness" begins to separate Robert and Alice, and the way is prepared for a fourth intrusion, one which Robert invites. To distract himself from the growing complexity of threats, Robert visits Herb Rutherford, a loquacious young English instructor whose tone is always ironic. His interpretation of Hemingway's suicide and his comments on humanity in general seem to offer Robert the vicarious toughness he seeks. But Robert senses that behind the "constant, bitter grin" he turns upon mankind, Herb is like Lubie, continually hurt and disappointed in life. Thus Williams' control over his raw material enables him to involve Robert in a gradual process of self-discovery, for in Lubie and Herb he sees polarized extreme tendencies in himself; it is the toughness, however, that he overtly encourages. In a parody of confession (reminiscent of the glib wise-guy talk between Jake Barnes and Bill Gorton in *The Sun Also Rises*), Robert comes too close to reality when he tells Herb: "Father, I committed the sin of toughness." On the verge of tears, he is enraged at himself.

Just before the episode with Herb,

Williams sets up the most magnificent moment in the novella. While Robert is discussing Hemingway's "The Killers" in class, a memory of his army days intrudes. A man nearly blew his face off with nitrostarch while doing a problem in mine detection. Neither Robert nor anyone else wanted to help him up, until a sergeant appeared and obscenely ordered the man picked up. Robert never forgot that strange, "crude and shaming way of expressing the man's humanity" in spite of the fact that his face was one sheer expression of blood. This motif becomes an extremely expressive element in the climax.

In Robert, Williams traces the progress of the average man's ability to dehumanize himself in order to exist placidly on the surface of society. The many things that have piled up in him recently cause Robert to sense that he has stifled, perhaps killed, something in himself. Why should a fairly decent man like himself be so thoroughly "bugged" by life? He conducts an interior inquisition and charges himself with not loving the human race. One day he cannot leave his study to face his students. "I don't know what's gone wrong with me lately," he tells Alice. He does not deserve, he feels, the love she gives him, and he violently rejects the ministrations of Lubie, "a loose-jointed jerk with diarrhea of the emotions." First Williams shows how self-loathing manifests itself in violence directed toward those we love most. When Alice greets him at the door with compassion, he rages at her; when she cries, he is so filled with an aching desire to hit something that he gives her a hard blow on the shoulder.

Then the author shows how guilt over the outward thrust against the beloved causes a reversal and drives the destructive impulse more deeply into oneself. Robert has tried to build himself "a little shrine to precision and logic" and to line it with "books in which serene minds speak calmly." But just outside the window is Mr. Sleeper's gutted mattress, emblem of human conduct. And every time he pulls out the drawer of his antique desk, he senses the weight at the back of his Colt .45, which he used to polish until it shone, as he now polishes his scholarly notes. Both reassure him that there is a cold, precise, orderly way to dispense with human threats to one's tranquillity. Discharged at twenty as a buck sergeant, he regretted not having been able to demonstrate his toughness in combat. Academically considering the question of suicide, he sums up, in Hemingway's style, a justification of it: "You shoot yourself when it doesn't feel good anymore to be alive." Thus Williams pulls his hero (and Robert, who begins as the anti-hero familiar to modern fiction, does become a genuine hero of considerable dimension) down to rock bottom: Robert can either kill himself or allow himself to be born again as a man.

The American grain against which he has always felt himself pushing, intellectually, is emotionally ingrained in Robert: "Kill the bastards! Stop all this talk-talk-talk-think-think-think and get it over with!" Though he yearns in his very muscles for the ease of violence as a solution, he knows it means "only death." He learns that toughness reverts to oneself. The SAC bomber is the epitome of violence-as-solution; and the violence dormant in the bomber sleeps in Robert also: on both a massive and an individual scale, the disruption of this violence is suicidal. Ap-

propriately, the jet is the catalyst that draws out of Robert a deeper and finer, but basically human, emotion. Jake Barnes and Holden Caulfield become blended in Robert Stiles.

The fifth intrusion becomes a means of salvation for Robert. One morning a jet flies so low that Robert, afraid it will crash, is anxious for the major. This is a minor preparation for the moment of compassion that Williams next presents. The bomber frightens the pregnant woman so badly that she falls, and Sleeper takes her to the hospital, leaving the repulsive infant in its pen in the yard for Robert to tend. Just as the baby is smiling and Robert is wavering between avoidance and response, a bomber flies over the pen and the baby goes into "the constrictures, the mechanical virtuosity of pure terror." As the bomber flies over again, Robert takes the baby into his arms: "He didn't know its name, but words came to him—words that didn't seem strange at the time, or ever, really, coming as they did from his limited vocabulary of tenderness. A "weird symbiosis" occurs. "The child's body and his body in that long moment seemed to be just one body, and in a way that was mindless and yet complicated beyond his understanding he took the child's fear inside his own chest and killed it there." Williams has an impressive talent for natural symbolism; as one responds purely to the experience, one intuits the symbolic significance of that experience—that the baby Robert holds in his compassionate embrace is symbolic of his own emotional rebirth.

The encounter, from which Robert could not turn away in the name of some notion of manliness, asked point-blank: are you or are you not a man

133

of feeling? But just as the bomber will return, Robert has not stifled forever the violence within him. Alice returns, moved at the sight of Robert comforting the baby. "Behind her rose the high white house, and the leaves of the rock maples billowed dark red before it, violent as fire": a compound image of the human situation, composed of gentleness and violence, contending on the threshold for a place by the hearth. The high new house is the one Williams has been building in Robert, both the temple of man and the temple of God are within him.

Two of the stories deal with adolescent confrontations with inclinations toward gentleness and violence. In the better of these, "The Buck in Trotevale's," the narrator, observing his infant son's gropings for an apple, remembers with a baleful nostalgia the summer when he was fourteen, working in a tedious small-town department store. The Jewish tailor's belief that all forms of violence are inhuman conflicts with Mr. Brown's belief that hunting is not an ignoble sport. But when a buck deer invades the store one morning and the police stupidly slaughter it, it is Mr. Brown who rejects the town where he is loved; the wailing tailor, cranky and unloved, stays because he has learned how to survive in a world without gentleness. Ethical ambiguity dynamically disturbs the boy's complacent sense of values. In "The Hand that Rocked the Cradle Has Kicked the Bucket," an even-tempered but potentially violent football player is drawn into a scandal by his rebellious roommate. "Jimjo had to come into his life and muck everything up, had to give him alternatives he couldn't ignore." He comes to accept Jimjo's code: "You had to outwit

the sons of bitches." But poor Cliff, ironically, lacks the wits and will soon resort to violence.

There are three stories about men in their late thirties who resemble, as does the boy in the deer story, Robert Stiles. In "Ten Years Out," a college professor's peace of mind is harried by the presence next door of a repulsive fraternity house. In "I Cannot Tell A Lie," an English professor's strained relationship with his wife and children is upset by the repeated demands of an alumnus for appraisals of his worthless poetry. He can hurt his son, who irritates him on the morning of his meeting with the alumnus, but he hasn't the nerve to tell the man the truth about his poetry. That night, his wife (who resembles the other wives in Williams' stories) confronts him with the emotional consequences of his cowardice: the boy has withdrawn into a little tent in his room. The father, the little sister, and finally the mother crawl quietly into the womb-like intimacy. "There they were, he thought, all their hearts beating in a row. But even then he was thinking that he could not tell a lie, that love is shadows of shadows, and sometimes even the smallest light could make it blind." This is a fine expression of Williams' poignant but unsentimental view of human love. A more pessimistic view is conveyed in "The Orphan's Wife." About to settle into domesticity, a lawyer revisits Paris where he was once intensely alive to life's possibilities. But all his friends are dispirited; Paris is gloomy, and he discovers that his wife is becoming a middle-class dead weight. After the high fervent flights of youth comes the long glide down into placidity.

"The Skier's Progress" is relatively

134

inconsequential, another occasion for that cliché critical observation "a light, sophisticated *New Yorker* story." But "Goose Pond" is a typically fine Williams story. An old man about to retire in comfort, secure from everything but death, "rages against the dying of the light" by going on a solitary hunt, with bow and arrow, in the mountains for a doe. Alone, he accomplishes a feat any young man would boast about. His feeling of oneness with the trees, the pond, and the wild Canadian geese is a momentary prelude to the restoration of balance between unease and crisis.

Author of *Ceremony of Love, Town Burning*, and *The Night of Trees*, Thomas Williams, assistant professor of English at the University of New Hampshire, has created a body of work that has received many honors and deserves serious critical attention. *Town Burning* was nominated for the National Book Award in 1960; the author was the recipient of a Guggenheim Fellowship for 1962-1963, and *A High New House* received both the first Dial Press Fellowship Award and the first Roos/Atkins award, the latter being the first national literary award presented on the West Coast and one of the largest given in the United States. One is tempted to run the risk of overpraising Thomas Williams. Perhaps one ought simply to conclude, in a calm voice, that his book is a gift.

David Madden

IDIOTS FIRST

Author: Bernard Malamud (1914-   )
Publisher: Farrar, Straus and Company (New York). 212 pp. $4.50
Type of work: Short stories and one short play
Time: Recent decades
Locale: New York, California, Rome, Milan

A collection of recent shorter pieces in the sensitive and yet gusty manner of one of America's finest delineators of character

This is Bernard Malamud's fifth book and second volume of short stories. His first collection, *The Magic Barrel*, won the National Book Award for fiction in 1959. The entire output so far, including the novels *The Natural* (1952), *The Assistant* (1957), and *A New Life* (1961), has won for their writer a following unstinting in its enthusiastic praise and deep respect. The name Malamud immediately suggests a master of the craft who puts a highly refined colloquial style at the service of humanistic themes treated sympathetically through subjects at once comic and pathetic. Malamud is the very best kind of liberal: his love of people is not a doctrine but a norm; it is not intellectualized but felt; it is not argued but represented. And his people are not idealized or satirized, but understood. For Malamud, pathos does not exist without respect, and comedy is a consequence of simple truthfulness. His style is the natural result of straight and uncluttered thinking about what is observable in his experience and, without bias, acceptable. What he is able thus to render in his seeming artlessness is a vibrancy that excites emotion and an incisiveness that commands conviction.

Malamud's audience has been large and variable. Something of its extent is suggested in the list of magazines where these stories found their original publication: *Commentary, Esquire, Harper's Bazaar, Partisan Review, Playboy, Saturday Evening Post, The Reporter, World Review* (London), and *New Statesman*. The scenic range of the stories is wide, but not variable; that is, four of them are set in Italy, the rest in New York and California. And the character types represented in the stories are multiple and various: a sick failure and his idiot son, a successful liquor merchant, a would-be artist who turns double-crook, a tailor, a scholarly professor, a teaching professor, a widow who adapts from grief to life, a failing grocer, an intellectual European critic, a retired actor, and a talking bird. So much for a chart of this fictional world and of the real world where the other may be known.

At the same time, there is a fundamental unifying element in the fiction which, far from imposing a limitation, actually effects another kind of universality. That element is the Jewishness of so much of the subject matter, so much of the idiomatic dialogue of the characters, and so much of the special wisdom inherent in the point of view of the narrator. A few of the stories here do not fit into that category, but it is not too much to say that one inevitably carries away from this book the impression that it is the wonderful work of a conscious Jewish artist who, even when he writes about people other than Jews, brings to bear that particular human understanding he has already shown to emanate from his own capacious Jewish soul. What is important to note about Malamud's Jewishness is that it is not sentimental,

not defensive, not disputatious; rather, it is the manifestation of a cultural quality warm, sensitive, comical, persuasive, and humanizing, producing as it does a spiritual aura which is so appropriate to the author's themes.

Actually, only eleven of the twelve pieces in *Idiots First* are short stories; the remaining one is a short play, "Suppose A Wedding." The title story demonstrates as well as any the imaginative way in which Malamud can convert realism into a kind of cross between farce and fantasy. The narrative is concerned with the desperate efforts of an ill and penurious father to raise money late on a winter night to send his idiot son to California. But in the final scene a struggle with the ticket collector turns into a meaningful drama of absurd, hysterical shenanigans.

"Black Is My Favorite Color" is an account of the irony of one man's fatal attraction to Negroes, who in turn nearly always reject him as a "Jew bastard." Out of simple feeling of heart he has appealed to them for friendship or love—in childhood and now in middle age. But he is doomed to frustration, and the refusal of his maid to eat lunch with him in his kitchen is the last straw. The inversion of minority prejudice works well as the motivating power of this very funny, very sad tale.

In "Still Life" there appears again one Arthur Fidelman, who may be remembered from Malamud's earlier story, "The Last Mohican." Here painter Fidelman shares a studio in Rome with a *pittrice*, Annamaria Oliovino, who in trying to break off an incestuous affair makes demands on him which ultimately reach the heights of burlesque.

"The Death of Me" tells of old Mar-

136

cus, a tailor whose prospering "into ill health" entails hiring an assistant tailor and a presser, one Sicilian and one Pole, who both hold the old Jew in their affection, but despise each other. At last Marcus' indulgence of their feud, his saintly efforts to convert them to love, end in martyrdom.

Yet another variation of moral perception is discoverable in "A Choice of Profession," the story of a college professor whose extensive knowledge about the past of a girl student dooms the relationship he idealistically desires. The title suggests several levels of meaning.

"Life Is Better Than Death" is a dialectical comedy of two mourners, she for her husband, he for his wife, who meet at graveside and then consider for a period of months whether a breach of faith with the dead constitutes adultery, and whether marriage destroys love. The questions remain interestingly unresolved.

"The Jewbird" is an ingenious parable of the self-conscious nature of persecution. There is witty, ironical interpretation of the fabulous bird implicit in the roles of the human creatures in this tale.

Fidelman appears a second time in this volume in "Naked Nude." As the pawn of a gang of art thieves, he dupes his confederates most cleverly in order to satisfy his personal vanity. In this story, Malamud devises a marvelously comic revelation of the ego of an artist manqué.

A more conventional treatment of pathos, but free of any touch of the banal or sentimental, is found in "The Cost of Living," a story of the shock of the intrusion of big business upon a little merchant—the chain store springing up next to the corner gro-

cery. There is a real sense of winter blowing through the lives of Sam and Sura Tomashevsky, but in the telling of their story there is neither outrage at the forces of the world nor resignation to the inevitable; instead, there is compassion in the face of the human condition.

"The Maid's Shoes" is the story of another man's vicarious involvement with others, this time on the part of an American professor in Italy who tries to shape the ethos of his house maid. Unlike Marcus the tailor, however, Professor Krantz does not suffer the martyrdom of the moral middle-man. The story ends amusingly in a recognition of man's pervasive irresponsibility.

The short play, "Suppose A Wedding," is a very funny comedy in the Yiddish manner about the family of a retired actor and the problem that revolves around his daughter's choice of a husband. Malamud's great gift for creating sharply distinctive character is nowhere more apparent than in this conventional situation comedy, which generates the hope that he may someday write more at length for the theater.

The last story in the book, "The German Refugee," is a deeply moving study of a displaced Jewish intellectual who in his attempts to master his psychic despair at the same time he attempts to master the language of his new land, comes to realize something beyond the power of any language to express, something more insufferable than any of his previous sufferings. Its placement at the end of the book suggests the ultimate power of this story.

There may be minor details in Malamud's writing which could incur a negative response—occasional vulgarities or crudities, perhaps a lapse of

137

tone, a jocularity too easy or too sudden—but such matters are minor and occasional. The dominant impression after five books remains: Bernard Malamud is a very good writer indeed, one who exercises sure artistry in behalf of a tremendous vitality.

Fred Bornhauser

THE ISLAND

Author: Robert Creeley (1926-   )
Publisher: Charles Scribner's Sons (New York). 190 pp. $1.65
Type of work: Novel
Time: The present
Locale: An island in the Mediterranean Sea

An American writer, guilt-ridden and impotent, moves through increasing alienation toward self-knowledge

Principal characters:
JOHN, an expatriate American writer
JOAN, his alienated wife
ARTIE, an English writer
MARGE, his pregnant and distant wife
ROBERT WILLIS, an English visitor
RENE LELY, a French visitor and painter
MANUS, a French publisher

Robert Creeley, an established poet, tries his hand at the novel in this book. He tells the story of a writer who, because of temperament, feels himself to be on the outside of life and needs to get inside it. Like the characters of Sherwood Anderson and Ernest Hemingway, or, more recently, of Albert Camus (especially his Mersault), he is a stranger, impotent in heart and imagination, hungry for love and experience, but immured in the loneliness and futility of his sensibility. Told from his point of view, the prose expressing his consciousness, the novel is bizarre in style; besides lacking normal dialogue—or the format for it —the novel sees everything as through a pane of ice, flat, remote, distorted, confused, obscure, while it reveals the protagonist's movement toward a moment of truth in which he comes to understand the extent and effect of his inability to live.

Artie, a British writer, drunk and on impulse, visits the protagonist, a man known only as John, who lives in isolation with his wife and children on a Mediterranean island. Artie's unexpected arrival from town at an early hour of the morning amounts to an explosive invasion of John's detached private world, or his island. This incident begins a series of episodes—involving other men, a town and its rituals, and various women—in which reality infringes upon John's sealed-off consciousness, challenging him to emerge from his hermetic sensibility to become engaged in life, but with each challenge he only sinks more deeply into himself, becoming more and more estranged from the world. To live he must escape from his solipsism, come

138

out of himself, by finding something within himself or in the world to which he can dedicate himself with passion and confidence. And he can only do that if he has accurate knowledge of reality, for life cannot be sound and strong unless it is nourished by truth. Clearly *The Island* is a novel in the tradition of American literature beginning with Emerson and continuing through Henry Miller, in which art is regarded as a means to intellectual and spiritual sanity because it, and only it, can produce the self-knowledge that frees man from the narrow arbitrary social and personal ideas he normally lives by. Art, or more specifically, in this case, literary art, shatters illusions and refreshes us with a vision of the hard facts of life. Although we learn that power, creativity, procreation, transitoriness, change permeate all that exists, the artists of this tradition regard such knowledge as liberating and exhilarating. Their attitude is based on the assumption that conformity to the higher reality, that transcendence of the ego, permits men to live true to their being, and since being is joyous self-affirmation, such conformity, as in its more traditional religious or Christian forms, frees man for difficult but glorious life. For Emerson, Thoreau, Whitman, E. E. Cummings, William Carlos Williams, Henry Miller, truth does not coddle man by satisfying his intellect's desire for fixed order and meaning or his heart's desire for moral absolutes and immortality; it confronts him with a challenge to abandon himself to freedom with all of the burdens and dangers it entails.

Although Mr. Creeley's novel is in this tradition and is based ultimately on this idea of man and art, it is less religious or metaphysical than the great works in it; instead, it is predominantly psychological. In this respect it is a mirror perhaps of the times, of the greater subjectivity and self-consciousness of the twentieth century American. His story is set this side of the final and larger truth, his protagonist having crawled so far into his shell that he can be aware of nothing beyond the pain of his existence. Dominated by fear, he cannot let go of his impotent sensibility; he cannot clear his vision sufficiently to become Emerson's "transparent eyeball," or open the vents of the self to let Thoreau's wind or Whitman's procreative urge blow through him. His story can tell, therefore, only of his agony, of his failure to transcend his puny self-consciousness. John testifies to an obvious decline in the fortunes of the American man; the mid-century American, in Robert Frost's diagnostic phrase, can see neither far out nor in deep. He is stuck with his own self.

To be sure, John has his moment of truth, which suggests that he may achieve some kind of breakthrough. John's sexual ineffectuality increases throughout the novel to the point where, out of self-defense, he accuses his wife, Joan, of sexual relations with Artie. Furiously, she hurls his typewriter to the floor, shattering it, and apparently his identity as a writer, one who reflects upon rather than lives life, and flees into the night. John goes in search of her and not finding her thinks she is dead. Overwhelmed by grief he confronts himself in self-recognition, acknowledging his guilt and impotence. When Joan turns up shortly thereafter, he reaches toward her, then withdraws his hand. Lest the reader miss the point of the novel, Mr. Creeley has provided a prefatory statement of his theme. "People want an island," he writes, "in which the world will be at last a place circumscribed by visible horizons. . . . This island is, finally, not real . . . time, even if it will not offer much more than a place to die in, nevertheless carries one on, away from this or any other island." Past achievements provide no insurance against the present or future; every moment is unique and demands of us a fresh response. One of the weaknesses of the novel is that it does not make that point, at least clearly. John learns, but he learns that the world remains the same; it is obdurately there and his self-knowledge, won through great suffering, does not relieve him of his burden of guilt or strengthen him. He has won a hard knowledge, but there is no indication that he is being carried, by his own will or time, beyond the island on which he has tried to hide from life.

Whereas the great works of the tradition to which *The Island* belongs look ahead, deriving exuberance from truth and freedom, Mr. Creeley's book in effect looks back, with the result that its tone is pronouncedly despondent.

There is little to hope for and nothing to rejoice in, not even as much as there was for Anderson and Hemingway. John is an even more desolate character, for instance, than Hemingway's Jake Barnes and his lost-generation colleagues. His knowledge of things as they are provides him with the heavy burden of having to move on, while all his instincts tell him to rest in the present shelter. Perhaps Mr. Creeley's novel reflects the present mood of America—our deep desire to quit while we are on top rather than continue with the nation and world-building first embodied in American literature by Emerson in the zestful confidence of a country in the making. At any rate, it testifies that our literature and life no longer have their roots in that kind of spiritual soul. The patriot who became an expatriate during the 1920's is now totally estranged from everybody and everything. Mr. Creeley has skillfully unbared this predicament in his pitiless portrayal of John as a man with no redeeming virtues, truth telling him nothing more than that life is one damned moment after another.

William R. Robinson

THE JACOB'S LADDER

Author: Denise Levertov (1923-   )
Publisher: New Directions (New York). 87 pp. Paperback, $1.55
Type of work: Poetry
    Poems by the author of The Double Image, Here and Now, Overland to the Islands, *and* With Eyes at the Back of Our Heads

Since the publication of her first book in London in 1946, Denise Levertov has moved impressively into one of the commanding positions in a generation of poets devoted to clarity of idiom and the cultivation of delicate insight. Erroneously she has been linked with the Beats. Though she is capable of a capricious wildness, she is more properly to be thought of not in connection with Ginsberg, Corso, and LeRoi Jones, but with the more careful and lower-keyed voices of Duncan and Creeley. In company with these latter two, she may be said to represent possibly the best achievement of the Pound-Williams line in the present situation of its development. At least as it appears now, these young poets recognize Williams particularly as their poetic father, with Charles Olson, the Black Mountain sage, as a compatible uncle.

Into Denise Levertov's verse come the impulses which have dominated the postwar movement: simple precision of speech, concentrated yet clear images of commonplace objects, and a tendency to avoid "rhetoric" and merge the values of prose and verse. Probably no contemporary poet manages *all* of these impulses with as much success as Miss Levertov. Probably this versatility in handling urgent notions of what poetry ought to be is precisely what has made her work so popular, and deservedly so. Yet, as the title, *The Jacob's Ladder,* suggests, Miss Levertov's poetry does not rest finally on mere mastery of a few modern techniques, but on deep bases of religion, myth, philosophical awareness, and even an existential frame of interpretation of the famous dream of Jacob. As epigraph to the book, she quotes *Tales of the Hasidim: Later Masters,* by Martin Buber:

Rabbi Moshe (of Kobryn) taught: It is written: "And he dreamed, and behold a ladder set up on the earth." That "he" is every man. Every man must know: I am clay, I am one of countless shards of clay, but "the top of it reached to heaven"—my soul reaches to heaven; "and behold the angels of God ascending and descending on it"—even the as-

cent and descent of the angels depend on my deeds.

It is this ground for poetry, this vision, which focuses the Levertov material on the simplest and profoundest human concerns and makes it possible for the poet

To stand on common ground
here and there gritty with pebbles

and to write quite naturally about "current events" such as the Eichmann trial. A sense of the wash of history and time under the present informs the first poem of the book, a sort of "argument" addressed to the reader, in which the poet declares that

. . . as you read, many gods
lie among lianas: eyes of obsidian
are watching the generations of leaves,
. . . the sea is turning its dark
pages . . .

Although the world Denise Levertov encounters is full of paper cups, trees, petals of flowers, and rye bread—the modern world of incidental minutiae —it is not finally the nominalistic universe of unrelated objects that one finds in a more uncompromisingly hard-headed poet such as William Carlos Williams. Rather, being both poet and woman, Miss Levertov calls to herself, and the reader, to desire

Not 'common speech'
a dead level
but the uncommon speech of paradise,
tongue in which oracles
speak to beggars and pilgrims . . .

A diffuse, soft-hearted mysticism mars such language, and the poet is far below her best when attempting such abstractions as the "speech of paradise." But as an example of the way this poet can make vivid a rather com-

141

mon protest against the spiritless quality of modern life, take this passage:

Man gets his daily bread
in sweat, but no one said
in daily death. Don't eat

those nice green dollars your wife
gives you for breakfast.

In this excerpt the fresh and totally unexpected closing image has a capricious and exact "truth" to it.

Short, bright lyrics composed of rapid images and quiet but fervid meditations make up the bulk of the book, along with several long sequences such as "Five Poems from Mexico," which keep, in their sequential parts, the brilliance and the bite of the shorter poems. Instinct and passion are the presiding and moving spirits in much of the work. She quotes D. H. Lawrence: "And virtue? Virtue lies in the heroic response to the creative wonder, the utmost response." Yet each poem is as carefully made as a cameo; or, in the case of the longer sequences, as finely crafted as a necklace of interlinked ivory figures, with casual sensuousness and a narrative ease that moves the reader's eye effortlessly from imagistic link to link.

In her poem "During the Eichmann Trial," Miss Levertov considers the defendant as some dark essence of a common human disease, and speaks of the inseparability of the public symbol and ourselves:

Earth cannot swallow
so much at once

a fountain
rushes towards the sky

* * * *

Pity this man who saw it
whose obedience continued—

he, you, I, which shall I say?
He stands

isolated in a bulletproof
witness-stand of glass,

a cage, where we may view
ourselves, an apparition . . .

The poem continues to embody a dramatic sense of the commonality of human beings.

Two of the most instructive poems in the volume, from the viewpoint of the poet's development, are "Overland to the Islands," from the 1958 book of the same title and "The Jacob's Ladder," which holds in this present volume the other end of a thematic thread running throughout this poet's work. Both poems are fables about the creative process itself. But this continuing concern is not an idle one because the poet identifies poetry with dream, with change, with a qualitative human advance. In "Overland to the Islands," a dog is used as the symbol of intuitive and intently perceptive movement: the dog disdains nothing on his haphazard way, and his attitude makes "every step an arrival." All time has become present. And the fabulous ladder into heaven becomes, in the poet's vision:

A stairway of sharp
angles, solidly built.
One sees that the angels must spring
down from one step to the next, giving
a little
lift of the wings:

and a man climbing
must scrape his knees, and bring
the grip of his hands into play. The cut
stone
consoles his groping feet. Wings brush
past him.
The poem ascends.

142

This latest book by Denise Levertov is almost uniformly excellent. It demonstrates one of the finest, most precise talents and one of the largest spirits among the poets now writing.

Robert Hazel

JOHN KEATS
The Making of a Poet

Author: Aileen Ward
Publisher: The Viking Press (New York). Illustrated. 450 pp. $7.50
Type of work: Biography
Time: 1795-1821
Locale: England and Italy

The biography of a distinguished Romantic poet, Shelley's Adonais, "forever young"

Principal personages:
JOHN KEATS
RICHARD ABBEY, a tea broker and Keats's guardian
FANNY BRAWNE, Keats's wife-to-be
FRANCES BRAWNE, her mother
CHARLES BROWN, a dramatist and writer
CHARLES COWDEN CLARKE, a schoolmaster
CHARLES WENTWORTH DILKE II, a scholar and politician
BENJAMIN HAYDON, a painter
WILLIAM HAZLITT, a literary critic and essayist
LEIGH HUNT, a poet and critic
FANNY KEATS, John Keats's sister
GEORGE and
TOM KEATS, his brothers
GEORGE F. MATHEW, a poet
JOHN HAMILTON REYNOLDS, a poet
JOSEPH SEVERN, a painter
JOHN TAYLOR, Keats's publisher
RICHARD WOODHOUSE, a barrister

John Keats, as Fanny Brawne once remarked, was fortunate in his friends, and it is due to the admiration of these friends—businessmen, lawyers, journalists, painters, physicians, curates—that so great a wealth of detail regarding his personality and genius has been preserved in the memoirs, journals, and letters of his contemporaries, each chronicler recording his impression of Keats's character with that sense of patronizing possession of truth which seems to be an especial trait of Keats's friends and admirers. What they noted and collected has permitted the late Professor Hyder E. Rollins to prepare two significant publications, the letters, memoranda, and criticism written by Keats's friends and relatives (*The Keats Circle*, 2 vols., 1948) and in 1959 *The Letters of John Keats*. The publication of such sources, impeccably and astutely annotated, presents a fresh opportunity to write a new study of the poet's life; the dust jacket indicates Miss Ward's biography as the "first full-scale" one in more than twenty-five years (if Dorothy Hewlett's *Adonais* is in mind here, it was published in 1937 and revised in 1950). Miss Hewlett's biography was directed to depicting the Regency and Georgian milieu of Keats; Miss Ward's is to show the development in Keats of the character of the poet, his self-creation as an artist in the vale of soul-making.

The factual details of Keats's life by their very multiplicity present biographical and critical problems which require in the biographer scrupulous tact in judging sources and sensitive psychological insight into Keats's human relationships and into his creative development as a poet; these qualities Miss Ward has in abundant measure. It is well known that the father, Thomas Keats, came from the West of England, became the head ostler at the Swan and Hoop Inn, and married his master's daughter, Frances Jennings, in 1794. Keats, born in 1795, was the oldest of a family of four sons and one daughter. Miss Ward is curious as to why Keats was so silent about his childhood, but she finds no evidence of an unhappy one. (Was his silence motivated by the shame of his mother's dereliction and hasty remarriage?) When John was eight or nine his father died; his mother remarried within two months, and later seems to have been somewhat ambiguously attached to the household of a Jewish merchant. This experience, observes Miss Ward, changed Keats from "an affectionate child to a rebellious schoolboy." He found affection and stability in the home of his grandmother, Alice Jennings, but the biographer discovers in this disaffecting adolescent experience the origins of Keats the poet. Keats's mother returned home and died of tu-berculosis in her early thirties, despite the agonized, devoted nursing of her oldest son.

The children's guardian after the grandmother's death, a prosperous London tea broker, Richard Abbey, urged the older brothers John and George to select careers; Miss Ward suggests plausibly that Keats's choice of a medical career (as apothecary-surgeon) was not forced upon him by Abbey, once the belief of biographers, but was rather his own decision and the issue of his experience with his dying mother and his resolute determination to face a world of reality. One of the most interesting parts of this biography is the narrative (Chapter 3) of Keats's gradual shift from his career as surgeon to his decision to become a poet when he became of age on October 31, 1816. The extreme concentration of the poet's literary career from the time he mounted the stagecoach to Southampton on April 14, 1817, to his burial in the Protestant Cemetery of Rome in February, 1821, was all too brief; the biographical narrative makes the most of the dramatic development of Keats's poetic genius, and of his "leap into the sea," the determination to write the long poem *Endymion* with the slenderest of financial prospects.

Miss Ward seems to believe that Keats's shift from medicine to poetry was partly due to an estrangement from his chosen profession because of an exceptional vulnerability to personal suffering, and partly to the necessity of assuming the pose of poet and artist to achieve some sense of stability in creative selfhood amidst the distracted uncertainties of early manhood. This speculation on Keats's motivation is of course dangerous, but essential for the biographer; Miss Ward's suggestions

144

seem more plausible and helpful in interpretation than the frequently alleged motive that Keats was merely stepping out of an uncongenial occupation. The months of 1816-1817 were indeed thereafter the happiest of his life, his poetic expectations being based modestly upon the praise of his friends. He was indeed, as Keats described himself, "a pet lamb in a sentimental farce."

The remainder of the biography is concerned with the maturing development of the poet and his relationships with his friends and with Fanny Brawne. The vignettes of his friends —Hunt, Hazlitt, Brown, Haydon, Reynolds, Severn—and his intimacy with his brothers Tom and George and with Fanny Brawne are vividly delineated, and the minute and immediate record of the poet's life during the brief, intense flowering of his poetic powers and their rapid decline is presented by Miss Ward in engaging, moving, and illuminating comment.

It would be difficult to chronicle all the fresh small insights and discoveries Miss Ward finds in her presentation; she is right, for example, in dismissing the absurd contention that in his steadily weakening condition from tuberculosis Keats ever seriously entertained a resolution to recoup his fortune by embarking as a surgeon on an East Indian vessel. Certain small reservations can be made of the biographical treatment. Has she left a fair picture of George's financial evasiveness, even with some adjustment of the portrait in the Epilogue? Has she clearly run down the sources of Keats's hostility to Christianity, beyond showing that Haydon and Bailey blamed the Hunt circle for his infidelity? Professor Michel Renzuli (*John Keats*, 1956) finds that Shelley is responsible for Keats's loss of Christian faith and belief in immortality. It is not at all clear that the grandson of Sir Charles Dilke did not behave more ambiguously in the publication of the Fanny Brawne letters than the Epilogue seems to imply. Miss Ward's treatment of Fanny Brawne's love for Keats is admirable and wholly just to the sincerity and devotion of her character.

In her discussion of the sources of Keats's creative inspiration, the central focus of the book, Miss Ward develops the thesis that the ultimate image of his poetic structure is "the face of his dead mother, shrouded in her coffin," a symbol of "Beauty that must die" and yet be miraculously brought to life again (cf. p. 340); the fundamental images of his poetry were shaped by the memories of this pale, beautiful (but faithless) woman and the sight of a mysterious beauty at Vauxhall Gardens in 1814. There is a restrained use of pyschoanalytic insights in the book that occasionally seems over-anxious to be modern, such as the likening of the early "Imitation of Spenser" to dawning consciousness and to the primordial sexual symbols of sky and water, but Miss Ward does make a case for the recurrence of allusion to the biological processes in Keats's imagery, such as the identification of food and love in his poems. Miss Ward rejects the allegorical interpretation of *Endymion*; her description of it as "unabashedly sensual" seems sensible. What especially reveals Miss Ward's aesthetic sensibility is the complex relationship she sees between sexual love, Keats's desire for "fellowship with essence," his hostility to the Wordsworthian "egotistical sublime," and his preference as a poetic creator for the annihilation of the poet's personality in a

145

poetic vision inspired by Shakespeare's "negative capability." She is fully aware of the relationship of this annihilation of personality to Keats's growing interest in the drama and to the writing of his play *Otho*, but she is of course informed of Bernice Slote's treatment of this aspect.

This must have been a difficult book to write because there are so many pit-

falls involved in close attention to the psychology of the creative act, but the biography is a distinguished achievement, perceptive, often very moving, and exceptionally successful in helping the reader feel poignantly the very pulse of Keats's daily existence.

John Keats was the winner of the 1964 National Book Award for Arts and Letters.

John P. Kirby

LAVAL
A Biography

Author: Hubert Cole (1908-   )
Publisher: G. P. Putnam's Sons (New York). Illustrated. 314 pp. $5.95
Type of work: Biography
Time: 1883-1945
Locale: France

A study of Pierre Laval, collaboration leader in the Vichy Government of France during the German Occupation of that country in World War II

Principal personages:

PIERRE LAVAL
MARSHAL PHILIPPE PÉTAIN
OTTO ABETZ, the German Ambassador to the Vichy Government
PAUL BAUDOUIN, a minister in Pétain's cabinet
YVES BOUTHILLIER, a conspirator against Laval
ADMIRAL DARLAN, a minister in Pétain's cabinet
GENERAL CHARLES DE GAULLE
ADOLF HITLER
GENERAL LOUIS MAXIME WEYGAND
EUGÉNIE LAVAL, Pierre Laval's wife
COMTESSE DE CHAMBRUM (JOSÉE LAVAL), Laval's daughter

On October 15, 1945, Pierre Laval was executed as a traitor to France by a firing squad of French soldiers at Fresnes. He had been tried before a special high court appointed by General Charles de Gaulle in the emotion-packed months immediately after the liberation of France by Allied forces. As the events are retold by Hubert Cole, there is reason to inspect, indeed to suspect, de Gaulle's motives, inasmuch as an election was in the offing

and the judges and jurymen were quite obviously in a frame of mind to find Laval, then a hated man, guilty of treason because of his collaboration with the Germans during the Occupation of France by the Nazis.

Numerous books about Pierre Laval have appeared in France, where several of his associates published defenses of his actions in the decade after his execution. Each of Laval's three lawyers published books pre-

146

senting him as they had come to know him during his trial and after. René de Chambrun, Laval's son-in-law, published a collection of documents concerning Laval's career during the Occupation, and Laval's own defense, written while he was in prison, has been published by his daughter Josée, the Comtesse de Chambrun. All these books, however, were written by Frenchmen. Hubert Cole's book is the first to be written in English.

Cole's styling of his book as a biography is something of a misnomer, for the title leads the reader to expect a full portrait. However, *Laval: A Biography* is a work that gives only minor attention to his life prior to his becoming the Président du Conseil under Marshal Pétain in the Vichy Government and his being named as Pétain's successor as the head of the Vichy regime in the event of the marshal's incapacity for his tasks. Also, a limited number of episodes are used to explain the career, the downfall, and the personality of Laval. While Cole's book is interesting as the first book in English on the subject, it really stimulates the non-French reader to look forward to a definitive study of Pierre Laval, who, though executed as a traitor, had been hailed in the United States by *Time* as the Man of the Year in 1931.

Cole shows the reader Laval as a man who hated violence of every kind, especially war. Laval believed that negotiation, especially when carried on face to face, was the way to settle all problems. And at negotiation he proved himself, throughout his career, a masterful figure willing to sacrifice a little in order to gain a great deal. While on the one hand his willingness to negotiate earned him hatred, espe-

cially during the years of the Nazi Occupation, on the other it enabled him to accomplish much. For example, Laval managed to save approximately ninety percent of the French Jews from the Nazis, whereas in other countries the Jews were practically decimated. As a negotiator of everything, Laval was a realist, and he came to be disgusted with anyone, foreign or French, who was motivated by ideologies. He found that such persons did not understand him, and he did not understand them. In fact, it seems that he and his career in the Vichy Government were damned by the very people who clung to more idealistic views of the relationships of a man to his country. At the time of his trial Laval seems to have been judged by the fact that he had collaborated with the Germans, not on whether that collaboration had been better or worse in its results for France and its people.

Like most biographers, Cole has a view of his man. He sees Laval as a man of courage and determination, disdainful of public and private opinion, who truly believed that a moderate, reasonable person could govern and guide a country, like France, which had gone down in defeat and was existing perilously in a world at war.

Because he loved his country, Laval fought for it in his own way. He himself, said: "I cannot live if I cannot tread the soil, the furrows, talk with peasants, the people of my home." He disconcerted and antagonized others, especially men in government, by his disregard for honor and glory. Marshal Pétain himself said that what he found most discouraging in Pierre Laval was the latter's lack of appreciation of spiritual values. People in high places were antagonized, too, by Laval's lack of social graces, his poor manners even at the table, and his untidy appearance. None of this criticism seemed to bother Laval, who in his pride assumed that he, and only he, could retrieve his beloved France from the low state into which it had fallen following defeat at the hands of Nazi Germany in 1940. He saw himself as a man of destiny and followed his own beliefs—although he was realistic enough to carry a vial of poison during the years between 1942 and 1945, poison he tried to use the morning of his execution to evade being shot to death by a firing squad.

In some ways Laval had astounding vision. Prior to World War II he worked long and vigorously in an effort to prevent the outbreak of war. He would have been willing to ally France with Fascist Italy had he been able to forge a ring of steel about Nazi Germany. He knew full well that France could not withstand a German onslaught, that Germany was too great an adversary, even in terms of population. During the war years Laval strove for an understanding among the West European nations about the future and the U.S.S.R. Laval foresaw that the Communists would become the real threat to peace in Europe, and so he tried to persuade the Allies and the Germans that they ought to band together against a worse enemy than even Nazi Germany. Laval was unafraid to predict to the German leaders' faces that the future would find much of central Europe, even much of Germany, in Communist hands. That Laval foresaw the future correctly everyone can now see for himself.

That Laval could have produced a workable plan to prevent the growth of Communist domination is, of course, another matter.

Perhaps one important sidelight for American readers of Cole's book is the insight it gives on the European view of the United States during World War II and after. Hailed for a time as the liberators of France, Americans have been disconcerted to learn that the French have no keen liking for Americans or the United States, although we in America have felt kindly toward France since the days of Lafayette and French help received during the days of the American Revolution. Cole's book reflects that both the British and the French distrust and envy America. Many Americans need to learn that the United States and its people are not universally liked and that our nation's policies and actions are not always pleasing to friendly nations, even two such long-standing allies as France and Great Britain.

Hubert Cole is not always careful in his book to make only such generalizations as his evidence warrants. In a few cases he offers sweeping opinions which cast a shadow of distrust over the entire work, inasmuch as such opinions gratuitously offered and unsupported cause the reader to question other phases of the writing. For example, Cole says at the end of his fifth chapter, "What Churchill had described as 'the unnecessary war' had been ended with the unnecessary bomb." The reference is, of course, to the United States' use of atomic bombs at Hiroshima and Nagasaki in August, 1945.

Gordon W. Clarke

THE LETTERS OF F. SCOTT FITZGERALD

Author: F. Scott Fitzgerald (1896-1940)
Edited, with an Introduction and notes, by Andrew Turnbull
Publisher: Charles Scribner's Sons (New York). Illustrated. 615 pp. $10.00
Type of work: Letters
  Half the available letters written by the American novelist F. Scott Fitzgerald to his daughter, his wife, his editor, his agent, his society and literary friends, and others

From Hollywood in 1940, the year of his death, F. Scott Fitzgerald wrote to Maxwell Perkins, his editor at Scribner's: "Even now there is little published in American fiction that doesn't slightly bear my stamp—in a *small* way I was an original." Two years earlier he had written to Perkins: "I have come to feel somewhat neglected. Isn't my reputation being allowed to let slip away?" All his books were out of print. And when Arthur Mizener's biography appeared in 1951, the situation was little better. Now his publisher is reissuing all his books as the result of a reassessment that has enshrined Fitzgerald with the giants of the 1920's: Hemingway, Faulkner, and Wolfe. "An author ought to write," Fitzgerald said prophetically, "for the youth of his generation, the critics of the next, and the schoolmasters of ever afterward."

The years between 1925 and 1929 had a stunning effect upon American fiction with the publication of *The Great Gatsby, The Sun Also Rises, A Farewell to Arms, The Sound and the Fury,* and *Look Homeward, Angel.* Also in this decade appeared Eliot's *The Waste Land* (1922); one may sense the influence of this thematically visionary poem in *The Great Gatsby.* With Hemingway and Wolfe, Fitzgerald recognized an essential affinity: the attempt "to recapture the exact feel of a moment in time and space, exemplified in people. . . ." Our picture of this era becomes more intensely fasci-

nating with every new biography and collection of letters about these three novelists and their editor, Maxwell Perkins. "What a time you've had with your sons, Max," Fitzgerald wrote in 1938. "Ernest gone to Spain, me gone to Hollywood, and Tom Wolfe reverting to an artistic hillbilly." In their works and in their legends these writers consciously expressed a dynamic poetic image of their time. Of his own contribution, Fitzgerald wrote to Edmund Wilson in 1918 while still at work on his first novel, *This Side of Paradise:* "I really believe that no one else could have written so searchingly the story of the youth of our generation"; and to Perkins he said later, "I don't know anyone who has used up so much personal experience as I have at 27."

Edited by Andrew Turnbull, whose biography of Fitzgerald appeared in 1962, these letters provide a many-faceted view of that "huge season" and of the man who led "the gay parade." It was a time so bemused by itself that he later said, "For me the past is forever." These letters show us the Fitzgerald of the St. Paul, Princeton, France, Baltimore, Asheville, and Hollywood years. As an insider who figures prominently in the letters himself (he was a childhood friend of Fitzgerald and the playmate of the writer's daughter Scottie) Turnbull is well qualified to write about Fitzgerald and to edit his letters. Unfortunately, those

149

to Fitzgerald's father and to his good friend Ring Lardner are not obtainable, but of those which are available, Turnbull has published half.

The organization of the volume is ingenious and imaginative. After a brief personal introduction and an adequate chronology, Turnbull opens with a large group of letters to the callow, romantic Scottie, covering the years 1933-1940. He next presents a brief group to Fitzgerald's wife Zelda (1939-1940). These letters provide an intimate view covering the dark years when Fitzgerald indentured himself to Hollywood to finance Scottie's education and Zelda's confinement in mental institutions. Of Zelda, he wrote to his daughter that "the insane are always mere guests on earth, eternal strangers carrying around broken decalogues that they cannot read." In a different mood he wrote to Zelda herself: "I ask only this of you—leave me in peace with my hemorrhages and my hopes, and what eventually will fight through as the *right* to save you, the *permission* to give you a chance." He endured in this same period the "dreary routine" and expense of his own illnesses. "What I am doing here," he wrote Scottie from Hollywood, "is the last tired effort of a man who once did something finer and better." His debts to his agent, his publisher, and to others were oppressive: "There had always seemed a little more somewhere and now there wasn't" seems an epitaph to his era.

In the 150-page section of letters to Perkins, many of which are among the most provocative in the collection, an entire creative span is covered. Both as an artist and as a proficient hack, Fitzgerald discusses in generous detail the machinery of publishing and the stages in the development of his books; and his comments on the personalities and writings of his contemporaries are often brilliant. Much briefer sections are devoted to major literary friends: Hemingway, who finally betrayed him; Edmund Wilson, who set his intellectual standards; John Peale Bishop, who introduced him to modern poetry, and Shane Leslie, who encouraged him to pursue his career as a writer. Other sections bring together letters to Christian Gauss, his teacher at Princeton; Harold Ober, his good friend and agent from whom he eventually became estranged, and to such society friends as Mrs. Richard Taylor; Mrs. Turnbull (Andrew's mother), whom he greatly admired and respected and who gave him "a sense of the continuity of life"; and Gerald and Sara Murphy, models for some of his rich, romantic characters. (The book includes excellent photographs of each of these correspondents.)

The volume ends with a 150-page section of miscellaneous letters to his family, to his school friends, to strangers who expressed admiration or asked advice about living and writing, to critics (James Branch Cabell, Gilbert Seldes, Alexander Woolcott, Dayton Kohler, Malcolm Cowley, George Jean Nathan, Henry Mencken), to fellow writers (Sinclair Lewis, Sherwood Anderson, Gertrude Stein, John O'Hara, Thomas Wolfe, Budd Shulberg, and S. J. Perelman), and to movie people (Helen Hayes, Joseph Mankiewicz). Many other writers, including Dorothy Parker and John Dos Passos, and movie people, Shirley Temple and Joan Crawford among others, are interesting figures in the letters. This section provides the broadest view, from 1907 on. There is also a serviceable index to persons and literary works.

By deciding against the strict chronological approach, Turnbull returns us again and again to focal events, and there emerges an impressive image of a complex, dual personality whose dramatic life, romantic in youth, tawdry in some instances, and pathetic in its "dying fall," strained his body and his creative powers to the breaking point (see *The Crack-up*). Eventually Fitzgerald came to believe that "life is essentially a cheat and its conditions are those of defeat" and that "the redeeming things are not 'happiness and pleasure' but the deeper satisfactions that come out of struggle." Unlike his other, more nearly autobiographical novels, his masterpiece, *The Great Gatsby,* is an artistically unified expression of his own disordered character, which could not hold two opposed views at the same time without cracking up. In *The Great Gatsby* he "found the intensity of art," and "nothing else that can happen in life can ever again seem as important as the creative process." From one point of view, the letters to Perkins and to Ober constitute a work record that shows how Fitzgerald's mediocre and second-rate stuff (for *Liberty, The Saturday Evening Post,* and *Cosmopolitan*) kept him from more important work and detracted from his reputation among serious readers. "In my new novel," he wrote to Perkins, concerning *The Great Gatsby,* "I'm thrown directly on purely creative work—not trashy imaginings as in my stories but the sustained imagination of a sincere yet radiant world."

Most of the letters have a polished literary finish that either proves Fitzgerald's fictive style was really quite spontaneous or suggests that his correspondence was with posterity. In contrast to the stiff letters of Joyce, Fitzgerald's letters run the gamut of human emotions and moods. They are frank, intimate, bitter, warm, gossipy, desperate, self-pitying, stoic, introspective, charitable, compassionate, irreligious, moralistic, kind, apologetic, grateful, and full of bizarre wit and humor. They remind one of the lively letters of John Keats or D. H. Lawrence.

Fitzgerald's disputes with Wilson, Hemingway, and Bishop over aspects of his private life which they publicized, with Perkins over Fitzgerald's estimation of other Scribner writers, especially the later Wolfe, and with Ober over money problems, reveal a great deal about all those involved. He writes often of the direct influences in life and literature upon his writing. He speaks of Compton Mackenzie, Keats, Norris, Conrad, Kafka with rare discernment, and he never quite recovered from the impact of Spengler, whom he read while working on *The Great Gatsby.* Also valuable are his reassessments of his own work; we witness the author's progress from an egotistical confidence in his first novel to a more mature confidence in *The Great Gatsby.* His various comments on the craft of fiction have a timeless relevance: "All good writing is *swimming under water* and holding your breath." He offered sound advice to young writers, whom he was always eager to assist, morally, critically, and practically. "This is to tell you," he wrote to Perkins, "about a young man named Ernest Hemingway. . . ."

Although he speaks of her, there are no letters to Sheilah Graham. But there is one moving letter in which he ends a relationship with a married woman. Like most people who squander money, health, talent, and friendships, he was

151

lavish with advice. With the authority of failure, but with a Chestertonian aptness as well, he advised Scottie, for instance, about her schooling, reading, writing, and romancing. "Just do everything we didn't do and you will be perfectly safe." Summing up his concern, he said, "I don't want to bury you in your debut dress."

His observations on the Hollywood of the 1930's—its writers, directors, stars, producers—indicate that he possessed the raw material to make *The Last Tycoon*, unfinished at his death, a major novel. Alternately elated and depressed as a script-writer who as-

pired to direct his own movies, it is in one sense appropriate that he died in Hollywood. For at his worst he hacked out strips of garish celluloid and at his finest he conjured up the image of America that the movies, potentially, are best able to project.

Reviewing *The Last Tycoon* in 1941, Stephen Vincent Benét wrote: "You can take off your hats, gentlemen, and I think perhaps you had better. This is not a legend, this is a reputation." At this stage in literary history, the biographies of the author and the new evaluations of *The Great Gatsby* suggest that F. Scott Fitzgerald is both.

David Madden

THE LETTERS OF ROBERT FROST TO LOUIS UNTERMEYER

Author: Robert Frost (1874-1963)
Publisher: Holt, Rinehart and Winston (New York). 388 pp. $7.00
Type of work: Letters

   A self-revelation of Frost as man and poet, in a collection of letters written to a friend over a period of almost half a century

Louis Untermeyer's editing of Robert Frost's letters, written to him over a span of forty-seven years, is important for two reasons. First, the collection tells the story of a warm personal and literary friendship between two men who did much to advance the cause of modern verse when it was new, Untermeyer through his anthologies that helped to promote the study of contemporary poets in the schools, Frost by his poems and his example, the purity of his devotion to the idea that poetry was worth a lifetime of dedication and effort. Second, the book presents an unretouched self-portrait of Frost as only those who knew him best ever saw him, a figure often sharply at odds with the public image

of the farmer-poet and cracker-barrel pragmatist that Frost himself helped to shape with Yankee shrewdness and playful delight in the contrarieties of men and things.

Perhaps the most remarkable aspect of this friendship was its duration, the longest of its kind in the history of literature. For writers, by and large, are an ungenerous, suspicious lot. Too often they are brought together by ties that prove only temporary—sudden enthusiasms, literary fashions, mutual admiration, or concern for some plight in which they find themselves or see their fellows—and they are likely to be swept apart just as suddenly by the abrasions and stings of their professional lives. The history of friendship

152

among writers is a long, sad story of misunderstanding, rivalry, grudges, betrayal. But the relationship of Frost and Untermeyer was one of respect and trust from the start. These letters show how much relish, good nature, loyalty, and healthy prejudice formed an unshakable bond between the poet and the anthologist, men of different backgrounds but common interests. This is not to say that all was harmony and admiration over the years. Always protective of his own art, Frost became convinced that Untermeyer was giving to criticism time that would have been better spent in the writing of poetry, and he spoke up in protest: "That's another thing I oppose in you. You just deliberately lose yourself in the ruck of Phelpses and all. . . . But it's foolish and it's dangerous. You should know better what you are after. For my part I live in fear lest I shall get so I can't tell politics and criticism from the warmth that called and clasped me to my kind. It wouldn't hurt you to cultivate the same fear in yourself." Nettled by Untermeyer's involvement in leftist causes, he administered another rebuke: "Why when you can write poetry like Jerusalem Delivered will you continue to mess with the Masses (or is it mass with the messes)?" On another occasion we find him subtly defending his own conservatism and skepticism: "You want to blow the candle to see if it won't give more light. All right, let me hold the candle so you can give it all your attention to blowing it carefully so as not to blow it out. And let me hold the matches too so that if you should blow it out we could form a society to relight it." Touches like these give the letters their human cast and feeling.

As Mr. Untermeyer recalls, his first awareness of Frost was seeing his name signed to "The Fear" and "A Hundred Collars," published in *Poetry and Drama*, a new quarterly issued from Harold Monro's Poetry Bookshop, in London, in 1913. Reading them, he was puzzled by the un-British effect of style and theme, so different from the prevalent patterns of Georgian verse then popular in England. In spite of their universality of theme, the poems seemed to him alien in idiom and scene, more in keeping with American speech and a New England setting. Later Lascelles Abercrombie informed him that Frost was an American living in England. His interest aroused, Untermeyer secured a copy of *North of Boston* when Frost's American publisher brought that book over from England. Untermeyer's review appeared in the Chicago *Evening Post* about the same time that Amy Lowell reviewed the poems in *The New Republic*. These two notices of his second volume greeted Frost when he returned with his family from England in 1915.

This review marked the beginning of their friendship. Frost's first letter, dated March 22, 1915, and written in reply to one from Untermeyer, declared: "There's not a person in New York I should have more pleasure in meeting than Louis Untermeyer." A month later Frost's tone had become more open and outgoing: "You see so well the necessity of our being generous to each other as fellow artists. I probably don't deserve all your praise, but you'll never be the poorer for having uttered it, and trust my enemies to discount it where it needs discounting." By the fall of that year they were calling each other by their first names and Frost was writing: "You mustn't be so intellectual with me. I shan't be at ease till we are on emotional terms where there is no more controversy neither is there any danger of crediting one or the other with more or less than we mean. . . . We shan't mean anything too profoundly much except perhaps that we are friends and nothing else matters between friends. That is the only sincerity: all else is an approximation."

It is easy to say now—and a few have suggested it, in the light of what happened later—that Frost was playing a far-sighted game of literary politics when he courted Untermeyer's friendship and favor. Certainly no one did more, except the poet himself, to establish Frost's reputation and keep his name before the public. As these letters reveal, Frost was a master of strategy in ploys of this kind, and on a number of occasions Untermeyer was a willing ally who used his friend's poetry to set standards or to batter lesser talents. But at the time of their meeting Untermeyer had not begun to compile the anthologies in which Frost came to figure so prominently. He was, in fact, a man trying to live in two worlds, that of business represented by his family's jewelry firm, and poetry. Perhaps Frost, trying to divide his time between writing, teaching, and farming, saw in Untermeyer's case a situation and a calculated risk similar to his own. Perhaps, too, Frost needed the reassurance that friendly support and helpful criticism could give. After his return from England he never lacked for fame, but there were times when he apparently doubted his ability to continue on the road he was traveling. For one thing, A Boy's Will and North of Boston had contained

poems written as early as twenty years before. "I tell you, Louis, it's all over at thirty," he wrote in 1916; he was then forty-two. "The poet in me died nearly ten years ago. . . . The calf I was in the nineties I merely take to market. I am become my own salesman." But Frost was also right when he said that he could "unfold as a personality at discretion," as he continued to do for almost half a century to come. There is nothing in these letters to cast reflections on Frost's sincerity or the value he placed on Untermeyer's friendship and help. In 1941 he wrote: "You know how I am about your Anthology. Being in it I look on [it] as having done more to spread my poetry than any other thing. I here put it in writing so I can't go back on it however our respective stocks may go on the market of the future." And in 1947 he wrote this: "No friend has ever released me to such letter writing."

These letters tell us a great deal about the life of art and the imagination, but much that was personal or crucial in the lives of the two men must be read between the lines or learned from the editor's notes and explanations. We get some knowledge, for instance, of Untermeyer's domestic crises, his marriages and divorces, his activities as an editor and lecturer, his own career as a farmer. And we see, though indirectly, how much of Frost's life was lived under the shadow of tragedies that would have destroyed a man without the gift of serenity in the face of all disaster. Events that shook his private life (the madness of his sister, the death of one daughter in childbirth, the tragic end of another, the insanity and suicide of his son, the sudden death of the wife whom he called "the unspoken half of everything I wrote") found no more than indirect expression in his poems. Only once or twice did he break out in bitter protest or, as at the time of his son's death, confession of failure. The man who learned to draw a sharp line between griefs and grievances confirmed in his poetry his belief that the experiences which move us most in the writer's personal life must in his work "be kept away down under the surface where the great griefs belong." "You've lost—time, if nothing else," he wrote. "I've lost. We've all lost. Having admitted that, let's say no more on the subject."

Fiction, drama, and most poems are the fables of man pretending, living in and expressing himself through the imagination; their symbol is the *persona*. History and biography are the record of man reporting. Letters are the voice of man speaking and as such the most direct and accessible of all literary forms. But their value, as has been pointed out, lies in the liveliness of their detail, the depth of their insights, and above all the imprudence of those who write them. Frost passes these tests successfully but in a manner so unmistakably his own that he stands apart from other writers with whose letters we are already familiar. He does not put us in the presence of an overwhelming personality, as in the case of D. H. Lawrence, whose letters seem to smolder and glow inwardly with the spirit of a visionary who is trying to reorder the world. Unlike Thomas Wolfe he does not substitute communication for the confessional as if his salvation depended on the ability to get everything down on paper. He does not, like Sherwood Anderson, make letter-writing an extension of his creative life, mixing fact and fantasy.

He lacks the large and generous vision which makes Keats's letters a rich commentary on life and art. He is not a conscious stylist in the way of writers who seem to be addressing posterity, not their friends. What we find in Frost's letters is the same working of mind and mood displayed in his poetry. Usually he begins with some observed or experienced fact and then proceeds, by puns, paradox, or metaphorical flight, to strip away layer after layer of meaning until the essence of things is bared. Whether his topic is poetry, politics, or education, he is completely ruthless in the process, with little regard for anyone who may be hurt along the way. Untermeyer comes close to the heart of this book when he says that Frost's admirers regarded him as "a benevolent, sweet, serene, and almost saintly person. He was none of these," Untermeyer adds; "he was proud, troubled, and frankly jealous."

He was also, on occasion, considerate and compassionate, but never toward other writers whom he regarded as rivals threatening his own poetic eminence or talents he considered unworthy of respect. He was harshest toward Edgar Lee Masters. The wordplay in the characteristic phrase "demolition of the masters" is only one gibe cast in the direction of the poet whose *Spoon River Anthology* had been a popular and critical success in 1915, the year in which Frost, also eager for fame, returned to America. Pound becomes the "Greater Garbler," a poet presenting "scraps of minor classics in Greek and Latin, but not a single idea of his own." Conrad Aiken is called "Comrad Aching" in one of the letters. Frost complains that "Anyone sharp enough to discover Archie Mc-

Leish's ruffled rhymes in all his archaeology ought to be able to find mine." Elinor Wylie receives his grudging admiration, for the wrong reason: "She was self-conscious artist enough to see her appointed task. It was to make a false heart ring false." The same attitude of prejudice and suspicion kept him from meeting Walter de la Mare and caused him to state that other respected poets were overrated. Yet he was capable of giving a helping hand to young poets, as he did to Merrill Root and Robert Francis. And late in his life he was influential in effecting Pound's release from St. Elizabeth's.

This pettiness in Frost, a cranky airing of personal grievances by a poet so conscious of pain and conditioned to human grief that he regarded his poetry as no more than "a momentary stay against confusion," is balanced in these letters by something more indicative of his real stature. Running through them is a spirit of play—with words, with ideas, with the awful imponderables of death and immortality. For play was a necessary condition of his life as well as of his art; it was another of his momentary stays against chaos. This playfulness may take the form of outrageous puns, verbal juggling with possibilities of determinism and choice, or the elaboration of an image shaped to the dimensions of inescapable truth. Frost had a metaphor for this kind of meaningful foolery. It is style:

I am not satisfied to let it go with the aphorism that the style is the man. The man's ideas would be some element then of his style. So would his deeds. But I would narrow the definition. His deeds are his deeds; his ideas are his ideas. His style is the way he carries himself toward his ideas and deeds. . . .

The style is out of his superfluity. It is the mind skating circles round itself as it moves forward.

Play, to Frost, was an attitude and act of grace, the spirit of give and take with which he accepted the facts of human weakness and mortality. It was, as Thoreau might have said, his armor against eternity. Frost called it his "lover's quarrel with the world."

Also characteristic of Frost is the way in which he made his letters a testing ground for his poems and those infrequent utterances on poetry he used to illuminate his public readings. The collection contains about three dozen poems, some old, some new, apparently sent to Untermeyer for comment or possible inclusion in the anthologies. A few are examples of his poetic foolery: a limerick, a parody of Vachel Lindsay, some nonsense verse, and several short pieces—reported—streaked with bawdry. (In Frost, as in Yeats, a strain of coarseness broadened in his old age.) Most of the poems were later printed, some with revisions or different titles, in his published volumes. A half dozen or so have never been included in any of his books. One is a poem on a religious theme of which three versions are given; perhaps Frost felt that he had never found its final form. Another is a long poem of 186 lines, written as a letter to Untermeyer in 1944, in which Frost was trying to explain, with a mingling of the whimsical and the sincere, his attitude of non-participation during World War II. Although the poem contains much that is purely personal, it deserves a place in his collected works because of the insight it offers to his stubborn conservatism and his individualistic refusal to enlist in any war, whether of politics or of class.

But in Frost things always went by contradictions. He was also the poet who wrote "The Gift Outright." As for his statements on poetry, they still ring true, unstaled by familiarity or frequent quotation in other men's books, because they are the pith without the theorizing of his poetic vision and practice.

This book makes plain what we knew all along but seldom said: that dark shapes move in the Sophoclean gloom at the heart of Frost's poetic world, beneath the outward serenity and natural simplicities of his verse. The dark woods are as much a part of that world as the pasture spring chang- ing from cloudy to clear. And he himself was not a simple, ordinary man uncommonly versed in country things and the bafflement in human nature. He was a person of deep and strange complexes, strong prejudices, wild moods, quirky insights. He despaired of finding absolutes in man or his society, but he continued to ask questions. He was a remarkable man and a remarkable writer. This book does not tell the complete story or present the full-length portrait, but it reveals an important part of both, in letters frankly written and honestly edited.

Dayton Kohler

THE LIBERATOR
William Lloyd Garrison

Author: John L. Thomas (1924-   )
Publisher: Little, Brown and Company (Boston). Illustrated. 502 pp. $8.50
Type of work: Social history
Time: 1798-1873
Locale: The United States

The definitive biography of William Lloyd Garrison and of his struggle to obliterate the social and moral evils in nineteenth century America

Principal personages:
    WILLIAM LLOYD GARRISON, editor of the *Liberator*
    HELLEN BENSON GARRISON, his wife
    WENDELL PHILLIPS,
    THEODORE WELD, and
    BENJAMIN LUNDY, Abolitionist leaders

The most recent study of William Lloyd Garrison, one of the most controversial figures in the reform movements of the nineteenth century, is a brilliant and penetrating analysis of the thoughts and actions of this great protagonist in his struggle for human rights. Professor Thomas evaluates his subject fairly and objectively in the setting of Garrison's life-span rather than by the ethical standards of today.

Early childhood weighed heavily in the formation of the personality and attitudes of the earliest spokesman of the reform movement in New England. William Lloyd Garrison was the son of an alcoholic father and a domineering mother who bordered upon religious fanaticism. The father made little or no positive impact upon Gar-

157

rison, for he deserted his rather large family before the boy could scarcely walk. All Garrison could learn of his father was through his mother, and she constantly instructed him to guard against his father's weaknesses for demon rum and tobacco. As a result of the influence of his mother, he was more comfortable in the company of strong-willed women than in the company of men.

The future editor of the *Liberator* was almost completely self-educated, and he was able to become an editor only because he struggled diligently, while serving as a printer's apprentice, to overcome his lack of formal education. As soon as he had completed his apprenticeship, Garrison became an editorial writer in Newburyport, Massachusetts. Because he was a conservative Federalist, his political views were in complete agreement with those held by the people of the community. However, the young journalist was not satisfied to remain an editorial assistant; more than anything else he wanted a newspaper of his own. Using borrowed money, Garrison bought the Newburyport *Free Press*. As editor and printer of the paper he began to attack such evils as Sabbath-breaking, free thought, dueling, prostitution, theater-going, and drinking. The newspaper failed six months after Garrison became editor, and he left for Boston immediately thereafter.

In Boston, although he was not too well received, he became active in the Abolitionist crusade. He met Benjamin Lundy and other leaders of the movement who aided him in solidifying his own views on slavery. From Boston he went to Baltimore to serve as an editorial assistant on Lundy's periodical, *The Genius of Universal Emancipa-*

tion. After the two encountered trouble in Baltimore, Garrison returned to Boston, where he again became associated with the leading Abolitionists of the city. Shortly after his return, with the aid of friends and borrowed equipment, he began a newspaper which would ultimately bring fame and success. The *Liberator* was dedicated to the immediate abolition of Negro slavery by every possible means. A perfect example of the aims, attitude, and crusading spirit of the editor is the statement printed on January 1, 1831:

I will be as harsh as truth, and as uncompromising as justice. On this subject, I do not wish to think, or speak, or write, with moderation. No! No! Tell a man whose house is on fire to give a moderate alarm; tell him to moderately rescue his wife from the hands of the ravisher; tell the mother to gradually extricate the child from the fire into which it has fallen;—but urge me not to use moderation in a cause like the present. I am in earnest—I will not equivocate—I will not excuse—I will not retreat a single inch—and I will be heard.

The circulation of the *Liberator* was quite limited, as only four hundred copies of this edition were published. However, Garrison received much publicity, and before long the *Liberator* was known in every section of the country, even though most of the people in Boston and New England disapproved of his editorials and refused to buy the paper. In time he came to be one of the men most hated and feared by the planter class in the South. But the *Liberator* received far more credit than was actually due it. Garrison was blamed for supplying the catalyst which started the Nat Turner slave revolt in South Hampton County, Virginia, at a time when not a single issue

158

of the *Liberator* was circulated in the South.

Garrison admitted that the *Liberator* was primarily a Negro journal because Negroes were his main financial supporters. In addition to Negro subscribers, there was a small group of white supporters. Most of these belonged to Quaker or other religious groups which condemned slavery, but there was a small group of wealthy supporters as well. Garrison depended upon placing the *Liberator* in strategic locations rather than on large-scale circulation. Before the end of his first year he was utilizing more than a hundred exchanges which insured wide-spread publicity. Southern editors found the organ highly offensive, and it was outlawed in many Southern states.

Garrison began to achieve notoriety. The Georgia Legislature offered a reward of five thousand dollars to anyone who would cause the arrest and trial of Garrison in Georgia. Numerous persons wrote him letters which included threats on his life. Senator Robert Y. Hayne wrote to the mayor of Boston asking that the *Liberator* be suppressed immediately. This act aided the cause greatly, for many people who had shown little inclination toward the anti-slavery cause came to believe that it was a struggle to prevent the loss of the basic freedoms.

Although Garrison had gained popularity, he still had to supplement the meager contributions if his journal was to survive. He began an attempt to raise funds by accepting engagements to speak in public. In addition, on November 13, 1831, the New England Anti-Slavery Society was formed in the hope that funds could be procured from its members. Even though both ideas achieved some success, the *Liber-*

ator was plagued with financial problems until shortly before the Civil War.

The year 1833 was a turning point with Garrison. He journeyed to England, where he was accepted by Bishop Wilberforce and the English Abolitionists as the leading American Abolitionist. Upon his return to the United States he became associated with such leaders of the American movement as Arthur Tappan, Theodore Weld, the Grimpke sisters, Benjamin Lundy, Theodore Parker, and Elizur Wright. It was with this group that Garrison helped to found the American Anti-Slavery Society.

Although Garrison continued to work with this group, he was disliked by most. One cause of controversy between the reformers was Garrison's demand that women be permitted to enjoy the same political and social rights that were extended to the male population. Additional strife was created because Garrison refused to support candidates or political parties, such as the Liberty Party or Free Soil Party, in an effort to achieve the aims set forth by the various Abolitionist societies. His refusal to permit his followers to utilize the ballot to achieve his goals was based upon his belief that politicians were corrupt and that all political parties, fighting sham battles for votes, had no real interest in seeing any reforms accomplished. He maintained this attitude until Abraham Lincoln issued the Emancipation Proclamation in 1863, at which time Garrison instructed his followers to support the Republican Party.

Living in a nation which permitted the institution of slavery to exist so embittered Garrison that he eventually destroyed a copy of the Declaration of

Independence and a copy of the Constitution. In this ceremony he declared himself no longer a citizen of a republic which would not abolish slavery. However, after the Civil War many people began to honor him as the first great leader of the Abolitionist movement. As a result, before he died, he achieved mass popularity.

The Liberator offers deep insight to the tensions and stresses of a decisive period of American history.

J. Perry Cochran

THE LITTLE GIRLS

Author: Elizabeth Bowen (1899-   )
Publisher: Alfred A. Knopf (New York). 307 pp. $4.95
Type of work: Novel
Time: The present
Locale: England

The ironic comedy of an elderly widow's search for lost time

Principal characters:
DINAH DELACROIX ("DICEY"), a poetically whimsical widow
SHEILA ARTWORTH ("SHEIKIE"), Dinah's former schoolmate
CLARE BURKIN-JONES ("MUMBO"), a fashion entrepreneur, the third of the schoolmate friends
MAJOR FRANK WILKINS, Dinah's elderly devotee
MAJOR BURKIN-JONES, Clare's father
MRS. CORAL, Dinah's hospitable neighbor
FRANCIS, a curious servant
WILLIAM and
ROLAND DELACROIX, the sons of Mrs. Delacroix

It is customary to assert that Elizabeth Bowen is possibly the greatest living English woman novelist in the tradition of Henry James and Virginia Woolf, and in several respects the comparison is a just one. Like Henry James and Mrs. Woolf, Miss Bowen teaches us a very genuine respect for the idea of tradition, for a social order which is a source of individual tribulation and frustration often, but which is nevertheless the custodian of important values still cherished by the person of discriminating sensibility. Throughout her career as a writer, Miss Bowen has been the leading exponent in modern British fiction of the intuitions of the feminine mind and of the sensibilities of the heart, and she has given her readers such wonderfully vivid and understanding portraits of feminine character as Karen Michaelis in *The House in Paris* and Stella Rodney in *The Heat of the Day*, composed in that fluent, subtle, poetic style which to some readers seems so admirable and to others so artificial, convolute, needlessly oblique in its syntax. In this novel the style is less mannered, more direct and colloquial, although not wholly without the characteristic double negatives and odd placement of the adverb: ". . . he sickened with love at the sight of his little daughter duly. . . ."

Her style, nevertheless, is one of the important means by which Miss Bowen gives her distinctive poetic perceptions "shape," by which she transforms so-

160

cial reality to a personal vision of some significant moral and imaginative pattern. She has defined the novel as a "non-poetic statement of a poetic truth," and often in her work this poetic truth resides in the revelation to her romantic heroines of the grave disparity between their absolute ideals and the living if corrupting reality of social experience. In the present work Miss Bowen has seemingly moved away from the persistent theme of the earlier novels, the trauma of innocent adolescence committed to a dream of love which leaves the heroine terribly vulnerable to the incursions of a tawdry milieu, but the attentive reader will nevertheless perceive a not unfamiliar pattern emerging in the plot: a protagonist widowed and unfulfilled in marriage pursuing an impossible romantic desire, not this time for ideal love, but for a meaningful relationship to the past, in E. M. Forster's sense of "only connect." After Dinah Delacroix, the protagonist, a widow living in Sussex, in a flash of recollection recalls a schoolgirl prank in which she and two friends were accomplices, she attempts to rediscover her friends and achieve the restoration of those tenuous links of adolescent affection and devotion with the companions from whom she has been separated for nearly fifty years.

The inspiration for this search for lost time comes from Dinah Delacroix's idiosyncratic undertaking (with her attentive bachelor friend, Major Frank Wilkins) to seal up in a neighboring cave a number of favorite objects expressive of the individual peculiarities of her friends, to be discovered by some far future race with "shattering" inferences as to the nature of these individual personalities which will sur-

vive the rigors of archeological research. Dinah has the sudden realization that she has somehow done all this before, a *déjà vu* experience. During the summer when she was eleven, in 1914, she and her two friends Sheila Beaker ("Sheikie") and Clare Birkin-Jones ("Mumbo"), fellow students at St. Agatha's in Southstone, had buried a coffer in the garden containing "secret" precious things and a ritualistic warning against disturbance, written in an "Unknown Language." Dinah undertakes to find her friends again by sending intimate and embarrassing notices to all the metropolitan papers. Sheila has been for years Mrs. Trevor Artworth, wife of the chief real estate broker of Southstone, and Clare, married and divorced, is again Birkin-Jones and owner of a chain of smart "Mopsie-Pye" shops. The three friends are once more united at Dinah's Sussex home, but Dinah finds her old schoolmates morose, aggrieved, and uncomprehending of her motives. Dig up that coffer again? Absurd. Besides, St. Agatha had "copped" it during a German raid in 1940, and it was no more. Nothing, that is, remained of that past; as Clare remarks, quoting *The Tempest*, "Into thin air."

In Part II the narrative shifts to the distant past of 1914; this section is most entertainingly written, and if the novel is to be· regarded as comedy, much of that aspect is here in the depiction of the vibrant, tempestuous relationships of the girls, in their remorseless scrutiny of each other which still survives during the Sussex reunion, and in the adventurous and hilarious plotting to secure and bury the coffer. Here Miss Bowen is at her best in catching the subtle overtones of the relationships of the parents and their children, the unspoken love of Major Birkin-Jones (killed at Mons, August 23, 1914) for Dicey's mother, Mrs. Piggott, the suggestion that Mrs. Piggott was perhaps being "kept" by her mother's cousin in Feverel Cottage, so redolent of English tradition and prewar security. The beach picnic in honor of Olive Pocock, turned twelve on 23 July, 1914, closes the section with an elegiac and nostalgic note— Dicey's parting from Mumbo and Sheikie for nearly fifty years.

The chief incident in Part III is the return of the three "revenants" to the garden at Southstone, now on a private estate, and their discovery that the coffer contains nothing of the past. When Clare refuses to yield to Dinah's pleas to stay with her in Sussex, the climax is reached in Dinah's attempted suicide (so we interpret the reference to Macbeth and Dinah's remark that she was "her father's child"; he had committed suicide).

It is part of the understanding of this book to see that to Miss Bowen Dinah Delacroix is an introverted romanticist characterized by a cloistered nostalgia for the past, in futile pursuit of its venerable security. "Life works to dispossess the dead," the author remarks in A World of Love, and this is evidently the interpretation of the book jacket of The Little Girls, where the novel is described as "anti-nostalgic," "a cautionary tale." Nevertheless, to accept without careful qualification this reading of the novel is to overlook the subtlety of Miss Bowen's ironic and compassionate sympathy for a character's search for self-fulfillment and personal identity. There are evidences of Dinah's gradual disillusionment throughout this part of the novel. Her contemplation in Sheila's home of the

watercolor of the long vanished picturesque High Street of Southstone concludes with the remark, "It might be better to have no picture of places which are gone. Let them go completely." That she has reached this resolution of her yearning for identity with the past seems evident in the last lines of the novel:

Turning to go, she thought of her last sight of the sands, from the sea wall: the wide sands and the running figure.

"Goodbye, Dicey," she said—for now and for then.

The sleeper stirred. She sighed. She raised herself on an elbow, saying, "Who's there?"

"Mumbo."

"Not Mumbo, Clare. Clare, where have you been?"

The last lines are comparable to the much disputed ending of The World of Love, wherein Jane, like Dinah, emerges from her commitment to the past; the parting on the sands at the picnic many years ago becomes symbolic of the separations and disjunctions that life sets up for human frustration.

In a very real sense, there is the artist in Miss Bowen sympathizing, nevertheless, with the artist in Dinah, who refuses to accept the possibility that the life of the individual is unmeaning, without connection, aimless lived through inconsequential fortuities and "prefabricated feelings" of the social environment. However mistaken the individual may be in his illusion, however tragic the consequences, it must be embraced; otherwise, as Dinah mumbles at the discovery of her attempted suicide, "It's all gone, was it ever there? . . . Nothing, No, no, no." In such a context, the despairing allusions to Macbeth (a less obtrusive

162

device here than in Virginia Woolf's fiction) become symbolic: " 'All is the fear, and nothing is the love'—that's *Macbeth*." Miss Bowen makes in her correspondence with Graham Greene a comment very pertinent here: "Even stories . . . which comment on or are pointers to futility, imply that men and women are too big or good for the futility. . . ." It is difficult to find such preoccupations with the tension and irony created by the mysterious incompatibility of ideals with reality either trivial, or snobbish, or sentimental.

John P. Kirby

THE LIVING SEA

Author: Jacques-Yves Cousteau (1910-   ), with James Dugan
Publisher: Harper and Row (New York). Illustrated. 325 pp. $6.50
Type of work: Natural-science narrative

A poetically written account of exploration of the sea and its bottom by the author, his crew members, and fellow scientists, operating first from the ship Calypso *and later in the "Diving Saucer"*

Captain Jacques-Yves Cousteau is not a meticulous scientist. For instance, he throws out the old theory that sharks lack maneuverability because one swam straight at him while he was skin-diving, swerved at the last instant, and took off in another direction; such inductive reasoning from only one example will make a plodding researcher grind his teeth. Neither is M. Cousteau (with James Dugan) a dramatic, climactic writer. While the development of the Diving Saucer may seem a great climax to oceanographers, it is no peak of excitement for the reader. And so eager is the author to be always slightly beyond the frontier in ocean science that he sometimes presents his material unfairly; when he writes about experiments in bioluminescence, he makes the reader feel that this, too, is a field never probed before, whereas chemists and others have been working intently on what the layman incorrectly calls phosphorescence for at least thirty years. It is also evident that Cousteau has never, flashlight in hand, been on an old-fashioned American bullfrog hunt: he is startled that a bright light can hypnotize a fish. But when all these trivial grievances are cast into the sea (where they belong), Cousteau —wearing, of course, the Aqua-Lung that he invented—pops up from the waves as a Poseidon among scientific writers. *The Living Sea* is a marvelous book.

Dryly stated, this handsome volume is an account of Captain Cousteau's adventures, assignments, discoveries, and just plain old jobs aboard the oceanographic vessel *Calypso* from 1951 to 1960. Most of the narrative takes place on or in the Earth's Last Frontier, the bottom of the sea, and some readers may find the prospect seems drear; but this prospect is brightened considerably by some twenty-four pages of magnificent color photographs, sixty-four pages of black-and-white photos, a map, and several attractive line drawings. These might be the accouterments of any good travel and adventure book, however, and the real thing that sets *The Living Sea* apart from similar works is its style, its colorful and sometimes lyrical use of words. Here is a sample:

> The coral took unexpected shapes and hues. There were skulls of dwarfs and giants; tufts of ohre and magenta mingled with petrified mauve bushes and red tubiporae fabricated like honeycombs. Superb parasols of acropora spread over idling fish that were painted with electric pigments of red and gold. Through this splendid tilted forest humpbacked sea snails traveled their winding ways. In reef recesses there were enough tridacna clams to furnish fonts for the churches of Christendom. Their shells were ajar, displaying swollen mantles painted like the lips of harlots.

Such descriptions send you scurrying not only to the unabridged dictionary but also to your sporting-goods store for the latest in Aqua-Lungs. Cousteau chooses words delightfully and wittily: note those harlots lounging so close to the fonts of Christendom.

The Living Sea contains plenty of excitement. One of the best episodes comes early in the narrative. The divers on the *Calypso* (they are all skin divers, of course; Cousteau is somewhat rough on what he calls hard-hat divers) decide to bring to the sea's surface the wreck of a Greek merchant vessel of the third century B.C. They have located the wreck in the Mediterranean at a depth of 130 feet, about ten miles from Marseilles. Cousteau skillfully presents the difficulties and the thrills of the operation. The freighter's cargo was chiefly amphorae (wine jars), both Grecian and Roman. Costeau resists the temptation to heighten the archaeological excitement when he almost casually mentions taking a sip or two from an undamaged amphora; not many writers would make

so little of a draft of what must be some of the world's most patiently aged wine.

Aside from what is revealed about Cousteau's own intriguing, ambivalent personality (proud, yet modest; poetic, yet scientific; brave, yet prudent), *The Living Sea* is short on human characterization, but the sea itself is, of course, the main character, and although its surface has been magnificently handled by many great writers, we are lucky that one of the earliest and best probers of its coral reefs, its wrecks, its bottoms, its weird and fascinating inhabitants is the free-swimming, keen-eyed Cousteau. Almost every book has a clown in it somewhere. There is one in *The Living Sea* also, and he (or she) turns out to be Cousteau's most charmingly developed character, Ulysses the grouper. The grouper is not a rare fish, but Ulysses is a rare grouper. He makes friends with the divers from the *Calypso* when they are on an expedition to the Seychelles, the Isles of Return, in the Indian Ocean north of Madagascar. While the divers are feeding and studying other fish, Ulysses gets so much in the way that he has to be caged. He is obviously petulant, then furious. The story of the grouper covers two stops of the *Calypso* in the Seychelles; the second part is a tale of grief and suspense, but ends happily, as should all stories about friendly, if bumbling, creatures.

The development of the Diving Saucer, told about with enthusiasm near the end of the book, is also filled with trouble and suspense. The Saucer can go deeper than free divers with lights; and apparently the deeper one goes the more beautiful the sea becomes. "Now the Diving Saucer," says Cousteau, "had placed us among the

164

most elegant chromatics of them all. About us the living forms were tinted suave pink, mauve, and white, with touches of lemon yellow." There is battery trouble, however, on an early dive of this new "ship"; but this story, like Ulysses', ends happily with the use of more conventional batteries and the improvement of electrical circuits. Cousteau leaves us with the feeling he has just begun to explore the ocean depths.

The Living Sea is filled with many unforgettable episodes: the tremendous leaps of dolphins in the Arabian Sea; the sounding of sperm whales as seen from under water (not even Captain Ahab ever saw that amazing spectacle); the accidental mangling of a baby whale by the propellers of the Calypso. Captain Cousteau is so stimulated by the unknown challenges of the ocean that his enthusiasm spills like salt water on the layman and the landlubber. One feat that he is very proud of is the firm anchoring of the Calypso above the Romanche Trench in the Atlantic. This record anchoring took five and one-half miles of braided nylon cable to hold his ship to the ocean floor some 24,600 feet below.

Readers of The Living Sea may find it difficult to resist using a phrase of Cousteau's that describes a dangerous emotional ailment of divers, for the term applies equally well to the pleasurable effect of this book: the rapture of the deep.

Preston Newman

LORD BYRON'S WIFE

Author: Malcolm Elwin (1902-   )
Publisher: Harcourt, Brace and World (New York). 556 pp. $8.75
Type of work: Biography
Time: 1792-1860
Locale: England

A fully documented biography of the wife of the famous poet and a detailed study of the break-up of her marriage

Principal personages:
    LADY BYRON (nee Anne Isabella Milbanke)
    LORD BYRON, her husband
    AUGUSTA ADA BYRON, their daughter
    SIR RALPH AND LADY MILBANKE (later Noel), Lady Byron's parents
    THE HON. AUGUSTA LEIGH, Byron's half sister
    LADY CAROLINE LAMB, Byron's mistress
    LADY MELBOURNE, Byron's confidante

The publication in 1961 of Doris Langley Moore's The Late Lord Byron and the ensuing controversy that raged for months in the staid columns of the London Times Literary Supplement demonstrate that the Byron mystery refuses to die. So here we have yet another book, the heart of which is that perennial question: what really caused the separation of Lord and Lady Byron that rocked London society in 1815-1816? Once again there has been a flood of interpretations and reinterpretations of the letters and remarks of these long-dead people.

The opening, for the first time, to

165

scholars of the vast accumulation of Byron papers assembled by the poet's grandson, the second Earl of Lovelace, and now in the possession of the Earl of Lytton, has made possible this revival of the mystery. The papers had been used by members of the family; and, indeed, the mere history of their use, involving family loyalties and feuds, sympathies and antipathies, presents to the reader, unless he be a Byron specialist, an almost impenetrable labyrinth. Mrs. Moore and now Mr. Elwin are the first outsiders to be given access to all of these documents. As a result, we know a vast deal more about the day-by-day happenings in that tempestuous ménage in Piccadilly. But has the heart of this mystery been at last plucked out?

The flamboyance of Byron's personality, even more than his fame as a poet, has tended to push his wife into a somewhat minor role in the story of his life. He dominates the scene; she appears and disappears in accordance with the waxing and waning of her relations with him. Yet she had a life both before and after her brief marriage. The present volume, then, is a full-length attempt to present this life and to view the fatal marriage somewhat more from her side of the story. The almost unbelievable mass of documents that she preserved—sometimes as many as twelve letters a day—is the basis for the book.

Her father was Sir Ralph Milbanke, the sixth baronet, whose sister, for whom Byron had the greatest fondness, was Lady Melbourne, mother of the future Prime Minister, whose wife, in turn, was the notorious Lady Caroline Lamb. The Duchess of Devonshire called Milbanke "old twaddle Ralph," but his portrait by Reynolds

shows a man with an interesting, almost handsome face. He was well-to-do and had a small but respectable political career. Anne Isabella's mother was the Hon. Judith Noel, a name which her husband took in 1815 in accordance with the will of Judith's brother, Lord Wentworth, so that the reader must adjust himself to the fact that the parents were called Noel after that date. Byron's feelings towards his mother-in-law can be judged from a comment, in 1821, in a letter to Augusta Leigh, that ". . . the old b——h will live forever because she is so amiable and useful." He always blamed Lady Milbanke for the breakup of his marriage.

Annabella, as the future Lady Byron was called, from a contraction of her two Christian names, had the usual upbringing of a daughter in an aristocratic family of that period. But two important facts emerge: she was the only child of rather elderly parents —both her father and mother were past forty when she was born—and she was intolerably spoiled. Whatever its other failings may have been, the spoiling of children was not among the weaknesses of Regency society. She seems to have been somewhat less than attractive: indulged, precocious, and from early childhood convinced that she could never be wrong in anything. One of her older friends referred to her as an "icicle." She went through two London seasons without attracting any great number of suitors. And then an ironic destiny caused her path to cross that of Byron.

The history of their meeting, their courtship, and their marriage has long been well known in its larger outlines, though never before has it been so thoroughly documented. It was inevitable that the two should meet, for the London society of those days was small, and everyone knew everyone else. Byron, in spite of his gaucherie, was a social lion at the time. He had already published the first parts of *Childe Harold* and had engaged in a hectic affair with Lady Caroline Lamb. Annabella met him in April of 1812. He felt free to marry, for the possible sale of Newstead Abbey promised a solution of his financial difficulties. These were great, for Byron was even more careless of money than was the usual young nobleman of the period. But to his surprise and, perhaps, relief, Miss Milbanke refused him, and he plunged into an affair with Lady Oxford. The period from July of 1813 to September of 1814 the author calls "Annabella in pursuit." Having rejected the lion of London society, the fashionable poet, the great lover, she changed her mind and began the game of luring him back. She succeeded all too well; he returned and was accepted in September of 1814, and in December he "reluctantly" traveled north for his wedding, loitering on the way. The fatal marriage was solemnized on January 2, 1815.

Here the reader may pause to consider the question of why such an unlikely marriage ever took place, for surely no more ill-suited couple could be imagined: a temperamental, undisciplined rake with a gift for poetry wedded to a solemn, humorless puritan with a gift for mathematics. Why did he ever marry her or she him? The answer is perhaps not too obscure: like all dissipated men, he was attracted by a woman who was the opposite of the sensual mistresses he had known; like all women, she had the ambition to reform a profligate and

the conviction that she could do so. Such marriages have been countless and have inevitably ended in disaster; this one has become famous because of the fame of the husband.

The largest part of the present volume deals with the brief period of April to December of 1815, during which the Byrons were living in a much too expensive house in Piccadilly. Because of the vast documentation that has now become available, we can follow the events in this miniature lunatic asylum day by day, even at times hour by hour. It was an incredible scene: duns at the door, Byron deeply involved with the affairs of Drury Lane Theatre and with brandy, the birth of Augusta Ada, whom he called "sole daughter of my house and heart." Finding the situation intolerable, Annabella investigated the possibility of having Byron declared insane; failing in this attempt, she left him forever on January 15, 1816. But—and this is one of the strangest events in this strange affair—she wrote him an affectionate letter from her parents' home, so that the subsequent news that she had gone for good came as the greater shock to him.

Then followed the terribly involved legal question of the separation. By leaving her husband, Lady Byron had put herself in an awkward position. Divorce in those days, though possible, was not easy; it could be granted only by the ecclesiastic court, and to appear before that tribunal would mean the presentation of evidence that might prove extremely embarrassing to the parties involved. On the other hand, since Annabella had deserted Byron, the possibility always existed that he might successfully claim custody of the child, a possibility that she regarded with horror. So there was a vast amount of maneuvering in an attempt to manipulate Byron into agreeing to a legal separation without a divorce, while well-intentioned friends were trying for a reconciliation. Byron was finally worn down; the decree of separation was signed, and, on April 25, 1816, he left England forever, in the midst of a scandal that, obviously, has not subsided after nearly a hundred and fifty years.

The great mystery, of course, has always been: what was the real cause of the separation? From 1816 until her death in 1860, Lady Byron devoted herself to but one purpose: to justify herself in the eyes of society for having left her husband. In accomplishing her purpose, she so beclouded the issues, laid so many false trails, that it is now almost impossible to get at the truth, and even Byron specialists are still busily arguing the case.

This much is clear: in this marriage were joined two such incompatible personalities that only disaster could be the outcome. Mr. Elwin, granting that Byron made an impossible husband, discounts most of the lurid "confessions" that the poet made to his wife on the grounds that Byron, realizing that Annabella had no sense of humor whatever, could not resist pulling her leg. And yet some overt act took place. What was it?

The story of incest between Byron and his half sister was first given wide currency by the meddlesome Harriet Beecher Stowe in 1870, and the tale was supported by Lord Lovelace in his *Astarte* in 1905. Yet Mrs. Moore, in *The Late Lord Byron*, pointed out that the "minutes" of the conversation between Lady Byron and Lady Caroline Lamb cannot be relied on be-

cause of Lady Caroline's well-known inability to tell the truth. In our own time, the tenth Lord Byron (a descendant of the poet's first cousin, George, who succeeded him as seventh baron), said that he was one of the few who knew the truth, that the cause of the separation was not incest, but that the true cause could never be divulged —a statement that brings us up against a stone wall. Two other causes for the separation have been advanced, each with its supporting evidence: that Byron compelled his wife to listen to minute descriptions of his affairs with prostitutes or that he compelled her to submit to unnatural sexual relations. If the second of these theories is true, one can understand why Lady Byron shuddered at the prospect of bringing the case into the ecclesiastic court. Among the three possibilities the reader must make his own choice.

There is one minor but interesting fact about Lady Byron after the separation, a fact that has been noted but not emphasized. In 1827 the death of Lord Scarsdale called the Barony of Wentworth out of abeyance, and Lady Byron became Baroness Wentworth in her own right. The Barony of Wentworth, created in 1529, was much older than that of Byron, created only in 1643; yet Annabella never claimed it and continued to be known as Lady Byron. Could she really have so deeply hated the memory of her husband if she chose to be known by his title rather than by her own much older one? Could she really have believed Augusta Leigh guilty of incest and yet continue to see and correspond with her almost daily for years?

This book is intended for the Byron specialist rather than for the general reader. Yet the author presents a memorable portrait of a woman whose life-long conviction was that she must always be right in everything and that everyone else must be wrong. Mr. Elwin ends his story abruptly with the signing of the deed of separation and passes over Annabella's remaining years in but a few paragraphs. One would like to know more about those years and more about the daughter,

Ada, Countess of Lovelace, that strange mathematical genius who must have shocked her mother by insisting upon being buried in the Byron vault beside the father whom she could not remember. Ada died in 1852. Lady Byron lived for eight more years, to complete what Mr. Elwin aptly calls that "unique monument of self-justification known as The Lovelace Papers."

Tench Francis Tilghman

A MAN AND TWO WOMEN

Author: Doris Lessing (1919-   )
Publisher: Simon and Schuster (New York). 316 pp. $5.00
Type of work: Short stories
Time: The present
Locale: England and Africa

A varied collection of short stories detailing the predicament of the individual in terms of his human relations and his environment

Doris Lessing's *The Golden Notebook* was one of the most impressive fictional performances of 1962, an exhaustive account of a twentieth century woman novelist's emotional and intellectual plight which attempted to convey the problematic relationship between life and art by alternating the personal entries of her notebooks with chapters from the novel which she was presumably writing. In her latest collection of short stories, *A Man and Two Women*, Mrs. Lessing again demonstrates those qualities of prose fiction which render her not only one of the most important women writing today but one of the significant voices, regardless of sex, in contemporary fiction. The short stories in this collection do not, unlike *The Golden Notebook*, individually represent Mrs. Lessing as a technical innovator, but, taken in the aggregate, they do suggest the range of her accomplishment and the degree

of technical control she maintains throughout that range.

To say that Mrs. Lessing's voice is a distinctly feminine one is neither to denigrate her achievement nor to imply that the masculine mind is a closed book to her, though it may be one which on occasion makes for unpleasant reading. The centers of consciousness in most of these stories are women, women as diverse as the lower-middle class heroine of "Notes for a Case History," the professional mistress of "Between Men," and the prosperous, intelligent neurotic of "To Room Nineteen," but Mrs. Lessing is quite capable of tackling the masculine ego, as the initial story in the volume, "One off the Short List," devastatingly testifies. Its hero is Graham Spence, "a member of that army of people who live by their wits on the fringes of the arts," a failure in career and in marriage who attempts futilely to salvage the shards

169

of his fragmented ego by projecting an image of himself as a bon vivant and seducer, seeking in the non-forthcoming recognition of that image compensation for his feeling of personal failure and defeat. The story concerns his one-day pursuit of Barbara Coles, a rising young stage designer whom he is interviewing for the B.B.C., and details his strategy of seduction, the collapsing ploys he uses to ingratiate himself and establish an easy familiarity with Barbara and her theatrical set, his conversational fumbles before and during the interview, his prolonged and desperate pass to which the girl finally submits only out of boredom and exasperation, his ultimate sexual failure, and finally his embarrassed attempt to pass himself off before Barbara's co-workers as her successful new lover. The irony is fierce, but so thorough is Mrs. Lessing's rendition of Spence's subterfuges, and rationalizations, his willful self-blindings to the reality of his pain and humiliation, that pity and recognition almost measure with contempt.

"A Woman on a Roof" is another study of male frustration, but it is the other side of the emotional coin. A young man working on a roof is attracted to a woman who sunbathes daily on a roof several buildings away, but the romantic fantasies which he centers upon her are destroyed when, upon his trying to make her acquaintance, they meet with the stony opposition of her total indifference. The situation is a nascent version of "One off the Short List"; however, what is self-delusion in Spence is innocence in the boy, and what appears understandable disgust in Barbara Coles becomes inevitable callousness in the nameless woman.

"Before the Ministry" deserts the relation of the sexes for the masculine world of politics. Two members of the rival factions of an African government meet before the Ministry in London and discuss which of their leaders, Mr. Devuli, the alcoholic leader of the old guard, or Mr. Kwenzi, the left-wing representative of the new order, is to represent the country in an interview with the Minister. The two exchange insults under the guise of formal diplomatic parlance until the arrival of their two leaders, Devuli, a tottering titan who accuses his adversaries of having attempted to poison him, ultimately submitting to the smooth pressures of Kwenzi while the latter's underling mouths irrelevant platitudes of statesmanship. Mrs. Lessing, trenchantly underlining the crumbling of human dignity before political expediency, views the frustrations and absurdities of public life with as keen an eye as she does those of private experience.

It is essentially the private life, however, which occupies Mrs. Lessing, and it is here that her talent most characteristically shines: in "Between Men," the increasingly drunken conversation of two kept women who are between affairs; in "Each Other," a scene between an incestuous brother and sister who preserve the pseudo-sanctity of their relation by refraining from climax; or in "Notes for a Case History," the record of a middle-class girl who knowingly rejects her own integrity and the man she is drawn to for a conventionally successful marriage. The longest and possibly the best piece in the volume is "To Room Nineteen." In it the seemingly happily married Susan Rawlings gradually becomes obsessed with the triviality of her married existence as well as the burden which everyday life with her husband and children imposes upon her and withdraws from them, seeking isolation and a mindless satisfaction of solitude, first in the anonymity of a seedy hotel room and finally, when her husband has pursued her even there, in suicide. "To Room Nineteen" is striking as an unconventional twist on the by now nearly bromidic theme of isolation, but even more so as a revelation of the madness which exists in the midst of the ordinary pattern of life, a madness induced by the realization of that pattern's blankness.

In "How I Finally Lost My Heart," Mrs. Lessing resorts to a rather fey symbolic gimmick which vitiates the story's effectiveness, but it is about the only time her hand falters. Her ability to render the very quality of environment is strong, particularly in the African stories, and in "The Sun Between Their Feet," a story in which nothing happens other than a woman's observing the activities of a dung beetle, she manages to convey the tremendous disparity between the human imagination and the reality of nature. But it is basically the human imagination and its ordinary frustrations which concern Mrs. Lessing. And it is in her revelation of the extraordinariness and the rich individuation of the ordinary that her authentic gift lies.

Donald L. Mull

MANDATE FOR CHANGE, 1953-1956
The White House Years: Volume I

Author: Dwight D. Eisenhower (1890-   )
Publisher: Doubleday and Company (Garden City, New York). Illustrated. 650 pp. $6.95
Type of work: Memoirs
Time: 1953-1956
Locale: Washington and the world

Memoirs in which the thirty-fourth President of the United States tells of the events, as he sees them, leading up to the sweeping mandate, and describes the problems and personalities of his first administration

> Principal personages:
> DWIGHT D. EISENHOWER
> KONRAD ADENAUER
> GEORGES BIDAULT
> WINSTON CHURCHILL
> ANTHONY EDEN
> NIKITA KHRUSHCHEV
> RICHARD M. NIXON
> HERBERT BROWNELL
> ALLEN DULLES
> MILTON S. EISENHOWER
> MAMIE EISENHOWER
> JAMES C. HAGERTY
> HERBERT S. HOOVER
> HARRY S. TRUMAN
> JOSEPH R. MCCARTHY

The account of the stewardship of President Eisenhower began officially on January twentieth, 1953, when he took the oath of office in Washington as the thirty-fourth president of the United States. So he declares in the first sentence in Chapter I. Chapter XXIV ends with his decision, on February 29, 1956, to run for a second term. In the intervening pages the author discusses with freshness mingled with humor and philosophy his many problems during those crowded years in the White House.

Although a number of the ex-Presidents of the United States, including the last three, have left useful memoirs, one critic calls this present volume something unmatched in presidential literature. Its honest writing reveals a personality differing greatly from his portrait by newspaper reporters and political associates. In looking not only at his victories but also at his partial and complete failures and in telling why he took the steps and what he thought he was accomplishing, Eisenhower reveals himself as a decisive, courageous man who, without arrogance or vanity, was motivated by deep faith and by a carefully evolved philosophy. Throughout the book, however, he never questions his judgments or goes back to reflect on those decisions.

For politicians who complained that he did not give enough help to candidates of his party in off-year elections, he states: "It is doubtful whether a President should intervene too intensively and directly. The President has a duty to exercise leadership in behalf of all the people." His role, he believed, was to explain issues, programs, and achievements in the hope that the majority of Americans would approve and would support the party's candidates and program.

To clarify the situation he faced, the author goes back in time in Chapter I, titled "Prelude to Politics." To a newspaper correspondent, Virgil Pinkley, he gives credit for the earliest suggestion, in 1943, that he run for the presidency. At the time he laughed off the idea, but in 1945 the proposal was repeated by President Truman, who offered support to Eisenhower in order to insure continuity of his own ideas. In view of that statement, the title, *Mandate for Change,* is a bit puzzling.

At the suggestion of Walter Winchell, twenty thousand communications flooded his office during one week in 1946, when he was President of Columbia University, urging him to run, with another deluge as time for the 1952 convention approached. However, rather than the voice of the people, it was the voice of his conscience, he says, as well as his feeling that many politicians were trying to limit the power of the presidency in matters vital to America and the world that persuaded him to enter the New Hampshire primaries of March 11, 1952.

Something of the strain as well as the humor of campaigning appears in the pre-election chapters. This chatty book is full of anecdotes that are both amusing and dramatic. We also get new sidelights on events after charges had been brought against his running mate, Richard M. Nixon, and on Eisenhower's share in steps taken to present the truth to the voters.

Chapter IV explains Eisenhower's thinking on international problems and the reasoning back of his earliest appointments and acts. His attempts to use Army methods in delegating power, both at the White House and in administration, explain some of the charges against him of failing to push his policies.

Book II opens with an account of Eisenhower's inauguration. Vainly the new President sought to make the inaugural parade short because he had, as he said, "marched in too many parades myself." (He had been among other things, a member of the West Point contingent in Wilson's inaugural in 1913.) He had better success in replacing the tall silk hats by Homburgs for the ceremonies, and he silenced those who stressed tradition by remarking that an even longer-standing tradition decreed tricornered hats and knee breeches. He explains that his lassoing by Roy Rogers during the parade had been prearranged several days before, as part of the high jinks of the Republicans' return to power. However, one quoted incident of the following day was to reveal to him the essential seriousness, as well as the loneliness, of his new office. General Omar Bradley, with whom he had been on an "Ike" and "Brad" basis since 1911, telephoned him and began the conversation with a formal salutation, "Mr. President."

Throughout the book the words "integrity" and "efficiency" contained in his first State of the Union Message are frequently repeated. The dedication to peace of this military man and

173

his religious faith are also constantly reiterated.

He knew he would have problems. Herbert Hoover, from his own experience, had warned him: "Some people will want you to lead them back at full speed to the 'good old days.' Others will want you to initiate welfare programs regardless of their effect on federal financial affairs and the nation's economy. To go back is impossible. Yet to allow present trends to go on is unwise; they will lead to disaster. All you can do is to turn away gradually from the path leading to paternalism until it takes a central course, and then stick to it. And both sides will dislike you."

Eisenhower's path, as he outlines it, was the "Middle of the Road," a course "that preserves the greatest possible initiative, freedom, and independence of body and soul to the individual but that does not hesitate to use government to control cataclysmic economic disasters that can be even more terrible than convulsions of nature."

His political promises continually occupied his mind, despite the slim Republican majority and its lack of practice in coöperating with the Chief Executive. His feeling that a leader should use reason and not force explains why so many of his projects met with only partial success. Too many cowardly Congressmen, he says, put their jobs and their constituents ahead of the country, and he offers as examples the fiascos in taxes, tariffs, and post office efficiency.

Problems of security concern him in Chapter XIII. Earlier he expressed his concern over the casual U.S. attitude toward communism. He writes of his feelings about the Rosenbergs and Dr.

Oppenheimer, as well as the 8,008 cases of security lapses discovered during 1953-1954, but mostly the chapter deals with McCarthyism. Accusing newspapers and television publicity of encouraging the senator's career of baseless accusations, he explains his own refusal to inflate McCarthy further by personal combat.

Much of the book, of course, deals with the many extensive foreign problems faced by the President during his first term. How and why he acted are explained with generous praise for those who aided him. "American political, military, and economic influence was being used to help solve old problems, preserve freedom, eliminate traditional antagonisms, and give confidence to weak and exposed nations. We had inherited many problems out of the past. In company with good friends and allies around the globe, from Seoul to Guatemala City to Teheran to London, these problems we have solved." In Latin American problems he acknowledges the assistance of his brother Milton, "a dedicated diplomat with such exceptional capability that were it not for the accident of his being my brother, he would certainly have been asked to occupy a high cabinet post in my administration." Throughout his book, Eisenhower takes particular pains to avoid suspicions of attempting to form a family dynasty. His son John would not have attended the inaugural had not President Truman ordered him temporarily returned from Korea.

National defense is the theme of the last part of Book IV. Because they wanted a military man in charge of national security, many had voted for Eisenhower in 1952. He wryly reports the difficulties of deciding on what

174

sort of defense to spend the national money, to keep equipment up to date in the face of the slogan: "If it works, it is obsolete." His conscientious efforts brought many charges that he was wrecking the Army and the Navy.

The story of any man's life gains in interest through the people with whom he becomes involved. Eisenhower had an unrivaled opportunity to meet and judge people. For this reason, his opinions of Churchill, Robert Taft, Arbenz of Guatemala, Mossadegh of Persia, Marshal Zhukov, and others offers much quotable material. Of the Russian Premier he says: "Khrushchev does not want peace, save on his own terms and in ways that will aggrandize his own power. He cares nothing for the future happiness of the peoples of the world—only for their regimented employment to fulfil the Communist concept of world history."

These memoirs were organized by Eisenhower's son John and Dr. William B. Ewald, Jr., who worked two years on the basic research. Helpful in understanding the text are sixteen appendices listing the members of the Cabinet under Eisenhower and providing the texts of Constitutional amendments, reports, and letters. Thirty-two illustrations and nine maps are also included. *Mandate for Change* is an engaging, personal, intimate book that reveals a man true to his concepts of morality. Perhaps he is too friendly to make a good historian, for his viewpoint is rosy and he is unwilling to condemn anybody. The book is not a great literary effort; some may find it monotonous and repetitious. But it is genuine and invaluable for those interested in knowing how the government is run.

Willis Knapp Jones

THE MERCY OF GOD

Author: Jean Cau (1925-   )
Translated from the French by Richard Howard
Publisher: Atheneum Publishers (New York). 310 pp. $5.00
Type of work: Novel
Time: The present
Locale: A prison in France

An existentialist novel which, despite its technical brilliance, reworks the familiar ground of the absurd world of Malraux and Sartre

Principal characters:
THE DOCTOR, a madman and murderer
EUGENE, a crane operator, drunk, and murderer
ALEX, a boxer, brute, and murderer
MATCH, a gambler and murderer

That Jean Cau was for a time Jean-Paul Sartre's secretary and that his first novel, *The Mercy of God*, won the Prix Goncourt are, perhaps, reasons enough for a serious consideration of the novel, and they are, at the same time, indications that this is a conservative novel, one more closely akin to the existentialist fiction of the forties and fifties than with the French *nouveau roman* or the American and European renascence of imaginative and fantastic fiction. Although Cau's novel exhibits some entirely successful technical innovations, his characters and themes belong to the existentialist tradition of Malraux, Sartre, and Camus. Cau's characters are also trapped in a world with "no exit," and they, too, are deeply concerned with problems made unanswerable by the silence of God, who either does not exist or does not choose to answer the cries of men.

The four central characters of this novel share a cell in a prison the location of which they do not know, and they are all murderers. They describe themselves as a madman, a drunk, a brute, and a gambler, and they are all totally involved in a double task: to create an imaginary external world in which to believe and to re-create their own past lives to discover the nature of themselves, guilt, sin, love, and, ultimately, of God. Throughout the novel and in a variety of ways, they attempt to establish an order to transcend the mutable and absurd world, a world giving rise to answerless questions which result only in despair:

Why, O Lord, why must earthly happiness be more fragile than the gut of a fish line, for perch, shaken by a swordfish? Why does the furious cyclone fall upon the happy isles, tearing away the palm fronds and strewing the yellow beaches with black coconuts? Why is the gentle poodle suddenly seized with madness? Why does the flower lose its perfume and the mother her child? Why does the satyr rape the innocent virgin who then, red with blood and shame, hurls herself from the top of the cliff?

The narrative technique of the novel is a reflection of the only answer the prisoners can find, aside from despair, for those questions—the establishment of a unity and order among themselves in which, to some degree, each prisoner becomes each of his cellmates. The novel is narrated in the first person, but the narrator is not one of the prisoners; he is, rather, all of them, a constantly shifting perspective which, because of the nature of the prisoners' relationships remains constant. Just as they have created an outside world (a world gone mad with war, death, and injustice) by means of imaginary newscasts by one of their number, so they have created their own cell world where one must answer all questions (but the truth of one's answer may vary from day to day) and where, as their mutual identity begins to blur and disintegrate their specific identities, "Everything we think happens."

However, unlike the hero of Jack Richardson's *The Prison Life of Harris Filmore*, who finds a perfectly orderly and happy life in a prison world, the prisoners in Cau's existentialist prison are forced by circumstance and their quest for the nature of God beyond the peace and joy of a selfless, group identity to an even more artificial and absurd order, one which seems to contain Cau's vision of man's position in a world faced with Pascal's frightening "silence of these infinite spaces." When a fifth prisoner is to be added to their cell, the prisoners fall into despair, fearing that their artificial order will become foolish in the eyes of a stranger, a man from an outside world about which they wish to know nothing beyond what they have decided for themselves. The Doctor, who is at once the smartest and the maddest of the prisoners, saves their world by suggesting correctly that the new prisoner

176

can be driven to suicide by their silence and their staring gaze.

In their elation over the success of their plan and the restoration of their orderly life, the prisoners lose all identity and become, for a winter, a new entity of four interchangeable parts: "Like God, plus one more . . . gentle, good, virtuous, transparent." But, with the coming of spring, their elation fades and, with it, their new communal God, and they continue their quest for the answers. They define themselves simply as criminals, and a criminal "is a man who realizes that love is impossible." Who, then, is God and of what will his mercy consist?

> God Himself doesn't know what mercy will inspire him on Judgment Day. "Is *that* what my humanity was? Is that what you are, my human beings? Poor wretches!"

The Doctor finally, after deciding that the universe is solipsistic and that he is the dreamer of it all, declares himself God. The others, out of fear or because being dreamed suits them, agree with the Doctor's decision, although they do not decide to worship him. They become, then, a new entity, the drunk, the brute, the gambler and the madman, a surrogate man, composed of murder and recognizing as God only its own damaged, dreaming brain. If the mercy of God and God Himself are unintelligible, then a human and therefore artificial God is, according to the Doctor, "logical, quite logical. He said it had to end this way."

Jean Cau has constructed, in this novel, another artifact of the existentialist mind like those of his former employer, Sartre, before him. Unlike so many of his American and European contemporaries, he places faith in neither the creative imagination nor the creative will, and, unlike his French contemporaries involved in the *nouveau roman*, he remains in the familiar precincts of a world absurd and beyond hope or despair. *The Mercy of God* is the novel of an artist. Like too many French novels, however, it is a work which grows out of no faith in art and, thus, of no faith in that part of men's nature, imperfect as it may be, which makes art possible and necessary.

R. H. W. Dillard

THE MOVING TARGET

Author: W. S. Merwin (1927-   )
Publisher: Atheneum Publishers (New York). 97 pp. Clothbound, $3.95; paperback, $1.95
Type of work: Poetry

A serious confrontation of the modern world, leading to a significant response to and reflection of this world in highly subjective, personally symbolic poetry

W. S. Merwin's poetry is vital and dynamic. Modern in form, condensation, and intensity, it is a description and a record of one human being experiencing the act of living: learning, feeling, doing, growing. As with most modern art, visual and verbal, the symbolism is personal because it seeks to express unique and individual responses to life. Furthermore, like most modern art, Merwin's poetry concerns itself with matters peculiar to the modern age. It is powerfully and penetratingly descriptive of sensations lurking in the recesses of modern minds and of the conditions of modern humanity. The anxieties, doubts, insecurities, and emotional defenses of man caught up in a dehumanizing urbanization and frustrated by the negation of traditional values are presented in Merwin's poetry as apparently and forcefully as in the wasteland poetry of T. S. Eliot. But Merwin's poetry, like Eliot's, is not a philosophical pessimism. Where Eliot's view is philosophical and theological in nature, Merwin's, though subdued, is in the strength of his capacity to face up to a disillusioning environment and in a positive faith in man's nature and destiny.

As a conscious experience of and response to environment, his poetry reveals a courageous and vital attitude toward life, in spite of an agony of uncertainty and dissatisfaction that reflects the fundamental unrest of the age. Contemplation, sensation, passion, unconscious forces, and intuition all unite in a composite effort to find values in the inexpressible complexities of life.

Concerned more with the fact than with the meaning of existence, or rather seeking to find the meaning in the fact, the purpose of his poetry is to describe not to appraise. For this reason no explication of the poetry can hope to be thorough or altogether adequate. It is not unusual for the reader to see in such poetry what he himself puts into it. Poe, Valéry, and, more recently, Brooks and Warren in criticism have made the public aware of and receptive to a self-contained poetry. It is

a poetry which allows for obscurity as long as that obscurity permits broad and significant perceptions outside of and beyond the logical position. If anything general can be said about Merwin's poetry, it is to say it has a serious, severe approach to consciousness and is challenging in technique and style, at times even obscure.

Though Merwin's poetry is not structured on an intellectual framework, its tone, high purpose, and import can be partially realized through an inquiry, though not without unavoidable inferences, into its impressions at an intellectual level which the poetry transcends. A thematic element most easily approached, in spite of its broad, unwieldy implications, is Merwin's concern with Time. His experience of Time, of its incomprehensibleness, its incessant march, its consequences, is the force behind both his exalting aspirations and his confusion. Time as a phenomenon or characteristic of life is viewed through several areas of reality. It is realized as a phenomenon of abstract laws, as an accumulation of events and sensations, or as a specific period of life captured in memory or anticipation. The experience of Time, of men in the act of filling Time, is one of uncertain aspiration and yearnings, of despair in the sterility and inanity of routine, urbanized living, or of a cautious hope never fully justified or realized. In many poems these experiences are united in one experience, thereby becoming in magnitude and power of theme almost inexplicable.

In "Home for Thanksgiving" the poet returning to a particular place is brought back to a time in the past. In memory he relives this past time, trying to weigh, now with the insight

178

of retrospection, the wisdom of his life. His uneasy, indefinite approval of his past decisions implies that one, in most cases, can no better appraise the past from the perspective of the present than he can predict the future from the present. In "Route with No Number" Time is translated into life. He identifies a few landmarks along the route of his life, a horizontal extension of Time becoming the structure for the exciting images which convey his condition and sensations along the way.

Many of Merwin's poems voice the archetypal searching and struggling of the restless, unsettled American hunting anchorage and certainty. Since the spiritual search usually involves as much an escape as a discovery, at least three areas of life are available to art that is concerned with this theme: the environment or condition to be escaped, the struggle itself, and the goal. Though a single poem may deal with all of these areas, it usually concentrates upon one. Poems which focus attention upon the situation to be escaped usually convey only a vague idea of what is better, principally because the poet necessarily delimits himself. The waste of *The Waste Land* and the hollowness of "The Hollow Men" direct attention upon that from which one would escape, although, if one is to accept Cleanth Brooks' interpretation of *The Waste Land*, the poet determines alternatives through contrast.

The same is true of many of Merwin's poems. In "Another Year Come," the invariableness, illusion, incompleteness, and distastefulness of life are looked on with both dismay and hopeful determination. This poem, the voice of a searching consciousness, fo-

cuses upon the negative motivations that prompt an uneasy quest. In "Recognition," a spirit of loneliness and unfulfillment is magnetically felt through the poet's painful attention to the insensitivity and even estrangement of his immediate environment. Notice, for instance, the appeal of these images: "The bird of ash has appeared at windows/ And the roads will turn away, mourning" and "I came home as a web to its spider." Notice the sense of isolation expressed here:

> I walked
> In on the mirrors scarred as match-
>   boxes,
> The gaze of the frames and the ticking
> In the beams. The shadows
> Had grown a lot and they clung
> To the skirts of the lamps.

In another place the poet says: "To-morrow/ Marches on the old walls, and there/ Is my coat full of darkness in its place/ On the door."

In "Resolution," his impotent world is realized in broader terms than in "Recognition" but still emphasized is the impotency. In this poem are images such as "Memory leaking feathers" and ". . . the feeling/ Runs ahead and hides in bushes with its knives pointed out" and "The clock dropping its shoes and/ No floor." These expose unidentified disturbances in the deep, intangible areas of sensation.

But neither Eliot nor Merwin turns his complete attention to the unlovely; both look to the discovery that the searcher must make. While the spiritual search may involve a quest for meaning or experience, Merwin's search is usually for both. In "The Continuo," studying the peculiar powers of the wind, he asks: "What can

179

you learn from it?" Nowhere is his overall stand more thoroughly stated, however, than in "Bread and Butter." He acknowledges, with some dismay, his frequent tribute to "the gods of abandon." Then he declares his resolute, positive attitude toward life:

I will not bow in the middle of the
  room
To the statue of nothing
With the flies turning around it.

In what he is, despite limitations, he finds the prophecy of what he is to be: "On these four walls I am the writing." And in his power to envision, in spite of crippled and ill-capable instruments of salvation, lies a tomorrow when

The broken boats will come in,
The life boats
Waving their severed hands,

And I will love as I ought to
Since the beginning.

A similar hope, in spite of past failures, is the emphasis of "Finally." As in Arnold's "Dover Beach," hope is found in an integrity of intimate companionship. The poet makes a plea for unity: "Let us share/ Understanding like a family name." Then he closes with a note of warm congeniality, beautiful in its sincerity and vividness of imagery, which voices a hope in the dark:

Come. As a man who hears a sound at
  the gate
Opens the window and puts out the
  light
The better to see out into the dark,
Look, I put it out.

When viewed in a composite picture, all of the various statements about life in these poems—about being, yearning, despairing, hoping—convey highly controlled impressions. Intellectually and emotionally alert to the disparities of life, Merwin bemoans the narrow, anemic, pantomimic life but never really loses sight of the eternal hopes of mankind; his optimism nourished by a fundamental aspiration and a masculine defiance of all that is demoralizing.

To see his poetry as philosophical statements, however, is to distort it. Its real merit is not in philosophical soundness or profundity but in the validity of the human experience conveyed. To oversimplify, the meaning comes through the experience rather than the experience through the meaning. How they make the reader feel is the criterion by which these poems must finally be weighed. Through the poet's sensitivity and responsiveness to life, he is able to express for most men dormant feelings waiting for a word in order to be realized fully and enjoyed. Merwin is unmistakably in tune with the melodies and variations of modern emotions.

But to say that Merwin's poetry is modern in technique is to cloud it with generalities, although most of the distinguishing characteristics of modern poetry may be found in his, of which obscurity, personal symbolism, and controlled formlessness are only the most obvious. His art cannot be approached with a rubber stamp and is best discerned when preconceived ideas and comparable poets are held most in abeyance. Although a desultory reading of Merwin's poetry may leave one with a feeling of formlessness and vagueness, a controlled and extensive reading discloses a fundamental, natural construction which serves as an index to his interpretation of life and to his symbolism. When one is aware of Merwin's point of reference and of his symbolic artifice, he has a key which unlocks the doors to the otherwise elusive significations of his concentrated language. As do many poets, he constructs a sensory realization of the physical environment which, through symbolic signification, projects and effectuates a spiritual (or subjective) state. The mind is held in rein by the objective world, and yet the objective world is stretched by the acting of the mind upon it. Penetrating and living into the world of things, Merwin attempts to experience as much of his humanity as is possible. His aspiring soul, his gravitation toward the invisible world, his unsatisfied humanity, are realized in terms of the restrictions, suggestivity, and limitations posed by his physical environment. For instance, in "The Ships Are Made Ready in Silence" is a breathtaking tension between the objective correlations and the inscrutable dreams and memories which, beginning with the suggestivity of the object, strain to burst free into the thin atmosphere of which they are a part. The result is a growing excitement that starts controlled and calmly and then breaks like a new world seen through the glow of dawn:

> At this moment I could believe in no change,
> The mast perpetually
> Vacillating between the same constellations,
> The night never with drawing its dark virtue
> From the harbor shaped as a heart,
> The sea pulsing as a heart,
> The sky vaulting as a heart,
> Where I know the light will shatter like a cry
> Above a discovery:

> "Emptiness.
> Emptiness! Look!"
> Look. This is the morning.

We can follow the poet as he scans the harbor and then turns his face to the sky. His painful disillusionment, growing out of his preparation for this scene (emotionally and mentally), reveals not only a physical setting, imaginary or real, but the drama of a mental impression as well.

Most of his symbolism is drawn from an urban environment. Windows, mirrors, doors, hooks, steps, and many other specific things and housing in its broader sense of cities are among the recurrent symbols given fairly consistent values. Windows, for instance, seem to symbolize our reserved confrontation of life, our limited, shielded communion with the outside world, and similar states and attitudes; mirrors symbolize our illusions, distorted views, and passivity; hooks are related to man's conformity, conventionality, and to routine conveniences that devitalize.

Although these are more or less conventional symbols, they become personal when they are shaped into symbolic metaphors, when they make up a language of their own by blending the object and the personal evaluation of the object into a new thing which presents in a single reference or episode the composite, personally subjective values and stimuli related to it. When these concentrated, organic images are joined and ordered in the making of a poem the result is electrifying. Many images are effective without an intended or necessary explanation on the rational level. Take, for example, "The clock dropping its shoes and/ No floor" or "I put out my

181

hand and the dark falls through it/
Following a flag" or

Ahead of me under
False teeth hanging from a cloud, his
Sign that digs for his house, Tomorrow,
The oldest man
Is throwing food into empty cages.

Usually the poem as a whole is self-explanatory because of the wholeness and finish of its emotional expression. One is enabled to "live out" the objective references through a basic familiarity with the essential inherent dynamics of these references.

Merwin's world is not a dichotomy of matter and spirit or body and soul, although it is a world, much like that of the transcendentalist, in which reality and meaning are synonymous. Because the experiencing self rather than the rationalizing self is the center of his poetic method, things and the interaction of things have not only a subjective coloring but also a subject correlary which is regulated to a certain extent by the limitations of the objective. His inability to realize his highest nature is his inability to escape or fully comprehend his lower but basic nature.

In this way he voices the modern, and at the same time the age-old aspirations and realizations of man, by artistically asserting the tension between what man is and what innately he craves to be, between the qualities and the values of reality. He is first of all a poet, obviously inspired and poignantly expressive, communicating attitudes and values in startling, compelling images, some of such rare beauty as to touch the most aesthetically dull, some of such pertinence and substance as to provoke the most thoughtless.

Charles Workman

182

MY LADY SUFFOLK
A Portrait of Catherine Willoughby, Duchess of Suffolk

Author: Evelyn Read (1901-   )
Publisher: Alfred A. Knopf (New York). Illustrated. 205 pp. $4.00
Type of work: Biography
Time: The sixteenth century
Locale: England and Western Europe

A sympathetic portrait of a strong-minded, charming woman of Tudor England

Principal personages:
  MARIA DE SALINAS, lady in waiting to Queen Catherine and wife of Lord Willoughby
  CATHERINE WILLOUGHBY, her daughter
  CHARLES BRANDON, Duke of Suffolk, the guardian and later the husband of Catherine Willoughby
  MARY TUDOR, the "French Queen," wife of Charles Brandon and foster mother of Catherine
  HENRY VIII, King of England
  WILLIAM CECIL, minister of Queen Elizabeth I and friend and counselor of Catherine Willoughby
  RICHARD BERTIE, the second husband of Catherine

My Lady Suffolk is a modest book. Only slightly over two hundred pages long, it does not pretend to be a formal biography. Although Evelyn Read allows some play of imagination and sentiment over her carefully gathered facts, she does not engage in lavish invention in the manner of typical writers of historical romance. She has lived so long and so imaginatively with the inhabitants of the sixteenth century that they seem more like her friends and acquaintances than costume pieces or puppets. In general she treats her characters with rare charity and gentleness.

Mrs. Read is the widow of the eminent historian Conyers Read, whom she assisted in writing his excellent two-volume biography of William Cecil, Lord Burghley. Her own book is a by-product of the larger work; it was suggested to her by her husband and is dedicated to him. Her knowledge of libraries and collections of official rec-

ords and the ready help given her by distinguished scholar-friends of her husband served her well in completing the research for this book.

Mrs. Read's fondness for her heroine is undisguised. Catherine Willoughby was the daughter of an English lord and a Spanish lady in waiting to Queen Catherine, the first of King Henry's six wives. Lady Willoughby's loyalty to the unfortunate queen apparently outweighed all her other emotional involvements. On the death of her father, little Catherine became the ward of King Henry's brother-in-law, Charles Brandon, Duke of Suffolk, known to readers of fiction and cinema-goers as the hero of *When Knighthood Was in Flower*. The young girl was devoted to her foster parents, the duke and his third wife, gentle Mary Tudor, widow of the French king. The ill-health and the untimely death of this affectionate foster mother must have caused the

183

young girl great grief; however, although probably only thirteen or fourteen years old, Catherine became the wife of the middle-aged Duke of Suffolk three months after the death of "the French Queen." "By sixteenth-century standards," writes Mrs. Read, "neither the speed with which the widower Duke of Suffolk remarried nor the difference in age between him and his bride was unusual enough to cause surprise."

The author's portrait of Charles Brandon is a favorable one. She writes: "Charles Brandon was said to be the only man Henry VIII ever really loved." Certainly, although Brandon and his wife respected Queen Catherine and disliked Anne Boleyn, the duke did not allow a rift to grow between him and his fiery royal brother-in-law. At the time of Suffolk's death Henry remarked that "in all their long friendship the duke had never attempted to hurt an adversary, nor had he ever said a word to injure anyone. 'Is there any of you, my lords,' the king added, 'who can say as much?' "

Mrs. Read stresses the intelligence and wit as well as the beauty of the young duchess, whose name was soon involved in romantic speculations. The author summarily dismisses the rumor that Henry VIII had his eye on the attractive young widow as a possible seventh wife. Rumors of several international suitors, however, receive more careful attention. The wit, though attracting many admirers, certainly made enemies for the duchess, who did not mind making adversaries appear ridiculous. She particularly alienated Bishop Stephen Gardiner, who repaid the debt of hostility with interest. She also had another quality which begot enemies: she was intensely religious and intensely partisan in her religion, being a militant Protestant. The most profound influence on her religious beliefs was Hugh Latimer, who became the Bishop of Worcester and who was burned at the stake in the reign of Bloody Mary Tudor. In her treatment of Latimer and many other figures, Mrs. Read shows a rare gift of bringing a character to life with a surprisingly small number of words. Had she filled out her sketches or embellished incidents, she would have produced a very large volume indeed.

After the death of Henry VIII, Catherine of Suffolk retired to her country home, with William Cecil as a not too distant neighbor. There was strong friendship and mutual respect between the two, but the duchess did not approve of Cecil's political craft of compromise. She was "a fighting zealot"; he was a practical politician and statesman, sympathetic toward the reformers of religion, but averse to fanning the flames of strife.

In her portrait of Catherine of Suffolk, the author does not hide some incidents of ungraciousness as well as of sharp-tongued wit. The pathetic orphan daughter of Sir Thomas Seymour and his wife Catherine Parr was made the ward of the duchess. She received no such tenderness and affection as her foster mother had received from Mary Tudor. There is no evidence of cruelty, but Catherine showed considerable coldness toward the child.

The greatest tragedy in Catherine's life was the untimely death of both her fine sons by Charles Brandon. The promising young scholars at Cambridge University died of the same disease within an hour of each other. About a year after this tragedy the

184

duchess married her gentleman usher, Richard Bertie. Their hairbreadth escapes and long exile from England during Bloody Mary's religious persecutions furnish material for vivid and suspenseful narrative; but the potential historical romance is treated with great economy by Mrs. Read. The adventures ended happily, however, and the family (there were then two children) returned to England in the reign of Elizabeth I. The duchess was loyal to the great queen, but held the same objections to her moderate and tolerant religious policy as she did to William Cecil's. Near the end of her life Catherine had the misfortune of an unhappy relationship with her daughter-in-law, the wife of Peregrine Bertie. Mrs. Read expresses regret that the duchess died before the daughter-in-law changed from a headstrong and difficult wife to a loyal and loving one.

The lack of sensationalism, the impression of quiet truthfulness, and the knowledgeable re-creation of inhabitants of a golden century give the book a definite appeal, particularly for readers surfeited with the unbridled bursts of purple passion and inaccurate pseudo-history stacked on many bookstalls.

G. Burke Johnston

THE NAMES AND FACES OF HEROES

Author: Reynolds Price (1933-   )
Publisher: Atheneum Publishers (New York). 178 pp. $3.95
Type of work: Short stories
Time: The recent past
Locale: North Carolina

Finely conceived and deeply moving stories by the author of the highly praised first novel, A Long and Happy Life

If someone had not already chosen *Fathers and Sons* as a title, it would serve almost as well here as *The Names and Faces of Heroes*. Both the dedication and the epigraph reinforce the discoverable fact: a son and his father are the subject of all but one of these stories, whether the subject is treated directly or obliquely. The epigraph is from a letter of William Blake: "I met a plow on my first going out at my gate the first morning after my arrival, & the Plowboy said to the Plowman, 'Father, The Gate is Open.'" The scene and the words are cryptic, but the suggestions are clear and powerful; one of the most profound of human relationships is subject to change. The image and the phrase imply a movement from obscurity to clarity, from constriction to freedom, from the confusion and difficulty of identification to a sure and blessed knowledge of who and what we are. The boy becomes a man by emulation of the eternal hero, the father, and of the lesser divinities who are linked by name or love to the father.

The one story which is not a part of the pattern is "The Anniversary," and it is the weakest in the collection. The most conventionally "literary," it does not have the stamp of Reynold Price's *style,* of his highest imagination. It is the only story we could imagine someone else having written. Lillian Belle

185

Carraway, an old maid, every year places flowers on the grave of her fiancé; this year she is accompanied by a little Negro boy, Wash, and she tells him the comic and sad story of her love affair. The details are right and the narrative is handled with impeccable skill and subtlety, yet in the context of the other stories "The Anniversary" seems insufficiently felt, lacking in intensity.

The six remaining stories are of a piece, each illuminating and enriching the other. "A Chain of Love" and "The Names and Faces of Heroes" are first and last in the volume, and the most brilliantly lighted scene in both is that of a deathbed, the dying father attended by his son.

"A Chain of Love" approaches this scene obliquely. The story concerns characters already made familiar by Price's novel, *A Long and Happy Life*: Rosacoke Mustian, her mother, her brothers Milo and Rato, her sister-in-law Sissie, Rosacoke's boy friend Wesley Beavers. Her grandfather, Papa, only a memory in the novel, is very much alive here; it is his enforced stay in the hospital which brings Rosacoke into fleeting touch with the Ledwell boy and his father. She and Rato have come to keep Papa company, and when she first sees the boy she mistakes him for her beloved Wesley. This mistake is quickly cleared up, but the chain of love has been forged, and Rosacoke is drawn into the sorrow and mystery of impending death across the hall. There is nothing she can do but offer flowers, the sorrow and mystery remain obscure, yet Rosacoke's feeling and sympathy are redemptive; they give meaning:

If he had to die wasn't that as good a way as any, leaving his living picture back here in that boy? But she hadn't

ever seen him alive really. She hadn't ever told him or any of his kind—out loud—that she felt for them. . . . That was why she spoke at last. . . . "It don't seem right," she said. "It just don't seem right. It seem like I had got to know him real well."

The title story moves to the heart of the mystery, the mystery of death, of identity, of human defeat and victory. Nowhere has Price's dense, convoluted, poetic style been better suited to the matter than in this story. A nine-year-old boy recounts, in the present, a winter's night spent with his father, riding home through snow. As he lies with his head in his father's lap he ponders his great problem, the need for a hero, "somebody who is what you are not but need to be." The faces of family and friends rise to his mind's eye; one face, the one which looks unswervingly into the dark before them, he discounts. It is too familiar; "you do not seek heroes at home." If the boy knew what Jesus' face looked like, that would serve, a "face that could change people's lives." The slow disclosure, the revelation, is made, and the miracle stands before the boy in the car's headlights: Jesus' face *is* his father's face. Before the evening ends, the boy sleeps and has a vision of the future, when he is a man standing by a hospital bed, attempting to hold the life of his father in his hands. As the father's life ebbs away, the boy, now a man, makes a vow: "I will change my life—will turn in my tracks on myself my foe with you as shield." The boy wakes; they arrive home, "together, whole. This one more time." What Rosacoke saw faintly the boy now knows, and he grows and lives from the knowing.

The other stories serve as variations

on this grand and simple theme. "The Warrior Princess Ozimba" tells of a Negro woman who plays a part in a ritual. The boy's family gives her a new pair of tennis shoes each Fourth of July, a gift offered out of the family's love and because of the woman's need. It all began years ago because "it pacified my father who was a boy then and who wanted to give her presents." Now the father is dead, and the son must bear the gift. The Warrior Princess, in her blindness and senility, denies the passage of time. This is the father bringing her shoes, and the son cannot bring himself to make the old woman understand: "I stood there those last few minutes, looking through sudden amazed tears at all that age and remembering my dead father."

"Michael Egerton" and "Troubled Sleep" are accounts of the young boy's experiences, his awakening both to his capacity for treachery and his need for a hero. "Michael Egerton" is the story of the boy's fellow camper, the son of divorced parents, deprived of a father, and abandoned by his friend. "Troubled Sleep" evokes the magic of childhood, its fears and stratagems. Falc is the cousin the boy loves and is deceived by, but love and need overwhelm deception. The two boys will die together in the light of the moon, will sacrifice themselves as Blood Brothers. The father finds them, living and breathing, and smiles down on them:

When they missed us from our bed and my father came out at midnight to lead us home . . . he found us in that secret place where he knew we were, and

all he could see, he smiled at—me in troubled sleep in the full moon still and Falc dark and gone like he didn't mean to return, but in each other's arms at least and breathing slow.

"Uncle Grant" is in many ways as rich and complex a story as "The Names and Faces of Heroes." Both stories illustrate Blake's belief that "All deities reside in the human breast," that somehow the human face and form are divine Love, Peace, Mercy, and Pity. The face of Uncle Grant, a Negro man loved by the boy's father, is the same face the boy discovers as a man on the postcard picturing "Amenhotep IV, pharaoh of Egypt in the eighteenth dynasty . . . the one true god, the streaming disc, the sun." "Uncle Grant" is the artfully simple re-creation of Grant Terry, who lived at times with the boy's family. The father and Uncle Grant are indelible images in the boy's mind. Both are now dead. Whatever their life was, it has been consumed by time. Their mystery is unsolved:

. . . Nobody knows why they sat there night after night at a hard kitchen table under a bare light bulb, talking on and on, and laughing. Unless they loved each other—meaning there would come times when they needed to meet, and they never explained the need to themselves.

The story, or portrait (perhaps it is not a "story" at all), achieves a kind of perfection: the man lives on in his loneliness, his pride, and most importantly, his trust. The chain of love links indissolubly father, son, friend. We cannot ask for more than this book of stories gives.

James Boatwright

187

NIGHT COMES TO THE CUMBERLANDS
A Biography of a Depressed Area

Author: Harry M. Caudill (1922-   )
Publisher: Little, Brown and Company (Boston). 395 pp. $6.75
Type of work: Regional history
Time: The 1600's through 1963
Locale: The Cumberland Mountains of eastern Kentucky

An imaginatively written biography of a depressed area, the Cumberland Plateau of eastern Kentucky, telling of early settlement, the Civil War, the famous feuds, the timber and coal industries, the moonshine wars, the union drives, human and natural waste, and the rise of the welfare state

Harry M. Caudill is one of America's angry young men and *Night Comes to the Cumberlands* is his testament. But unlike most of his British counterparts and his American contemporaries, Caudill's rage is sparked on the anvil of profound commitment where he hammers out an instrument with which to help raise up his depressed area, the Cumberland Plateau of Kentucky. A Whitesburg lawyer with six years' service in the Kentucky House of Representatives as an advocate of progressive conservation and education legislation, he writes out of personal involvement; his people have lived in the plateau from the beginning. No wonder he subtitles his book "A Biography of a Depressed Area" and dedicates it "to the Kentucky coal miners whose trials and tragedies are its central theme," for perhaps in no other part of America are people and place so completely one ecological organism. In no other area are the spectacular ironies of American history so painful, the promise of the good life so mired in poverty. As an eloquent appeal to the American conscience, *Night Comes to the Cumberlands* is a major achievement in a venerable American tradition. With

something of Harriette Arnow's feel for history, of Steinbeck's dramatic power, of Upton Sinclair's reformist zeal, and of James Agee's lyrical empathy, Caudill has created a supreme metaphor of the failure of the American Dream and the American Character.

"The Cumberland Plateau region of Kentucky," writes Caudill, "is a serrated upland in the eastern and southeastern part of the state. Its jagged hills and narrow winding valley cover some ten thousand square miles. It embraces nineteen counties and portions of a dozen others." Its half a million inhabitants are "drawn from some of the oldest white stock to be found north of Florida." The Kentucky mountaineer's "forebears had dwelt in or on the edge of the Southern Appalachians for generations before the Declaration of Independence was penned." The regional past "resulted in a land of economic, social and political blight without parallel in the nation." The purpose of Caudill's book "is to trace the social, economic and political forces which produced the vast 'depressed area' of eastern Kentucky." Much of this region's history is the story of coal:

Coal has always cursed the land in which it lies. When men begin to wrest it from the earth it leaves a legacy of foul streams, hideous slag heaps and polluted air. It peoples this transformed land with blind and crippled men and with widows and orphans. It is an extractive industry which takes all away and restores nothing. It mars but never beautifies. It corrupts but never purifies.

But the tragedy of the Kentucky mountains transcends the tragedy of coal. It is compounded of Indian wars, civil wars and intestine feuds, of layered hatreds and of violent death. To its sad blend, history has added the curse of coal as a crown of sorrow.

This long quotation may provide an impression of the heat and tension of Caudill's style.

Recognizing the crisis that this region's problems posed for the nation, President Kennedy had planned to visit the area to view conditions for himself. Caudill enables the reader to make that journey in Kennedy's stead. The reader may see what Kennedy, typical of most Americans, was *surprised* to see, when he visited West Virginia in 1960, "conditions of squalor, ignorance and ill health which could scarcely be equaled in Europe or Japan or, perhaps, in parts of mainland Asia." Nor is the helplessness and hopelessness of the mountaineer true of eastern Kentucky alone. "What I shall say about the Kentucky coal miner applies, with local modifications, to the entire coal-producing area of the Southern highland," which includes parts of Maryland, Virginia, West Virginia, Alabama, and Tennessee. The juxtaposition of the "dark and bloody ground" of the Cumberland Plateau to the Tennessee Valley Authority, the nation's magnificent monument to the wisdom of a "system-

atic conservation program," is an appalling irony which should force the nation to confront a region away from which it has always turned its gaze.

Secretary of the Interior Stewart L. Udall's foreword to this cry of alarm is pertinent, harmonizing with the tone of the book. In a succinct introduction, Caudill relates the genesis of his study, inspired, appropriately, by irony: he served as commencement speaker at an eighth-grade graduation in a cramped, squalid coal camp school where the ceremony was opened with a lusty singing of "America the Beautiful."

The book is divided into eight parts, but like a modern tragedy it falls severely into three acts. In Part I, Caudill relates the story of how our forebears —theologically, economically, and politically disinherited, as indeed they remain today—sowed in the harsh wilderness seeds of "home sweet home." Part II is the story of a land divided by the Civil War and the famous local feuds produced by it; Caudill also cites minor forward steps taken in the areas of religion, education, politics, and health.

"The coming of the coal men" is depicted in Part III. But the first of the grand-scale spoilers attacked "the lordly trees." The "most momentous single occurrence in the history of the Cumberlands" was the intrusion of the railroads which cut a path for the outpouring of coal. A century after the settlement of the frontier, the railroads and the coal companies created "alabaster cities," and to the "big bosses" the rugged individualist willingly surrendered his freedom and self-reliance. In this section Caudill also describes the customs and habits—social, religious, sexual, cultural—of the mountaineer whose way of life was to

189

change with such violent suddenness. The years of "boom and bust" are chronicled in Part IV. The greatest coal boom lasted from 1912 to 1927. Prohibition encouraged mass practice of the ancient art of moonshining and caused an era of mayhem that recalled the horrors of the feuds. The Great Depression created conditions favorable to the strong thrust of union drives. One of the legacies of the Thirties was a political machine well-oiled with welfare benefits and welfare psychology. Part V describes the progress from "bust" to the second great "boom" made possible by World War II.

Having set the stage for the final act of the tragedy, Caudill assails the interdependent evils of "waste and welfare" in Part VI. New highways were constructed to accommodate automation and the proliferation of truck mines. These forces not only wantonly ravaged the landscape but also darkened horizons for the miner as well. The "welfare state" has risen on a foundation composed of swarms of illegitimate children and men who, having given up hope of working, aspire to "total disability" and the "dole" it brings. Part VII is a description of "the purple mountain majesties" that greed has literally moved—mostly into the rivers that flood annually. Gigantic augers, raking out tons of inferior coal to feed mammoth generators, some of which belong to TVA, are, ironically enough, the most recent instruments employed in "the rape of the Appalachians." "The scene today" is generally that of a vast wasteland of natural and human resources. A chapter called "The Politics of Decay" provides a close-up of a county judge's typical day.

Caudill presents an epilogue in Part

VIII, entitled "The Future." In "The Case for a Southern Mountain Authority," he offers a twelve-point prescription for the region's chronic ills. He pleads for a public works program which would give the people an active role in their own rehabilitation. The new federal aid program, announced late in 1963, is by its nature a means of treating the present agony, rather than curing or preventing its causes.

The book also contains a map and seventeen photographs. While the photographs have a journalistic excellence, the book's true pervading tone requires a visual enhancement similar in quality and attitude to Walker Evans' in *Let Us Now Praise Famous Men*. In such a book as Caudill's the absence of footnotes is a virtue, but an imaginative index would have proved helpful.

The winter of 1962-1963 in eastern Kentucky was one of union strife— with gunfire, explosions, and roving bands of pickets—of starvation, massive relief drives, and record snow and cold. "New hatreds gripped the hills as the hopeless antagonists grappled over the skinny carcass of what had once been a rich coal industry." On the morning of March 11, 1963, photographer Billy Davis recorded from a helicopter the spectacle of two towns, Lothair and Hazard, flooded by the double lash-like curves of a river overburdened with the waste of mines and the eroded soil of stripped mountainsides. In the autumn of 1963 prolonged drought and idle malice set thousands of acres of the region's remaining timberland ablaze.

"The plateau," Caudill concludes in a postscript, "almost unnoticed, continues to lurch toward a day when perhaps 80 per cent of its inhabitants will be Welfare recipients—charges on the

190

national purse" and conscience. But the enormous national attention given his book makes it possible for him to qualify the word "unnoticed."

David Madden

1918: THE LAST ACT

Author: Barrie Pitt (1918-   )
Publisher: W. W. Norton and Company (New York). Illustrated. 318 pp. $5.95
Type of work: Military history
Time: 1918
Locale: North Western Europe

A definitive study of the last year of World War I, covering the attempts of the Central Powers to force the issue and the ultimate victory of the Allies

Principal personages:
MARSHAL FERDINAND FOCH, the Supreme Allied Commander
FIELD-MARSHAL PAUL VON HINDENBURG, Chief of the German General Staff
GENERAL ERICH LUDENDORFF, First Quarter-Master General of the German Army
FIELD MARSHAL SIR JOHN FRENCH, Commander of British Forces in Europe
FIELD MARSHAL SIR DOUGLAS HAIG, Member of the Supreme War Council
MARSHAL HENRI P. PÉTAIN, Commander-in-Chief of French Forces
GENERAL JOHN J. PERSHING, Commander-in-Chief of American Expeditionary Force

This book, written by a man who first saw the light of day while the history of his subject was being made, is a brilliant and penetrating study of World War I. Mr. Pitt, above everything else, has the facility of making history come to life on paper. Although he himself did not participate in any of the action, he has been able to present a clear, concise, and completely objective chronicle of the events between December, 1917, and November, 1918. Fortunately for the reader, Mr. Pitt has included far more material than the title of his work indicates.

According to the author, Europe went to war with great joy and complete confidence of victory after a brief struggle. Each major nation had spent long years preparing to assume the of-

fensive without giving any consideration to techniques which would have to be applied in the event of a stalemate. When the offensive system failed during the first weeks of the war, both sides were forced to improvise, and the doctrine of attrition supplanted the spirit of the offensive. As a result, for the remainder of the war the soldiers of both the Central Powers and the Allies were forced to live underground in a system of trenches which extended from the English Channel to the Swiss border.

By 1918 the joy of war had been replaced by fear and hopelessness. The long years of struggle had been costly on the home front as well as on the war front. Civilians had been called upon to make sacrifices that they had never

191

expected to be imposed by the authorities. Lack of food and fuel had become acute as early as 1917 in Germany and Austria. Hunger, by 1918, was no longer a problem; the problem was starvation. A few persons had grown rich as a result of the war, but the bulk of the population had been financial losers during the years of conflict. The gloom, which was in every European nation, filtered down from persons in high offices to the lowest citizen. There was no longer any pleasure in war; the generals simply wanted to get on with the grim business at hand.

As 1918 dawned, Hindenburg and Ludendorff decided that this was the year for victory. The reason for renewed German hope was the collapse of Russia, a national debacle which would permit the concentration of all troops on the Western Front. Another factor which made 1918 the year of decision in the minds of the German General Staff was the arrival of the American troops in France. It was decided that if Germany were to win she must strike before too many Americans could be ferried across the Atlantic and into combat.

Until 1918 the Allies had fought as individual nations, each under its own commanding general, but in 1918 a Supreme Allied Commander was selected for the first time. At the suggestion of Sir Douglas Haig, Marshal Ferdinand Foch was given this command. It was hoped that with a Supreme Allied Commander better coördination and greater unity could be obtained. Under a single command no side campaign or small operations would be permitted in order that a battle offensive could be uniformly maintained in Western Europe.

As stated earlier, long before 1918 both combatants had developed a system of trench networks. However, none of the trenches were constructed as they should have been. Part of the problem was attempting to build trenches under combat conditions, and the rest was the weather. Trenches in the summer were unsanitary nests which were covered with swarms of flies, lice, rats, and other kinds of vermin. In the winter they became mud holes filled with slime. Only during weather cold enough to freeze the mud did they offer any relief, and then those out on guard duty suffered from the cold. Such an existence as this was sure to break a man's spirit after a short stay in the trenches.

According to Mr. Pitt, another psychological factor which helped to break the spirit of front-line troops was enemy shelling. In trench warfare the element of surprise was discarded and when an attack was scheduled, the area to be taken was pulverized for several hours by artillery fire before the infantry emerged from the trenches to move against enemy positions. The infantry receiving the artillery bombardment was filled with anger and fear and a feeling of utter helplessness while under attack. They could only sit and wait it out in the hope of being able to return to the fire-step of the trench and repulse the advancing enemy when the artillery barrage began to lift. Many soldiers were killed under the impact and concussion of the exploding shells, but far more suffered mental breakdowns which left them helpless and useless in battle. The author's explanation of trench construction and trench warfare is brilliant, far surpassing anything that this reviewer has previously read on the subject.

When General Ludendorff decided

192

to assume the offensive in the early morning hours of March 21, he began the operation with the most concentrated artillery bombardment the world had ever known up to that time by ordering almost six thousand guns to begin firing on a forty-six mile front. This was the signal that Germany was attempting to break the stalemate. Initially, it appeared that the German offensive was highly successful, and that St. Quentin was to be the beginning of the end for the Allies. However, it was soon realized that the German troops were not equipped materially or spiritually for the task at hand. The troops were war-weary and had no stomach to do much more than go through the movements of attack after the first two days. Supplies of munitions and foodstuffs, vitally needed if the attack was to be maintained, failed to arrive. Then, too, Ludendorff began to lose his confidence and to make untimely changes in his battle plan at the most inopportune times. As a result, by April 1, the German General Staff began to prepare for another offensive movement.

On April 9, the German war machine began to attack Lys. Again it appeared that the Germans would achieve success during the early stages, but once more the Allies managed to break the force of the attack. The fighting thus far in 1918 had been extremely costly. According to Mr. Pitt, Germany had lost 56,639 killed and 252,186 hospitalized between March and May. Allied losses during the same period were 28,128 killed and 181,338 wounded.

The last offensive thrust of the Central Powers was to be unleashed in the battle of Chemin-Des-Dames in May. The Allies managed to stall the offensive, with the American Expeditionary Force taking the brunt of the German fury. The author is of the opinion that the Americans fought much better than anyone had expected; what they lacked in battle experience they made up in confidence and courage. At Château Thierry the Second Division beat back the German offensive. General Pershing, who had refused to integrate his forces into units of the Allied Army, may well have done a wise thing because the success of the Americans served to boost the sagging morale of French and British troops.

The second Battle of the Marne served as the turning point of the war when the Allies assumed the offensive in August of 1918. From this time on the Central Powers began to deteriorate rapidly. By November 1, 1918, it was realized that Germany could not continue the war for any length of time. Her armies were being slowly pushed back to her borders; she was virtually fighting alone; and because of the Allied blockade both her civilian and military populations were slowly starving.

The author describes the attempts of the General Staff to stop the war and improve the German position. President Wilson exchanged diplomatic correspondence with the German authorities but refused to be duped by them. The kaiser was forced to abdicate when the General Staff capitulated and the leaders of the new German Republic asked for an armistice.

Mr. Pitt discusses the aftermath of the war in his final chapter. He limits himself to military matters and does not include consideration of economic, social, or political problems. He briefly explains how the German military machine, which Hitler inherited when he came to power, was constructed. He also discusses the attrition of the armies of the victors through the development of a defeatist attitude in France and a growing isolationist attitude in the United States.

Mr. Pitt has written in this superb account of World War I a work of documented accuracy and historical insight.

J. Perry Cochran

NOTEBOOKS: 1935-1942

Author: Albert Camus (1913-1960)
Translated from the French by Philip Thady with a preface and notes by the translator
Publisher: Alfred A. Knopf (New York). 224 pp. $5.00
Type of work: Notations and comments

A diary of the observations and reflections and of the creative explorations underlying the French writer's published works

One of the prices of success, of becoming famous, is that one's entire life tends to become public property. For writers like Albert Camus, a foremost figure in the literary world since about 1940, as well as for movie stars and presidents, public acts are not enough for their audience; they only whet the appetite for an intimate and complete knowledge of the man. Heroes, fictional or real, inevitably must serve the purpose of allowing each of us in our solitariness genuine contact with another's humanity and through them with our own.

The quest for the man Albert Camus, who died in 1960 at the early age of forty-six, will proceed apace now, thanks to his considerateness. He kept a literary diary from 1935 to 1960, and in 1954 he had a typewritten copy made, apparently with the intention of publication, of his first seven notebooks. This volume includes the first three, covering the years between 1935 and 1942. The remaining four will be published in two volumes in the near future, but no decision has yet been made about publication of the remaining notebooks for the years 1956-1960. Camus complicates the task by eliminating personal matters from his diary

and restricting it to the life of his mind, but he opens up sufficient behind-the-scene activities to provide the quest after the man with an impetus that will endure for some time to come.

Notebooks opens with a long entry, dated May, 1935, in which Camus writes: "A guilty conscience needs to confess. A work of art is a confession, and I must bear witness. When I see things clearly, I have only one thing to say. It is in this life of poverty, among these vain or humble people, that I have most certainly touched what I feel is the true meaning of life. Works of art will never provide this and art is not everything for me. Let it at least be a means." The book closes with the entry dated February, 1942: "Cf. Marcus Aurelius: 'Wherever it is possible to live, it is possible to live well.' 'What prevents a work from being completed becomes the work itself.' *What bars our way makes us travel along it.*" Between these extremities exists a cornucopia of varying descriptions, quotations, insights, criticisms, and reflective and literary ideas. Nevertheless these two entries, whether or not by accident, reveal the definitive characteristics of Camus' mind—his main theme, as it were.

In an essay titled "Why I Write," written about sixteen years ago, Camus dissociated himself from those thinkers committed to the absurd and proclaimed his purpose to be, after the model of the Platonic myth of the cave, to turn and look into the fire from which his being as man and artist issued. Typical of the intellectual in the twentieth century, he had an acute sense of himself as estranged from all the possibilities of authentic experience, but he also had an implicit faith that such experience, in essence good, could be attained. Consequently, he envisaged his task as that of peeling off the imprisoning layers of falsity to release the power contained in the vital center. Poverty, life at its most rudimentary, for this reason fascinated him. Landscape, especially the brilliant, oppressively hot landscape of his native Algeria, elemental in its primitive force and vastness, obsessed his imagination for the same reason. And he could write, in Notebooks, against striving for exalted attainments: "We haven't time to be ourselves. All we have time for is happiness." And again, this time against the need to assert oneself, he wrote: "The innocent is the person who explains nothing." To live well, then, was to abandon the rock Sisyphus rolls up the mountain and to draw strength and peace from being.

More clearly than any other modern writer Camus could envisage and aspire after happiness, and his greatest achievement has been to remind modern man, burdened with anxiety and nothingness, of that possibility. But this contribution is not the whole man. In fact, Camus, despite all his close scrutiny of pleasure, was not a sensu-alist. Rather, he was a moralist. A work of art is a confession, and so his entire career was devoted to expunging his guilty conscience. His conscience barred his way, so that he had to travel along what barred it. He could not do what came easiest, could not turn his back on a challenge. When something pressed against him, he had to push back; Sisyphus' rock was a challenge he was unable to resist, not a necessity of his existence as a man. Perhaps writing was itself a stone; perhaps it got in the way of his living well. At any rate, his eye was focused on living, on acting and doing, art and thought being means, not ends in themselves. Because he invested so much in living well, morality, the essence of action, was his obsession, and because of this obsession, and his courage, he could create a moral vision of happiness within the limitations of life on earth.

The moralist, or the man who seeks to live well and therefore makes art and thought an adjunct of life, does not sufficiently commit himself to the mind to produce towering artifacts of the intellect or imagination. He sacrifices system and scope of vision to pragmatic moral insights. Certainly Camus did, and because he did Notebooks is superbly suited to his temperament and style. His mind plays over a wide range of subjects and events yet always illuminates them with quick, brilliant glints of light emanating from his empirical, moral involvement in life. The book places him more firmly than ever in the pantheon of such great modern moralists as Henry David Thoreau and George Orwell.

William R. Robinson

195

NOTES FROM A BOTTLE FOUND ON
THE BEACH AT CARMEL

Author: Evan S. Connell, Jr. (1924-   )
Publisher: The Viking Press (New York). 243 pp. $6.00
Type of work: Narrative poem
Time: The past and the present
Locale: The high seas, north and south

A *narrative poem in the form of a spiritual odyssey written in the Augustinian allegorical tradition*

In *Notes from a Bottle Found on the Beach at Carmel*, Evan S. Connell, Jr., has boldly and simply accomplished what was only recently called the impossible. He has written a long, complex, subtle book-length modern poem which is at once readable and worthy of admission into the small group of major poems written in our time. Known as a gifted short story writer and novelist, Connell's interest in poetry and, more important, his ease and ability in handling complex verse forms and conventions, were virtually unknown until a version of this poem appeared in *Contact*. That initial appearance and now the publication of the full poem in book form should have startled the small, tight little world of poets still lost in settling the issue of the formalists versus the so-called beats. The book has largely been ignored in the world of poetry, for it jars safe assumptions and rattles skeletons in closets. It has come upon the scene unannounced like a poor relation, lacking the usual letters of recommendation signed by such worthies as John Ciardi, Donald Hall, or Robert Bly. Still, curiously, the book has not been ignored by the public. Its sales have been steady and regular. It has found an audience.

The basic fable of the poem is clearly established in the title. It is, indeed, a work in the form of notes, snippets and fragments written by an archetypal seafarer and addressed to whom it may concern. He, the narrator, is at once all voyagers, all sailors and, as well, the author himself. The poem ranges wide and free among cultures and traditions, in time and space; and in the modern fashion established by Eliot and Pound its method is chiefly allusive. But it is just possible (time will tell) that Connell's achievement, though based on the pioneering of these masters, will prove to be greater. If this poem were to be indexed and footnoted, it would surely equal the *Cantos* in its multiplicity of allusive reference; yet Connell's allusions are not so much personal as representative of the fiber of our modern intellectual culture. Thus *Notes* is accessible to the intelligent, educated reader. It should also be noted that the book bears a definite relationship to the work of James Joyce. Like *Finnegans Wake*, it is a nightmare of all human history, all recorded time being, as in a dream, simultaneous, equally valid, and dramatic. Yet, somehow, Connell has managed to create a dream which is more universally the troubled dream of Western man in the atomic age.

The reason for the universality of the poem must surely lie in the fact

196

that, even though it is radical and altogether modern in decoration and details, its general metaphor of the life of man as a blind pilgrimage, a sea voyage without chart or destination, is one of the oldest in our literary history. During the transition from paganism to Christianity Saint Augustine preserved this image as a valid one for the Christian era. In the history of English literature we are familiar with its implications from the Anglo-Saxon "Seafarer" (to which Connell frequently alludes) into our own time with such poems as Joyce Cary's *The Drunken Sailor*, a poem which in many ways parallels Connell's. Connell is obviously aware of the tradition to which his poem belongs, for he invokes on several occasions Saint Augustine as the patron saint of the poem.

Not surprisingly the basic theme is human suffering in all ages, from Babylonian sacrifice to the modern concentration camp, to reveal the evidently irremediable loneliness and cruelty of the human animal. As the voyage continues, one by one all hopes and illusions are stripped away from the seafarer. Nothing makes sense or has meaning except the lonely voyage itself. At the moment of truth, however, the naked existential corner from which no man can flee, Connell turns back to the example of Boethius and Saint Augustine, achieving a resolution which must be called a triumph in a world without victories. It is the wisdom and triumph of Job.

What holds us here?
Why are we preserved?
There is no hope.

In this, our extremity,
I see how foolish we have been.

And the final line of the poem, "Submit to Providence," is precisely the Boethian choice, the more profound because, in spite of its merciless view of the ashes of human history and absurdity, it is a *free* choice.

Although the *matter* of *Notes* is complex and cumulative in the sense that bits and pieces cannot be easily abstracted from the texture of the whole, still it is characterized by lucid writing in verse. There has been no attempt to make the *manner* correspondingly difficult. Line by line, stanza by stanza, the verse is clear and coherent. There is no virtuoso writing for its own sake which might conceivably detract from the total impact. Basically, Connell uses a wide variety of free stanzaic forms. Periodically for the sudden intrusion of abstract speculation he employs a quick one- or two-line epigramatic statement, as though it were a marginal note to the action of the poem.

All is possible to those who believe

. . . . . .

I do not think too highly of men; nor too lowly.

. . . . . .

He is nowhere upon the mountain
where we had thought
to find Him, nor among galactic systems.

Variation is created by differences in length of line and stanzaic unit. Familiar verse forms are not used and Connell does not rely upon the obvious devices of poetry. Instead, he bases his form upon direct statement and the various rhythms of the spoken language. The possibilities of the form are exemplified in this passage, spoken by a concentration camp victim who returns to the scene of the crime:

197

The keeper explained with an apologetic smile there was not much to be seen any more, it had been so long. Brush and weeds had overgrown the odd cylindrical hut. I did not tell him I had seen it once, or that I almost accepted his invitation to enter, to hang up my clothing on a hook and refresh myself with a shower from the painted nozzles.

I did not tell the keeper I had ever seen this place, since he failed to recognize me. I am touring your country, I said, and of course such things as this are invariably interesting.

Connell has written a long, religious poem at a time when both the long poem and the religious symbols which are its life blood have been declared defunct. This book will surely be discussed and studied for years to come.

George Garrett

OLD RED AND OTHER STORIES

Author: Caroline Gordon (1895-   )
Publisher: Charles Scribner's Sons (New York). 256 pp. $4.50
Type of work: Short stories
Thirteen stories, set mostly in the South, by a distinguished novelist and critic

One of the most influential of recent short story anthologies is *The House of Fiction*, edited by Allen Tate and Caroline Gordon. The editors, disciples in theory and practice of Flaubert and Henry James, show scrupulous care for the craft of fiction, and they reserve most praise for those writers who approach the craft with intelligence, integrity, and subtlety.

Miss Gordon's longer fiction shows that she has taken a similar approach. Her first novel, *Penhally*, was published in 1931. *Aleck Maury, Sportsman*, which at least one critic (William Van O'Connor) considers a "masterpiece," appeared in 1934. The title character appears in many of the stories in the present collection, including the best known of Miss Gordon's tales, "Old Red." Katherine Anne Porter has said that *None Shall Look Back* (1937) is the best novel about the Civil War.

Miss Gordon's first collection of stories, *The Forest of the South*, was pub-

lished in 1945. *Old Red and Other Stories* is not a gathering of stories written since that volume; stories appear here that were published as early as 1933. Four of the thirteen have never appeared in book form before, one of which ("One Against Thebes") is to be the second chapter in Miss Gordon's work-in-progress, *A Narrow Heart: The Portrait of a Woman*.

Miss Gordon is a Southerner and her stories are Southern, almost without exception. When she moves out of this familiar territory—as she does in "Emmanuele! Emmanuele!"—the result can be disastrous. This is a thinly disguised story about André Gide and his wife, and if one did not know the key, it would surely be a meaningless exercise. Reviewers have asked, and rightly, why Miss Gordon has attempted to tell a story that Gide has already related with great artistry.

The other stories are set in the West and the South, and they present a uni-

198

fied, consistent, and artfully worked vision of life. "The Captive," a bloody, dramatic recital of Indian torture, scalping, and kidnaping, wanders farthest in theme and setting, but the narrator of that story evokes images of her girlhood in "the Roanoke country." Like most serious Southern writers, Miss Gordon is deeply concerned with the land, with time, with the tragic, pathetic, or victorious attempts of the characters to cope with both. Arthur Mizener has defined what is to be sought, what is ideal in the workings of this triangle:

. . . The best Southern writers look at life with a clear understanding . . . that the most meaningful and valuable world we can live in is the longest known and most familiar, that the past must be cherished as part of the present, and that the most important thing to do with the life we actually live from day to day is to love it. Love it adequately and yet without illusion as to its real nature; live it on these terms, and one makes of it, whether he knows it or not, an art, as Aleck Maury makes an art of his life of hunting and fishing in Old Red.

Aleck Maury is the central figure in many of these stories. He establishes a norm of behavior and belief, and those characters whose lives vary from that norm most often come to grief. He is sometimes the central character, sometimes the father of the girl who serves as narrator. The world of fishing and hunting, of lures, guns, and dogs, horses and mules, of autumn leaves, rivers, and waterfalls may sometimes, as in "The Brilliant Leaves," be a setting for tragedy, but it is the world of real value.

The intruder who comes to destroy this world takes various forms. It is sickness that drives Maury's friend Bob Reynolds to suicide in "One More Time." He drowns himself in the beloved Blue Hole, the fishing spot that is the center of the world of real value. Human passion is the most familiar form the intruder takes. In "The Presence," Jim Mowbray is "as fine a wing shot as ever lived, as gifted a handler," but his infidelity destroys his wife: "But here was a kind of death. She lay there like a shot bird." Its absence can be as destructive; Cousin Tom and Cousin Eleanor in "The Petrified Woman" play out their pathetic story before the uncomprehending eyes of the children gathered at the cave for the reunion. Wood and cave, family gossip and the loving recital of genealogy are the stable background to the desperate scene that the children witness. The Petrified Woman of the carnival is for them only an occasion for secret jokes; for Tom it is an image of his atrophied marriage. "Some women are just petrified in spots," Cousin Tom said. "She was petrified all over."

The finest story in the collection is undoubtedly "Old Red." Aleck Maury is a complex character: a classicist, he is not naïve about human history and motive. But he knows that abstract knowledge can be a trap. He considers his son-in-law, Stephen:

Poor boy, dead to the world and would probably be that way the rest of his life. A pang of pity shot through Mister Maury and on the heels of it a gust of that black fear that occasionally shook him. It was he, not Steve, that was the queer one. The world was full of people like this boy, all of them going around with their heads so full of this and that they hardly knew what they were doing.

Maury is proud, and he knows that his

pride and his instinctive allegiance to his own nature, and its likeness to the laws of the natural world, are his salvation. The symbolic figure of the fox develops naturally in the story, and both he and the fox *see* the world, know it, and know how to cope with it. The fox flees the foxhound (which

"remains at heart a wild beast and must kill and gorge and then . . . kill and gorge again") and finds salvation under Pinnacle Rock. Aleck Maury leaves his daughter, his son-in-law, memories of his dead wife: "Thirty minutes after he got off the train he would have a fly in that water."

James Boatwright

ON REVOLUTION

Author: Hannah Arendt (1906-   )
Publisher: The Viking Press (New York). 343 pp. $6.50
Type of work: Philosophical study

An examination of the nature of revolution and the part that it has played and will probably play in world culture

Americans looking with distaste, if not horror, on revolution, forget that our own nation began with a revolution almost two centuries ago. Reminded of our government's origins, we often reply to the effect that the American Revolution was different. One of the aspects of Dr. Arendt's book is that she shows how the American Revolution *was* different and that America's singular success in establishing a stable and lasting government is in large part due to that difference.

Citing eighteenth century writers, Dr. Arendt shows that in colonial America there was no grinding poverty, except for the Negro slaves, nor was there an absolutist government that the colonials sought to unseat. People were not lacking, she notes, in the fulfillment of their basic needs for food, shelter, and clothing. The American Revolution, when it came, did not pass into the control of people suffering utter poverty. The American Revolution remained a middle-class revolution. The colonials were essentially Englishmen accustomed to a constitu-

tional monarchy; they rebelled because they were being deprived of rights enjoyed by other Englishmen. When they removed themselves from the authority of the British government they instituted a relatively similar government in which power was restricted. As colonials they had experience in establishing a government in a new environment, so that the creation of government was not for them a new and alien experience. Indeed, as the author notes, before adopting the federal Constitution the original colonies had individually created and adopted state constitutions.

By comparison, in Europe, from the time of the French Revolution on, and in other parts of the world too, revolutions have been against absolutist forms of government, monarchies and dictatorships of one kind or another. Such forms have been succeeded by equally absolutist forms, usually after the lowest classes in the society have seized control of the revolutionary movement from its middle-class initiators and leaders. Such lower-class people have failed, suggests Dr. Arendt, even to understand what freedom is or what participation in government ought to be; thus their revolutions have ended inevitably in despotism and failure.

In one of the most thought-provoking sections of *On Revolution*, Dr. Arendt suggests that lower-class ideals, molded by poverty and want, have come to the American scene and now endanger the future of American government. In the eighteenth century people understood that happiness, as it was associated with government, was public happiness as opposed to private welfare. This concept was so taken for granted, says the writer, that in the Declaration of Independence it was deemed unnecessary to use the word "public" in the statement about "life, liberty, and the pursuit of happiness." It was understood, she maintains, that public happiness, the opportunity to act, to be seen and to be recognized by one's equals on the political scene, was intended. The danger, in her opinion, comes from forgetting this meaning of "happiness." She accepts the view that this concept has in large measure been forgotten, and she proceeds to examine the reasons for and the results of that forgetfulness.

Migration during the latter part of the nineteenth century and during the early decades of the twentieth century, Dr. Arendt points out, brought hundreds of thousands of poverty-stricken, uneducated Europeans to America, people who knew nothing but utter deprivation and want, coming as they did from the lowest socio-economic classes. These people knew nothing of "public happiness" and could not, says the writer, because their only interpretation of "happiness" was personal and material. For them the pursuit of happiness was the search for food to eat, clothing to wear, and shelter from the elements. These matters they understood; they became the basis of political values. The children and grandchildren of these people have brought a change to American thinking, suggests Dr. Arendt, so that in our time people are interested not in the pursuit of public happiness but in the pursuit of private welfare—seeking a happiness that is personal, selfish, and based on the accumulation and use of things. Such is the origin indicated in *On Revolution* for the wave of hedonism rampant in our America. It comes, is the suggestion, not from a new generation of people who have rediscovered hedonism for themselves; it comes from people who remember too well their ancestors and are all too like them in their values and ideals.

Historians too often have misled us, with the result that people generally have a wrong concept of revolution. The events of violence, the rebellion, have captured the fancy of both the historian and the common man. In the action of the events of any rebellion there are drama and emotion to stir the heart and grip the spectator and the student of history. But the violence of rebellion is only the first part of a revolution. It can be sterile or even lead to disaster. Once the old regime is gone, and rebellion's aim is to topple the old regime, a new and stable government is the goal. If the goal is not achieved, the rebellion has been fruitless. While people throughout the world have proclaimed a desire for freedom and self-determination, history shows us that few have achieved the goals. Rebellions have occurred and regimes have fallen; but the people quickly have

201

found themselves under a new order much like the one that fell. The rebellion has succeeded, but the revolution has failed.

Dr. Arendt sees revolution as the prime political phenomenon in the future, inasmuch as war has become an absurdity in a society where nuclear weapons have made it possible for both sides to achieve mutual annihilation. As a result we must begin to understand revolution as we have not in the past. Part of our understanding must be the way in which a revolution can be truly successful in establishing a government that will continue with stability and with the ability to keep people part of its action. Everyone must have a place for political action based upon his abilities. Everyone, the writer submits, must have an opportunity to participate in government in some additional manner other than voting on election day. Merely voting, whether in a free country or under a dictatorship, in a multi-party or in a one-party situation, is not enough for people if they are to pursue "public happiness." Politics has become a career, so that space for public action is closed, maintains Dr. Arendt, for everyone but the professional in politics. What is needed is grass-roots councils where people have opportunity for political action and status. This suggestion, she carefully points out, is not original with her. The idea is an old one. Thomas Jefferson in his later life thought that some system of "ward" councils was most important to our country for the very purpose of supplying political space for everyone's political activity.

On Revolution is in every way a thought-provoking book. It challenges the reader to think as he reads, and to read slowly and carefully. A vast amount of knowledge and thought has been assimilated into these pages. It may well be that future generations will consider this one of the most thoughtful books and one of the most important books on politics in this century.

Gordon W. Clarke

ONE DAY IN THE LIFE OF IVAN DENISOVICH

Author: Alexander Solzhenitsyn (1919-   )
Translated from the Russian by Max Hayward and Ronald Hingley, with an introduction by Max Hayward and Leopold Labedz, and a statement by Alexander Tvardovsky, editor of *Novy Mir*
Publisher: Frederick A. Praeger (New York). 210 pp. $3.95
Type of work: Novel
Time: A day in January, 1951
Locale: A labor camp in Siberia

The chronicle of a day in a Russian concentration camp, with an expanding significance which comprises a startling view of man and society

> Principal characters:
> IVAN DENISOVICH SHUKHOV, convicted of treason, formerly a carpenter
> ALYOSHKA, a Baptist prisoner
> BUYNOVSKY (THE CAPTAIN), recently convicted
> TYURIN, a prisoner and boss of Shukhov's Gang 104
> PAVLO, his assistant
> FETYUKOV,
> CAESAR MARKOVICH,
> SENKA,
> KILGAS, and
> TWO ESTONIANS, prisoners
> LIEUTENANT VOLKOVOY, the disciplinary officer

Alexander Solzhenitsyn is part of the *nouvelle vague* of post-Stalin Russian letters which includes Pasternak and Yevtushenko. Khrushchev has condemned the "personality cult" of Stalin and is sponsoring a mass "rehabilitation" program for long-term political prisoners, convicted during the purge of the late 1930's and the period of World War II. Having been in prisons and concentration camps since 1945, Solzhenitsyn was rehabilitated in 1957, and his novel obviously grew from most direct experience. As a social document it reveals both the insane injustices and cruelties of the Stalin regime and the new liberality of Moscow, for the novel (unlike *Doctor Zhivago*) was published and well received in Russia.

But *One Day in the Life of Ivan Denisovich* transcends the documen-

tary and takes its place with more universal novels which use social and political upheaval to lay bare the human condition, novels like *The Red Badge of Courage, The Enormous Room,* and *Darkness at Noon.* All of these books isolate and focus on a single man in the unusual situation of war or imprisonment, all see the world through that man's eyes, and all give startling and fresh insights into the structure of the universe and the psychology of man.

As Crane did before him, Solzhenitsyn offers an extremely realistic work. Almost one-quarter of the sentences deal with the twenty-below-zero cold and means of protecting oneself from it, and another quarter of the book recounts the complex intrigues by which Shukhov acquires enough food for himself. An awareness of the passing of time permeates the narrative. The book begins with a pre-dawn reveille and ends with a count of the length of Shukhov's sentence: 3,653 days. The sun and the moon play important roles in Shukhov's life because they mark the beginning and end of each workday. The January day spanning the time sequence of the novel is a sunny one, and this simple fact elicits comments from the prisoners. The Russian word for the rays of a sunburst as seen in a mist is the same word used for a fence post, and this bitter pun develops:

> "We don't mind posts," said Kilgas, and he laughed. "As long as they don't stretch barbed wire over them. . . ."

Later the mist vanishes, but the sun gives no warmth:

> "It's only cows who get warm from the sun in January," Shukhov said.

Again, discovering that the Soviet Government has dictated that the sun is highest at one o'clock rather than noon (because of daylight saving time) Shukhov remarks: "Did the sun come under their laws too?" This statement serves as a good example of the whole tone of the novel, a naïveté underlined by a pervasive irony.

In his rapid, penetrating sketches of character Solzhenitsyn follows Cummings' method in *The Enormous Room*. Some characters are described with a single obscenity, some by their names themselves (Volkovoy, from *volk*, "wolf"), some by phrases (". . . that scavenger Fetyukov" or ". . . Stepan Grigoryevich, a loudmouth know-it-all who never stayed still himself and never let his patients alone"), others by an ironic sentence: "The Captain was used to giving orders and he always talked to people like this." Unfortu-

nately, however, his manner of speaking led the Captain into ten days of half-rationed solitary confinement in the "cooler" for insulting Volkovoy. A prisoner invariably contracted tuberculosis after ten days in the heatless cooler. In the straightforward narration of events, from pitiful breakfast to a day of bricklaying to pitiful dinner to bed, in the deathly cold under the constant eye of the guards, these glimpses of character illuminate the life of Shukhov. Working with his fellow prisoners, the tightly knit community of Gang 104, Shukhov can forget the cold, forget his wife whom he has not seen in eight years, and forget his ceaseless hunger.

The high points of the novel are the brief, singularly laconic statements about the prisoners' pasts. Tyurin's story, which marks the center of the book (lunch time) is told "without pity, like it wasn't about himself." Just before his capture, Tyurin kidnaped his brother from his home and gave him to "a gang of young thugs."

> ". . . and I said, 'Listen here, gentlemen of the gutter, take this kid brother of mine and give him an education. Teach him how to live.' . . ."
> "And you never saw your brother again?" asked the Captain.
> The boss yawned.
> "No, I never saw him again." And he yawned once more.

Shukhov was convicted of treason because he had been captured by the Germans. After his escape he was condemned to ten years in forced labor camps; he knew he would never see home again.

The circumstances of life in Shukhov's camp reduce the social animal to his simplest form. The philosophy of the prisoner must be extremely practical in order for him to survive. Shuk-

204

hov learned this philosophy during his first year in camp, from an old hand, a twelve-year gang boss:

> "It's the law of the jungle here, fellows. But even here you can live. The first to go is the guy who licks out bowls, puts his faith in the infirmary, or squeals to the screws."

Licking up other men's unfinished food could lead to disease, and "squealing to the screws" (informing) could lead to a cut throat. On the one hand there must be individual cunning:

> It was every man for himself. Who is the prisoner's worst enemy? The guy next to him.

On the other there must be self-sacrificing teamwork:

> That's how it was in your gang. The higher-ups had a job to get a prisoner to work even in working hours, but the boss only had to say the word, even if it was the meal break, and you worked. Because it was the boss who fed you. And he wouldn't make you work if he didn't have to.

Shukhov's religion is a simple theism. When asked if he believes in God he replies:

> "And why not? When He thunders up there in the sky, how can you help but believe in Him?"

The waning of the moon, says Shukhov, is caused by God's breaking it up into stars to replace the ones that fall. When confronted with the organized martyrlike religion of the Baptist Alyoshka, Shukhov balks. His final statement on the subject, which seems to sum up the general Russian attitude, is denial:

> "Look, Alyoshka," Shukhov said, "it's all right for you. It was Christ told you to come here, and you are here because of Him. But why am I here? Because they didn't get ready for the war like they should've in forty-one? Was that my fault?"

Religion is as foreign to Shukhov's world as are Caesar Markovich's discussions of Eisenstein's film-making.

Solzhenitsyn's theme is clear. Man is first of all a biological animal: take away his material comforts, leave him physically naked, and one is forced to conclude with King Lear that ". . . unaccommodated man is no more but a poor, base, forked animal as thou art." Sophistication in man consists in more and more elaborate techniques for acquiring food and warmth. Shukhov succeeds in these pursuits during the day given to his story. He has almost doubled his normal food ration, and he has not been thrown in the cooler. "Nothing had spoiled the day and it had been almost happy."

But the novel ends with the unspoken question that all Russians, all men, are asking today: What of tomorrow?

Stephen Barney

THE PALACE

Author: Claude Simon (1913-   )
Translated from the French by Richard Howard
Publisher: George Braziller (New York). 252 pp. $4.50
Type of work: Novel
Time: 1951 and 1936
Locale: Barcelona

A novel in which memories of the Spanish Civil War mingle with the present to determine the full extent of reality for the central character, who is visiting Barcelona after a fifteen-year absence

> Principal characters:
> THE CENTRAL FIGURE, a student in the Republican army in 1936
> THE AMERICAN, a volunteer in the Republican army
> THE RIFLE, an Italian soldier and assassin
> THE SCHOOLTEACHER, a Republican official

The fiction of those younger French writers who have, to whatever degree, been involved in the recent renascence of the French novel (*le nouveau roman*) are of particular interest to American readers not only for the intrinsic merit of the books, but also because of the evidence they offer of the tremendous impact of two American novelists, Henry James and William Faulkner, on much of the most advanced and stimulating work being done in that form today. The novels of Michel Butor and Alain Robbe-Grillet have shown this influence in their use of time and in their careful attention to a precisely controlled and restricted point of view, but the novels of Claude Simon, of which *The Palace* is the most recent, are most clearly a part of the James-Faulkner tradition, in form, content, and even manner. In his earlier novels, and especially in *The Wind* (1959), *The Grass* (1960), and *The Flanders Road* (1961), Simon exhibited a Jamesian preoccupation with the human nuances of particular events and a Faulknerian attitude toward the immediacy of the past and the involvement of the past in an eternal present.

These attitudes have developed his style as well as the pattern of his ideas to their most ambitious and original level in *The Palace*, a novel in which the past is as immediate and as much a part of the present as the particular objects, people, and events which would normally be considered to constitute that present.

Simon's prose is perhaps the obvious place to begin any discussion of *The Palace*, for in the manner is the key to what may seem puzzling about the matter. Simon's prose is a nearly perfect representation of his vision of the texture of life itself. His sentences are long (longer even than Faulkner's), in the present tense, and unified by participles; any specific event is, thus, syntactically involved with the past events which preceded it and the possible events to follow it—one of Faulkner's techniques developed to its logical culmination. Simon has moved beyond Bergsonian duration of time, the principle behind the earlier novels, and composed this novel with static scenes, totally experienced and expanded to the limits of perception and comprehension. The result is a construct in

206

which time and memory have disappeared into a present sensorially rich with the past, a subjectively eternal present. The length of the sentences, then, involves present and past, and the use of participles and the present tense communicates the immediacy of experience, present and past, in a revolving continuum indicated by the epigraph of the novel, significant beyond its humble origin in the *Dictionnaire Larousse*:

Revolution: the locus of a moving body which, describing a closed curve, successively passes through the same points.

The idea of revolution also dominates the imagery of the novel: birds wheel about the square; a revolving door is at the center of one episode; stairs turn through the center of the palace of the title; and the city itself (Barcelona, the dust jacket suggests) was "apparently torn by something that had come out of, or rather that it had wrested, expelled from itself, more (blood and ordure) like a kind of childbirth, or perhaps an abortion, whose effects were distributed centrifugally, as the fragments of a bomb fan out from its explosion point." The structure of the entire novel, like that of any single sentence, is a revolution, or series of revolutions, as memory carries the central character's present through the events of his past.

The central figure of the novel is visiting Spain in 1951, fifteen years after he had been there as a student and as a volunteer for the Republican cause. Those days in 1936 were the high point of his life, a time when, despite the violence and chaos, men were "still exuding something invincible, something indestructible (not a belief, a faith, nor even a conviction, still

less the certainty of being right: merely knowing that, good or bad, things could be otherwise)." Since that time he has come to feel alienated, apart even from his own past. As he sits in a park opposite the palace, which had been the Republican headquarters and has been converted into a bank in the years following the war, he allows his mind to recover several events which occurred on two days in 1936: the funeral of a murdered general, his being told of an assassination by the Rifle (an Italian volunteer), the leaving of an American for the front, and his frustrated attempts to find out about the American's departure. The memories simply make his alienation more complete; he is overcome by an awareness of mutability and of loss, as if "they had left him there, abandoned him to slow desiccation, his flesh gradually crumbling to dust without anyone's noticing."

The central character fails to come to terms with a past which had failed him, and present and past fuse at the end of the novel in a whirling vision of futile search amid disintegration and decay. Simon weaves all of the characters and images of the story together in these last pages into a brilliant realization of the hero's despair, "like those flocks of anxious, plaintive and wild birds he saw fluttering endlessly as they wailed over something invisible, some carrion, some dying beast, some monster, some sick Leviathan already beginning to decompose though still alive." These images lead to the central character's culminating vision of the city and of everything that he values, "exhausted, expiring, without hope that it can ever end, draining away in a tiny, incessant and futile hemorrhage: not even cut open, stabbed, nothing but a little blood seeping, endlessly trickling through a tiny and invisible fissure in the very center of the body."

Claude Simon's achievement is a brilliant one within the proper scope of the novelist: he has made no philosophical statement about the human condition; he has, rather, presented in the highest of artistic terms the patterns of a particular human consciousness trying to come to grips with the movement of time and the irreparable loss of youth, idealism, and the past. If the mind of the character at the center of this novel is confused, the hand of the author is always sure and certain. Claude Simon, whose name has yet to be fully recognized in this country, is a worthy successor to the tradition of James and Faulkner; his is as true a talent as *The Palace* is a brilliant example of the art of which that talent is capable.

R. H. W. Dillard

PARNASSUS CORNER
A Life of James T. Fields, Publisher to the Victorians

Author: W. S. Tryon (1901-   )
Publisher: Houghton Mifflin Company (Boston). 445 pp. $7.00
Type of work: Biography
Time: 1817-1881
Locale: New Hampshire, Boston, New York, and Europe

The story of the junior partner of the famed Ticknor and Fields, "the most distinguished publisher's imprint in America," and of Boston's Old Corner Bookstore, the gathering place of the most distinguished American and English gentlemen of letters

Principal personages:
> JAMES T. FIELDS, publisher, lecturer, poet, essayist, and editor
> ANNIE ADAMS FIELDS, his wife, hostess to the Victorians
> WILLIAM DAVIS TICKNOR, senior partner and astute business manager of the publishing firm
> CHARLES DICKENS, their friend and intimate, last of the great men
> HENRY WADSWORTH LONGFELLOW,
> JAMES RUSSELL LOWELL,
> OLIVER WENDELL HOLMES,
> RALPH WALDO EMERSON,
> WILLIAM MAKEPEACE THACKERAY,
> CHARLES READE, and
> THOMAS DE QUINCEY, writers who contracted for their books with Fields

Warren S. Tryon, professor, historian, editor, and author, is not the usual historian, nor is Houghton Mifflin Company the usual patron. The latter, an outgrowth of the great publishing house of Ticknor and Fields, has published *Parnassus Corner* in a replica format worthy of the Ticknor and Fields imprint; the former has made readable and inspiring a biography and cultural history of a great man in great times for literature. The whole is a tribute to a most worthy institution, the American publisher. The documenta-

208

tion is exact, complete, resourceful, and the writing is in the sound tradition of literary journalism.

The sketchy early life of James T. Fields, an almost rags-to-riches story so sentimentally dear to Americans, sheds very little light on what a cheerful, accommodating, resourceful bookseller and publisher he would become. Endowed as he was with excellent health, good looks, strong principles, how could he have failed? His faith in himself was unquestioned; his first and only employer never doubted him either. The teen-age boy, never an intimate or a close friend of the employer whose partner he later became, not only polished up the handle on the seven-to-seven open door of America's most famous bookstore, but also ingratiated himself to its patrons first and later to authors throughout his life. His industry never slackened in those early years, no matter how menial his tasks. As a young bookseller he learned his greatest lessons in merchandising and circulation, experience which helped him to transfer the bookseller's trade into a publishing industry. He loved and read books, wittily and enthusiastically endorsed them and their authors, and formed the great tie between the top and the bottom of the title page.

As the reverential young man he was soon known and loved by Longfellow and Holmes, Lowell and Whittier in America; and as an Anglophile he then went on to cultivate Tennyson, the Brownings, Hunt, De Quincey, and above all Dickens. He was the first great publisher on either side of the Atlantic to consider the author first, who weakened the ties of patronage and opened the market to copyright protection, who with great aesthetic appreciation and taste made the hand-somest books of the period. Even during depressions he managed with the solid support of his great mentor-partner to keep solid business feet on the rock of Whig enterprise.

So ebullient and talented was he that his early life promised to be in letters and not printer's ink, and his devotion to the lecture and lyceum both educated and advanced him. Called on to write commemorative odes (" 'We are lost!' the captain shouted" is the most parodied but not one of his better verses) and satirical disquisitions, he performed with verve and to great applause. His several volumes of poems, essays, travel, and biography were extremely popular in his own day and worth reading even now. But it was as friend, editor, and publisher of the finest writers of his time that he achieved an immortality with the names he loved and promoted.

His climb was not without reverses. He suffered personal losses and occasional lapses into anguish and melancholy which would have retired a less strong-willed editor and publisher. His fiancée died suddenly of tuberculosis; her sister, whom he married a few years later, died of the same disease; his mother's lingering illness debilitated him; and his closest friend, Charles Dickens, died during his great reversal of fortune. The treachery of trusted friends who publicly accused him of sharp practices was the blow that drove him into retirement after forty years in publishing. To escape the blight these charges cast on his spirit, he returned to the lecture stage until ill health forced him into completing a work sketchily begun and greatly needed. He wrote a series of essays on the lives and works of the great men he knew so well, studies not valuable as criticism but informing as biography. He had an almost indiscriminate love for those he knew, and while his judgment was good his motives were often puerile. Also, the manner in which he promoted books, the first "hard sell" in book dealing, made his method suspect. Fields himself never questioned his practices or the questionable matter of contracts which brought misfortune to his later years. He dealt in justifications and rationalizations of a particularly personal kind and shaved the edge of truth while remaining within the law. But this is all.

In his properly Bostonian house in Charles Street his second wife, who survived him by thirty-five years and continued to entertain famous literary figures, graciously extended his influence. Her greatest moment was as hostess to Charles Dickens, who in turn entertained majestically his devoted friends on their last grand tour. No one can doubt that this deep regard was genuine, but we now wonder at the excessive manner.

As editor of the *Atlantic Monthly,* the discoverer of an even greater editor in William Dean Howells, Fields extended his influence into the modern era. Both Henry James and Mark Twain were somewhat halting admirers of the indefatigable couple; neither could resist the Fields' good nature and kindly devotion. Nor could they fail to observe with Holmes that the master craftsman made all their lives possible and pleasant. Hawthorne, Fields' most important discovery and most devoted disciple, never ceased recounting the benefits received from both Ticknor and Fields. Ironically, his widow later joined in the hate campaign against the firm for imagined slights. Without Fields, *The Scarlet Letter* would have been a sketch merely. Even though nothing is said of the relationship of Fields and Thoreau, *Walden* might have been a vanity publication lying in Concord along with the peptic philosopher's first book.

It is easy for us today to see the too sentimental manner, the Philistinism of that Victorian and Augustan time. It is easy to smile at—or criticize—the weaknesses and the excesses. Men like Fields and Dickens are fair game to some modern critics, a workshop for the Freudians. The troubling thing is to look around for another corner on Parnassus, only to find the giants gone, the wares modernized.

William Tillson

PEKING AND MOSCOW

Author: Klaus Mehnert (1906-   )
Translated from the German by Leila Vennewitz
Publisher: G. P. Putnam's Sons (New York). 522 pp. $6.95
Type of work: Political science and history
Time: 1917-1962
Locale: Asia and Europe

An outstanding student of Communism simplifies the Sino-Soviet problem for the general reader by contrasting China and Russia over centuries

Principal personages:
CHIANG KAI-SHEK
SUN YAT-SEN
CHOU EN-LAI
MAO TSE-TUNG
V. LENIN
J. V. STALIN
NIKITA KHRUSHCHEV
DWIGHT D. EISENHOWER

Klaus Mehnert is frequently considered Germany's leading authority on both Russia and China. He has lived many years in both countries, whose languages he knows. He accompanied Konrad Adenauer to Moscow in 1955, and in 1959, under a Ford Foundation grant, he made his thirteenth trip to Russia and his ninth to China. Out of youthful experiences in Moscow and his years as journalist there, he has written *Youth in Soviet Russia* (1933), followed by *Stalin vs. Marx* (1952) and *The Soviet Man and His World* (1961). Now comes the present volume (first published in Germany in 1962) in an excellent English translation by Leila Vennewitz.

Many Americans look upon the cold war as a clash between democracy and communism, an individual bloc of a billion people. To Mehnert, however, the present struggle is a three-way conflict between the West and two different forms of communism. In the pages of this book, he reveals communism as diverse, quarrelsome, and conflict-rid-

den, and he finds a parallel between it and the political and spiritual contest of Rome and Byzantium in the fourth century, with possible results to the civilized world as far-reaching as were caused by that schism.

His first chapter poses questions that he attempts to answer in the four sections of this study:

To what conclusions are we led by a comparison of the Chinese and the Russians as to the present and future relationship of the two nations?

What are the powers of resistance—of the susceptibility—of the Chinese and the Russian people toward communism, yesterday, today, and tomorrow?

Is communism the logical crowning of each people or is it a complete contradiction of all that is Chinese or Russian?

To those who see the Tartar in every Muscovite, Klaus Mehnert's insistance that there is nothing "Asiatic" about the Russian people will be upsetting. His introduction, differentia-

211

ting the national characteristics of each, even though the characteristics have changed with time, states his theme. Again and again in the four chapters of Part I titled "Peoples," appear the phrases: "in contrast" or "as antithesis." Innumerable anecdotes from his personal experience illuminate the differences, beginning with a description of a volatile Russian family living beside the author in a Shanghai apartment building, whom he contrasts with their immutable Chinese servants.

The Chinese, Mehnert states, have a "shame culture." As the antithesis of the Westerner, who suffers from an inward feeling of guilt even when no one knows about his crime, the Chinese "loses face" only because his crime has been observed. Another difference, the author suggests, is that a Westerner, faced with a conflict, is likely to ask: "Which side is right?" The opportunist Oriental will wonder: "Which side is likely to win?"

Stressing the Chinese lack of consideration for, or interest in, others, their capacity for finding happiness in adversity, and their tolerant attitude even toward exhausting work, Mehnert shows why the attitudes of the two peoples toward communism is so different. His chapter on heritage continues his thesis: "In its spiritual heritage, Old Russia is, of all the peoples of Europe, the antithesis of Classical China." Some critics believe that Mehnert has somewhat romanticized Russia's Slavic past and the peasants' love of land and God, but there is no denial that the individualistic Chinese displays no interest in world salvation that could be turned, as in the case of the Russians, into the Communists' secular doctrine of salvation. Perhaps, suggests the author, the Chinese bend before

the inevitable when required to demonstrate in behalf of some absolute goal or some non-Chinese people. He quotes an anti-Communist who shrugged off the movement with the patient comment: "It will pass. Even the rule of the Manchus lasted less than three hundred years."

By his comparison of the two societies the author shows the difference in the growing media in which the seeds of communism were planted. Russian obligations degraded those subjected to them, almost to the status of slaves. Lenin, as liberator and spokesman for the masses, held up as models to the peasants the developing middle class in order to inspire the workers to seek a life of dignity and equal rights. The Chinese peasant, in contrast, was an individualist, never held in servitude by either family or clan so closely circumscribing his life. From the author's personal observation and from his reading of old and modern Chinese writers he believes that the Oriental civilization could have gone on peacefully if disturbing Western influences had not impinged upon it. The first Communist article published in China, he points out, stressed the fundamental equality of all men before God and appeared in a Y.M.C.A. magazine. Eventually the ensuing liberalism became communism. Mehnert charges the West, especially Japan in the war of 1937, with being responsible because the educated younger generation was driven inland, away from the liberalizing Western influences of the coastal region. This help given communism is confirmed by another book published in 1963, Arthur Young's *China and the Helping Hand: 1937-1945.* It was inevitable that the penetration of the modern world into Russia and China should bring immense changes with it; that it should lead to communism, however, was not inevitable. Why, then, did it take that form?

The course taken by the revolutions in the two nations, as outlined in Part II, "Revolutionaries," was quite different. Why did both end as Communist states?

As the author describes the Marxist image of history, capitalism puts an end to feudalism as the bourgeoisie gains power. Then, during the ensuing industrial revolution, the proletariat overthrows the bourgeoisie and establishes a dictatorship which is to be followed by the ideal classless society. In Russia, this change was accomplished during the "ten days that shook the world." In China, the struggle of Mao Tse-tung lasted a quarter century, despite his utilization of many of the Russian techniques. The contributions and resistance of the Chinese social classes, the peasants and workers, the middle class, and the intelligentsia, are discussed. But Mehnert shows how the Chinese standard of living fell as few of the workers were brought into the party because of the leaders' suspicion of them. In Russia, after Stalin's reign of terror, the proletariat became state employees and eventually the Russian standard of living rose.

In the attitude of literary people, as described in one interesting chapter, "The Troublesome Intellectuals," national traditions again produced differences. Following Stalin's death, Russian writers and artists had more freedom and yet generally followed party lines; in China, following Mao's "Let flowers of many kinds bloom" speech, the temporary freedom brought only critical literature. Brainwashing and the attempted re-education of the Chinese are also considered in this chapter, along with the amusing failures of the various "campaigns," the anti-fly, the anti-bedbug, and the anti-sparrow campaigns which, starting because the birds ate some of the grain, ended with the crop failures of 1959-1961 because these pests, previously checked by the birds, took over.

After stressing differences, in Part III, "Neighbors," Mehnert reports Mao as the pupil and imitator of the men in the Kremlin. The two nations should have proceeded toward a "socialist brotherhood," but the unbrotherly creditor-debtor relationship and Stalin's scorn for Mao, whom he termed a "margarine Communist"—that is, an imitator and not the real thing—caused a hardening of the Sino-Soviet frontiers. Readers will remember newspaper accounts of the recall of Soviet experts and the end of friendly interchange of students. The Russians resented accepting soy beans in return for modern machinery; the Chinese feared that the Russian Communists were too free and relaxed, too close to the West.

Part IV, "Partners and Rivals," is the least satisfying section of Mehnert's study. At the start he acknowledges the difficulties in obtaining adequate and accurate information about present-day China and compares it with censored Russia of the Stalin period. Under a harsh dictatorship of the Stalin type, with few travel visas and with Red China publications, smuggled into Hong Kong, scarce and costly, Mehnert faced many handicaps in reviewing the issues and the consequences of the Peking-Moscow feud. He indicates that the Russians began to realize that the Chinese people's enormous poten-

213

tial of spiritual strength "could enable them to catch up with the evolutionary head start of Soviet Russia."

The moment came, says Mehnert, when Khrushchev in February, 1956, "wiped out the Stalin myth and thus removed the moral and psychological basis for Moscow's hitherto undisputed claim to leadership in the Communist world." He made the separation absolute in October, 1959, when he disclaimed responsibility for acts of the People's Republic of China. China was eager to assume equality. Its commune of April, 1958, had been, in the eyes of many historians, no less significant than the Russian Sputnik of October, 1957. An account of how the Chinese had accomplished the short cut to communism fills thirty pages. The result of equality was an increased aggressiveness of both branches, first against outsiders, then toward each other.

In the final six pages of this study Mehnert tries to visualize the future of Sino-Russian rivalry. He believes the present relationship can be summed up in a single phrase: "I love him because I must." This affection will last only till each feels able to go it alone, and so Mehnert advises the West never to relax pressure against both types of communism, by trying to demonstrate to the citizens of both nations an alternate way of life, by helping to make India, Pakistan, the Philippines, and Japan showcases of the results of democracy. But if the break between the two eventually occurs—and the nearer China comes to possessing nuclear weapons, the more the men of the Kremlin will be seeking realignment —then, Mehnert believes, the West will be wise to stand with Russia because China presents the greater threat to world peace and prosperity.

Forty-two pages of chapter notes refer to some of the twelve hundred books and thousands of newspaper and magazine articles consulted; twelve additional pages contain a selected bibliography. This book is a meaty, stimulating, and important contribution to the solving of one of the toughest of world problems.

Willis Knapp Jones

THE PRICE OF GLORY: VERDUN, 1916

Author: Alastair Horne (1925-   )
Publisher: St. Martin's Press (New York). Illustrated. 371 pp. $5.95
Type of work: Military history
Time: February-December, 1916
Locale: Verdun, France

A *penetrating study of the bloody and protracted battle which occupied most of 1916 during World War I*

> *Principal personages:*
> FIELD MARSHAL ERICH VON FALKENHAYN, Chief of German General Staff
> RUPPRECHT OF BAVARIA, Crown Prince of Bavaria and Commander of the German Army at Verdun
> MARSHAL JOSEPH JOFFRE, Commander-in-Chief of the French Army
> MARSHAL PHILIPPE PÉTAIN, Commander of French forces at Verdun
> GENERAL ROBERT NIVELLE, Commander of the Second Army of France
> FIELD MARSHAL CONRAD VON HÖTZENDORF, Commander of Austrian forces

The Price of Glory is superior military history, in many ways the most penetrating study of the Battle of Verdun to date. Judged by any standards, it is likely to become one of the classics of World War I history. Alastair Horne, who possesses the rare ability of writing solid history that surpasses most fiction in suspense and readability, has written as much about the actions and attitudes of the participants as he has of the monumental and devastating struggle. This is a study of persons caught up in a great historical event as well as a carefully documented account of the movements and strategy encountered in the ten-month deadlock.

In the early chapters the reader is introduced to the military commanders who will make the vital decisions in the coming conflict. Erich von Falkenhayn, who had replaced Helmuth von Moltke as Chief of the German General Staff on November 3, 1914, after the failure of the German forces to achieve victory in the Battle of the Marne, decided that the most promising method of ending the war was to let France defeat herself. Early in December of 1915, Falkenhayn began to draw up plans for his operation. It was a rather simple plan; the Germans were to capture the apparently well-fortified French positions near Verdun, and the French Army was to be destroyed when the attempt was made to recover the lost positions.

This scheme was based upon the knowledge that the bulk of the ranking officers of the French Army believed without reservation that success in any engagement required assuming the offensive, to regain any lost territory. Through her espousal of the total offensive, the strategy of *l'attaque à l'outrance,* France would be bled white.

In conjunction with this plan was the decision to wage an unrestricted submarine war against British shipping to prevent supplies from reaching Europe and thus to bring England to her knees.

Von Falkenhayn decided upon Verdun because Crown Prince Rupprecht of Bavaria commanded the army located in that sector. The crown prince and his Chief of Staff, General Knobelsdorf, agreed in principle with the plan; however, they favored fighting over a more extended area. This was only the beginning of a series of disagreements which would plague the operation and ultimately cost von Falkenhayn his command, perhaps Germany's last chance to win the war.

According to Mr. Horne, the German plan was not to pit infantry against infantry, but to utilize artillery against the helpless French troops. To this end von Falkenhayn had to amass a tremendous store of materials before he could begin the operation. The utmost secrecy was maintained while men and materials were moved into position. Reserve forces were stationed approximately one hundred miles to the rear lest they be committed to battle prematurely—a discretion which would ultimately cost the Germans dearly.

The French, under General Joffre, were unaware that the German Army was building up forces in the area of Verdun. Then, too, the French were so confident that the Germans would not attack at this point that they had not bothered to return a number of guns which had been removed earlier in the war. German security was so well maintained that the French did not learn of the planned assault until the eve of the event. Even at this late date, fate intervened to assist the French because the snow which fell during the night of February 11-12 prevented the

Germans from beginning their attack according to their timetable.

More than 1,220 artillery pieces were concentrated along a front of only eight miles. The assault force was assured that it would achieve the objective without opposition. The shells rained on the helpless Frenchmen for twelve hours on February 21, almost without let up. Late in the afternoon, the first massive German attack was launched. The awesome bombardment had not been as successful as von Falkenhayn predicted, for by that time the French were able to offer considerable resistance. However, by February 24, the superior weight of the German assault had forced a rupture in the French defenses. This breakthrough permitted the German Army to capture Fort Douaumont.

Once the French line had been broken, the French position became desperate. But von Falkenhayn also had problems because he was unable to move up his big guns as rapidly as had been anticipated. Another problem which plagued the German commander was whether to call up the reserves in an effort to capture the town of Verdun. Von Falkenhayn had neglected to inform his forces that he had no desire to capture Verdun and wanted only to fight for limited objectives. He had not informed the infantry of his plan because he feared that it would lower the morale of his forces. Had he committed his reserves at this time he could, in all probability, have taken Verdun.

The French forces at Verdun were rapidly becoming so disorganized that they no longer resembled an army. In an effort to halt disintegration, General Joffre elevated General Pétain, probably the ablest French battle leader in World War I, to command of the Second Army, which was given the task of holding Verdun. Pétain's task was made more difficult when he was ordered not to evacuate the right bank of the Meuse River because retreat meant giving advantage to the enemy. Had the evacuation been permitted, a natural barrier would have aided the French. But it also would have aided the Germans when the French began their counterattack.

Fate now played a cruel trick on von Falkenhayn. At the time when he expected the French to begin their attack which would permit him to "bleed them white," one of the few French officers who did not agree with the total-offense theory was placed in command of the defense. Instead of taking the offensive, Pétain began to shore up his defenses. In rapid order he reorganized his forces and the troops regained their confidence. He began a system of rotation which pulled units back for rest; he sent cooks to schools where they could learn to cook, and he ordered that the French remain on the defensive until such time as they had the manpower and matériel to assume the offensive.

Pétain's plan was not fully realized because General Joffre insisted that a start be made to recapture lost ground almost as soon as the German offense had bogged down. General Nivelle was given this task, and until Pétain stopped this action it appeared that von Falkenhayn would achieve his objective. It was only after a thorough reorganization of his forces and the buildup of matériel that the French could be successful in removing the Germans.

It is ironic that General Nivelle emerged as the liberator of Verdun, while Pétain was overlooked. However, after people began to study the battle, Pétain emerged as the "Savior of Verdun."

The deadlock of this battle was unique in many ways: the flamethrower was used for the first time in modern warfare; airpower was utilized as a fighting arm for the first time, and artillery was used to support attacking infantry for the first time. Verdun, in the opinion of Mr. Horne, was the most crucial and destructive battle of World War I. The lengthy deadlock caused the French military leaders to embrace the theory of fortification. No longer did they advocate the doctrine of the total offensive. Their planning for total war now placed reliance on the construction of heavily fortified defense positions—hence the Maginot Line of World War II.

Sharing Field Marshal Montgomery's opinion, Mr. Horne states that the French Army never fully recovered from the terrible losses suffered at Verdun. This struggle may well have been the reason why France failed to fight more effectively during World War II. The price of glory was costly at Verdun in 1916, and those who survived could never forget it. And it is hoped that this book is the beginning of a long series of volumes covering World War I by Mr. Horne, who promises to emerge as one of the ablest writers in this field of history.

J. Perry Cochran

THE QUIET ENEMY

Author: Cecil Dawkins (1927-   )
Publisher: Atheneum Publishers (New York). 214 pp. $4.50
Type of work: Short stories
Time: The present
Locale: The American South and Southwest

An uneven collection of seven stories by a young woman of strong and original talent

By this time the reading public is undoubtedly weary of being told of the Southern Renascence, of the remarkable phenomenon represented by William Faulkner, Thomas Wolfe, Robert Penn Warren, Allen Tate, William Styron, Eudora Welty, and others. With the publication of each new work by a Southern writer, *Time* is struck with wonder that a benighted region of injustice, illiteracy, and ignorance could continue to produce good writers. The attitudes of both the reading public and *Time* are understandable, but the stubborn facts keep obtruding. A disproportionate amount of the best fiction and poetry of the twentieth century has come from the South, and despite the lugubrious warning of various commentators about the invasion of the North and of Northern ways, there seems to be no sign that the "renascence" is finished. No list of important young writers would be complete without the names of James Dickey, Reynolds Price, Flannery O'Connor—and this newest addition, Cecil Dawkins.

Flannery O'Connor praises this collection; they are "fine, strong stories." Such praise should come as no surprise to the reader familiar with the work of Miss O'Connor, for the stories of the two women are similar in striking ways. The characters are usually Negroes and middle- or lower-class whites. Inarticulate, strangled voices, mouthing suspi-cion, fear, greed, cynicism, and occasionally, a fervent hope—this is how the characters are remembered. Rarely does one character understand another (the protagonist of Cecil Dawkins' "Eminent Domain" is literally deaf). They are either "rationalists" or adherents to an atavistic faith. What is most terrible in the world of these characters is the *meaninglessness* of their lives. In such lives violence and cruelty are the norm, the expected: in Miss O'Connor's "Good Country People," the fraudulent Bible salesman dupes Hulga by putting her artificial leg out of reach; in Miss Dawkins' "The Quiet Enemy" Bitsy's lover kicks her in the stomach and brings about a miscarriage.

Of the seven stories that make up the collection, the title story is the most finished and powerful. Ostensibly the chronicle of the hero's search for an ugly woman, whom he could sleep with without payment, it is finally a story of desperate need, desperately expressed, and finally unfulfilled. Money is the only sure value, the absence of money the real sin:

He felt that the constant drain made by the simple needs of food, shelter, clothing, and women was the quiet enemy, the deadly enemy, that most let slip up on them from behind and rifle their pockets. He had seen to it that this enemy would not, in his case, find an easy mark.

The terrible pity is, of course, that he comes to realize the untruth, the inadequacy of his ethic, but he is powerless by then. He and Bitsy meet like two brutes; they begin to soften, to become human. But it is too late, and his pathetic murmuring of "love" is met by Bitsy's raucous laughter.

The other stories do not quite attain this level, but some of them are very good. "Eminent Domain" concerns an old, deaf Negro woman whose farm must be sold to the government to make way for a dam. She understands nothing of what the government man tells her, however, and signs the papers with an X unwittingly. Enter Jethro, a footloose young Negro who stops at "Old Momma's" for a meal. He takes over, convinces the authorities that he is Old Momma's son, draws out the money deposited in her name, and comes back with a pick-up truck to load Old Momma and her belongings into it, so that they can begin their trip to New Orleans. In a subtly narrated sequence, we discover that Old Momma thinks Jethro is the devil; the trip is for her a trip to hell, for Jethro a journey to paradise. She contrives a way to bring them both to destruction.

"A Simple Case" is a Flaubertian title, and the story is an honorable example of a true craftsman's work. Harold Widkins is a simple man, but one who is aware that his life is a role in a drama he does not fully understand. He comes in from the fields one day to find a burglar in the kitchen. After Harold kills the intruder, he immediately feels a sense of failure; the event is not what it should have been, given the setting and the actors: "Harold stood looking down at him, feeling, in spite of the accuracy of his shot, in some vague way disappointed." The

drama of life becomes more and.more farcical. It turns out that the burglar was insane, harmless, the gun he brandished was unloaded, and the end of his trigger finger was missing: "The trouble with life, [Harold] had often felt, was that you never had any practice for the big things, and that was why it was so easy to make a fool of yourself." The story reaches its tragic and comic climax when Harold meets the parents of the boy at the funeral home; after this confrontation, his life can never be quite the same.

"The Mourner" is a story of an exile who must return home, to the South, for the funeral of his grandfather. The complicating element is that the man's family is Italian, his mother a sad and frustrated woman who has never recovered from her husband's desertion. She clings pathetically to her exiled son, and the family plays her a painful trick: when he leaves for San Francisco after the funeral, she accompanies him, happy in her possession, unaware that she will ride only as far as the first stop. Miss Dawkins becomes convincingly rhetorical in the closing lines of the story, which describe the son's feelings:

He allowed himself the pillow of her, for soon they would emerge from that steep place onto a plain and he would be alone. The clacking wheels turned and churned and birth is not a thing of ones, one spasm, one swelling, one hour of pain, one cry. Between the wombs of woman and the grave, upon this belly earth, the fetus re-enacts itself a thousand times; breath tears and struggles in its caul; the shroud awaits; the angel of despair spreads wings like nets to catch the risers; bear your birth, the angel said. He allowed them both this sleeping moment before the rent, the breaking tears, the cry, before this mon-

219

ster he was riding bore him off again to peace and loneliness.

Of the remaining stories, "Benny Ricco's Search for Truth" demands serious attention. The title is badly ironic; his search leads him, once a "good Catholic," into despair and finally to an abject, mechanical faith, which he professes by kneeling before a statue of "the former governor of his state." The other two stories, "The Buffalo Farm" and "Hummers in the Larkspur" are both failures. "The Buffalo Farm" is about The Bomb and involves an unfulfilled wife (Jimmy) who, unable to accept the empty, materialistic values of her husband, turns, at the moment of the test bomb's explosion, to the false prophet in the desert. An overheated, self-conscious exercise, its faults are shared by "Hummers in the Larkspur," a story totally unlike the others in the collection. It is the only really comic story, but the comedy does not, finally, work. All of the ingredients are here: the gossiping ladies with absurd Southern names, the strange and unmanageable mulatto girl, the town's idiot boy, the Cultured Visitors, and the daughter who says *maman*. What would be in Eudora Welty's hands a strong but delicate narrative becomes, when treated by Miss Dawkins, only sentimental and fey.

James Boatwright

RAISE HIGH THE ROOF BEAM, CARPENTERS and SEYMOUR, AN INTRODUCTION

Author: J. D. Salinger (1919-   )
Publisher: Little, Brown and Company (Boston). 248 pp. $4.00
Type of work: Novellas
Time: June 4, 1942, and 1959
Locale: New York City and a girl's college in upper New York state

Two further episodes in the story of the Glass family, in which Buddy goes to Seymour's wedding and does a character sketch of him

Principal characters:
SEYMOUR GLASS, the oldest son, bridegroom, and poet
BUDDY GLASS, the second son, wedding guest, and fiction writer
MURIEL FEDDER, the bride
RHEA FEDDER, the bride's mother
HELEN SILSBURN, the bride's aunt
EDIE BURWICK, the bride's matron of honor
BOB BURWICK, Edie's husband, a lieutenant in the Army
THE BRIDE'S DEAF-MUTE UNCLE

One of those writers who sacrifice range for the rewards of concentration, J. D. Salinger has so repeatedly reworked one theme that his stories are now readily identifiable by their typical ingredients and established pattern. Whoever he may be, the protagonist suffers from a physical-moral sickness resulting from an acute sense of himself as simultaneously superior to the common lot of men, dedicated to an ethical purity beyond their awareness and appreciation, yet inseparably linked to them by his moral being. Disgusted

220

by phoniness, selfishness, and self-complacency to the point of nausea, he seeks disaffiliation from humanity so that his conscience may be chaste and whole. But to be moral is to be responsibly related to other human beings, so that his self-centered desire for moral purity, which inclines him to repudiate his fellow man, only increases his guilt. What appears to be a loose leash for moral realization turns out to be a strangling moral bond. To escape his dilemma he must be saved from himself by the love of another or he must dirty his soul by humbling himself before those he has been contemptuous of, shining his shoes, as it were, for the Fat Lady.

Opposite him, as his antithesis in temperament and as moral ideal (though this character can sometimes be the protagonist of a story), is the selfless man, a saint, who, despite of or by reason of his extraordinary powers of understanding and goodness, dies because he is too finely tuned for the coarse music of mundane human life. Whereas the saint is, so to speak, on the outside and perishes from lack of nourishment, being unable to transmute the stuff of life into a liquor assimilatable by his ethereal blood and yet is not sufficient to himself either, the protagonist is on the inside, feels himself imprisoned, and desperately wants to escape. The two characters approach each other from opposite poles, aiming seemingly at a union which will heal the schizoid moral world they inhabit. On the contrary, they end up being more completely and intensely what they initially were, driven apart rather than reconciled, more aware than ever of their separateness and autonomous identity.

Salinger's fiction is devoted to persistent close scrutiny of this moral matrix from which issues man's transcendental ethical awareness and aspirations and his radically conflicting moral tie to other human beings. (Incidentally, Salinger inherited his theme from Emerson and Thoreau, who identified man's spiritual being with his conscience and were deeply disturbed by the dichotomy between his private and public, or solitary and social selves, and with whom he shares a taste for Oriental thought.) Caught in the cross current of these countervailing moral powers, Franny, the protagonist of a story bearing her name, cries out, "I'm sick of ego, ego, ego." Distressed by her own, tortured by the vicious competition for self-aggrandizement characteristic of human social life, she longs for a holiness which will absolve her of her egotism. But her ego is puny compared to that of Buddy Glass, her brother, Salinger's *persona*, and the narrator of these latest two stories (published originally in 1955 and 1959) about the Glass family. Buddy's greater quantity of ego results from Salinger's desire to use him as a vehicle to explore even further than he yet has into the mysterious moral darkness where the contrary impulses of self-exaltation and self-annihilation vie for supremacy.

In "Raise High the Roofbeam, Carpenters," Buddy, in the army and recuperating from pleurisy, appears in New York on June 4, 1942, to attend Seymour's wedding. But Seymour, the saint of the Glass family, does not appear, so that Buddy is left to spend the day with four wedding guests, all but one of whom, a dwarfish deaf-mute, are of the despised middle class. The matron of honor does succeed in winning some grudging admiration from

Buddy for her moral energy and indignation, but only because these are qualities of his own that he values highly. Otherwise he is acutely aware of the extreme degree to which he is set apart from them by his intelligence and sensitivity. Supporting him against them, or so he assumes, are the deaf-mute (Holden Caulfield, it will be remembered, wanted to disaffiliate from humanity by pretending deaf-muteness) with whom he has a natural affinity, and Seymour, whose diary is in Buddy's hands. To Buddy's dismay, Seymour reveals that he loves Muriel Fedder because she is undiscriminating and he is marrying her to undergo a rebirth through assuming responsibility, and knowing its joys, for the first time in his life. Boo-Boo, the oldest daughter in the Glass family, recognizing intuitively that Seymour's motive is a desire to enter into and share the life of common mortals, provides the title of the story in a message on a bathroom mirror to signify that mundane life will have to be generously expanded to accomodate Seymour, a being of heroic proportions. Buddy, on the other hand, upset by the revelation of Seymour's motive and feeling betrayed, adds a large quantity of alcohol to physical exhaustion, collapses into sleep, then later awakens miserable and alone, abandoned finally by the deaf-mute also, left with nothing but his ego and more completely alienated than ever.

The second story, though stylistically the cruder, is Salinger's profoundest treatment of his theme to date. Ostensibly an introduction to Seymour, it is as much an introduction to Buddy, who confesses to upstaging his brother because of "my ego, my perpetual lust to share top billing with him." Actually, the story defines their contrasting temperaments by setting them over against each other, which is their natural arrangement anyway; and since both are artists, Seymour a poet and Buddy a fiction writer, the story defines the nature of art, the essential difference between poetry and prose, and the human predicament of the artist who practices them. Because of his talent, intelligence, and sensitivity, the artist stands apart from the common lot of men; at the same time the fact that he publishes, performs before an audience, as it were, involves him in their life and forces him to acknowledge a responsibility to them. Thus, Buddy worries about communicating, agonizes over his relation to his reader, and in general suffers with great intensity from man's inherent moral dilemma, present in a salient form in his vocation. Employing a distinction much like Edgar Allan Poe's, Salinger allows the poet a higher order of moral being: Seymour, like a figure in a Zen story quoted by Buddy, sees through the external to the spiritual mechanism or essential, inward qualities. Incapable of the selflessness necessary for such power, for directly perceiving the poetic current that runs through things, the fiction writer cannot escape his ego and so his art predominately displays his subjectivity. However, Buddy, like other Glass children before him, learns from Seymour the secret of art, which is to put the whole heart into a work, to be fully yourself.

Salinger's fame, seemingly out of proportion with his small output, has resulted from a brilliant style capable of deftly and vividly expressing moral disgust and spiritual dryness, and hinting of holy silences. But in these latest stories, especially in "Seymour, An Introduction," his prose is obviously labored and flat, all the poetry gone out of it. Buddy admits as much to be true, insists that his style must be "gluey," and thereby indicates that Salinger deliberately chooses to write badly. The reason for this effect is that to be wholly himself Buddy, the egotist, must be his self-conscious egotistical self, must accept his burden as artist and play the fool for his public. As an artist, his task is to take the risks entailed in exploring the moral abyss of the gifted, excluded man and to report his discoveries to the community. He is a kind of hero and clown, savior and scapegoat, whose gifts for others are himself and his brother Seymour, the contrasting moral ideal of saintliness, which he can admire and present in his art but never himself achieve.

William R. Robinson

THE RISE OF THE WEST
A History of the Human Community

Author: William H. McNeill (1917-   )
Publisher: The University of Chicago Press (Chicago). Illustrated. 829 pp. $12.50
Type of work: History

A universal history of man in which the author presents a new interpretation of the inter-relationships of cultures and of the development of the historical processes

At first glance, or even after having read the first half of *The Rise of the West*, winner of the 1964 National Book Award in history and biography, it appears that Professor McNeill's title is something of a misnomer and that his work should more properly be entitled *A History of Civilization* or some equivalent in comprehensive outline. It is only after looking upon the work as a whole that the keenness of his thought in selecting his title becomes evident. In essence, his study of cultural developments and conflicts leads the author to the conclusion that these cultural movements have culminated since 1500, and most particularly in the nineteenth and twentieth centuries, in an era of Western cultural dominance of the entire world and of much older and better established cultures. This culmination, in his eyes, indicates a much greater faith in the West and in Western culture than has been expressed by the "prophets of doom" of the past and present. Professor McNeill writes: "The rise of the West seems today still far from its apogee; nor is it obvious, even in the narrower political sense, that the era of Western dominance is past." Such is his assertion in his introduction of the era of Western dominance, and in his conclusion of the same section he says that present trends indicate the creation of a stable, world-wide cosmopolitanism. He adds: "But no matter how it comes, the cosmopolitanism of the future will surely bear a Western imprint. At least in its initial stages, any world state will be an empire of the West. This would be the case even if non-Westerners should happen to hold the supreme controls of world-wide political-military

223

authority, for they could do so only by utilizing such originally Western traits as industrialism, science, and the public palliation of power through advocacy of one or another of the democratic political faiths. Hence, 'The Rise of the West' may serve as a shorthand description of the upshot of the history of the human community to date."

Although *The Rise of the West* is not a complete departure from earlier interpretations of the development of civilization, it does offer new interpretations. Finding the beginnings of civilization in the economic, political, and military activities of primitive peoples, Professor McNeill places more emphasis on the economic factors, and far more on the military, than have most cultural historians. He feels that economic surpluses make a strong political system possible and that developing military technology enables the political system to survive or not to survive in the face of external and internal challenges. He also sees civilization as a unity, springing from the soil of the Mesopotamian region and spreading east and west to the Nile and the Indus, and from thence to the Aegean and to China. He emphasizes the similarities rather than the differences of Middle Eastern, Indian, Chinese, and Western civilizations; and he insists that there is no question of their common origin. Rather, he says, it is a question of the "density and intimacy" of their contacts with one another. Western civilization, for example, resembles the civilization of the Middle East much more closely than it does that of India because the West derived its origins from the Middle East and because its contacts with India have been more sporadic and less intimate than its contacts with Middle Eastern culture. Chi-

nese civilization, on the other hand, despite its apparent uniqueness, owes its beginnings to the cradle of civilization via ideas conveyed across the steppes by nomads who were probably themselves uncivilized. Professor McNeill maintains that although the style of Chinese writing is unique, the very idea of writing originated in the Middle East much earlier and must have been communicated to the Chinese along some route of travel or trade. Although the uniqueness of Chinese script might be used with equal force as an argument for the separate origin of Chinese civilization, *The Rise of the West* shows many other points of contact between early China and areas to the west, and the book presents fairly convincing proof that if China was unique, she was only rarely completely separated from other civilized centers.

In contrast to other interpretations which have divided history into cultural and national periods, *The Rise of the West* divides it into three major periods and twelve minor periods. The first of these had its beginnings in prehistory but picks up the thread of history about 3,000 B.C. and carries it down to 500 B.C. This period Professor McNeill terms the Era of Middle Eastern Dominance. He describes the origin and consolidation of civilized communities in Mesopotamia during this time and the spread of civilization to peripheral areas such as Egypt, the Indus Valley, and Crete. During the same period a civilized cosmopolitanism came into existence in the heartland of the Middle East. This cosmopolitanism was to become the model of civilization throughout the world.

Professor McNeill's second great period extended from 500 B.C. to A.D. 1500; he refers to it as the period of

Eurasian Cultural Balance. During this two-thousand-year period high civilizations flowered in the West during the Classic Age; in the Middle East with its Persian, Sassanian, and Muslim empires; in India, under the Guptas; and in China, under the Ch'in, Han, Sung, and T'ang dynasties. This was also the age of the great universal religions: Christianity, Mahayaha Buddhism, Hinduism, and Islam, all indicating, according to Professor McNeill, similar emotional needs among civilized societies having the same origins, after having reached approximately the same level of development. He also believes that, because of the high political organization everywhere, the connections between civilized areas became intimate enough between 500 B.C. and A.D. 200 to justify his term: the closure of the Eurasian Ecumene. Here, perhaps more than at any point prior to the nineteenth century he finds the justification of his thesis of the unity of civilization. It is certainly true that during those centuries reasonably close connections did exist between the major centers of civilization. Finally, he sees common problems of barbarian onslaught threatening all civilization during that same period. All civilized centers resisted the barbarians, but none emerged unchanged from the experience. He describes the sub-period between 600 and 1500 as the time of response and recovery of the civilized areas from the effects of barbarian invasions.

Professor McNeill's third great period extends from 1500 to the present; he calls it the era of Western Dominance. During this period he sees the West, although starting about the same level, or slightly behind, other centers of civilization, forging ahead and tak-ing over unquestioned leadership of the world. His chief explanation for this phenomenon is the Western mind, shaped by the ages of civilization and left relatively unfettered by the after-effects of the Renaissance and the Reformation. (By contrast, Indian, Chinese, and Middle Eastern thinkers were rather seriously encumbered by the essentially stagnant and unchanging concepts of Hinduism, Confucianism, and Islam.) Western thinking, then, was free to develop in a truly unique fashion; and Western man, by virtue of his relative immunity to pestilence, his innate pugnacity, and his developing economic sense, quickly spread Western ideas throughout the world. Professor McNeill's assertion that non-Western bodies were affected by the West long before non-Western minds felt any influence is so obvious, when once considered, as to be a truism. In essence, then, the West did come to dominate not merely the civilized world, but the known world, and it did so through a combination of superior political and economic organization, based upon real intellectual progress and backed up by vastly superior military and naval technology.

The Rise of the West is a lengthy, useful, thoughtful, and scholarly work. Although, as any work of this kind must, it leaves many questions unanswered, it certainly does attempt to answer other questions and does so very well indeed. Professor McNeill makes wide use of archaeological and sociological, as well as historical, sources; but he admits the lack of reliable sources in archaeology and history in some areas. Certainly much work remains to be done before a definitive world history can be attempted. It is, however, a pleasure to read the work of

225

a man learned enough to try to weave such apparently obscure subjects as Tamil bardic art or Sarmatian animal art into the fabric of Western civilization.

Howard Mackey

THE SAND PEBBLES

Author: Richard McKenna (1913-   )
Publisher: Harper and Row (New York). 597 pp. $5.95
Type of work: Novel
Time: 1925-1927
Locale: China

A novel about the crew of an American gunboat patrolling a tributary of the Yangtze River during the Chinese revolution

Principal characters:

> JORIS K. HOLMAN ("JAKE"), an American sailor
> FRANCIS MARION BURGOYNE ("FRENCHY"), Holman's friend
> EDITH ECKERT, a young American missionary
> PO-HAN, a Chinese coolie
> MAILY, Frenchy Burgoyne's Chinese wife
> LIEUTENANT WILLIAM COLLINS, captain of the U.S.S. *San Pablo*
> LYNCH,
> HARRIS,
> CROSLEY,
> "RED DOG" SHANAHAN, and
> FARREN, crew members aboard the *San Pablo*
> MR. CRADDOCK, a missionary and teacher, Edith Eckert's superior

The Sand Pebbles, Richard McKenna's first published novel, was the Harper Prize Novel for 1963. The title, a somewhat enigmatic one, is taken from the nickname the American sailors aboard the U.S.S. *San Pablo* give themselves, deriving it from the name of their ship. The *San Pablo* is an old Spanish-built craft taken by the American Navy at the time of the Spanish-American War and refitted for use as a gunboat on Chinese inland waters. For more than two decades before the opening of the story the vessel has patrolled the Siang River, a tributary of the Yangtze River, and Tungting Lake, in Hunan Province, hundreds of miles upstream from Shanghai and the China Sea.

Although *The Sand Pebbles* recounts the adventures of the gunboat and its entire crew during 1925-1927, the story centers about Jake Holman, a Navy enlisted man who loves machinery and finds contentment in the engine room of his ship. The novel opens with his appearance aboard the *San Pablo,* and his death while on duty protecting American missionaries closes it. Of all the crew, only he has his life prior to the *San Pablo* shown in flashbacks. The central character through whom the reader focuses his view of the action throughout most of the story, Holman is the author's most highly developed character, a man in his middle twenties who has served in the American Navy eight years. During that time

226

he had earned high efficiency ratings and several letters of commendation for difficult engine-room repairs. But Holman is not a typical sailor; he hates the military side of Navy life and finds happiness only with the machinery he loves and understands. Because he has little regard for discipline or shipmates, he has been transferred from ship to ship until he arrives aboard the little gunboat for another tour of duty. Aboard the *San Pablo*, through helping an intelligent and intellectually curious bilge coolie, Po-Han, to learn about machinery and its functions, Jake Holman becomes aware of the sympathy he can have and needs to have for other human beings. The humanization of Holman is continued after the death of Po-Han by the influence of Shirley Eckert, a teaching missionary at China Light Mission, an independent Christian mission in Hunan. In Miss Eckert, Holman finds finally a woman he can respect and love. The end of the novel depicts the death of Holman, which comes when he remains behind to cover with a rifle the flight of Shirley Eckert and others from an armed Chinese mob attacking the mission.

On another level *The Sand Pebbles* is the story of a whole ship's company which almost comes to disaster because the crew are permitted to hire coolie labor to perform almost all the duties of the sailors. Service aboard the gunboat seems almost ideal to most of the crew. Their jobs are practically taken over by the Chinese, and the ship has been remodeled to house them. The scraping, cleaning, and painting of the ship are done by coolie laborers. Chinese maintain the engines, stoke the furnaces, cook the meals, and perform personal services for the American crew. The men have come to depend upon the Chinese, but when the revolution breaks out and the Chinese flee the ship, the sailors, reduced in number over the years, have to perform their own jobs and care for themselves. While the crew of the *San Pablo* rises to the occasion, there is clearly the warning by McKenna that such social dependence, in the Navy at least, weakens and cripples the persons who permit themselves to turn over their work to others and, as a result, become physically, mentally, and morally flabby. McKenna says that Navy men seemed particularly susceptible to becoming the prey of moral stagnation aboard the China gunboats. Those who liked the life there stayed on and on, often till the age when they could retire and settle in Chinese river towns. Those who disliked the life, he says, left as quickly as they could effect transfers.

There is also a political level to this novel. The adventures of the Sand Pebbles, as the crewmen of the *San Pablo* call themselves, are told against the background of international politics. The men and their ship are a political pawn used by the United States, as one of the treaty powers, to protect American lives and interests in China. Businessmen in China are depicted as approving the arrangement, missionaries as opposing it. With the coming of the revolution in 1926-1927 the Chinese are openly and actively opposed to the presence of the gunboats, as well as other foreign privileges exercised in China. The Navy men, long used to "showing the flag" to express American power, at first cannot understand the refusal of their civilian leadership to let them fire at the Chinese at the first sign of outrage. The enlisted men, in particular, fail to understand that one era in history is closing and another is being born, that the old China is gone and that a new nation is emerging. Accustomed to warlords, the warlords' irregular troops, and coolies, the men cannot understand that the Chinese Nationalists have different notions and different political goals. Failing to recognize the inevitability of change, they do not begin to realize the strife between the Kuomintang and the Communists which only begins to appear in the novel as the jostling of factions and their leaders for power. McKenna does not establish his own commitment on the political backgrounds of the story. In so doing he relinquished an opportunity to make this aspect of *The Sand Pebbles* meaningful in any way but as a milieu for his story.

A great deal of fiction about the military and naval service has appeared in American literature since the end of World War II, often exploring strange nooks and crannies of the defense establishment. The lives of men in the various services in time of war and in time of peace have been a fruitful source of material for these novels. *The Sand Pebbles* explores a heretofore unknown bit of service life. As such an account it is good. A detailed and convincing picture of life aboard a China gunboat is presented. But some readers, at least, may be disappointed that the novel does not accomplish more than it does. They will regret that Richard McKenna has not explored further the psychological, political, and moral possibilities of the story he has told. Other readers will be content with the lively story well told, and this *The Sand Pebbles* certainly is. McKenna's narrative skill is great: he portrays characters who function persuasively; he dramatizes action with clarity and zest; and he provides a picturesque background for a story which excites a reader's interest.

Gordon W. Clarke

THE SCHOOL FOR DICTATORS

Author: Ignazio Silone (1900-   )
Translated from the Italian by William Weaver
Publisher: Atheneum Publishers (New York). 244 pp. $5.00
Type of work: Socratic dialogues on political themes
Time: 1938
Locale: Zurich, Switzerland

Satiric and ironic dialogues give instruction to an aspiring dictator through examining the history of totalitarianism and citing the examples of many dictators

Principal characters:
>   MR. DOUBLE YOU, a pseudonymous would-be American dictator
>   PROFESSOR PICKUP, his ideological adviser
>   THOMAS THE CYNIC, a political refugee

This is a revision of the first version of this book published in 1939 when Ignazio Silone was a refugee from Mussolini's Fascism. He had chosen exile in Zurich, the city which serves as the book's locale. He was then already known for two of the best and most moving political novels of the century,

228

Fontamara and Bread and Wine. Both had shown the impact of Fascism upon the peasants in the area of Pescina, Silone's birthplace in the rugged mountain territory of central Italy. The School for Dictators, being a treatise rather than art, was frankly polemical. It was meant to defend democracy and to provide a critique of Fascist and Nazi ideology. It was also an attempt, writes Silone in a preface to the new edition, "to expose their falsification of history . . . and to define the social factors which facilitate totalitarian enterprises in the present age."

In the 1950's Silone wrote two new novels. In the 1960's he wrote another and turned also to the rewriting of his earlier work, a practice employed notably by James, Whitman, Yeats, and others. After rewriting Bread and Wine and Fontamara, he took up The School for Dictators. He began to rewrite the book because he felt that though military defeat had destroyed the leaders of Fascism and Nazism, their meaning had not been universally grasped. Moreover, dictatorship still existed and not very many democrats understood the factors increasingly favorable to totalitarianism in the modern age. Cutting material that was now documentary, Silone dwelt "more fully and more insistently on the conditioning of political forms in present-day mass society." He would not be surprised, he wrote, if many readers found the book pessimistic, but he affirmed nonetheless that "The spirit of freedom will survive: of this I am convinced."

Beginning with the epigraph, "How little wisdom rules the world," he devotes the first of his fourteen chapters to an introduction of his three characters. Mr. Double You is temporarily detained in Zurich by minor illness. A former machine politician hoping to become American dictator, he is traveling incognito in Europe in an effort to learn if a technique of dictatorship really exists. His ideological adviser, Professor Pickup, is the inventor of pantautology, a science whose basic tenet is, "Everyone is himself and can be nothing else but himself." The two know more about practical politics than at first appears, but they are fundamentally uncultured and naïve. The greatest satisfaction of their trip thus far has been their success in purchasing Columbus' egg from a Genoese collector. To while away part of his enforced stay in Zurich, Mr. Double You asks the author for lessons in totalitarianism. The author declines, but suggests instead Thomas the Cynic— thus named because "he has a horror of euphemisms and a habit of calling things by their right name." The remaining thirteen chapters consist of Socratic dialogues among the three men.

With questions that are sometimes obtuse and sometimes acute the two Americans serve as straight men for Thomas the Cynic. He is urbane, adroit, and learned, quoting both the ancients and moderns in his discourse. As exemplars of the practice of the art he most often cites Napoleon, Mussolini, Hitler, and Stalin. Whereas the two Americans constantly drop names of the famous men they have interrogated on their European trip, Thomas cites the great theorists from de Tocqueville to Marx. Although these discussions necessarily lack the coherence of political essays, they gradually produce a clear impression of Thomas' interpretation of the history of totalitarianism: contemporary conditions, because of mass media and mass men, are growing more and more conducive to what Silone calls "the totalitarian degeneration of public life." Moreover, errant human nature has always been such that the clever man can exploit it for his own purposes, particularly if he knows the theory and technique of totalitarian politics—something quite as unknown to most old-style politicians as politics itself to the layman.

Thomas emphasizes these points to the empirically-minded Mr. Double You. Mussolini and Hitler soon had at their mercy the men whose political and social theory stopped at 1914, the cynic tells the American. And, like most successes in this area, they were obsessed with power for its own sake. Like Lenin, the man who best exemplified this trait, "all the most successful politicians have been opportunists of genius." Characterizing the Fascist movement, he calls it a "counter-revolution against a revolution that never took place." It was born, he tells his listeners, of the anxiety of the middle class which saw its position threatened by technical progress, the disillusionment of members of the working class crushed in ill-organized attempts to seize control, and the capitalists' fear of expropriation of their wealth. He documents his analysis with both theory and fact.

Each chapter deals with a small constellation of related ideas or phenomena. Thomas gives an outline for a coup d'etat after an abortive revolution. In the next day's discussion he deals with common characteristics among dictators: failure in artistic careers, foreign origins, and physical and moral defects. Thomas then deals with the party structure which the aspiring dictator must build and the way in which craft and flexibility are vital, whereas a positive and logical political program is an absolute handicap. The most important conclusion at this point, he tells his hearers, is, "don't be discouraged. . . . Don't be in a hurry. Have faith in the possible rebarbarization of humanity."

The rest of the dialogues are occupied with Thomas' discussion of the way democracy devours itself, with such know-how as the art of double-dealing, and with cautions about the dangers of conspiracies and revolts. It concludes with a brief treatment of plebiscites, the interrelation of state and party, and the uses of scapegoats.

This book, as reviewers were quick to realize, is in the tradition of Machiavelli's *The Prince*, for all Silone's irony and his use of fictional characters. The author's own consciousness of this quality is clear in his attempts to broaden the scope of the book through his revision so that it will have an even wider applicability than it did in 1939. Some passages suggest today's headlines: "I'm thinking of a totalitarianism along Jacobin lines, openly democratic in its ideals and anti-democratic in its methods, because of the backward condition of its masses. This may be the most practicable form for the democratic leaders of colonial peoples, when they achieve independence."

Although there are occasional turgid passages, they must be expected, one supposes, in a book which deals with phenomena as complex as these. And though the Socratic form precludes the tightly reasoned discourse, it makes the presentation of these matters a good deal more interesting. This two-week course in totalitarianism may become a modern classic. It is too bad that the otherwise excellent American edition of Silone's text contains several bad typographical errors and fails to provide the reader with an index.

Joseph L. Blotner

THE SEED AND THE SOWER

Author: Laurens Van Der Post (1906-   )
Publisher: William Morrow and Company (New York). 256 pp. $4.50
Type of work: Novel
Time: World War II
Locale: Southeast Asia

A series of vignettes demonstrating the differences between men yet the sameness that occurs during periods of great stress

Principal characters:
    JOHN LAWRENCE, an English officer and prisoner of war
    ROTTANG HARA, a Japanese sergeant and prison guard
    JACQUES CELLIERS, a South African commando officer
    HIS CRIPPLED BROTHER
    YANOI, a Japanese prison commander
    COLONEL HICKSLEY-ELLIS, a senior British officer and prisoner

Laurens Van Der Post uses the old device of the flashback to bring together two novellas and a short story that while not a novel in the usual sense of the word do have a common thread that ties them together. That thread which builds around the relationship between two widely dissimilar characters can perhaps best be described in the author's own words:

We may not be able to stop and undo the hard old wrongs of the great world outside, but through you and me no evil shall come either in the unknown where you are going, or in this imperfect and haunted dimension of awareness through which I move. Thus between us, we shall cancel out all private and personal evil, thus arrest private and personal consequences to blind action and reaction, thus prevent specifically the general incomprehension and misunderstanding, hatred and revenge of our time from spreading further.

In summary this concept holds that evil rides the world, that man's inhumanity to man is practically limitless, that cruelty is the natural lot of man, but that there is a point in the lives of some men when, in their relationships with other men, the beauty that can be found in man is able to rip away the callousness of the façade and shine through the darkness.

Two of the three pieces in this novel have their settings in Japanese prisoner-of-war camps during World War II.

The first, entitled "A Bar of Shadow," was first published as a separate novella in 1956. It concerns a strange relationship between a Japanese sergeant, Rottang Hara, and an English Army officer named John Lawrence. Rottang is a Malaysian word for *cane* and Hara, a prison guard, had been given this name by Japanese troops because he always carried a large cane which he used to beat both the prisoners of war in his camp and his own troops as well. Even though Lawrence suffered

231

more at Hara's hands than did any other prisoner, he always excused the abuses by referring to the fact that Hara was the natural product of Japanese culture. He was "humble enough to accept implicitly the promptings of his national spirit. He was a simple, uneducated country lad with primitive integrity unassailed by higher education and really believed all the myths and legends of the caste so deeply that he did not hesitate to kill for them." The acts of Hara that seemed to Western eyes to be those of an insane, cruel martinet were a natural part of Hara's soldierly make-up. While Lawrence was not the senior English officer in the camp and was not therefore responsible for the activities of the English prisoners of war, Hara seemed to turn to him as the responsible party more than to the English colonel who was, under the Geneva Articles of War, the responsible officer.

When, after the war, Hara was tried and sentenced to die by a war crimes tribunal he was unable to comprehend the reason for his trial or his sentence. He had done nothing that many others—on both sides—had not done during the war and had done nothing to the prisoners that he would not have done to his own men under the very rigid Japanese military code of conduct. Why, then, he asked of Lawrence, who visited him in his cell following the trial, was he sentenced to die?

With this question, Van Der Post brings into light the entire issue of the validity and efficacy of the war crimes trials held by the Allies following World War II. Certainly Hara, and most of those tried following the war, had been true to their soldier's code. They had fought for their country with every resource at their command; they had conducted themselves, for the most part, in accordance with established rules of military discipline that required a subordinate to follow religiously the commands of a higher officer. Were these war crimes trials really not the trial of the vanquished by the victor? In Hara's case, Van Der Post states the point very well when he says, "He may have done wrong for the right reasons but how could it be squared by us now doing right in the wrong way?" Many people have asked this same question since World War II without receiving an adequate answer. Perhaps all that one can answer is the response given by Lawrence to Hara's question of why he had been sentenced to die. That answer was:

You can try to think only with all your heart, Hara-san, that unfair and unjust as this thing which my people are doing seems to you, that it is done only to try and stop the kind of things that happened between us in the war from ever happening again. You can say to yourself as I used to say to my despairing men in prison under you: "There is a way of winning by losing, a way of victory in defeat which we are going to discover." Perhaps that too must be your way to understanding and victory now.

This theme of victory from defeat, of winning while losing, recurs constantly through the three items in this work of fiction. It is a part of the optimism which Van Der Post seems to have for the future of the human race in spite of the low state to which it sinks at times.

"The Morning After," the second novella, builds upon the duality scene in two different settings. The first part, a very moving story, concerns the relationship between two brothers raised in South Africa. The first, Jacques, is tall, fair, handsome, brilliant in school, outstanding in athletics, a leader from his earliest days. The other is his younger brother, a dark stocky boy with a hunchback. Through the years of boyhood and adolescence these two played a game that each of us has lived through. The older boy, looked up to by his brother, represents in large measure the cruelty that is close to the surface in all of us. His acts of bravery in defending his crippled brother are mostly those which bring acclaim and admiration to himself. In those instances when he could have really helped the youngster, he failed, deliberately and consciously. His failures to act in those instances, his inner cowardliness, bring a measure of internal conflict upon Jacques, causing a feeling of despair.

When war broke out, Jacques joined the army immediately, hoping by this action to bring peace to the inner conflict within him which was looking desperately for some escape. The crippled brother stayed home. Quickly distinguishing himself in battle, Jacques arrives in Palestine on a training mission and meets a monk who, sensing the other's inner conflict, brings the peace that Jacques so badly needs. After a brief visit home in which he asks his brother's forgiveness for all the harm that he has done, Jacques returns to the battle and becomes a prisoner of war. It is in this setting that the second story takes place.

Again Van Der Post depicts the strange duality in a relationship that grows up between Jacques and the Japanese prison commander, Yanoi. This relationship, which ends tragically when Jacques is executed by Yanoi af-

ter an act of incredible bravery, is almost a repetition of that which developed between Hara and Lawrence. Jacques, like John Lawrence, was a student of Japan's culture and was able to understand and appreciate the conflict between Western and Eastern mores and customs.

The method of execution, almost inhuman to the other British prisoners of war, was to bury Jacques to the neck in dirt and permit him to starve. Yet in this very act Yanoi showed his admiration for the bravery of his victim: ". . . even in the manner they killed Jacques his enemies acted out their unwitting recognition of the seed of his deed, for they did not only bury him alive but planted him upright like a new young growth in the earth." Yanoi, following Jacques' death, snipped a lock of his hair to be sent back to his ancestral home, there to rest with other honored mementoes of the past.

The short story concerns a chance and charged meeting between a man and woman in the last days before the fall of Java. As can happen only in war, the chance meeting ends with a brief but passionate affair in a hotel room. Yet this is not in the modern vogue of clinical descriptions of intimate scenes; it is instead a moving love story demonstrating that the relationship between a man and woman can rise above the level of sex for sex's sake. Each of the people here encountered feels a need to help another in the desperate futility of defeat. In helping, each found the serenity and peace that can come only rarely but which helps to inspire one for the rest of his life.

The man and woman in this story never saw each other again, nor did either really expect to. For one short night each had played a part that na-

233

ture had planned; this was all there was and all there needed to be.

The title of the book and its principal theme come from this statement:

Wind and spirit, earth and being, rain and doing, lightning and awareness imperative, thunder and the word, seed and sower, all are one: and it is necessary only for man to ask for his seed to be chosen and to pray for the sower within to sow it through the deed and act of himself, and then the harvest for all will be golden and great.

Thus in defeat there is victory, in death lies the seed of a new and better life. *The Seed and the Sower* is a moving work by an author of merit.

Frank K. Gibson

A SENSE OF REALITY

Author: Graham Greene (1904-   )
Publisher: The Viking Press (New York). 119 pp. $3.50
Type of work: Short stories
Time: The future and the present
Locale: Contemporary Europe and an imagined future Europe

A group of short stories, most of them set outside a definable time or place, concerned with the inter-relationship of the religious impulse and life in Europe as it is and might become

A writer of fiction who is a Catholic convert rather than a Catholic writer of fiction, Graham Greene has perplexed, dismayed, and delighted readers of all faiths since his first popular success with *Orient Express* (1932). After the first three novels he did not publish and the varyingly successful *The Man Within, The Name of Action,* and *Rumor at Nightfall,* all of them written before *Orient Express,* he has been taken seriously by good critics and read avidly by the greater public that does not read criticism. Until the publication of *A Sense of Reality,* he has been less successful as a writer of short fiction than as a novelist, although there are few who have read it that do not admire his long short story "The Basement Room." It is true also that critical severity demands that one say there have been nearly as many rises and falls aesthetically in his novels as in the short fiction collected in *Twenty-one*

Stories (1954) and *A Sense of Reality.*

The Man Within (1929), his first published novel, displayed an unusual combination of detective-story pace, a serious exploration of man's sense of guilt, and the nightmare atmosphere that reality sometimes seems to assume. Though some of these qualities can be found in his other fiction, few will deny that *Brighton Rock* (1938), *The Power and the Glory* (1940), *The Heart of the Matter* (1948), *The End of the Affair* (1951), *The Quiet American* (1955), and *A Burnt-Out Case* (1960) stand out among the too many entertainments, novels, essays, and plays he has written. Nothing he has written can be read without reward; indeed, his poorest novels and stories are superior to the vast majority of current novels, and the best of his entertainments, such as *The Ministry of Fear* (1943), are more seriously reward-

234

ing than such pretentious novels "with a message" as the late Lloyd Douglas' *The Robe*.

In *A Sense of Reality*, one finds again interesting and subtly differentiated dramatizations of Graham Greene's running quarrel with the contemporary world and a continuation of his presentation of "the real" as nightmare and the nightmare as real. Although critics whose intelligence I respect disagree with me about this, I feel that both "A Discovery in the Woods" and "Dream of a Strange Land" are inferior to "A Visit to Morin" and the masterly "Under the Garden." "Dream of a Strange Land," a fantasy about two survivors from the preferable Edwardian world, is too slick an evocation of a similarity between the modern world and an insane asylum. Although it is somewhat better, "A Discovery in the Woods" seems a little usual and sentimental in its accounts of children who live in a world populated by deformed survivors of atomic warfare. Its intentions are unquestionably serious, but it is difficult to lament unsentimentally, as Liz does in the story, the disappearance of giants who are six feet tall and have beautiful straight legs. Perhaps this difficulty arises because Mr. Greene has not succeeded in that most difficult of not impossible tasks, a vivid and valid evocation of a future that can only be imagined reluctantly.

His brief short story, "A Visit to Morin," is one of his best short pieces. It describes with remarkable effectiveness the pilgrimage of a young wine-seller to a Catholic writer who no longer believes in either his books or his reputation.

The dramatic confrontation of Dunlop, the wine merchant, and Morin is tremendously effective, although Morin makes a statement that is curious theology. Morin confesses that his "lack of belief is a final proof that the Church is right and the faith is true" because he experimentally cut himself off from the Church twenty years before to see whether his faith would wither as the priest said it would—and it has.

By far the best of Greene's stories in the volume is the novella "Under the Garden." In it Wilditch tries to recall his lost childhood (a perpetual preoccupation with Greene) in order to recover his sense of reality. He recalls, or thinks he recalls, a visit to a cave when he was a young child. There he meets a man who lives out of time. The man who lives out of time, who might symbolize Jehovah or at any rate Greene's conception of Him, sees the earth Wilditch inhabits as a combination of apparent ugliness and beauty which is really only beauty to the God-oriented, just as God, incomprehensibly, comes out of nothing without any formulable antecedents. The confrontation of the man in the cave and his past is actually a dramatization of Wilditch's confrontation of himself as he really is and of the changelessness of the fearful and wonderful world man views so variously in different eras.

The search for reality and its discovery under the garden is evoked with a robust naturalism which makes it clear that Greene, like all of us who are aware, is still a seeker rather than a burnt-out case, as he seemed to feel himself to be in his latest novel. Because it contains "Under the Garden," *A Sense of Reality* is as valuable a volume as Greene has written. It might even be said to epitomize his central and continuing search, his healthy obsession about the nature of reality, that

235

he writes about in his essay, "The Lost Childhood." Indeed, "Under the Garden" could have been called "Return to the Lost Childhood" because of its preoccupation with the remembered and irretrievable past the wise face squarely as death's inevitability impinges closer and closer upon one's sense of mortality.

Harvey Curtis Webster

73 POEMS

Author: E. E. Cummings (1894-1962)
Publisher: Harcourt, Brace and World (New York). 86 pp. $4.50
Type of work: Poetry

Another volume from the precise, unorthodox pen of a revolutionary poetic talent

This twelfth book of E. E. Cummings' poetry, published posthumously, serves as a fitting tribute to one of America's distinguished writers of our time. Aside from his poetry he published three plays, two journal-novels, two books of art, and an autobiographical book of lectures. He always described himself as both poet and painter (*Peesahtel y Hoodozhnik*, as he says in *Eimi*, a journal of his travels to Russia), although his painting has not been well received. His poetry has revolutionized American letters, and no poet writing in English would wisely ignore his amazing advances in the raw technique of putting words on a page. He was a precise, accomplished craftsman.

Having published nearly eight hundred poems in his books, Cummings might be considered a fast, facile writer. Such a view would encourage rapid, superficial reading; a quick unbinding of the usual syntactic knot and that's that. Norman Friedman, in his *E. E. Cummings: The Art of his Poetry*, has offered proof to oppose this notion. A single poem by Cummings had almost 150 pages of drafts before it was completed. The poem, at each stage of its development, was typed at the top corner of each page. Then the page was covered with notations of rhymes, stanza forms, trial lines, trial stanzas, regrouping of stanzas. No one could approach Cummings' work lightly after seeing this exhibition. His method of creation was the opposite of Robert Frost's, which is characterized by few changes in the drafts. The fact is that Cummings spent more time writing poetry than most poets have done.

It has become so traditional to defend Cummings' pictorial, iconoclastic typography that a few words may suffice here. In the Foreword to *Is 5* (1956), Cummings stated his first principle:

> At least my theory of technique, if I have one, is far from original; nor is it complicated. I can express it in fifteen words, by quoting The Eternal Question And Immortal Answer of burlesk, viz. "Would you hit a woman with a child?—No, I'd hit her with a brick." Like the burlesk comedian, I am abnormally fond of that precision which creates movement.

His readers have been precisely hit by Cummings' bricks ever since. Dryden's Crites noticed that a new art or science may in one century arrive at a great perfection. If the candid admis-

236

sion of shock value as a new art—or at least a new criterion of art criticism—is Cummings' great innovation, he has certainly perfected it.

Examples of most of his techniques are found in 73 *Poems*. There are verbal pictures, such as in poem 61, which describes a snowflake

```
(a
   li
      ght
         in
 g)
```

and poem 66, commenting on a newspaper reader, has to be read as one reads a newspaper. Poem 10 contains an unusually complex usage of word-splitting for the sake of puns:

```
                . . . you
& i(be
ca
us
e It's we)
```

"I be" and "us" are added, for obvious reasons, to "I (because . . .)." Cummings often begins a cliché to stop it in midstream:

onehundredpercentoriginal sin
cerity . . .

Punctuation and capitalization work for him as he sketches golden leaves

```
t
ReMbLiN
g
,;:.:;,
```

And we find the famous ruptured syntax, of which poem 12 is a beautiful example. But the list of devices extends on and on.

If singlemindedness is the mark of greatness, Cummings is the modern world's greatest poet. The striking edge

of his brick is always fresh, but its substance remains constant. Cummings has expressed his theme succinctly at the end of *i: six nonlectures* (1953):

I am someone who proudly and humbly affirms that love is the mystery-of-mysteries, and that nothing measurable matters "a very good God damn": that "an artist, a man, a failure" is no mere whenfully accreting mechanism, but a givingly eternal complexity—neither some soulless and heartless ultrapredatory infra-animal nor any un-understandingly knowing and believing and thinking automation, but a naturally and miraculously whole human being —a feelingly illimitable individual; whose only happiness is to transcend himself, whose every agony is to grow.

His poetry develops this theme in several ways. Some poems encourage us to love by expressing its sweetness, as in poem 7:

it's
so damn sweet when Anybody—. . .

loves. Others discourage us from automation, as in poem 62:

now does our world descend
the path to nothingness . . .

which ends ("—arise, my soul; and sing") on a note of affirmation. Some lyrics offer us examples by which to grow, as in poem 14:

a great
man
is
gone. . . .

or poem 22:

annie died the other day . . .

Honing a crumbling brick is tricky work, as is evidenced by an occasional dull edge. When he chose to write in

237

a more or less conventional form, Cummings most often shapes a sonnet. 73 *Poems* has an unusual proportion of sonnets, fifteen of them. Poem 36 is Cummings at his best in the form. Using fewer than the normal number of disruptions, it connects twilight with death in moving strokes. The poet allows the natural logic of the sonnet to work for him. On the other hand, poem 45, which has a real Shakespearian ring, contains several of Shakespeare's common mistakes; its back is broken and the end couplet jars.

Cummings is a radical reactionary preaching a strict return to the life of the New Testament. His poetry is steeped in the Biblical, classical, and English tradition. He has given new meaning to ancient precepts, and he has redefined forever the stance of the artist. 73 *Poems* belongs to a body of literature which has the elixir of immortality.

Stephen Barney

THE SHOES OF THE FISHERMAN

Author: Morris L. West (1916-   )
Publisher: William Morrow and Company (New York). 374 pp. $4.95
Type of work: Novel
Time: The near future
Locale: Rome

> The story of a Ukrainian Cardinal who becomes the first non-Italian in centuries to be elected to the Papacy

Principal characters:
KIRIL LAKOTA, Pope Kiril I
VALERIO RINALDI, Cardinal Camerlengo
CARDINAL LEONE, Cardinal Secretary of the Holy Office and Dean of the Sacred College
CHARLES CORBET CARLIN, Cardinal Archbishop of New York
JEAN TÉLÉMOND, S.J., a priest-palaeontologist
RUDOLF SEMMERING, Father General of the Society of Jesus
KAMENEV, Premier of the Soviet Union
THE PRESIDENT OF THE UNITED STATES
GEORGE FABER, the Italian correspondent of the New York *Monitor*
CHIARA CALITRI, George Faber's mistress
CORRADO CALITRI, her husband
RUTH LEWIN, a young Jewish widow

It is hard to imagine a novel that has had accrued to it a greater interest by the events of history following almost immediately on its publication than has had this story of some future Pope. The death of Pope John XXIII brought to a dramatic climax the world attention that had become increasingly focused on the Vatican during that Pontiff's lifetime, and the fever of speculation concerning the successor to the throne of Peter, always a thing of world-wide scope, rose to heights unprecedented in modern times. It was in these extraordinary moments in the Church's long history that *The Shoes of the Fisherman* made its appearance on the literary scene.

238

For the general reader the private apartments of the Vatican make a somewhat exotic setting for a story. It is within these sequestered regions of the vast papal residence, those not commonly known to the public, that a large part of *The Shoes of the Fisherman* is set. Morris West should be well qualified for his task. Author of the widely read and highly praised *The Devil's Advocate* (1959), Australian Mr. West, himself a Roman Catholic, has also been Vatican correspondent for *The Daily Mail,* an assignment which has given him the opportunity to collect the data necessary for the presentation of a technically correct picture of the workings of the Papacy.

When the novel opens, the Pope is dead. Three days hence he will be sealed in a triple casket of cypress, lead, and elm, and consigned to eternity. Meanwhile, the Lord Jesus Christ is without a vicar on earth, and the Governor of the Conclave is busily engaged in assembling, from around the globe, the princes of the Church, eighty-five in number, whom he will lock inside the conclave chambers until they have elected a new Pope.

Many readers will find Mr. West's description of the choosing of a new Pontiff one of the high points among his accounts of ancient Vatican procedures. This particular election does not take long. When the white smoke issues from the Sistine Chapel, the princes of the Church have chosen the first non-Italian Pope in centuries, the youngest of their number, and a stranger, fifty-year-old Kiril Lakota, a Ukrainian recently escaped after seventeen years of imprisonment and torture and made a Cardinal "in the breast" by the late Pope as he lay dying. When challenged with the ques-

tion, *"Acceptasne electionem* [Do you accept election]?"* Kiril, stunned and stricken, answers, *"Accepto. . . . Miserere mei Deus. . . .* I accept. . . . God have mercy on me!"*

The inescapable loneliness that is part and parcel of the human condition does not exclude the servant of the servants of God. More than with the papal proclamations or the public acts of the Pontiff, the author is concerned with the lonely pilgrimage of the man, Kiril Lakota, as he seeks out the human love and companionship that finally come to threaten his detachment as priest and bishop. (Some readers may see in the sensitive priest-scientist, Jean Télémond, a man whose qualities of mind and spirit tempt Kiril to an attachment beyond that which he has for any other, a striking resemblance to the celebrated palaeontologist, Pierre Teilhard de Chardin.) But Kiril discovers, with dismay, weaknesses within himself which, because he is greater than other men on earth, are a greater menace to his immortal soul as he faces the need to make, alone, awesome decisions whose consequences can affect millions both inside the faith and out.

The exact years of the telling of *The Shoes of the Fisherman* are not named, but they cover a period little different from our own with the world an armed camp whose member nations walk a tightrope between war and peace. From things said, and the sequence of events, the reader may well imagine Kiril Lakota as a Pontiff whose reign follows closely on that of Pope John XXIII. Kiril as Pope, finds himself, in the interests of peace, in secret correspondence with the President of the United States and his former gaoler and torturer, Kamenev, now Pre-

239

mier of the Soviet Union, world leaders who might well be successors to John Kennedy and Nikita Khrushchev.

But Kiril, Vicar of Christ, Viceregent of the Almighty, with a dominion spiritual and universal, has not only to do with the princes of the Church, the heads of states, and the affairs of the Church Holy, Universal and Apostoloc. He is also Metropolitan of an Italian see whose congregations, by historic tradition, feel themselves first claimants on his presence and on his services. Through the story of Kiril the Pontiff, the author has woven the stories of individuals of the city whose joys, sorrows, dying, intrigues, frustrations, backslidings, and searchings after faith become the concern of Kiril, Bishop of Rome.

Toward the beginning of the novel, Kiril, in a conversation with one of his cardinals, regrets the splendor with which he must be crowned and the need for wearing a crown at all. The cardinal replies: "Wear it, Holiness. . . . Wear it for the day, and do not trouble yourself. Soon enough they will crown you with thorns!" At the end, Kiril the Pope kneels at the altar in an agony of deciding. The decision which must be made may well have grave consequences for the Church and for the world, but neither the support of his cardinals nor the prayers of his people can lift from him the terrible burden of supreme authority which demands that he decide and decide alone. In the papal diary, preserver of at least "a vestige of privacy, humor, perhaps even sanity in this noble prison house to which [he is] condemned," Kiril the Pontiff writes:

. . . I am calm now because the moment of decision has come and passed, and I cannot rescind the choice I have made. But the calm is at best a truce: uncertain, embattled, dangerous to him who rests in it too confidently. . . .

Where do I go? Where do I turn? I am called like Moses to the mountaintop to intercede for my people. I cannot go down until they carry me down dead. I cannot go up until God elects to call me to Himself. The most I can expect of my brothers in the Church is that they will hold up my arms when I grow weary of this lifelong intercession. . . . And here is the shape of another mystery: that I who am called to spend so much find myself so poor in the things that are of God. . . .

Many readers of *The Shoes of the Fisherman* will compare it with another novel of the papacy, Frederick Baron Corvo's *Hadrian the Seventh* (1904). That there should be similarities in the two is inevitable. Age-old trappings of office, demands made upon administrator, priest, and bishop, the awesome burden of supreme authority would be the lot of any man who ascends the throne of Peter. It is in the characters of the two protagonists that the similarity ends. In contrast to Hadrian's self-chosen isolation and ironic detachment, born of years of hopes deferred, unremitting and unrewarded toil and bitter frustration in the face of the Church's failure to recognize his undoubted talents, are Kiril's dread of solitude and his agonizing love born out of the depths of the pain and humiliation that he has seen in others and has himself endured during his years of torture and imprisonment. Mr. West's novel, in spite of its many merits, does not have the sense of unity nor attain to the brilliance of its predecessor. Nonetheless, he, like Baron Corvo before him, has given us the portrait of a man of singular gifts of

mind and spirit for which the reader
has cause to be grateful in the midst
of the despairing mediocrity of so many
of the subjects of contemporary fiction.

Margaret Bowman Tilghman

THE SICK FOX

Author: Paul Brodeur (1927-　)
Publisher: Atlantic-Little, Brown and Company (Boston). 305 pp. $4.75
Type of work: Novel
Time: The present
Locale: A small village in the Pfalz

*An ambitiously complex first novel by a young writer about the delusion of a
young American officer in postwar Germany*

Principal characters:
> HARRY BRACE, an officer in U. S. Military Intelligence
> MATHIAS, a shepherd
> LISL WEBER, Brace's mistress
> WEBER, her husband, an innkeeper
> KONRAD ZABERN, a millionaire, the most prominent citizen in the
> district
> GRETA, Zabern's wife
> THE GÄNSEREI, the old men of the village

One of the half dozen outstanding
books among some fifty-odd American
first novels of 1963, *The Sick Fox* attracted much deserved critical attention for its young author. Paul Brodeur
is at present a staff writer for *The New
Yorker,* and a portion of *The Sick Fox*
appeared there first, in somewhat different form. Not surprisingly, the book
reminds one, particularly in its earlier
section, of much *New Yorker* fiction:
one finds the same "alienated" protagonist, the same scrupulously Jamesian
narrative point of view, the same preoccupation with the picturesque values
of a foreign setting, the same amateur
sociologizing, the same tendency to regard all material surfaces as somehow
significant of a profound psychological
meaning, the same disturbingly claus-
tral tone. Perhaps the single unexpected
element in the book is its overlay of
Ambleresque suspense, for on its top-

most layer *The Sick Fox* is really an
adventure story.

The hero of the book, Harry Brace,
is an officer stationed near Weiersheim,
a remote village in that hilly back-
woods region east of the Rhine, the
Pfalz, which the Germans themselves
refer to as "behind the moon." As the
local representative of U. S. Military
Intelligence, Brace is free to come and
go pretty much as he pleases; his job
is to guard an underground nuclear
storehouse known as the Site, to keep
an eye on some rapidly deteriorating
Army property reserved for use in war
games, and to maintain an incidental
finger on the political pulse of the
populace. Having adapted himself as
much as possible to his environment
and having successfully cut himself off
from interference by his superiors or
by other Army branches in the area,
Brace is happy in his job, perhaps too

241

happy: he has come, like so many other conquerors of the region in the past, to think of Weiersheim and its wooded hills as somehow "his." His failure to reckon on the historic temperament of the Pfalz has resulted in delusion, and the extent of his delusion is, of course, the major theme of the book.

The first crack in Brace's comfort comes at the very outset of the book when for some reason not entirely known to himself, apparently a respect for a fellow creature who is, like himself, completely alone, he spares the life of a sick fox. His mercy, it turns out, was a mistake, for the fox is rabid and Brace's failure to act at this crucial point eventually brings into corrective play, first, the entire machinery of local German officialdom, then that dangerous system of tribal loyalty, epitomized in the concept of the *comitatus*, which is peculiar to the Germans and which has historically always acted to reassert the permanence of an atavistic way of life against the transitoriness of all conquerors. Brace discovers in the end that the land is not his, that it can never belong to him or people like him, that instead of owning anything, in fact, he is a landless nomad, a sick fox bound to the world of men by his own weakness and able to survive only as long as men will let him.

Brace's initial delusion is fostered in part by the fact that he believes himself so thoroughly to have dominated the life around him: he speaks German fluently, dresses like a German, exercises German authority; he fishes in local streams, skies the local hills, plays tennis with Greta Zabern, the wife of Konrad Zabern, the leader of local society, and occasionally sleeps with Lisl Weber, the wife of Weber the inn-keeper, a DP from Königsberg who is active in a movement to reclaim and reunify the former territories of Germany and who owes his affluence chiefly to Lisl's habit of passionate submission to conquerors like Brace. Eventually Harry Brace seduces Greta Zabern; and her final refusal to run away with him, a refusal, that is, to accept Brace in place of her husband, confirms the dawning realization that he has remained outside the land he thinks he governs, that he is, after all, only another in the endless stream of passing conquerors.

Brace is not alone in his alienation, however, for it includes even other Germans, those who have come from regions outside the district behind the moon and who find themselves equally landless foreigners. Among the German outlanders are Weber, who in the end leaves Lisl and returns to live in the East, and, most important, an old nomadic shepherd named Mathias, who enters the district in the course of wanderings he has carried on for more than the Mosaic forty years. Like the sick fox, Mathias becomes for Brace a symbol of himself; he finds this nomad, whose suspected Jewishness makes him almost an Ahasuerus, strangely sympathetic, and the American undertakes, at the expense of good relations with the static peasants of the village, to give him protection against the local bureaucracy with its obsessive interest in property rights and regulations. Mathias stands for the anarchy in Brace and for a time Brace is successful in his defense. He shelters Mathias, ironically, in an abandoned POW stockade built for U. S. Army war games and defies the local authorities in exactly the same way that the robber barons, besieged in their castles,

242

had defied them hundreds of years before.

Meanwhile, however, Konrad Zabern learns of Greta's unfaithfulness and resolves to avenge himself on Brace by mobilizing the absolute faith of the *comitatus*, invoking the tribal loyalty of the peasants to him as their chief. Using the rabies scare as an excuse, he leads the *comitatus*, a ragged army composed largely of the Gänserei, the old men who keep a deathgrip on the property of the village, up to the stockade. There they kill all of Mathias' sheep, while Brace stands by, furious and armed but helpless in his false position as a supposed alien overlord to do more than threaten Zabern's life. The killing of the sheep exposes Brace's weakness in the face of forces whose source lies far back in history and which centuries of occupation by army after army have not been able to efface. At the end of the book, his offer to Greta—which we see as Brace's futile attempt to avenge himself, in turn, on Zabern—having been refused, Brace requests to have himself withdrawn from behind the moon. His final words to his superior attain an ironic ring that echoes his whole position of involuntary non-commitment in a community where total commitment to the land and to a leader is the only acceptable norm:

"Nothing compromised," he said, and hung up the phone.

Brace has been a fox among the geese, the Gänserei, the old men who run the village and whose peasant immobility can be stirred only by a call to loyalty like Zabern's. The basic conflict of the book, then, is the conflict between the peasants and the nomads of the world. With great skill Mr. Brodeur creates an atmosphere of curious looming danger by hinting that this conflict is permanent and universal, that the foxes of the earth represent an element of freedom and independence that the geese can never know or understand, that geese have ways of destroying this freedom and of defending themselves against a fox. He demonstrates ultimately, in fact, that it is the foxes who are threatened by the geese, for the geese outnumber the foxes and are organized, while the foxes, in their homeless anarchy, have no place to turn for help and only themselves to depend upon. Brace's life behind the moon has really been a kind of game for him, a game of fox and geese played out against a background of reality in which he has no part, a game that he could neither continue forever nor win. Temporarily released from the usual responsibilities of a man in society, he has been allowed to play his game of useless Intelligence only until the time when society should turn on him, reverse the roles, and call a halt; when he fails to kill the fox, he makes his decision for a freedom more absolute than society will allow and therefore, in the end, it repudiates the game, killing Mathias' sheep and driving Harry Brace out as it has every sick fox since Cain.

Mr. Brodeur has constructed a highly provocative book and one that is almost sure to survive its season. Obviously a deeply considered work, it raises no new notions of technique or theme, and its chief fault, perhaps, is a certain rigidity in adhering to what appear to be *The New Yorker* rules, a stiffness and an overscrupulousness of thought and expression excluding a good deal of what one feels *The Sick Fox* might have had to say had it been allowed a

little looseness of articulation. One
would like to see what Mr. Brodeur

can do in a second novel and one
would like to see it soon.

John Rodenbeck

SIR WILLIAM

Author: David Stacton (1925-   )
Publisher: G. P. Putnam's Sons (New York). 352 pp. $5.95
Type of work: Novel
Time: 1782-1803
Locale: Sicily and England

A comic novel based on the famous love affair between Lord Horatio Nelson and
Lady Emma Hamilton

Principal characters:
ADMIRAL HORATIO NELSON, the renowned naval hero
SIR WILLIAM HAMILTON, the aging English ambassador to Naples
LADY EMMA HAMILTON (nee Emily Lyon), Sir William's wife and
    Nelson's mistress
CHARLES CAREVILLE, Sir William's nephew

We all enjoy watching the great drama of life unfold before our eyes, and one aspect of this eternal drama that has a special attraction for us is the illicit love affair between prominent personages. The romances of the Hollywood stars excite attention, and we delve into the past for examples of properly adulterous "courtly love." One of these almost mythological legends of love on the sly is the story of Admiral Horatio Nelson's affair with Lady Emma Hamilton, a woman who, unlike her forgotten husband, now occupies a place in all the encyclopedias for her invaluable contribution to the British war effort against Napoleon. Sir William Hamilton, Emma's old husband, has been almost completely forgotten by everyone except David Stacton, a young American writer whose novels are only now beginning to enjoy in America the fame that they have been acquiring abroad for a number of years.

The fact that Stacton's novels are gaining popularity slowly but steadily

is easy to understand, for his literary method takes a time to grow on the reader. His style is intentionally old-fashioned and learnedly clever, and his scenes are so pithily short that they flash by in an endless procession; in fact, his episodes resemble extended epigrams. Furthermore, his perspective is unique: he tells the story of this notorious love affair from the viewpoint of the aging Sir William, a broad-minded man too old (or too wise) to mind being cuckolded. Sir William thinks of Nelson almost as a son, and the two men go fishing together whenever Nelson is not making love to Emma. The three of them are one big happy family, so affectionately close that Stacton refers to them as *tria juncta in uno.*

Stacton systematically deflates all the idealized aspects of the Nelson-Emma legend romanticized by so many writers in the past. He reminds us that at the time of the passionate liaison, Nelson had only one arm, one eye, no teeth, and very little hair. He also re-

244

veals to us that Emma had been the mistress of Sir William's nephew when she was sixteen. But there is something strange about Stacton's Emma in the light of her rather warm reputation in real life. The odd thing is that in this book she has absolutely no sexual desire. She allows herself to be taken advantage of by quite a few men, but her motives for giving in are a vague mixture of bourgeois money-hunger, laziness, and an inability to say "no" because she always likes to be obliging. Thus we see that this novel has no dashing hero or passionately devoted heroine, even though Emma is quite passionate about one activity—eating. The whole love affair is as unromantic as a freezing rain. For one thing, Nelson takes a hundred pages to get up enough courage even to start the affair. Emma's attitude toward the tender romance can be summed up in the following laconic conversation about Nelson's troublesome wife, Fanny:

"I cannot live without you," said Nelson, who was, alas, sincere.
"You silly boy, you do not have to," said Emma, who was, alas, now not. "We can all four visit back and forth." It was still her hope that Fanny might be induced to sponsor her at Court.

The total effect of the novel depends mainly on Stacton's completely unromantic retelling of a romantic story rather than on his positive creative genius. But merely taking an irreverent attitude toward a traditionally sentimental story does not in itself make great literature. Stacton has an original outlook on his story. But has he really created a worth-while novel while displaying his unique outlook? A mere negation of romantic traditions is not enough. Has Stacton, who is exploding the romantic myth of the old legend, made his version of the story worth reading in itself? The answer is yes, for the most part. Stacton's style and grasp of character reveal his artistic originality and sustain the reader's interest till the end, in spite of an obvious inability to find any great "theme" to give his comic story real meaning. His style is a mélange of puns, epigrams, and paradoxical turns of thought, and his episodes are a series of piquant snapshots which etch memories into the reader's mind after they have been read. In his mixing together of epigrams and puns, Stacton achieves just the right balance of solid wisdom and frivolity to make him a member of that small but powerful league of intellectually sophisticated and urbanely loquacious comic writers, the marvelous group that includes Swift, James Joyce, and Vladimir Nabokov. The only trouble is that Stacton, in spite of his marvelous verbal gifts, does not yet have the ability to tell a truly compelling *story*; he has not yet developed that dramatic ability which vitalizes the novels of the three great comic writers just mentioned. Stacton's plot is sometimes hard to follow, but this fact does not necessarily mean that the book is profound, and the reader finally tires of cryptic references and verbal games which are a substitute for a really engrossing plot. The narrative has the condensed complexity of a poem, and yet its very complexity emphasizes the thinness of the story. In the middle sections of the book, the reader begins to feel that Stacton has not really written a novel at all, but merely a collection of endlessly witty and finally tiresome tableaux. And yet, toward the end, the

245

dramatic effect of Stacton's handling of the story begins to accumulate, and the ending makes the whole book glow in the reader's memory in a clear, pleasant light. The middle sections are a letdown after the immaculately structured beginning, but toward the end we realize that Stacton is really justified in asking us to read his version of a tale that has already been told many times. For very few writers have created quite the same dramatic effect that Stacton ultimately attains.

Stacton's characterizations are at first disconcerting, for at times the personalities of his characters seem lost under the coating of epigrammatic description and sophisticated satire. And yet these characters, like the plot, have a cumulative effect on the reader; at the end we realize that Stacton has captured the essences of their personalities, even though he has not tried to delve into their souls. Nelson, of course, comes across as a tired, unheroically middle-aged man who possesses a quite believable sense of integrity. Sir William, the most passive and therefore the least sensational member of the trio, is a focal point of sanity and tolerance. Like Emma's shrewd mother, he is an outsider, a "watcher" of other people's lives. In spite of, or perhaps because of, Stacton's lack of sentimentality, Sir William ultimately becomes an endearing character, and Stacton ironically makes us mourn for the urbane old man by telling us suddenly of his death.

Emma is a hilarious character, but she is not a caricature; the laughter she inspires comes from the fact that she is completely real. In his chronological development of Emma, Stacton shows how a natural, vulgar, lower-class girl becomes a society-blinded po-seur. She is "God's masterpiece, a silly woman." Telling us that women are "professional actresses," Stacton uses the historical Emma's love of posing like classical statues (she called these poses her "Attitudes," and she performed them for all her guests; when she was pregnant, she would give the performances sitting in a chair) in order to show us that her whole personality really became a "gallery of statues." In this fashion Stacton has impressionistically captured the essence of Emma's personality, and at his hands she becomes a wonderfully life-filled embodiment of the vulgar, avaricious, and childlike bourgeois woman. And Stacton realizes that, unlike Mrs. Bloom's, Emma's vulgarity is not sexual. Thus Emma becomes a unique but quite believable figure, a vulgar woman who sucks in food and money like a sponge but who could not care less about sexual pleasure because "she was that rare thing, a sexually satisfied woman." In the end, she walks away into history singing a hopelessly silly song.

Stacton's humor, like Nabokov's, is refreshing because it is not bitter. His epigrams are sharp but never childishly angry, and he fortunately realizes that a mature satirist does not have to fill his book with "messages." He strips his characters of their pretenses, but he does not despise them. He tries to be completely honest about these people, and he causes us to admire their good qualities: "Emma was without malice, and so, unsuited to the polite usages of society." Little remarks like that one make his characters seem real and rounded. Little bits of clever psychology appear on every page ("Sir William . . . was quite willing to laugh at his own passions, given he might do so reminiscently"), and Stacton relieves his clever humor with several poetic idyls, touching descriptions of lonely people sitting by themselves in reverie. His descriptions of George Romney, the tragically inept painter, are really moving, and he adds depth to the novel by casually telling us and Emma that forgotten Romney has died. Stacton's structural method, though repetitive and thus often tiring, has professional polish, and his clever use of montage adds to the flowing-surface effect of the novel. Stacton smoothly weaves historical material into the story through the use of letters and brief con- versations, and he emphasizes the humorous fact that historical events do not always seem important to the people taking part in them.

Sir William is not a deep novel, and it is not a lyrical novel. Instead of delving into the souls of his characters, Stacton gives us a light, impressionistic, cumulative picture of their essential personalities. It is, as the reader looks back on it, a very pleasant book, a promise of more fine work to come from a writer whose ironic and humorous "message" is summed up in the last sentence of the novel: "Life is a dream."

Michael Campbell

SPECULATIONS ABOUT JAKOB

Author: Uwe Johnson (1932-   )
Translated from the German by Ursula Molinaro
Publisher: The Grove Press (New York). 240 pp. $4.50
Type of work: Novel
Time: 1955
Locale: East Germany and West Berlin

A proletarian hero is driven to his death by the inhuman social and political conditions of his world

Principal characters:
    JAKOB ABS, a train dispatcher in Dresden
    GERTRUDE ABS, his mother, who flees to the West
    GESINE CRESSPAHL, an East German girl working as an interpreter
        with NATO
    HEINRICH CRESSPAHL, her sixty-eight-year-old father, a cabinet
        maker
    JONAS BLACH, an assistant professor of English philology in East
        Berlin
    HERR ROHLFS, an agent of the East German secret police

The dehumanization of man has been a popular, if not overworked, theme among Western social scientists, artists, and critics for some time. Taking note of this fact, Communists have insisted that dehumanization is a bourgeois phenomenon, the inevitable consequence of a decadent class society in which the individual is exploited by the abstract demands of the economic system, and claimed that the socialist state, on the contrary, protects and enhances the person. Accordingly, the Communists have consistently prohibited their artists from experimenting with the techniques of *avant garde*

247

Western art and required that they celebrate the proletariat in the officially sanctioned style of social realism. In *Speculations about Jakob*, Uwe Johnson, who came to the West just before his book was published, takes advantage of the techniques of cubism to expose the truth about life in a socialist state that the Communists have been so anxious to hide.

Speculations about Jakob is not an easy novel to read. The physical action, to be sure, is simple enough. Jakob Abs, a twenty-eight-year-old train dispatcher, is recruited by the East German secret police to contact Gesine Cresspahl, who has defected to the West and taken a job with NATO. Because they had lived together in the same house for several years and were like brother and sister, Jakob will supposedly be able to help persuade Gesine to pass information to the Communists. The contact is made but nothing comes of it. Although Gesine loves Jakob, she refuses to return to East Germany or to aid the secret police. Jakob is then mysteriously killed by a train while crossing the tracks on his way to work. His death is puzzling because it occurred on the morning after his return from West Berlin, where he had visited Gesine, and because as a train dispatcher he was familiar with the schedules and had walked daily across the tracks.

The simplicity of the physical action is deceiving, however, for it is never directly narrated. Johnson employs a montage of rapidly shifting points of view and time perspectives so that little of Jakob and few of the events are ever seen up close or directly. The novel is therefore an intellectual mystery in which the hunt is on for the truth about Jakob Abs by characters within the story as well as by the reader. Because almost everything seen is refracted through the mind and memory of someone, and because, as Johnson takes care to remind the reader on several occasions, opinions are not reality, Jakob eludes his pursuers, his reality becoming lost in the labyrinths of their separate, detached minds. Thus the title of the novel—Jakob is an object of speculation known remotely from various points of view but never directly perceived for what he is in and of himself.

The novel, in form as well as in theme, is based on a vision of a radical disjunction between perception and fact, reason and reality, self and society. This disjunction permeates every aspect of the story. The family, once a stable social unit founded on intimate human relations, is broken apart, first, by the death of Jakob's father, in the war, and Gesine's mother, and then by the departure of both Gesine and Jakob's mother to the West, leaving the male remnants of a surrogate family the two fragments had constituted. The intellectual, represented by Jonas Blach, dwelling in the abstract realm of theory, has no affection for his family and nothing to contribute to solving the real problems of his fellow men. The government agent, Herr Rohlfs, is kept away from his wife and child by the demands of his job, which by nature entails the sacrifice of personal considerations to the state's purposes and ideology. Most telling, however, is the absence of love in the lives of all the characters but especially in that of Jakob, who is apparently loved by two women but loses both because of politics, one being "progressive" and the other defecting to the West. In short, every person's life is invaded and cor-

248

roded by superpersonal forces to the extent that all the traditional bonds between men—love, trust, honesty, and the like—have been destroyed, so that no longer does anyone experience himself or others as persons. Each is locked in the barren cell of himself.

And that includes Jakob, too. Despite the difficulty of getting an unobstructed look at him, Jakob emerges from an accumulation of details and opinions as a man possessing abundant humanity. He is the triumph of Johnson's artistry. Nevertheless, *Speculations about Jakob* is the story of Jakob's death, of his progressive disillusionment and hopelessness. Descended from Pomeranian farmer stock, he has a solidity and freshness, a vigor and practical-mindedness reminiscent of his soil-tilling ancestors. Where others think about ideology, he worries over his job, deeply concerned that it be done right and that all his ability go toward solving problems that cause his fellow man discomfort. Caught up in the machinations of politics, Jakob's frustration with bureaucratic inefficiency increases; his personal relations are destroyed by the duplicity he is forced to practice; and finally he understands the degree to which the individual is pushed around by the state, by the superpersonal mechanics of an industrialized and urbanized society. He is driven to his death by the discovery that there is no place for him or for what he values in the modern world.

Should the reader be inclined to look for evidence of the failure of communism in Johnson's novel, he will be disappointed, not because communism is not portrayed as failing, but because what is revealed as the truth about East Germans is a truth that cuts across national and ideological boundaries. Johnson has succeeded in generalizing the division of Germany into the plight of men everywhere in the twentieth century. A superbly controlled novel, *Speculations about Jakob* moves from the smallest detail and personal fact to the largest political and spiritual realities with classical objectivity, clarity, equanimity. Blending epistomological realism with social realism, Johnson writes with a cool, steady eye, recording precise perceptions honestly, unflinchingly. He is an artist of impressive intellect surveying an irrational world with reason, and revealing, soberly and quietly, the sterile ground of modern society. Where so much of modern fiction has had its strength sapped by the disintegration of the external world into the absurd, his novel is rooted in Greek and German humanism, deriving from them a firm image of the wondrous creature that man was. But Johnson does not take refuge in nostalgia. There is only the grim fact coolly perceived. The writer provides little pleasure and no inspiration for the proletariat, nor for anyone else either. She (meaning Gesine, after Jakob's death)—"she didn't look as though she has been crying; that's a point we do want to make," Johnson insists in his concluding sentence.

William R. Robinson

SPRING OF THE THIEF

Author: John Logan (1923-   )
Publisher: Alfred A. Knopf (New York). 74 pp. $4.00
Type of work: Poetry

New poems by the author of Cycle for Mother Cabrini *and* Ghosts of the Heart, *and editor of the magazine* Choice

One must confront carefully, and with open senses, the work of a poet who has been universally praised since his first publication. Among the estimable critics who have nominated Logan on a ticket of contemporary excellence are Tate, Ransom, Fowlie, Kunitz, Fitts, Whittemore, Ciardi, and James Dickey. Represented here are at least two modern critical persuasions at considerable variance with each other, and it is a tribute to Logan's talent that he draws approbation from all camps. His verse echoes a deep religious sense and search embodied in carefully wrought forms, a quality which endears him to the more conservative readers allied with the sensibility of Eliot and Maritain. At the same time, he inherits the highly-developed Symbolist influence that makes him acceptable to readers who continue to make a point of the allied, though not coincident, values of Donne and Baudelaire. Further, in the later poems, Logan has "opened" his idiom, achieving a kind of freedom sought also, lately, by other excellent contemporaries such as Robert Lowell and James Wright; and this choice has satisfied those who exalt the Whitman-Pound-Williams conviction in verse. Yet even here Logan's poems at their seemingly most free do not abandon the tight sense-sound structure which the skillful worker naturally gravitates to, and Logan reaps the simple rewards of solid craft. Even in his less impressive poems, he suffers no technical failure. In

short, he has been from the first a true "pro"—but not finally subject to the slighting connotation ordinarily attached to professionalism in a romantic era such as this. Logan's work is neither facile nor over-studied; it bears the marks of struggle with idea and feeling goaded and cajoled into appropriate, hard-won forms.

A Catholic, Logan has as much in common with Donne as with Hopkins, as much with Hart Crane as Merton. The earlier writers are mentioned because Logan displays the educated poet's appreciation of history and tradition. Here is an erudite poet who has done graduate study in philosophy, who is also strongly involved with the most current quirks of contemporary feeling and idiom. He writes as easily of the Cisco Kid as of Aquinas. And to share Logan's insight into a kind of Chaplinesque pathetic reality, take this brief passage from "The Thirty-Three Ring Circus":

Kids on bicycles
gathering bottles
and a dozen bent,
thirty-five-cent fans
from the Orient.

By a dead bon-
fire lies the charred
button down
shoe of a clown.

Between the well
and the hill
is the skull
of a doll.

250

Logan's voracious intellect leads him to quote from Kierkegaard and Camus, a "Source Book of Animal Biology," a Turkish military captain, and Hart Crane—any source which can feed a strong and random imagination. Half-tame, half-wild, he ricochets off many walls of poetry. In a religious vein he writes:

I thought (and before it was too late)
my heart had begun to turn, that was
shut to love, for I was adamant
as saints, and tough as the martyr's heart,
as a wooden statue of a god,
where my father sat in the straight pew,
my mother bowed to the stone, bearing
flowers she had cut out of the earth
of my life. Ah the candles bloom cold
in the earthen air of early Mass . . .

Then he turns to an absolutely secular celebration of the refurbishment of earth through the senses and acts of a little girl:

Oh I have felt these same
yearnings in myself—
the tiny dark and yellow
hairs lit with wet
at the center of the May Day
violets Elizabeth held
in her seven-year-old fist
some six or seven years before
the grace she gave the afternoon . . .

Logan's quiet but powerfully religious, and orthodox, use of verse, carefully breathed, paced, and spaced, with natural rhythms in short lines which bespeak utmost sincerity, comes in "The Wooden Mirror":

I wait beside the fount.
My God whispers in the box
where a fellow sinner still confesses.
Again my mind caresses
with my hand the iron fence
that protects or that ornaments,
out of art, caution or some

paradigmal wisdom,
the dish kept for our baptism.
I had forgot this fount
has eight sides of highly rubbed wood,
each with a Gothic arch in relief
leading nowhere
but to my own natural face
shadowed in its mirror . . .

There is a great deal of cumulative force in Logan's work. The images reinforce one another from poem to poem as one goes along. The title poem, "Spring of the Thief," shows the easy progression of the most passionately held theme: spring, regeneration, Christ killed and buried, the thieves of the Crucifixion prayed for, the thief representing us in our local and modern criminality and absurdity. It is even suggested that the Christ, taken and rejected, is significantly flanked by a "true" thief who is part and parcel of the divine situation, coupled imagistically with the Christian Hero:

Again at last the late November snow
will fill those fields, change this hill,
throw these figures in relief
and raining on them
will transform
the bronze Christ's brow and cheek,
the white face and thigh of the thief.

Here we discern the identification of the holy and the debased, and farther back in history, the association of the thief, with his "white face and thigh," with the figure of Pythagoras, who in Yeats' rendering became "golden-thighed," true to the myth and a symbol of intellect.

If any recent poet can be said to be Gentile, Greek, and Jew, he is probably John Logan, with his fluent progress in verse, his concentration on seriously pertinent themes, his historically trained allusions and symbols. Logan's present achievement and the general enthusiasm it has aroused have put a burden on him. His next book will have to be exceptionally strong.

Robert Hazel

STAND UP, FRIEND, WITH ME

Author: Edward Field (1924-   )
Publisher: The Grove Press (New York). 77 pp. $2.50
Type of work: Poetry

Sprightly and very frank poems which, though tinged with self-pity, are fresh, unaffected, and full of many wise comments on modern life

When applied to a man, the adjective "sprightly" suggests a middle-aged gentleman with a slight paunch who moves briskly and wittily about, doing things with the vigor of youth and the precision of age. Yet not many men like to be classified as sprightly, with its implications of middle age and beyond, and not many poets like to have the word applied to their work, often with the implication of a lack of depth and of that quality all poets think they must have—"seriousness." But Edward Field's *Stand Up, Friend, with Me,* the Lamont Poetry Selection of 1962, practically demands being called sprightly, in all the complimentary connotations of the word.

The opening section of the book is called "Greece" and immediately there appears a kind of gentle joshing, a sort of low-key satire, both disarmingly presented in a clear-cut style, unembellished with vain attempts at wisdom through obscurity. Take "Donkeys," for example: this poem deals with the paradox of man's insensitivity as compared with a donkey's sensitivity, for Mr. Field sees donkeys not as creatures full of stubbornness and comical heehaws but as a kind of paradox within themselves, "with their sweet eyes and ridiculous ears." In these lines the poet gets in his sly dig (or kick) at mankind:

And if I tried to explain to them
Why work is not only necessary but good,
I am afraid they would never understand
And kick me with their back legs
As commentary on my wisdom.

In the title poem of this first section Mr. Field seems as charmed with things Grecian as any happy American tourist. He finds the bodies of modern Greeks as beautiful as the ancient ones that were ennobled in statuary, but with this reservation: those Greeks who come to America and then return home seem altered. "I suppose," says the poet, "they sacrifice their gods to a foreign one/And lose their own divinity." And so America gets the kick this time. In "Prologue" the poet shows his technical skill by a remarkably effective example of moving from the general to the particular. He starts out with the universe ("Look, friend, at this universe"), particularizes to the earth, to an island, to a village, to a house, to himself ("Look, friend, at me").

Field has his flaws. One is illustrated in "A Bill to My Father" (in Part II: "A View of Jersey"), which

252

contains a complaint from a young man, while he is typing up bills for a firm, that his father has never given him the attention and/or the love he deserves as a son. The poem rambles on for quite a number of lines; its entire "message" can actually be summed up in one sentence: my debt-ridden father responds to written bills but ignores one overdue account—his unpaid bill to me. Such a paraphrase, of course, is not poetry, but it suggests that the poet might try the discipline of condensation, perhaps even of rhyme and metrical regularity. Another flaw in Field's work is the touch of self-pity that poets experience in this evil, ugly, commercial world; such feelings come out in "What Grandma Knew," a naïve complaint about the office where the poet is employed. Answering his "favorite" question, "Why must I work for a living?" Mr. Field says:

If you're famous, life is fun;
If you're not, you live like others do,
And go to the same death of the heart
Long before the hairs finally all fall out
of your head.

The reader wants to pat Mr. Field on the head and say, Come, come now, not all the non-famous have their hearts die; even in Manhattan there may be a few cheerful souls with the vigorous outlook on life of Edgar Lee Masters' Lucinda Matlock; read Masters' poem, fellow, and buck up! Field himself gives us hope that he may not always deplore the contrivances of urban life, which is his not-so-happy hunting ground, for in "The Telephone" he praises this instrument that provides him—hungry as a bear coming out of hibernation—with "the human voice and the good news of

friends." Perhaps someday he will have a good word to say for diesels, even subways. Other striking poems in Part II are "Spring" and "Poem for the Left Hand," both of which illustrate Field's great skill in building to a climax; in the latter the poet expresses relief at having lost a hand, for in the past he had been an unnoticed emotional cripple, but now he is obviously maimed. The climax states:

Knots are too difficult for one hand to
be bothered with:
Now I cut them through and laugh for
the liberation.

Edward Field's choice of a title for Part III—"Graffiti"—is somewhat unfortunate, for W. H. Auden has used the same heading in a recent book, and Field is not yet of Auden's stature. There are good poems here: "Sonny Hugg and the Porcupine," in which Sonny has his difficulties in cuddling his new-found friend; "Trees," in which the poet expresses his fear of trees (Field scrupulously avoids the bucolic in his poetry) because of their size and their "terrifying view" of outer space; and, best of all, "Graffiti" itself, in which the poet tells us (in startlingly frank words) what little kids do to improve the signs in subways; Field slides smoothly into expressing pity for these children who are headed for adulthood, "a winter that will freeze them forever. . . ."

"A New Cycle" is the heading for the last section of the book, and here are poems of a new type, mostly about people. The title poem, however, goes back to the old father-son relationship; it tells of a bicycle—Mr. Field is fond of puns—his father bought for him when he was a boy. The bicycle opened up a whole new life: a paper

253

route, pocket money, dances, "sexual adventures that would have made my father's hair/ Stand up in horror had he known." The poet ties this memory to his thirty-fifth birthday, the end of another seven-year cycle, when he finds himself with "nothing to do and no ideas for the future." He pleads for another bicycle to change his life once more. The poems about people range from tributes to Chopin and Fidel Castro to a light-hearted description of Mark Twain and Sholem Aleichem at Coney Island, two elderly men having fun in the surf even though their humor and love have failed to make the world a better place. The poem on Castro, while lively enough, seems somewhat dated: it brings in the black man's troubles, the Jew's troubles, and makes much of the significance of Castro and Khrushchev bear-hugging in Harlem. Is the poet enamoured of Castro or is he merely kidding? A poem near the end of the book is a birthday piece for Field's younger sister and is undistinguished

from similar child-growing-into-woman poems, except that the poet has added the fillip of sex and a number of scatological terms. Also, Sonny Hugg (a favorite character of the poet) pops up again in "The Sleeper," an amusing account of Sonny's efforts to turn the frail, diminutive poet into an athlete.

Stand Up, Friend, with Me is a fine book of poems: fresh, different, moving, frank. In summation, however, Mr. Field leaves himself open if not to criticism, at least to strong suggestion. He needs to condense, to be less abject in the face of the world's treatment of "sensitive" people and of Jews, and to remember that frank statements and terms about sex and other body functions do not always make good poetry. This view is not dictated by prudery, only by a feeling that even the best gimmicks wear out. But for the present we have *Stand Up, Friend, with Me* and we are pleased to stand up, Mr. Field, with you, and all for you.

Preston Newman

THE STORIES OF WILLIAM SANSOM

Author: William Sansom (1912-   )
Publisher: Little, Brown and Company (Boston). 422 pp. $6.00
Type of work: Short stories
Time: Recent decades
Locale: Great Britain and various Continental settings

A collection of thirty-three short stories which represent the author's range through eight separate volumes

As a novelist, William Sansom has never quite come into his own. Few readers of modern British fiction have given more than cursory attention to his six works in longer form—*The Last Hours of Sandra Lee, The Cautious Heart, The Loving Eye, A Bed*

of *Roses, The Face of Innocence,* and *The Body.* Whether this neglect is due to Sansom's expense of talent "on themes that are basically trivial, or on characters who are unduly shallow," as the critic Frederick Karl has charged, or whether it is due to some other failure on the part of either the author or his readers, the fact of neglect remains. The truth of the matter would seem to be that Sansom is a member of that group of writers so much at home in the short story that they cannot successfully project their visions of experience on the large cineramic screen of the novel. One thinks of such writers as Maupassant, Katherine Anne Porter, and Eudora Welty who share this quality, just as with respect to the reverse principle one thinks of Robert Penn Warren.

In her introduction to the present volume, Elizabeth Bowen states the case with different emphasis, but arrives nonetheless at a conclusion which takes similarly into account the nature of generic specialization: "Incidental short stories of writers by nature given to greater space, or by need bound to the synthesis of the novel, generally warrant attention and give pleasure. Some have the *éclat* of successful command performances. Few quite misfire. Few fail to merit the author's signature or to bear the particular stamp he gives any work. Yet such stories, recognizably, are by-products. One does not feel that they were inevitable. In this, they differ essentially from stories by the short-storyist *par excellence*: the short-storyist by birth, addiction and destiny. Such is William Sansom."

There are here some thirty-three examples of his art, taken from eight previous collections of short stories, and reprinted in chronological order, so that it becomes convenient as well as possible to consider the development of his "best work." Such an analysis reveals an easing of manner with a concomitant flexibility and security of style, and an expansion of subject matter which frees the tightly conceived

locus of the earlier fiction and embraces more subtly at once a more comprehensive and more suggestive range of human experience.

There was a time, some twenty years ago, when a fashionable critical tag to affix to the name of Sansom was "the English Kafka." Stories of prisoners forced to wring wet cloths dry, only to have the pits where they worked flooded as soon as they were through —such stories seemed indeed Kafkaesque, revealing as they did the plight of man in a world in which perverse forces, inexplicable and inscrutable, could lead only to frustration, futility, agony. From a longer vantage point in time, it is possible to say that this mode does not represent the quintessence of Sansom's work. Indeed, no blatant story of universal dilemma appears in the present collection. On the other hand, some tales, both early and late, can be said to manifest a bad-dreamlike unreality in the midst of familiar phenomena, and so in this one respect resemble the nature of Kafka's work; one realizes now that to make more of a comparison would be misleadingly shallow and distortive. The point is that they are not Kafkaesque but Sansomesque stories, that they derive from a far from atypical twentieth century sensibility which combines depressive terror with mild comedy, an often grotesque unbalance of man in society with a fearful symmetry somewhere in the universe.

Sansom's stories are endowed with a wonderful sense of particularity. The word Miss Bowen finds to apply most accurately to their pervasive quality is *sensation*. This is an acceptable generalization. It is borne out in such stories as "The Wall," in which a wartime fire-fighter in London is confronted with the sheer physicality of a wall of bricks collapsing like a perforated card upon his head, and "The Vertical Ladder," in which a youth who has taken a dare mounts to dizzying heights on a storage tank, finds the last steps to the pinacle platform have rusted away, and in a state of vertigo not only cannot descend but can barely cling to the perilous place he is; or in such later stories as "Among the Dahlias," in which an "ordinary" man panics when he meets a lion loose on the path of a zoo, but despairs when he is ignored by the king of the beasts, and "To the Rescue!" in which a commercial man leaps into the sea to save a child, turns back because the current is too strong, and feels hurt when he is snubbed by the man who does perform the rescue. An immediacy of very particular sensation is felt by the reader, whose reaction is one of empathy. The major development to be observed in the more recent stories is an increase in psychological complexity and implication, a movement from a sensation of danger and its attendant fear to a pathetic, almost comic, sensation of despair and loneliness.

Hitting with keen critical certainty on virtually all the distinctive points to be made about Sansom's short fiction, Miss Bowen also remarks on the great importance of scene, quite literally the descriptive passages which evoke landscape or architecture. A number of stories are so integrally bound up with scene that it is hard to imagine their transplantation; all of them are noticeably, significantly scenic. A perfect example of the scenic mode is "Episode at Gastein," in which a winter spa is as important *qua* place as the hotel in the motion picture, *Last Year at Marienbad*. An ironic tale of an aging aristocrat, Ludwig de Broda, whose infatuation with the charming Fräulein Laure Perfuss seems requited until the certainly not inevitable intervention of a young skiing master, this is one of the longest, best developed, and most successful pieces in the collection. But throughout, the consideration of highly civilized human experience is made so subtly and yet so precisely in conjunction with the effect of mountains, snow, view, and cold that person, place, and thing are altogether inextricable. Geographical setting of the stories is various, and in every case—Scotland, London, Provence, Scandanavia—something of what must surely be a consciously scenic conception of human event is demonstrable. And, needless to say, the quality of sensation is not thereby excluded, but coexistent and contributive.

Another element in these stories deserving of mention is Sansom's comic sense, sometimes in a very broad form. This effect is most particularly apparent in such a story as "A Contest of Ladies," in which a retired actor's seaside home, decorated like a hotel to make a veteran itinerant feel at home, is mistaken for a commercial hotel by a bevy of entrants in a "contest of beauty," with hilarious and ultimately romantic (even hilariously romantic) results. The sureness and effectiveness of Sansom's touch in handling comedy are the more remarkable for their manifestation in an author who is so adept at handling a nearly opposite mode—melodrama. "Various Temptations," the story of a lonely, foolhardy, and humane girl who, fully aware of the rampaging of a prowling strangler, effects a full and—up to a point—satisfying relationship with a shadowy man who enters her window late one night, reveals the author's refined gift of projecting terror and suspense.

The critical reader of this book is not struck by any absolute consistency of performance. The stories are more or less interesting in theme, more or less extensive in scope, more or less powerful in effect; but they are all considerably skillful in execution, and as a group they represent the work of a unique English storyteller.

Fred Bornhauser

TELEPHONE POLES
and Other Poems

Author: John Updike (1932-   )
Publisher: Alfred A. Knopf (New York). 84 pp. $4.00
Type of work: Poetry
  Poems ranging from the absurd to the wryly personal and the intelligently perceptive, by a distinguished young novelist and short story writer

Each book of fiction published by John Updike tends to line up the reviewers in opposing camps. One group praises him as a deeply insighted novelist and short story writer concerned with the predicament of man under the strains and temptations of his human condition, a craftsman who creates his effects with subtle skill, lucid vision, and stylistic brilliance. The opposition is willing to concede Mr. Updike's virtuosity and grace of language, but it regards their use as a waste of his talent on characters and themes of little relevance to the larger issues of life. It is much the same with his poetry. It imposes order on chaos and nonsense; it is entertaining and sometimes instructive. It is faddish in *The New Yorker* manner; it is merely adroit. But on one point this divided criticism agrees. His first book, *The Carpentered Hen*, and his latest, *Telephone Poles*, belong in the category of light verse and as such may be taken more or less for granted.

There's the rub. It has been said that light verse is the poetry of sad and desperate men, written for frivolous readers. If this statement is true, it admits Mr. Updike to some interesting and rather reputable literary company ranging from the Elizabethan poetasters and wits to Lawrence Durrell. Whether from some inner necessity or plain delight in doing the unexpected, most of the great poets wrote light verse at one time or another, though none made it the master bias of his work. It is only in our own time that light verse has become suspect, perhaps because of change in the climate of sensibility or the commitment of modern writers to certain accepted styles. For poetry as it is written today is for the most part a grim and serious business, as Robert Frost was indicating when he said that he played euchre while T. S. Eliot played Eucharist. Nowadays poetry is, allowing for some overlapping, oracular, incantatory, psychological, metaphysical, critical, religious, introspective; and its practitioners wear their private symbols instead of their hearts upon their sleeves. Its theme is the loneliness and terror of the soul, the relationship of man to himself or to eternity. Light verse, on the other hand, gives us a picture of man in society. Its subject is manners, not the dimensions or resonance of man's moral being.

Aside from literary fashion or critical prejudice, there is one valid charge to bring against light verse: it makes the will do the work of the imagination. Sir Walter Raleigh reads the plea of Marlowe's passionate shepherd to his love and writes the nymph's reply. Byron proposes a toast to Thomas Moore or cocks a snoot at John Bull. Lewis Carroll invents the Jabberwock. Oliver Wendell Holmes lends an heirloom punchbowl or has the portrait of an ancestress repaired, and he commemorates these occasions in graceful verse. Ezra Pound parodies a medieval lyric, "The Cuckoo Song." So it goes. Clearly these works belong to a lesser canon of poetry, but this is not to say that they do not add to our understanding or appreciation of the contemporary experience.

Perhaps the critical disfavor in which light verse is held today results in part from the fact that it is a slippery and protean form, almost impossible to catalogue or pin down. It may be a letter, a toast, a satire, a parody, a nonsense rhyme, or almost anything else. It can employ, as Louise Bogan has pointed out, a battery of traditional techniques and effects which the modern sensibility denies the more serious poet. But the true criterion of light verse is neither subject nor form, but style. Years ago Frederick Locker-Lampson tried to define poems of this type. According to him they should be "short, elegant, refined, and fanciful, not seldom distinguished by chastened sentiment, and often playful. The tone should not be pitched too high; it should be idiomatic, and rather in the

conversational key; the rhythm should be crisp and sparkling, and the rhyme frequent and never forced. . . . The poem may be tinctured with a wellbred philosophy, it may be gay and gallant, it may be playfully malicious or tenderly ironical, it may display lively banter, or it may be sarcastically facetious . . . but it must never be ponderous or commonplace."

W. H. Auden is another critic who has given some attention to this type of poetry, though he approaches it from the historical point of view. In his introduction to *The Oxford Book of Light Verse* (1938) he argues that in the more traditional societies of the past poetry was likely to be "light" because the poet and his readers shared a common background of custom and belief, so that major poets as well as minor ones "were able to express themselves in an easy manner, to use the speaking voice, and to use as their properties the images of their everyday life, i.e., social life." In Auden's view the Industrial Revolution marked the first real break between the poet and his audience. Aware of the disruption of community life and knowledge produced by a changing society, the Romantic poets announced that the world was too much with them, grew self-conscious, and turned inward to private areas of imagination and sensibility.

If all this sounds solemn and portentous it is intended only to show that John Updike's poetry represents a recognized genre within a minor but clearly defined literary tradition. The qualities marking the poems in *Telephone Poles* are elegance, wit, and proportion. His forms are modestly in keeping with their sources. A newspaper headline, an article in the encyclopedia, a name that strikes his fancy, a washing machine, or some experience as commonplace as a toothache or a drive home from a party—any of these may become an occasion for poetic comment in graceful rhythms. The name of Upperville, Virginia, a place that he has never seen, strikes his fancy and the result is a poem beginning:

In Upperville, the upper crust
Say "Bottoms up!" from dawn to dusk
And "Ups-a-daisy, dear!" at will—
I want to live in Upperville.

Names seem to fascinate him. Notice of a book written by an Indian author, M. Anantanarayanan, causes him to drift off into fantasy that invokes the hypnotic rhythms of Coleridge:

I picture him as short and tan.
We'd meet, perhaps, in Hindustan.
I'd say, with admirable elan,
"Ah, Anantanarayanan—

I've heard of you. The Times once ran
A notice on your novel, an
Unusual tale of God and Man."
And Anantanarayanan

Would seat me on a lush divan
And read his name—that sumptuous span
Of "a's" and "n's" more lovely than
"In Xanadu did Kubla Khan"—

In "Kenneths" he considers Kenneth Rexroth, Kenneth Patchen, and Kenneth Fearing, and admits his confusion by stating that "their mothers/ Perhaps could distinguish their sons from the others,/But I am unable." He brings events in the news to poetic scrutiny. A dispatch from Antarctica stating that "Mr. Aldez, a cloud physicist, came down last year to study air-

borne crystals" progresses from literal statement to fantasy:

That cloud—ambiguous, not
a horse, or a whale, but what?—
comes down through the crystalline mist.
It is a physicist!

In 1960, Life printed an exchange of remarks between Ernest Hemingway and Fidel Castro after the dictator had won the Hemingway fishing tourney. This report inspires a "meditation" in which Mr. Updike finds himself as much bemused as if he had "opened/a copy of 'Alice in Wonderland'/in which the heroine does win the croquet contest/administered by the Queen of Hearts."

In many of these poems Mr. Updike walks a narrow line between pungent comment and mere cleverness, and sometimes he fails to keep his balance true. Then we are likely to get little more than puns or play with words, as in "The Fritillary":

The fritillary,
Fickle, wary,
Flits from plant to plant with nary
A forethought as to where he
Alights, a butterfly.

The best of the poems are those in which he deals with the harassments and embarrassments of the urban middle class. In these he is capable of going beyond musing contemplation or barbed comment into an area where he moves us to responses of sensibility for which we are not prepared. Consider, for example, the self-searching in "Thoughts While Driving Home":

Was I clever enough? Was I charming?
Did I make at least one good pun?
Was I disconcerting? Disarming?
Was I wise? Was I wan? Was I fun?

259

Did I answer that girl with white shoulders
Correctly, or should I have said
(Engagingly), "Kierkegaard smolders,
But Eliot's ashes are dead"?

And did I, while being a smarty,
Yet some wry reserve slyly keep,
So they murmured, when I'd left the party,
"He's deep. He's deep. He's deep"?

"How middle class," we may say; or, "How pseudo-intellectual." Then the stab of recognition comes: "How true" —at least true to one part of man's deep-rooted anxieties and insecurity. In a number of these poems Mr. Updike crosses the undefined borderline between "light" verse and "serious" poetry, always with fine effect that matches form to feeling and illumination to subject. From *Telephone Poles* it is possible to take a group of poems as good as anything of their kind in the work of his generation: "Comp. Religion" (a chilling piece if we consider all that the poet implies in a surprisingly Eliotic vein), "The High-Hearts," "The Short Days" (an evocation of the suburban scene), "Seagulls," "Shillington" (the writer's birthplace), "Les Saints Nouveaux," "Seven Stanzas at Easter," "The Great Scarf of Birds," and the title poem.

"The High-Hearts" is typical of Mr. Updike's mingling of the fact noted and the meaning extracted, a poem in which he transmutes scientific truth— the fact that man's erect posture allows him to hold his heart higher above the ground than any other animal except the elephant and giraffe—into wry comment on the human effort:

Poor man, an ape, anxious to use his paws,
Became erect and held the pose because
His brain, developing beyond his ken,
Kept whispering, "The universe wants men."
So still he strains to keep his heart aloft,
Too high and low at once, too hard and soft.

Telephone Poles is a book of light verse, but as these examples show it should not be taken for granted or lightly dismissed, even though its texture is uneven and its contents are not likely to be booked for the sort of immortality that critical anthologies and literary scholarship confer. But Mr. Updike is his own man for all that, with the ability to entertain, to illuminate, and to ruffle our complacency because he strikes so close to home. This is what writers of light verse have always done.

Dayton Kohler

260

THE TENANTS OF MOONBLOOM

Author: Edward Lewis Wallant (1926-1962)
Publisher: Harcourt, Brace and World (New York). 245 pp. $4.50
Type of work: Novel
Time: The present
Locale: New York City

A profoundly humorous novel centering its focus on a great awakening which takes on the accents and intensities of a religious conversation to human dignity without ever departing from the secular indignities of the human condition

Principal characters:

NORMAN MOONBLOOM, a real estate agent for four apartment houses
IRWIN MOONBLOOM, his brother, the owner of the buildings
GAYLORD KNIGHT, the janitor
BODIEN, an unlicensed plumber
EVA, MINNA, and LESTER BAILY, two doting aunts and a nephew
ARNOLD and BETTY JACOBY, an aged couple
MARVIN SCHOENBRUN, a fastidious homosexual
STANLEY KATZ and SIDONE, bohemian jazz musicians
SHERMAN and CAROL HAUSER, a couple approaching middle age
AARON and SARAH LUBLIN, Jewish refugees
BASELLECCI, an Italian teacher
JERRY WUNG, a Chinese beatnik
BEELER, an elderly widower
SHERYL, his daughter
KRAM, a hunchback retoucher of photographs
WADE JOHNSON, a schoolteacher
LENI CASS, a divorcee
J. T. and MILLY LEOPOLD, a retired carpenter and wife
ILSE MOELLER, a German emigrant
KARLOFF, a hundred-year-old Russian immigrant
SUGARMAN, a philosophical candy-butcher
JOE PAXTON, a Negro homosexual writer
DEL RIO, a boxer
LOUIE, a bachelor
JIM and JANE SPRAGUE, a young expectant couple

Published posthumously (Wallant died of an aneurysm in December, 1962, leaving this and another novel in manuscript), *The Tenants of Moonbloom* seems to be one of the truly superior novels to appear in the last few years. Although the reviewers were respectful and generous in their reception of the novel, it has not as yet managed to attain a very wide audience. The acerbities of its plot, the grotesquerie of its characterizations, and the slyness of its humor may very well mitigate against any real widespread popularity. Wallant's early death, furthermore, and his failure to fit into any of the current fashionable modes of writing have thus far denied him an access to that audience which is most likely to respond to him. Although he was Jewish and specifically concerned with the treatment of Jewish themes, he is not a "Jewish writer" in the same sense as Bernard Malamud or Philip

Roth. And although his work trafficks at the very heart of the existentialist intersection, he cannot be categorized with Heller, Pynchon, or Donleavy as practitioners of "the absurd." *The Tenants of Moonbloom* falls between both camps, occupying its own lonely place that it has carved out for itself. It is possible, paradoxically, that this achievement of solitude is also the rare achievement of art and *The Tenants of Moonbloom* may continue to live after the fashions have consigned much that is now more popular to less favored positions.

As Wallant's third novel, it represents a distinct technical development over his earlier work. In particular, the major structural crudities which marred *The Human Season* (1960) and *The Pawnbroker* (1961) have been eradicated or bypassed. *The Tenants of Moonbloom* folds itself tightly within the arc of Wallant's sure capacities as a novelist. He discards both the time-flashback techniques of the earlier novels and the limiting constriction within the reflecting consciousness of an older broken personality. The focusing figure of this novel is Norman Moonbloom, the agent of the convulsed miseries and frustrations of the four apartment houses which he serves. At the beginning of the novel, he is one of the unliving, moving through life inside an envelope of secure detachment. He is a thirty-three-year-old virgin—both physically and psychologically—unawakened, unhurt, and unjoying. Around him whirls the heterogeneous constellation of grotesques that are the tenants of his houses. They are sordid, posturing, desperate in their pain, humorous and dignified in the artifices they erect to ward off an acceptance of total

squalor. Moonbloom moves through them week by week, collecting the rents, hearing their human cries like "the ear of God," but without heed, without life.

The action of the novel is basically a chronicling of Moonbloom's reveille; a crude violent violation of his detachment which forces him to bear witness, to become alive himself. The "ear of God" who is privy to all the petty complaints and profound disclosures of his tenants suddenly finds himself *listening*. The envelope has been burst; he is no longer asleep, he is ravished by the shock of existence. "Otherness" crushes him into the private being of selfhood and he discovers that *being* is unbearable unless it is put to some work. "Perhaps I'm trying to give a name to what is happening," he explains to himself as he undertakes the gargantuan renovation programme of painting, rewiring, repairing, cleaning, and ordering the four buildings in his charge. Nor does he fool himself as to the efficacy or motives of his actions. The child of one couple accidentally strangles to death, one tenant attempts suicide, another dies. Moonbloom himself is successfully seduced by one of the tenants for a reduction in the rent. All his paint and carpentry will not alter a deformed physique, a remembered betrayal, an impossibly frustrated desire. His struggle for cleanliness and physical decency is only secondarily for the benefit of the tenants; it is primarily a means to work himself on the new calendar of his becoming.

The double renovation of the houses and Moonbloom reaches a climax in the rebuilding and plastering of the toilet wall in Basellecci's room at the end of the novel. Basellecci, dying of incurable cancer, had earlier blamed his disease on the tumorous bathroom wall, and with the medical reports pointing to the true cause he had succumbed to severe depression. Fortified on Strega and vermouth, Moonbloom, the plumber, and the janitor remake the wall in a drunken transcendent choreography of pain and joy, finding in a community of laughter a human acceptance and antidote to the inhuman absurdity of man's fated condition. The grip of the cancer is not denied, nor is the human fraternity assured any but the barest duration, but the wall shines with white plaster and the remembrance of a sacred joy.

However, rich in grotesque density and humor as The Tenants of Moonbloom is (the effects of the remodeling of the houses will be to make their assessed valuation prohibitively higher than Moonbloom's brother can afford), the aims and achievements of the novel go far beyond its restricting grotesqueries. Wallant's realism is psychological and introspective, not reportorial, and this realism is at the service of an evocative overarch of symbolism. "A name to what is happening" is as much a description of Wallant's own building attempts in the making of his novel as it is for Moonbloom laboring in the cumulative filth and disorder of his Augean tenements. The reader is inex-

orably drawn into Moonbloom's metaphor, himself forced to burst the barrier of detachment and work at his own psychic renewal. On this level the novel scores a signal success; within the severe aesthetic limitations in which such a statement can be true, Wallant's readers all become tenants of Moonbloom, exposed to the raw slash of "otherness" and led to a perverse joy in their own augmented selfhood.

It is fashionable today for fiction to be ambiguous, problematical, contemptuous of traditional pieties, and irreverent in its embracement of absurdism as the irrational rationale for everything. These may all be legitimate positions from which to write novels, but they may also be lazy avoidances or cowardly failures to face up to resolvable questions. Wallant faces directly each of the problems which emerges from his work. The absurd and the problematic figure in his novel as inescapable but not dominating elements. He is able to wrest a form out of the chaos of our contemporary experiences which goes beyond a queasy burlesque nihilism, which accents human possibilities rather than niggling determinisms, and which communicates itself in the tones of a sacred laughter that is within the reach of the human voice and spirit.

Earl H. Rovit

THE TEREZÍN REQUIEM

Author: Josef Bor
Translated from the Czech by Edith Pargeter
Publisher: Alfred A. Knopf (New York). 112 pp. $3.50
Type of work: Novel
Time: World War II
Locale: Terezín, a prison ghetto in central Europe

A novel telling of the physical and spiritual struggle of Jewish prisoners to produce a work of art

Principal characters:
RAPHAEL SCHÄCHTER, the Czech conductor
ELIZABETH, an accomplished vocalist
MARUŠKA, a vocalist with a bitter past
CHERUBINO, a vocalist with a bitter future
EICHMANN, a Nazi genius of destruction

When Lanier said, "Music is love in search of a word," he might have said that music is love that has found its word, for to those who have ears to hear music is its own language, volant and flexible, confined only by the harmonies that complement the human rhythms of mind and emotion. Like Wordsworth's nature, it speaks a variable language, expressing the non-verbal sensations, speaking to or for the calm or the restless, the ordered or the confused, soul.

The Terezín Requiem is a story, basically true, of a human state that only music could express and of the music that did. At Terezín, a ghetto prison camp maintained by the Nazis during the war, a number of outstanding Jewish artists were confined. One among them, a Czech conductor named Raphael Schächter feeling the need himself and sensing it in his compatriots, began the almost futile task of organizing these displaced, persecuted artists into a productive, purposeful group.

That some diverting beauty was imperative was easy to see. Schächter, with the eye of the pure artist, saw to his own amazement that time, occasion, and resources had united in Terezín to produce a work of overwhelming power.

Here everyone hungered and thirsted after art, longed feverishly for every tremor of deep human feeling, all the more passionately and fervently as the world in which they had been forcibly imprisoned became more unthinkably repulsive and barbarous. Here a conductor would not be hampered by jealousy and the changing whims of spoiled prima donnas; every artist would be glad and grateful for the last place in the choir. Nor would any concert agency attempt to instruct him in what the public likes and dislikes. Here he could create a work whose artistic limitations would be fixed only by the quality of the conductor himself.

But even Schächter himself could not explain why he chose Verdi's Requiem, conspicuously out of place in this situation and among these people. Verdi's work no doubt expressed some of the deepest values of Roman Catholicism, but these were all Jews who

264

had their own values and who now, if ever, needed some personal expression. When Eichmann heard that the Jews were planning a performance of the Verdi opus, he was convulsed with mirthful laughter. If its selection was a mystery to the Jews themselves, it was ludicrous to him.

But behind the selection was indeed a mystery of humanity as profound as the music it yearned for. The inspiration to devote to Verdi what was for many the last, for all the only succoring, hours of life came out of the agony, indignity, and tragedy of life itself, and out of the flicker of hope that burned in the impenetrable darkness. For this life, too, was in search of a word, and the music of Verdi's Requiem was that word. However, "it was to be a new, a different kind of requiem, with a fanatical faith in historical justice here in this world. Only such a requiem could they sing here in this world."

This new kind of requiem that sang of an earthly hell and of a heavenly earth. The cosmological superstructure of the requiem was recognized in Terezín through imposing parallelisms. The hell was Terezín; heaven, the land of faith, was the restoration of justice with its impartial rendering of punishment and rewards. Life, then, to these people was parallel to the music; its subject matter became theirs, intensely immediate and real. All could understand the words of the *Offertorium:* "Deliver the souls from the pains of Hell and from the deep pit; save them from the mouth of the lion, nor allow the dark lake to swallow them up, nor darkness to enshroud them." Living in anticipation of destruction, always in sight of the horrors of persecution, seeing loved ones snatched to an irrevocable doom, their silent prayers were for their people in the jaws of destruction. When the solemn chords of the requiem were struck, how like Terezín were the images of that dark world and the deep pit. The inscrutable powers of evil, the horrors of continuous agony, man naked and consumed, were shadows in the dark world of Terezín. The mysteries of human suffering and forbearance directed these people to a new requiem, because these mysteries had to be resolved in the here and now.

But the requiem is a song of hope. Fundamentally and devoutly Christian, it sings of a spiritual and mystical deliverance and of a New Jerusalem. Just as this paradise is of another world, so the paradise of earthly peace and justice was at least of another time and in another place. Regardless of the object or promise of their faith, they too, in accord with the faith voiced in the requiem, believed in a light and a glory and in a victory of man's spirit over his Hell.

The power of the requiem, then, is not the imposition of its dreadful and magnificent cosmic picture but the human element in response to the severity of its world. The real music of the requiem sung at Terezín was the music of the various personalities that lived its significance and knew intuitively the mysteries of its language. From the slow, painful training and practicing came what were actually two pieces of music. One was the requiem itself; the other was a more subtle and deeper music, the melodies and variations of humanity. Besides the general magnitude of feelings and sensitivities represented in the large choir, the soloists and Schächter represent

265

several specific elements of humanity, each in its own way so intense and immediate as to have composed, as each performed his role, a fundamental chord of the greater music of which each was a living part. Without naming all, these were the key parts of the human song: Schächter, the voice of creativity; Elizabeth, the voice of sacrificial devotion; Maruška, the voice of gentle hope; Cherubino, the voice of courage. With these voices was blended the full scale of basic human feelings and sensations.

Schächter was a perfectionist whose art had been perfected by suffering. His was the agony of a compulsive creator, the pain of inspiration burning in the birth of creativity. A music to release the souls of these persecuted people, something the likes of which the world had never heard—that was the ambition that drove him and haunted him through the almost impossible demands of his undertaking.

Obviously many of the difficulties of producing the great work of music came out of the hostile and unusual situation in which he labored. Although he was allowed to rehearse without harassment and was given reason to feel that he would have a chance to present his performance when he was prepared, the inhuman and sadistic elements naturally associated with a prison camp inevitably preyed upon the helpless musicians. His first problem was smuggling equipment into the camp, an act which took ingenuity and courage. Certainly these artists displayed an abundance of both when they undertook to smuggle in three bass violins. The real problem, however, was the Nazi machinery that had dared to regulate the fates of human beings. Many of the artists were among those selected periodically to pack the transport trains, bound for no uncertain fate. Others, themselves exempted from such a destiny, chose to follow their families rather than remain without them; the Nazis refused none. With the rows in his choir frequently left gaping and his carefully chosen soloists suddenly snatched away forever, again and again Schächter battled the futility of his task and the formidable problem of finding well-trained, qualified soloists. But time and again he found them, blended them masterfully into their roles, and hoped. In his hope was a part of the power to be voiced in the music and part of the strength of his creative impulse.

He achieved his goal not only by mastering his external barriers but also by submitting to the internal forces peculiar to the creative instinct. His oppressing need for ultimate expression attacked him through his artistic senses, forcing him to perfection. In almost every part he recognized a flaw or weakness in the vocalist or the interpretation. There could be no flaw and no weakness. The tone of tragedy had to voice tragedy as only these people knew it, and the song of victory had to be a miracle that by its power would assuage and deliver the souls if not the bodies of the choir and of the pain-muted audience listening to the last song of humanity. Nothing but the ultimate expression would do for this artist who knew the depth of human feeling. Like the indefinable charm of music itself, always guiding him when his training or common sense failed, was a mystery of his own nature which knew the truth and the beautiful in music. But his agony was the agony before all great victories—

the dream, the determination, the tension—and was of the music of aspiring, creative humanity, antagonistic variations and tones contending, music swelling, throbbing, soothing, sustaining, now thundering with the turbulent drumming of strained emotions, now a diminuendo, calmed in the quietude of soothing and restful fulfillment, until the harmony, molded from many sounds, was a triumph in the hall of disaster:

Holy, Holy, Holy, Lord God of hosts. Heaven and earth are full of thy glory. Glory be to thee, O Lord, Hosanna in the highest.

Taking great care in selecting the singer for the mezzo-soprano part, Schächter discovered among the prisoners a well-known and accomplished artist who had sung in Verdi's Requiem many times. Elizabeth was in Terezín with her husband, whom the Nazis had left a helpless cripple and who now depended upon her for his welfare. She agreed to sing the part, but she had hardly begun to rehearse before her role as devoted wife called her to a personal requiem found in sacrificial love. According to the command, "in the interest of the inhabitants of the ghetto . . . who would thereby be enabled to enjoy a better life," all the helpless, ill, and crippled were ordered to the transports. When Elizabeth did not appear for rehearsal all knew that this great artist could have been seen making her burdensome way to the transports trundling a clumsy cart on which lay her maimed husband because she had to share with him his unchosen fate. All knew that her last performance would be by far her greatest.

Another person who had an impor-

tant role in the music of Terezín was kind and gentle Maruška. Having endured tragedies and shocks unusual even to her companions of bitterness, hers were the knowledge and the wound that only music could relate or soothe. She did not come into a major part easily, for Schächter, in an impatient moment, at first had unkindly rejected this slender, meek creature. In the sun of her undaunted good will, however, for his unkindness he was to reap both the torture of his error and the joy of restitution. Maruska's character and personality formed a sweet undertone for the uneven or violent tones and moods around her. Her gentle, forgiving spirit and her thoughtfulness were reassuring and consoling. Although her bitter past had left her slightly confounded and weakened, she became the light and power in the final victory song.

Then there was the one they called Cherubino, who found a major place in their ranks in a most unusual way. One day he dashed panting into the rehearsal room and, wild-eyed with fear, fell in among the open-mouthed Hosannas. Closely behind him, wielding a club and in a state of furor, rushed an SS man. Having seen only the back of the man he pursued, and suspecting him to have joined the choir, he searched every face to catch a faltering voice. Detecting none, he stormed out with Hosannas pursuing him. But Cherubino's voice was not for the choir. His was the angelic voice for which Schächter had been frantically searching to fill an important solo part. He had come among them unannounced like a gift from heaven which even the SS could not deny them.

He was to go as suddenly, however,

for he was finally discovered and summoned before the commandant. No one had to be told what his fate would be. He would be tortured unmercifully until the mercies of death released him. His last hour was spent with the choir where his last hope had been. These cultured, talented voices now felt the need to voice the sad but steadfast music of this wretched angel among them. Schächter, as sensitive to humanity as to music, chose the "Recordare," the women's part. They began with a tremor, gathered strength, and found a glorious consolement in the music above despair. The last part was Cherubino's, still the pure, sweet voice:

> Groaning 'neath my sins I languish,
> Lord have mercy on my anguish.
> Me unworthy, Lord, lean o'er me,
> Lest the flames of hell devour me.

Then he was gone.

These were the personalities whose talents and lives expressed major rhythms of a betrayed and persecuted people. But these were not the only ones who found themselves in Verdi's Requiem and the Requiem in themselves. When the performance was given, those who could not sing heard the music with the same surrender and fulfillment as their companions in the choir. They were all made people of light by their darkened world, made responsive to a new creation more a part of their being than reality itself. All, somehow more strongly through the mysteries of suffering, felt the beauty of sacrificial love, hope without malice, and courage without regret.

Even Eichmann heard and could not laugh, for he knew that this was a different kind of requiem, that it was a fortress above despair and a refusal of a people to die.

Charles Workman

THE TIN DRUM

Author: Günter Grass (1927-   )
Translated from the German by Ralph Manheim
Publisher: Pantheon Books (New York). 589 pp. $6.95
Type of work: Novel
Time: 1899-1954
Locale: Poland and Germany

A vast satiric novel in which the history of modern Germany is seen through the eyes of a self-willed dwarf

Principal characters:
> OSKAR MATZERATH, the narrator and hero
> AGNES MATZERATH, his mother
> ALFRED MATZERATH, her husband
> JAN BRONSKI, Mrs. Matzerath's cousin and lover, possibly Oskar's father
> MR. BEBRA, a circus midget and universal artist
> ROSWITHA RAGUNA, his shorter associate, the most celebrated somnambulist in all Italy
> HERBERT TRUCZINSKI, neighbor of the Matzeraths
> MARIA TRUCZINSKI, Herbert's youngest sister
> GREFF, a greengrocer
> LINA GREFF, his wife
> SISTER DOROTHEA KÖNGETTER, a trained nurse, a neighbor of Oskar in Düsseldorf
> GOTTFRIED VON VITTLAR, whose testimony leads to Oskar's arrest; later Oscar's friend

The past year has witnessed the publication of several excellent novels dealing with wartime Germany, among them the American-born Rudolph von Abele's *The Party* and the British Gabriel Fielding's *The Birthday King;* but by far the most impressive of the novels about Germany comes from Germany itself, *The Tin Drum,* the first book by the young novelist Günter Grass. To say that *The Tin Drum* is about as auspicious a novelistic beginning as *Buddenbrooks* is to suggest little more similarity with Mann than that of length and quality, for *The Tin Drum,* though it shows some signs of being a curiously gnarled hybrid variety of the German family chronicle, though in fact one can trace its lineage back to a multitude of traditions, is a novel which, like most of the great ones (which is not necessarily to say that it is quite in their company), cannot fit neatly into any fixed category, which is a category in itself.

The narrator of the novel is Oskar Matzerath, who tells his story from the insane asylum in which he is being held for a murder he did not commit. The question of Oskar's sanity is a little pointless. In the light of the mad world around him, his violent, bizarre outlook is the only vision imaginable. Oskar's story begins in 1899, when his Kashubian grandmother, sitting in a potato field, conceals under her wide skirts from the view of pursuing constables the fugitive Joseph Koljaiczek, and thereby conceives Oskar's mother. The incident, in its wild humor and eroticism and its suggestion of political chaos, is endemic of what is to come. In 1923, in the free city of Danzig, Agnes Koljaiczeck marries Alfred Matzerath, a citizen of the German Reich, and introduces him to her Polish cousin and lover, Jan Bronski, with whom he becomes fast friends. Thereafter the amazing Oskar is born: "I may as well come right out with it: I was one of those clairvoyant infants whose mental development is completed at birth and after that merely needs a certain amount of filling in." Oskar is promised a drum for his third birthday, the drum which in its many avatistic recurrences will allow him mutely to voice his protest against the meaninglessness of a world which formulates its destructive nonsense in empty language and to re-create the history of his consciousness, to recall in the varied music of the drum the rhythms of his mind's apprehension of the world around it, apprehensions earlier accompanied by the drum. It is also upon his third birthday that Oskar decides to stop growing by a sheer act of will, to remain with his three-year-old body and his totally conscious mind for the rest of his life: "I remained the precocious three-year-old, towered over by grownups but superior to all grownups, who refused to measure his shadow with theirs, who was complete both inside and outside, while they, to the very brink of the grave, were condemned to worry their heads about 'development,' who had only to confirm what they were compelled to gain by hard and often painful experience, and who had no need to change his shoe and trouser size year after year just to prove that something was growing."

Oskar's refusal to grow is the as-

sertion of his individuality against a world which, misconstruing him, would force him into an alien pattern. About the same time he discovers his ability to shatter glass with his voice, a talent which becomes not only a means of destruction, the venting of his hostility and outrage, but also an art whereby he can cut in the window of a jewelry shop a neat hole through which Bronski, upon whom he heaps the filial affection he does not feel for his more mundane father, can snatch an expensive necklace for his beloved Agnes.

The later period of Oskar's recorded existence is crammed with outlandish events. His mother witnesses a revolting scene of eels being extracted from the head of a dead horse submerged in water, perversely forces a diet of fish upon herself, and dies. Oskar becomes fascinated with the hieorglyphic scars on the massive back of Herbert Truczinski, his friend, but Herbert, who works as a Maritime Museum attendant, grows enamoured of a ship's wooden figurehead called Niobe and, in an attempt to make love to her, is instead impaled to her by a double-edged ship's axe. Jan Bronski is executed after an S.S. raid on the Polish post office where he has gone with Oskar, and Oskar is overwhelmed with guilt for the death of his mother and the man who was probably his father. In one of the most superbly preposterous seduction scenes in literature, Oskar becomes the lover of Herbert's youngest sister, Maria, and fathers her child. Maria then marries Alfred Matzerath, and Oskar turns to the ampler comforts (he is as prodigious sexually as he is diminutive physically) of Lina Greff, whose latent homosexual husband shortly, upon receiving a summons to appear in court on a morals charge, commits a fantastically elaborate and grotesque suicide. Oskar then goes on to join Bebra's troupe of entertainers and becomes the lover of the timeless Roswitha Raguna. When the Russians invade Danzig, Matzerath, to conceal his affiliations, swallows the Nazi party pin which Oskar has shoved into his hand and dies. Again Oskar feels responsible for the death of a parent. Before long, against his will, he begins to grow and to develop a hump. His postwar life takes him to West Germany, where he is at various times a black marketeer, a model, and a nightclub entertainer, and eventually to Düsseldorf, where a destiny not his own catches up with him in the guise of the accusation that he has killed Sister Dorothea, the woman in the room next to his. The testimony of Vittlar, which is meant to save Oskar, although Vittlar has earlier thought him guilty, ironically damns him, and Os-

kar submits to being judged insane and atoning for a guilt not strictly his, even though he is finally to his own sense guilty by implication, an emblem of the modern world even in his isolation from it.

The Tin Drum is a surreal-picaresque, a mock-epic chronicle of Western Europe's (and by extension the world's) twentieth century madness, a sardonic, shocking, hilarious reflection of a world in upheaval, a world in which values become inverted and indistinguishable, in which the tragic is at the same time the comic, and the agonizing the ludicrous. *The Tin Drum* violates all modes of decorum—its chaos is the outward appearance and inner principle of the world it seeks to capture—but the imaginative vitality of its creation is somehow its own decorum, and of itself an affirmation in the face of the dissolution which it postulates.

Donald L. Mull

TO MIX WITH TIME

Author: May Swenson (1927-   )
Publisher: Charles Scribner's Sons (New York). 183 pp. Clothbound, $3.50; paperback, $1.45
Type of work: Poetry
New and selected poems by the author of Another Animal, *contained in* Poets of Today I, *and* A Cage of Spines

Whenever one is tempted to make the summary judgment that poetry has gone downhill sadly among the women since Edna St. Vincent Millay and Elinor Wylie, Louise Bogan, and Leonie Adams, he stubs his toe on books such as this one by May Swenson. He must also remind himself of some of the poetic daughters of Marianne Moore, including Elizabeth Bishop

and Carolyn Kizer. And, very possibly, in this new constellation of young women there is no brighter and steadier light than that of May Swenson.

May Swenson is a special case in contemporary verse by virtue of her many assimilated influences, made carefully individual in her own forms, and the wide range of her ideas. She is capable of using her own modifica-

271

tions of Cummings' visual eccentricities on the page, of approaching the page as if it were susceptible of becoming an etching or a watercolor. She loves word-play and sometimes reminds the reader of Gertrude Stein's delightful fiddling with abstract patterns of language that border on nonsense, but stop short, remain intelligible. She has never attempted, during the anti-intellectual period since Dylan Thomas, to give up her essential concern with philosophy. More than any other young poet we have, she carries over successfully from the 1920's a sense of the excitement of ideas and of being experimental. In speaking of the universe she writes:

```
            O.K., let's say I'm
    out     and
    in      the
    round   free
    world:
    Back    there's the tight aluminum
                sphere
            I jumped
    out     of, slammed the door like an
                icebox.
            A clean landscape
    around  me, an inch or two of
                "snow"—
```

This pattern is not mere caprice or frolic because the gap, the alley down the page separates two worlds: on the left the world of philosophic drift and wonder—"out," "in," "round," "Back," "out," "around"; and on the right side of the page a world of concrete description of a parallel and sensible world.

The variety in this book is difficult to convey in a short space. The reviewer is like a man in a large, profuse garden, trying to point out all the flowers to a guest. The basic intelligence which forms an admirable trellis

for the display of talent is not aridly intellectualized. There is a dark strain in the work, evident in the passionate repetitions and vigorous rhythms of Miss Swenson's description of a bull, invited by a matador to die:

> Death invited to break his horns
> on the spread
> cloth. To drop his head
> on the dragged flag on the sand.
> Death's hooves slipping
> in blood, and a band
> of blood down the black slide.
> Death's tongue, curved in the open
> mouth
> like a gray horn, dripping
> blood. And
> six colored agonies decking the summit
> of his muscled pride.

A passionate response and an alert eye are required for the making of such a brilliant concluding image of the death symbol, surmounted by the gaudy pikes left by the picador; the result is a genuine triumph of modern imagery. Perhaps it is Miss Swenson's ability to open her eyes repeatedly on this high plane of seeing that has prompted Mark Van Doren to call her poems ". . . brilliant and interesting. That they are *interesting* is for me the main thing. . . ."

In another kind of poem, such as "Instead of the Camargue," which is one of her longer pieces, Miss Swenson handles the fashionable travelogue, the "I too have traveled on a fellowship in France and Italy" type of poem without letting it slide into the usual banality. What saves the poem is its richly baroque style, as in the following excerpt:

> This windy porch
>
> held, as well, an ancient cemetery. . . .

272

A very rich and rewarding group of poems about France and Italy, a truly ornate and decorous group that reminds one of Roman fountains and statuary itself, concludes with a historically informed passage describing the Pantheon with its sunken ramp full of starving cats and its columns "bitten with age, their bases dark and urinous."

Miss Swenson can be wittily light, assembling a multitude of program notes, as it were, to the great realistic swirls of the modern city. She describes the Museum of Modern Art in New York as a place where one need not go into the galleries at all to see modern "art," for one can just sit in the lobby and see a tremendous human college, and contemporary Garbos and Chaplins appear in a "mesmeric experimental film." When she rides the "A" train, she feels like a ball-bearing in a roller skate. A city cat does not understand snowflakes, tries to bat one of these "white insects" against a windowpane; but the flake has "no body and no buzz," so the cat decides to sleep until the world puts itself right again. There is, of course, a degree of social comment in such jocular images, especially in the following direct criticism of a dehumanized society:

If there is a flaw in May Swenson's work so far, it is only that so many of the poems seem to display their eccentricities very obviously. But this may also be a result of her equally obvious delight in exploiting every property of language, and the reviewer would be ill-advised to condemn such a tendency in a young poet whose work offers such a vivid re-creation of so much varied experience.

Robert Hazel

THE TRAVELLERS

Author: Jean Stubbs (1926-   )
Publisher: St. Martin's Press (New York). 200 pp. $4.50
Type of work: Novel
Time: 1959
Locale: Blackminster, an industrial town in the north of England

A fully peopled and diverse novel of character and circumstance, cast in the mold of Dickensian comedy and fantasy

Principal characters:

BEN MACKINTOSH, a young artist in revolt against his middle-class background
MAIR MACKINTOSH, his bride
TERESA CHAMBERS, a fat, foolish, good-natured woman
JIMMY BROADSTAIRS, her unofficial husband who cleans and does the cooking
RAZORS STRAUSS, her second unofficial husband, a lazy, greedy young man
MRS. D'ARBY, an aged, penniless gentlewoman
DOMINIC BRADLEY, her great-grandson
NELLIE HIGGINS, a domestic
NED HIGGINS, her worthless husband
JANET and
ALICE, their daughters
CAROL MARTIN, a quietly resourceful mulatto nurse from the West Indies
RITA SLOAN, her friend, a limpet in human form
CHARLES CHANTINALL, a sinister hunchback and master of machinations
RUFUS and
BOULTON NAB, the owners of Prospect House
ALBERT SIDEBOTTOM, the proprietor of a market stall and Razors' employer
HILDA SIDEBOTTOM, his wife
MR. DHAL, an Indian peddler
MULDOON, an art student

A second look at *The Travellers* confirms the earlier impression that this novel deserves more careful attention than it received at the time of its publication. The first and most obvious thing to be said about it is that it is written in none of the fashionable modes of the moment, for it is raffish, innocent, melodramatic, and worst of all chastely sentimental. The second is that it is clearly a work of promise.

Those conditioned to the language of book reviewing will know at once what is likely to follow: the book is a definite accomplishment; it employs interesting devices of style; the texture is uneven but the writer's willingness to take risks with theme, character, and form will not allow it to be called merely apprentice work; it promises a great deal for its author's future.

In the case of Jean Stubbs all of

274

these trite statements are undeniably true, but to say them and then stop would be doing scant justice to her performance. The most interesting, and the most promising, thing to note about *The Travellers* is its virtue as an example of the way in which the young novelist willing to be instructed may still learn much from Charles Dickens, not by way of accommodation or imitation but as an illustration of literary tradition establishing a link between writers of two generations separated by time, environmental change, and resulting differences of sensibility. It should be said at the start, however, that the Dickens who stands in the shadows behind this novel is neither the gross sentimentalist nor the passionate reformer loved by the Victorians. This Dickens is the great novelist who was also a great poet: the master of comic invention, the character-monger who filled his books with a sense of the rich variousness and unpredictability of human nature, the creator of atmosphere and symbolism who makes us uneasily aware of such obsessive images as the prison and the Clennams' ramshackle, shored-up house in *Little Dorrit,* the river and the dust heaps in *Our Mutual Friend,* the convict's irons and the crazed old woman in her decaying bridal finery confronting a young boy in *Great Expectations,* the fog rolling through the opening chapters of *Bleak House* and the rain falling on Lincolnshire and in lady Deadlock's heart alike. It is now possible to read Dickens' novels for their sweeping poetic power that orders both the nature of experience and the shape it must take for the display of outward drama and internal coherence. And this, though on a lesser scale and with

muffled resonance, is apparently the the way Miss Stubbs wants her novel read.

Consider, first of all, her setting, a dilapidated mansion in what was once the elegant part of an English industrial town. In 1800 the district was called "The Flowery Fields," now almost forgotten, but the old mansion is still referred to as Prospect House, even though it overlooks no brighter prospect than a grimy slum. A stick of bombs falling during World War II had shaken its crumbling walls and rotted floors, but it still stands because the town council has never got around to ordering it torn down. Its owners are Rufus and Boulton Nab, brothers, who inherited it from their father. Unable to sell it and not knowing what to do with it, they fill it with an odd lot of tenants willing to put up with a great deal of discomfort in return for cheap rent. The place is in the last stages of disrepair. Choked fireplaces smoke; soot pours down the chimneys; boards break through; bricks fall; cockroaches scuttle frantically when doors open. The tenants of Prospect House are the unknown, the disreputable, the outcast, the gone-to-seed; they match the house they live in.

We have viewed this scene many times before in other writer's novels —the slum and the tenement, symbols of the alienated life, the dead end of the human effort. Miss Stubbs never points, never nudges her reader's elbow as many of her contemporaries do. The world of the novel is not Heartbreak House or some other structure of allegorical meaning, yet the note of metaphor is unmistakable. If the reader has a sudden sense of familiarity with Miss Stubbs's old house and its atmosphere of ruin and decay, the reason is not hard to find. It is an image of our own inner world, the nightmare landscape in our fantasies of disaster and tumble-down despair.

Do not make the mistake, however, of supposing that Miss Stubbs is a solemn or portentous writer. She is a richly comic novelist, lyrical and down to earth at the same time, and her true quality comes through in the characters she creates. Roughly, her people fall into three classes: those who, like Mrs. D'Arby, have come down in the world; those who, like Ben and Mair Mackintosh, are at the bottom and trying to start up; and those who, like the Higgins family, have nowhere else to go because they are merely what they are, "wretched, beetle-ridden statistics" of poverty. Mrs. D'Arby, crippled by arthritis, indomitable, lives on the ground floor with Dominic, her small young great-grandson. She had been born in Prospect House in its great days and she has no intention of leaving it now. Her possessions show the present condition of her life, a mixture of things bought in the cheap shops and relics of Edwardian elegance. Her chief concern is her great-grandson; she is afraid that he will turn into another of the street loafers and Teddy boys whom she thinks typical of the modern age. Next to her live Mrs. Chambers and her two husbands, both unofficial because Mrs. Chambers never got a divorce from her first. On the first floor the Mackintoshes, newly married, set up housekeeping with only hope and devotion to art to sustain them; their marriage is as shaky as the old house. On the same floor are the improvident Higginses, born of generations of poverty, citizens of the new Welfare State. On the top floor quiet, sensible Carol Martin, a West Indian nurse, lives with a fiercely possessive, jealous friend. Their neighbor is Charles Chantinall, a hunchback of Mephistophelian appearance who brings an atmosphere of mystery and brimstone into Prospect House when he establishes himself there with his cat, his poems, and his wine.

The Travellers tells the story of the old house during the last year of its tenancy. The things that happen are very much what one might expect. Mrs. D'Arby dies in the night after a party the Nab brothers give in honor of her eightieth birthday, and Rufus Nab adopts Dominic. Mair Mackintosh gives up painting, works in a store, loses her baby, and almost loses her husband as well. Carol Martin and her friend separate. Mrs. Chambers' caretaker-cook husband, driven by jealousy and Chantinall's sly suggestions, runs away. When she suffers a bad fall and is hospitalized, Razors Strauss finds another protector in Hilda, his employer's widow, after Albert Sidebottom suffers a fatal heart attack. Ben Mackintosh wins an art prize that another student has rejected. Like a stalking cat, Chantinall prowls in and out of these people's lives, leaving behind him a trail of trickery and evil. Chantinall dies after being stoned during a student riot and is "buried as he had lived, with much colour and ceremony and loneliness: with many people to attend him and none to love him." The Mackintoshes go off to make a new start in another part of England.

All this sounds simple enough, but the novel is hard to sum up. Chantinall is a *papier-mâché* character, all too obviously a villain and easily dismissed. The process is not so easy with the rest of the novel because it follows no straightness of line. Poetic prose is here, delicately and expertly handled, falling into tricks at times but at its best imaginative and evocative. As for story, there is not much of that in the strictly novelistic sense. Instead, Miss Stubbs gives us a swift parade of situations and events, all presented from a somewhat stylized and oddly personal point of view. Personalities merge or clash and consequences follow. On the author's part there is a great deal of zestful delight in improvisation, in the idiosyncrasies of human character, in the rough and tumble of life lived on the margin of the social experience.

These matters bring us back to Dickens once more. Like him, in her somewhat disjointed effects, Miss Stubbs suggests the separateness in which most people live. Her people meet, speak, or go about their business in a jostling world, but too often they remain solitaries. They speak to themselves or the world, but seldom to one another. (The separation of Ben and Mair is as much the result of their failure to communicate as of Chantinall's interference.) When they do speak it is often in a monologue, with all the Dickensian overtones of Albert Sidebottom's sales pitch:

'Nah then, ladies, wot am I bid for this teapot, sugar and cream? *Five pound ten?* Designed for royalty. Wot's 'arf a crown between friends? *Five seven six?* You'll 'ave me on t'dole—I give that much for it. Come on, nah, wot'll you gie the vicar a sup o' tea out on if you don't buy this, eh? *Five five?* Think of the mother-in-law, bless 'er 'eart. *Five two six?* We'st go bout supper tonight, Roz. *Five,* ladies and gentlemen. *Five,* only? Was that a sign from the lady in blue? I'll come to supper wie you, dear. Tell me when your 'usband's on night shift. Call it *four seventeen six.* You sir,

make it up wie the missus, she does 'er best. Gie 'er a treat. *Four fifteen?* Yes, missis? NO? All right then. *Four ten. Four ten?* 'Ere I'll tell you wot, you come up 'ere and auctioneer, missis, I'll go 'ome and gie the old man 'is dinner! *Four ten.* Am I bid? Any more for any more? Going then, at *four ten.* Going to the lady for *four ten.* Going, going, going, GONE! Gone to the lady in the fawn coat. Wrap it up for 'er, Roz, afore we're out of business. There you are, missis, a set to be proud on, at less than wot I paid for it. And if ever you want a job I'll gie you one. You can teach me summat! Thank you. And now to the next. I've got six clocks 'ere and every man jack of them spankin' new. Nah, I'll tell you wot I paid for 'em. I'm not 'ere to rob you, ladies and gentlemen. I 'aven't been on Stothert Market for thirty-five year and learned nowt. SERVICE, that's my motto, and proud of it. You'll be on your knees to me in twenty year when these clocks is tickin' on the parlour mantelshelf. Fetch 'em up, Roz. Nah ladies—it's the ladies that rob me, you know. They beat me down. Still, that's better nor my owd woman—she beats me up.'

Or they hold conversations with things —again the Dickens touch—as Jimmy Broadstairs does when his mistress and her younger lover drive him to moods of jealous rage:

'Why do I do it?' whispered Jimmy to the casserole in the oven. 'He's a cheap, pimpled pimp. Why do I do it? Tell me that.'

'Because of Theresa,' winked the sugar on the apple pie.

Stew fumed into his little, hot, dark face.

'Love's a let-down,' whispered Jimmy. But it gave him a sense of purpose.

'Kill them!' glittered the carving knife.

'Poison them!' pricked the pepper pot.

277

The artist in Jimmy drew him up, incorruptible.
'Not with *my* cooking,' he said.

This is as good as Dickens in its use of the pathetic fallacy to suggest subtle relationships, the merging of the animate and the inanimate, between people and things. The style is appropriate to the level of interest and meaning the writer must sustain.

It may seem strange to give so much space to a novel that all too clearly reveals its influences. But *The Travellers* is a rather special novel and Miss

Stubbs is a talented writer. One has the feeling that she is restoring to the English novel something that has been missing in late years. What we find in this book is a sharp sense of the improbable and the farcical in human experience. Like the older picaresque writers, she deals in effects of adventure melodrama, and criticism cleansed by a lively sense of comedy. And beneath her surface fun her work is always serious, as the best books in the English comic tradition have always been.

Dayton Kohler

TWO SIDES OF AN ISLAND

Author: Martin Halpern (1929-   )
Publisher: The University of North Carolina Press (Chapel Hill). 54 pp. $3.50
Type of work: Poetry

A striking first book of poems dealing with many places, written in the author's own individual style, and characterized by an intriguing "double viewpoint" on life

In *Two Sides of an Island,* Martin Halpern's first book of poems, we find a good but troubled poet at work. We are told on the dust jacket, in the deep, apocalyptic style that only anonymous writers on dust jackets are permitted to use, that this "book as a whole has a central pattern: a movement back and forth between two polarities, 'two sides' of experience" and that "frequently the poems are animated by a tension of conflict between these polarities." Nonsense! Mr. Halpern merely feels at this stage of his career that there are very few "pure" experiences in life: joy without pain, laughter without sorrow, life without death. He may not say it in so many words, but in poem after poem the feeling is there. From the title poem, in which drowning and escape from drowning are juxtaposed, to the last

piece in the book, "The Osprey," in which two Maine honeymooners are driven from their "fern-forested island" by a mother hawk protecting her nestlings, the reader is kept unsettled by Halpern's divided viewpoint, by his (to borrow a word from psychology) ambivalence. Not all poetry is meant to be soothing and reassuring, however, and Halpern leaves his disturbed and ruffled reader with the satisfaction of having read some fine poems.

Martin Halpern is what might be called a "place" poet; that is, his ideas seem to come out with a change of scene. Harvard, Rome, Nevada, Provincetown, New Hampshire, California —all these places and others stimulate the writer. *Two Sides of an Island* is not by any means a dressed-up travelogue and these shifts of scene back up the impression of an emotional and

278

physical wanderer who hopes to settle down eventually somewhere on the earth, somewhere in time and space, in some place where his nagging ambivalence will leave him alone.

This first book of poems is remarkable in another way. There are no bad poems, no imitative or vague pieces which the maturer poet may regret. And there are many fine ones. The title poem sets the tone. A "spent swimmer" is faced with two possibilities in regard to the shore he is weakly struggling toward: it may be a smooth, unclimbable cliff or it may be a sandy beach welcoming his collapse. The poet hopes the swimmer is saved, but he ends the poem with this disturbing question:

> Well, how many heroes
> Who differ, we guess, in degree from
> us who project them,
> Have gasped thus, gained that grant,
> and woken squinting,
> Through yesterday's terror and dreams
> of dismal Avernus,
> Sunward—all humanly touched and
> tempted by
> Some island maid's humane, betrayable
> eyes?

By bringing in the heroic and the romantic the poet keeps before us that other possible fate: the swimmer vainly trying to climb up that "tide-smoothed and slime-shellacked" wall of rock. In "The Myopic Musician" the poet asks us to listen to Bach on the phonograph; the music comes to us with a grace, he says, never trusted to sculpture or painting. Thus he asks:

> Is hearing, least
> Possessive of senses, therefore the only
> sense
> Eternity is safe to dally with?

Is impermanence the only permanent thing? "The Two Nevadas" deals more straightforwardly with this same sort of paradox. After describing the flat, unfeatured landscape of the state as contrasted with its "neon oasis" of bars and gambling joints, the poet then says his automobile driver

> Must cover a couple of hundred unset-
> tled miles
> More of that first Nevada, to earn his
> will's
> Refreshment in a light not neon,
> But of the ever gaining, certain sun.

The second section of this book is called "From an Italian Journal: 1956-57." Halpern responds to Italy with a series of colorful poems ranging in subject matter from love to a traffic accident to an Italian production of "Tristano ed Isotta." In "With a Camera in Taormina" the poet searches for a photographic composition involving a cypress, a flowering almond, Mount Etna, and the sea. He finds the parts but not the whole. He praises the parts "And days when one must cull, compose,/ And frame such facts to pose a paragon." Halpern is the disappointed searcher, even in photogenic Italy. "The Trams of Rome" (with no mention of Respighi) gives the poet a chance to display his light, satiric touch. The trams prompt him to comment on Roman history, the different sections of the city, and the endless invasions of tourists; they also remind him of the year, when he was a boy in New York, the trams were removed from his borough:

> On some of the streets
> The tracks stand yet, a source of won-
> der to younger children,
> To most adults a driving hazard in
> slippery weather.

279

The third section titled is "Weathers, Without and Within." Halpern picks the time of low tide for his "Meditation on the Beach in Provincetown." The night before, this beach had been his "resting place and plaything," but now there are rocks, logs, and dead fish exposed on the mud. He feels as if "an affluence has ebbed from shore and will." One of the most provocative parts of the poem deals with a woman who tells him how childbirth, passion, and even dying are controlled by the tides.

Halpern likes to take familiar designations for poems and treat them in a different way. For instance, in the section on Italy he titles one poem simply "Ode" and it is quickly evident that he is not attempting an ode at all, but is writing about one vivid incident that has moved him greatly. The effect of the poem is heightened, however, by the title. And his "Elegy During a Convalescence" is different from all other elegies. While he is sick, the poet gets a letter telling him of the passing of an old, ill man whose death is neither unexpected nor grief-producing. The effect of the news on the poet is jumbled in with the sound of rain outside until he drifts off to sleep; when he wakes, he is "healed to true mourning as the bright dawn broke."

Near the end of *Two Sides of an Island* are two delightful poems: "On the Year's First Picnic," which plays around with Emerson's belief that "beauty is its own excuse for being" and with other ideas; and a lilting "Rake's Song," which builds skillfully to love's climax. But the final poem, "The Osprey," is far more provocative, for here at the end of the book is a loud, clear echo of its beginning. The honeymooners, like the swimmer in the title poem, are concerned with an island, this one being deserted and, if they care to pretend so, "undiscovered." But an osprey protecting her nestlings circles them; they pick up rocks to defend themselves, especially their faces, from the attack of her claws as

> . . . she banked off leftward
> and down, veered back
> And set bent watching beak and un-
> sheathed claws
> In orbit round and around the exposed
> sun's disc,
> Not twenty-five feet from our eyes.

The honeymooners vainly try to communicate to the hawk that they will not disturb the nestlings and that "there was room on this island for more than one/ Large love." She finally drives them to their skiff and away from the island. This poem is far different from another on a similar theme—Robert Frost's "Two Look at Two." Both Frost's and Halpern's worlds are complicated, but Halpern's is far less reassuring.

Two Sides of an Island is full of poetry that thinks rather than sings, but Halpern can be lyrical when he chooses. And his style is his own. If he is able to resolve enough of his dichotomies so that they do not become monotonous and if he can keep his pleasing variety of tone and subject matter, surely a distinguished future lies ahead.

Preston Newman

THE UNICORN

Author: Iris Murdoch (1919-   )
Publisher: The Viking Press (New York). 319 pp. $4.50
Type of work: Novel
Time: The present
Locale: An imagined part of England
An exciting story by a first-rate novelist whose concern with moral problems illuminates her art

> Principal characters:
> HANNAH CREAN-SMITH, who is confined to Gaze Castle
> PETER CREAN-SMITH, Hannah's absent husband
> MARIAN TAYLOR, the governess at Gaze Castle
> EFFINGHAM COOPER, in love with Hannah
> GERALD SCOTTOW, Hannah's "keeper"
> DENIS NOLAN, a pagan-like visitor at Gaze Castle
> MAX LEJOUR, a representative humanist, owner of Riders Castle

Anyone who thinks his conception of the novel, especially if it is a conventional one, *the* form a novel should follow, will not like *The Unicorn.* Others, who recognize that "the novel" is a flexible enough concept to include *Robinson Crusoe, Don Quixote, Pride and Prejudice, Ulysses, Point Counter Point,* and *The Castle,* will feel that *The Unicorn* is well worth the reading (though their huzzahs may not be loud). A vocal few will find *The Unicorn* (like *Finnegans Wake*) so happy a hunting ground for meanings within meanings that they will write long articles and perhaps books about it, for the novel certainly tantalizes, perplexes, or intrigues by its many ambiguities of meaning that are (as usual) rather too loosely tied to a plot that has enough material for the excitement of an Ian Fleming thriller. Most intelligent readers probably will, if they get past the first of the seven parts, continue to get the mitigated delight Iris Murdoch has offered in her preceding six novels—especially since they may know this novel will maintain, probably, her po-

sition as a peer of Angus Wilson and Muriel Spark, the two most exciting novelists to publish for the first time within the last decade.

Fortunately Miss Murdoch has stated explicitly what she intends her novels to do, as Granville Hicks pointed out in his excellent review in the *Saturday Review.* A "Christian fellow-traveller" with Sartre, an "existentialist at heart," she has been trying since her first novel, *Under the Net* (1954), to arrange about the still center of reality dances that reveal even what the philosophers call reality better than, say, her own excellent book about Sartre in 1953. Though reading all of her books fascinates more than it annoys by ineptitude, their overhurried following of one another has had too many ups and downs. Her first two novels. *Under the Net* and *Flight from the Enchanter* (1956) gave nearly pure delight, though the plots roamed as wildly as any picaro and the "truth" was expressed with such hilarious ambiguity that she could tell one reader he misinterpreted

281

Mischa Fox in *Flight from the Enchanter* and then say that she was not sure he was wrong.

Her novels preceding *The Unicorn* can be grouped more usefully than they can be ranked. In her two most distinctive novels, *Under the Net* and *Flight from the Enchanter*, partially in *The Sandcastle*, (1957) the mode is comic, though *The Sandcastle* and *The Bell* (1958) approach the conventional English traditional form most closely and are something of a bridge to her most recent manner. (One says this hesitantly since it has been said that the novels were not written in the order of their publication.) *A Severed Head* (1961), better on the stage than between hard covers because of its dependence upon pattern, *An Unofficial Rose* (1962), *The Bell*, and *The Unicorn* all apparently follow, too casually, the form of the traditional novel, but they always suggest a circling or dancing around metaphysical "truth" and an effort to catch it. If one comes to any of her last four novels with usual expectations, the most satisfactory are likely to be *The Bell* and *The Unofficial Rose*, *The Unicorn* the least. A tolerance for Kafka and Aldous Huxley and Rex Warner (in his early fiction) will help the reader to accept and therefore enjoy all of them.

In terms of plot simplicity, *The Unicorn* goes its intriguing, unbelievable course almost conventionally. There is the "interesting" counterpointing of sections that tell the search of Marian and Effingham for possession and knowledge of Hannah Crean-Smith, the centered figure about whom the action revolves. Marian, a "relative innocent," comes to Hannah and Gaze Castle without knowing what her real job is to be. Effingham, in love with Hannah and several other women, not unnaturally perplexed by his multiple relationships and his education, comes to see his old tutor and Hannah. The novel alternates between their points of view and an account of their actions.

Though exposition is too often crushed and the novelist takes less pains than either Huxley or Kafka or Sartre (whom she resembles as novelist also) in making the actions of the characters plausible, the activity is enough for several *Hamlets*. The story deals with homosexuality, heterosexuality, Hannah's husband's fall from a cliff and his miraculous survival, Hannah's death, fights, intrigues, a presumedly actual murder, and a murder one may presume to be actual. To talk about it more would confuse further rather than clarify what is actually an intriguing, imperfect fictional explanation of metaphysics to which the plot is necessary and to which it adds interest, even when it is managed imperfectly.

The reviewer cannot resist the temptation to suggest the meaning or meanings of the allegory that sometimes hides behind and sometimes obtrudes in this novel. Marian is untutored humanism seeking God; Effingham is sophisticated, dissatisfied humanism on the same search; Max is the wise, almost contented, humanist; Peter Crean-Smith, Hannah's husband, is either God or Christ (he is resurrected from death and his second coming is expected after the plot's disastrous climax); Jamesie and Violet Evercreech are everyman and everywoman; Denis Nolan is the masculine, pagan principle. Hannah may well represent something like man's anthropomorphic conception of God, Hardy's

282

unconscious will, the Anglican Church, or all three (even God and Christ seemingly upon occasion). These identifications suggest both the tantalizing Iris Murdoch succeeds at and her failure to avoid needless ambiguity. Perhaps this is to judge over-harshly a novel that suggests the search of a variety of representative schools of thought looking for a knowledge of the Prime Mover and still remains an arresting novel. The importantly representative search is plausible even if the characters often believe that their search has been fruitful only in that it has been valuable for its own sake. To the reader the search suggests that our own weak fantasies of a Willer (or Will) that may be only partially conscious may someday discover and contribute to a conception of a fully conscious Willer.

Miss Murdoch is endlessly an ambitious seeker, as The Unicorn shows best. Perhaps she should slow down, pack in less, write more carefully—advice that would apply equally well to Kafka, Huxley, and Sartre whom she resembles honorably. Cliché writing such as Hannah's "scarcely human cry of agony" is almost inexcusable as is her far too frequent use of "almost" dialogue such as Effingham's "Violet hates her," which is followed immediately by "No, Violet loves her. . . . But it comes to the same thing," is inexcusably paradoxical in anyone but Ivy Compton-Burnett, as is the too frequent banality of the conversation, exposition, and description. One often feels that Miss Murdoch should and could overcome her difficulty in bringing the passions the news her reason imposes through obscure symbolism and a too definitely imposed skeleton of ambiguity. One would like to see the ambiguity maintained, though within bounds, the free-wheeling of her first three novels retrieved and utilized even better. Still, each of her novels intrigues more than it upsets. One is certain that Miss Murdoch is on the track of something worth searching out even if it is unknowable, hopeful that the form that contains her complex ambiguity will be mastered. Finally, one is convinced that The Unicorn, or her least novel for that matter, is worth our while because it is always on the track of what the humanist, Max, quotes from Aeschylus:

Zeus, who leads men into the ways of understanding, has established the rule that we must learn by suffering. As sad care, with memories of pain, comes dropping upon the heart in sleep, so even against our will wisdom comes upon us.

For the tolerant reader who agrees with E. M. Forster that a novel is "a fiction of a certain length," such a quest dramatized is ample reward, especially since Miss Murdoch's dramatization sometimes makes us feel and always makes us think about ultimate moral and metaphysical problems.

Harvey Curtis Webster

V.

Author: Thomas Pynchon (1936-   )
Publisher: J. B. Lippincott Company (Philadelphia and New York). 492 pp. $5.95
Type of work: Novel
Time: The present and 1898-1919
Locale: Norfolk, New York, Alexandria (Egypt), Florence, German West Africa, Valletta (Malta)

A novel presenting the ancient and universal themes of mutability, loss, and eternal quest in terms of comic fantasy, metamorphosis, and triumphant American buoyancy

Principal characters:

BENNY PROFANE, a schlemiel and human yo-yo

HERBERT STENCIL, a young man searching for V. and his father's past

McCLINTIC SPHERE, a jazz musician

PAOLA MAIJSTRAL HOD, a deserted wife who assumes the role of Sphere's girl Ruby

SIDNEY STENCIL, an agent for the Foreign Office in search of V.

HUGH GODOLPHIN, explorer and discoverer of Vheissu

V., the eternal woman, the objective of every quest

Thomas Pynchon's *V.*, winner of the William Faulkner Foundation's award for 1963 as an "outstanding first novel," is in every way a novel of its time, of the 1960's. Kenneth Rexroth's essay, "Disengagement: The Art of the Beat Generation," seemed to define the pattern of the most obvious literary attitudes of the 1950's: disengagement from the world, transcendence through attention to and awareness of the self, and a "cool" oriental detachment and isolation which extended even into personal and intimate relations. McClintic Sphere, a jazz jusician in *V.* who is faced with the same confused conditions which led to the disengagement of the Fifties, realizes a different method of managing those conditions, an extension of the "cool" attitude:

. . . the only way clear of the cool/crazy flipflop was obviously slow, frustrating and hard work. Love with your mouth shut, help without breaking your ass or publicizing it: keep cool, but care.

With this novel, Thomas Pynchon joins the ranks of those novelists whose commitment is not to the hep or the cool nor to any system or theory beyond the necessities of literature itself, and *V.*, with such novels as Vladimir Nabokov's *Pale Fire*, George Garrett's *Which Ones Are the Enemy?* and those of Henry Green and Lawrence Durrell, is an artifact of the human spirit, a proper achievement of the human imagination in its own terms, those of art. This novel, then, like a painting or a sonata, is best appreciated for its texture, not its text; it uses the universal themes of literature —the quest for a lost vision of purity, mutability, the human desire for connection and communication—and shapes these into new forms and patterns, using devices as ancient and universal as the themes themselves: comic fantasy and metamorphosis.

V. is, at first glance, a novel with two plots, but Pynchon brings these two together thematically and, in the course of the novel, actually. One is an account of a group ("The Whole Sick Crew") of rootless people in New York, central among them, Benny Profane; the other consists of Herbert Stencil's attempts to re-create ("stencilize") the past of his father, Sidney Stencil, and his father's search for a mysterious woman known only as V. Eventually the two strands of the novel come together in Malta where both plots are resolved as much as any plot in the extra-realistic tradition can be. The Profane parts of the book remind one of Joseph Heller and the Stencil sections abound with echoes of Durrell, but the book is as fresh and unique as the works of either of those two writers and is certainly a more imposing achievement than Heller's overblown Catch-22.

The novel is unified, as all novels must be, by themes and techniques. If the novel is about a quest for a lost vision of purity, then it is concerned with the condition of living in a mutable world, a condition which, as Ovid noted in the opening lines of the Metamorphoses, is best presented artistically by metamorphosis, the telling of "things that change, new being out of old." In both plots, metamorphosis is a normal condition. In the "real" world of New York, characters shift from job to job, lover to lover, constantly seeking, seldom finding; McClintic Sphere's girl, Ruby, is really Paola Maijstral Hod, who finds her lost husband, Pappy Hod, and her father, Fausto Maijstral, on Malta where Stencil has taken her on his search for V., who had been encountered by Fausto Maijstral himself. In the Stencil sections, V. is a creature of change, appearing in a variety of forms: an English girl (Victoria), a saintly rat

(Veronica), Botticelli's Venus, a German trollop (Vera Monroving), the city Valletta, a lost country (Vheissu), an Italian woman of means (Veronica Manganese), a bad priest, and, of course, the Virgin herself.

But metamorphosis does not offer the sole pattern of the book, for the novel does have direction, a direction which is also a part of the theme of the quest. The past, to Stencil and to the reader, is richly colored, a time of action and life. The events of the past in which Stencil is interested occurred in Egypt (Alexandria, of course) and Florence, German West Africa and Malta, the sewers of New York, and Vheissu; the present is colorless by comparison. Life seems to be running down and becoming mechanical and artificial: even V. becomes less human and more mechanical, first with a false eye (inside of which was a tiny watch with "Darker green and flecks of gold . . . fused into twelve vaguely zodiacal shapes, placed annular on the surface of the bubble to represent the iris and also the face of the watch") and finally (as the bad priest) torn apart by children who reveal her to be completely artificial. ("Surely her arms and breasts could be detached; the skin of her legs be peeled away to reveal some intricate understructure of silver openwork. Perhaps the trunk itself concealed other wonders; intestines of parti-colored silk, gay balloon-lungs, a rococo heart.")

Unlike many English and European novelists (Arnold Bennett, Virginia Woolf, Marcel Proust, Claude Simon) who have been driven to despair or have concerned themselves with despair when they involved themselves with mutability and time, Pynchon is a writer in a very American tradition,

285

one which grows from the works of such disparate writers as Poe and Melville, Whitman and Faulkner, Nabokov and Stevens. Pynchon's characters are battered by experience, but they are not stopped. Profane, who has not learned anything from his experiences, finally finds a girl with whom he can run, hand in hand, into "the abruptly absolute night," and Stencil finds that the trail of V. does not end in the dismembered corpse in Valletta, but continues on. The novel ends, in every way, in the sea, a world of continual flux and change, but a world endless and perpetual.

Imagination is the guiding force of the world in *V.*, and it is imagination that gives the novel its life, that makes it more real than the "realistic" tradition. Along with *Pale Fire, Do, Lord, Remember Me,* and *Ship of Fools,* this novel marks a rebirth of true genius in American fiction, for these books are certainly the finest novels to appear in this country since Faulkner's novels of the early 1930's.

R. H. W. Dillard

VERDI
His Music, His Life and Times

Author: George Martin (1902-   )
Publisher: Dodd, Mead and Company (New York). Illustrated. 633 pp. $12.00
Type of work: Biography
Time: 1813-1901
Locale: Italy, France, England

A biography of Giuseppe Verdi which blends the history through which he passed with a discussion and analysis of the music he wrote

Principal personages:
GIUSEPPE VERDI
ANTONIO BAREZZI, a patron of music and Verdi's father-in-law
VINCENZO BELLINI, an opera composer
ARRIGO BOITO, an opera composer and one of Verdi's librettists
CAMILLO CAVOUR, an Italian nationalist leader
GAETANO DONIZETTI, an opera composer
MARGHERITA VERDI, Verdi's first wife
CONTESSA CLARA MAFFEI, the lifetime friend of Verdi
EMANUELE MUZIO, Verdi's secretary and pupil
POPE PIUS IX, known throughout the book as Pio Nono
GIUSEPPINA STREPPONI, Verdi's second wife
RICHARD WAGNER, Verdi's great musical competitor

Americans and Englishmen who are music lovers, but who happen to be untrained in music, have had no lack of good, non-technical books about Giuseppe Verdi. Francis Toye's excellent biography and operatic study has been readily available for more than thirty years. In the last eight years four fine and rather lengthy books on Verdi have appeared. In 1955, Carlo Gatti's austere and scholarly biography gave us the authoritative word of Italy's leading Verdi scholar. Vincent Sheean's enthusiastic and historically per-

286

ceptive *Orpheus at Eighty* (1958) was an exciting best seller. Frank Walker's, *The Man Verdi* (1962) tried to depict the subject "through the stories of his relationships with some of those who knew him best." This year, in covert recognition of the sesquicentennial of Verdi's birth, George Martin's, *Verdi, His Music, His Life and Times* has been published. What is the explanation for all of these books? It is, of course, the fact that the operas of Verdi are the core of the repertoire in any opera house in the United States and England. It is a fortunate fact, for Verdi was a consummate artist, clearly the equal of his great contemporary, Richard Wagner. Verdi's finest operas as well as the *Requiem* are unassailable as great art, and we should be thankful that they also appear to be enduringly popular.

Verdi was born in 1813 in Le Roncole, a small village in what was then the Duchy of Parma. His parents were peasants, and although he lived to be eighty-seven, enjoying many decades of fame and wealth, Verdi never freed himself entirely from his origins. Public attention never ceased to embarrass him. He often responded gracelessly to honors and awards, and he was impatient or angered with the demands which the world made on him as a famous artist. Verdi never lost the peasant's superstitious reverence for land, and as soon as his earnings permitted he purchased a farm in his local *paese*.

His father, Carlo Verdi, was among the first to recognize his son's musical abilities. He bought the boy a worn but still serviceable spinet when Giuseppe was only six years old and also arranged for him to learn to play the village organ. By the time he was ten, Verdi was Le Roncole's organist as well as a student in the nearby town of Busseto, where his family sent him to live. He studied music in Busseto for the next nine years and earned in the process the admiration of Antonio Barezzi, a moderately successful merchant and Verdi's future father-in-law. It was Barezzi's generosity and faith which sent the nineteen-year-old Verdi to Milan for further musical training with an aged but respected composer, Vincenzo Lavigna. At twenty-four, Verdi was a husband and father, Busseto's *Maestro di Musica*, a composer of six published songs, and the possessor of one unproduced opera, *Oberto*. This work had been rejected at Parma, but in Milan it came under the scrutiny of Bartolomeo Merelli, the impresario of La Scala, who was impressed by its musical qualities and willing to gamble on its success. The opera was produced on November 17, 1839. It was indeed a success with both the audience and the critics, and Merelli immediately offered to Verdi a contract for a new opera which the young composer was more than willing to sign. Without knowing it, in fact, Verdi had already succeeded as a composer, for he had proved that he could write exciting, appealing music which was also good theater.

Between 1840 and 1852 Verdi wrote sixteen operas. The worst of these, *Giovanni d' Arco, Alzira*, and *Attila*, are almost never performed and justifiably so. Only three, *Rigoletto, Il Trovatore* and *La Traviata*, are recognized as masterpieces. The others are solid, second-rate works with many pages of superb music and an abundance of memorable arias. At least half of them are still worth the expense of their production.

George Martin points out that these

287

early operas suffer frequently from silly plots and tawdry verses, but Verdi's ability to overcome these obstacles and maintain a quality of dramatic veracity, or rather, a valid thematic substance in the particular dramatic situation, has made them endure. This thematic substance is the notion that if good people had learned the truth sooner and had been able to act upon it, they would never have been overtaken by the tragic circumstances and events which invariably engulf them. Mr. Martin feels that the most interesting and certainly the most daring of these operas is *Macbeth*, in which, for the first time, Verdi employed melodic recitative extensively. Instead of traditional and expected climaxes of crescendos and fortes, the surprised audience was frequently led to climactic whispers and restrained tempi.

The most productive but not the happiest decade in Verdi's life ended in 1852; he later referred to these ten years as "the years in the galley." His fame was now world-wide, and foreign requests for new operas reflected the international popularity of his work. During the next two decades he wrote six operas, four of which had their *premières* outside Italy. *Les Vepre Siciliennes* (1855) and *Don Carlo* (1867) were first given in Paris, *La Forza del Destino* (1862) in St. Petersburg, and *Aida* (1871) in Cairo. He also participated in the making of the new Italian state as a member of its parliament, and he finally married Giuseppine Strepponi, his mistress of many years. *Aida*, his final opera of this period, came perilously close to being his last. The opera was, of course, fabulously successful from the beginning and it remains so. But Verdi, although adored by most of his fellow country-

men and besieged by publishers and impresarios, was growing keenly aware of the changes in musical composition and particularly the phenomenal impact of Wagner's work. Young Italian composers, of whom the most prominent was Arrigo Boito, nettled Verdi with their criticism that his recent works were either mostly poor and anachronistic or sometimes good because they were vaguely imitative of the German titan. Verdi winced angrily under this criticism ("A fine result after thirty-five years to wind up as an imitator!!!") and ceased composing operas. Although he was not deeply impressed by Wagner's music, he recognized that he must compose differently. Confronted with the difficult task of accommodating traditional Italian opera, which he had already greatly reshaped, to the new idiom of the music drama, he found his solutions to this problem in *Otello* (1887) and *Falstaff* (1893), both done as a septuagenarian and both serving as his two greatest achievements. But it took Verdi sixteen years to progress from *Aida* to *Otello* and another six to go from *Otello* to *Falstaff*. Meanwhile, he composed his *Requiem*, a work more dramatic than liturgical, but not operatic, in honor of the novelist and poet, Alessandro Manzoni, who died in 1873.

The final chapters of Mr. Martin's book are the most impressive. They are pervaded with the gloom and loneliness which increasingly surrounded Verdi as he came to know the meaning of outliving all of his companions and associates. Even the death of Pope Pius IX disturbed Verdi. The reactionary Pio Nono had ruled for thirty-two years, and Verdi, whom Mr. Martin classifies as an agnostic, wrote to his friend the Contessa Clara Maffei: "Everyone is dying! Everyone! And now the Pope! . . . Everything that he had done, good or bad, has helped the country. . . . So may this poor Pope have peace!" The contessa and Verdi's wife were his greatest comforts during these years. But they were even more important in a directly musical way. For it was they, along with Verdi's publisher Ricordi, who brought Verdi and Boito together.

Verdi was not easily persuaded to work with Boito. As Mr. Martin shows, he had not forgotten the criticisms which Boito had hurled at him earlier. When Boito first suggested their doing an opera based on a Shakespearian play, Verdi demurred. But he soon found that he could not easily resist Boito's intelligent and skillful scenario for a proposed *Otello*, nor his later libretto. Finally, the old man accepted the challenge. Verdi composed his great *Otello* with more than usual care and over a two-year period. The audience which came anxiously to the the *première* was not altogether certain that the seventy-three year old maestro would succeed. Mr. Martin, like the audience, like the critics, like young Arturo Toscanini who occupied a desk in the cello section on that evening, has agreed that he did succeed. The writer concludes that *Otello* is "the greatest of Italian romantic operas," and that Verdi achieved in it "the sort of musical drama at which he had aimed since *Macbeth*."

Falstaff followed in 1893. It was only Verdi's second comic opera, the first he had attempted since the conspicuously defective *Un Giorno di Regno* of 1840. Martin evaluates *Falstaff* as an opera with neither tunes nor recitative. The musical unit has become the "melodic phrase, which lasts only as long as the verbal phrase requires." It is a work of orchestral brilliance and musical and dramatic clarity despite its being verbally the most dense of Verdi's operas.

Verdi realized that *Falstaff* would be his last opera. He was in his eightieth year. He continued to compose, however, and his *Quatro Pezzi Sacri* is moving religious music filled with calm and resignation. In 1897 his beloved wife died, breaking the last link with his past as well as the most meaningful bond with his present. Gradually but perceptively he moved toward death. In January, 1901, Verdi suffered a stroke and died.

George Martin has, in his own words, "tried to present Verdi as a man and musician set firmly in the history of his times." He is therefore following the trend among Verdi biographers of writing a great deal about those things which might have shaped Verdi the man, but which had little discernible influence on Verdi's musical genius or his artistry. In fact, Mr. Martin has emphasized, more than any other biographer, extramusical factors, and he has amplified them to a questionable degree. His biography is, among other things, a short history of the Italian unification movement. It contains numerous long digressions on papal diplomacy, the Industrial Revolution, and international diplomacy. The crudities of the writing are sometimes shocking. ("She was in the unenviable position of being a prima donna with a failing voice, relatives and illegitimate children.") The crudities of his musical analysis are sometimes even more shocking. Verdi's pure melodies, conceived to express great sentiments, but notably free from saccharine sen-

timentality, are described as "catchy"
tunes. The rhythmic structure of the
Requiem's "Libera me," is compared to
"savages around a fire stamping away

their fears." But in spite of these surface defects the book remains instructive, enjoyable, and at times deeply
moving.

Philip Evanson

THE WAPSHOT SCANDAL

Author: John Cheever (1912-   )
Publisher: Harper and Row (New York). 309 pp. $4.95
Type of work: Novel
Time: The present
Locale: St. Botolphs, a New England town; Proxmire Manor, a Westchester suburb,
and Talifer, a missile research base

*A novel continuing the story of the Wapshot family as told in a variety of episodes
ranging from the realistic to the broadly farcical and the tragic*

> Principal characters:
> HONORA WAPSHOT, matriarch of the Wapshot clan, a Yankee indi-
> vidualist and an anachronism in the modern world
> COVERLY WAPSHOT, her good-hearted, well-meaning nephew, a
> public relations worker at the Talifer Missile Site
> BETSEY WAPSHOT, his wife, a woman of whims
> MOSES WAPSHOT, another nephew, a stockbroker and an alcoholic
> MELISSA WAPSHOT, his wife, a modern Circe disguised as a subur-
> ban matron
> EMILE CRANMER, the grocery boy who becomes Melissa's lover
> DR. LEMUEL CAMERON, the atomic scientist in charge of the Talifer
> Missile Site
> MR. APPLEGATE, the rector of Christ Church in St. Botolphs, also
> an alcoholic
> GERTRUDE LOCKHART, a Proxmire Manor matron driven to drunk-
> enness, promiscuity, and suicide by the failure of her house-
> hold appliances
> NORMAN JOHNSON, an agent of the Internal Revenue Service

"Change," says a character in one of
Willa Cather's novels, "is not always
progress." This seems to be John Cheever's opinion as well. Almost half a
century ago Miss Cather quietly offered the automobile as a symbol of the
standardization and mediocrity spreading across the American landscape. In
The Wapshot Scandal, a plot-loose and
fancy-free sequel to *The Wapshot
Chronicle,* Mr. Cheever shows the
world of the drive-in, the motel, the

supermarket, and the thruway to which
the automobile has brought us:

The Moonlite Drive-in was divided into three magnificent parts.
There was the golf links, the roller
rink and the vast amphitheater itself,
where thousands of darkened cars
were arranged in the form of an ancient arena, spread out beneath the
tree of night. Above the deep thunder from the rink and the noise from
the screen, you could hear—high in

the air and so like the sea that a blind man would be deceived—the noise of traffic on the great Northern Expressway that flows southward from Montreal to the Shenandoah, engorging in its clover leaves and brilliantly engineered gradings the green playing fields, rose gardens, barns, farms, meadows, trout streams, forests, homesteads, and churches of a golden past. The population of the highway gathered for their meals in a string of identical restaurants, where the murals, the urinals, the menus and the machines for vending sacred medals were uniform. It was some part of the autumn night and the hazards of the road that so many of these travelers pleaded for the special protection of gentle St. Christopher and the blessings of the Holy Virgin.

In the darkness of the amphitheater, on that same autumn night, four teen-agers sat naked in a parked car while they drank whiskey from paper cups and watched without interest a taste-less movie. ("I want to put on inno-cence, like a bright new dress," the ac-tress on the screen exclaimed. "I want to feel clean again.") The drive-in at night has become the sacred grove for youth's casual rites of love. Then, "Halfway through the feature, they got dressed and, with the cutout open and the radio blaring 'Take it Easy, Greasy,' roared out of the Moonlite onto the Ex-pressway, jeopardizing their lives and the lives in every car they passed (men, women and children in arms), but gentle St. Christopher or the mercies of the Holy Virgin spared them, and they got Émile safely home." This image of the careening car and its reck-less passengers stands close to the heart of Mr. Cheever's novel, for The Wap-shot Scandal is, among other things, a wryly comic fable of modern man's

inability to master his environment or to use his knowledge and the tools of his civilization for the improvement of himself and his society.

Like a number of his contemporaries who deserve to be called serious writers, John Cheever chooses to cast his fiction in the mold of comedy. In fact, the continuing presence of the comic spirit in the novels of the Fifties and the Sixties is a sign that a literary move-ment of sorts is under way. In no sense, however, are these writers to be thought of as a school, as that term is used in literary history and criticism. At the same time, collectively, they suggest that the comic vision may be the best angle from which to view the existen-tial concerns, hostile realities, and moral ambiguities of the world we live in today. (Wasn't it Kierkegaard who said that "the comic interpretation is always the concluding one"?) Tragedy instructs us in the nature of death, the Dionysian, fated end of man; but in a world darkly overshadowed by threats of violence and disaster tragedy has lost much of the meaning and force it held in earlier, more ordered times. Comedy, on the other hand, consoles us with the grace of innocence and the power of love for the cold fact of our mortality. This is its function in Mr. Cheever's novels and short stories where the comic vision is largely of a conditioning order, mediating between a quality of truth that life reveals and a quality of the imagination at work reshaping the familiar world into something strange and new.

Used in this manner, the comic mode serves Mr. Cheever's purposes ad-mirably. As a picture of the way we now live, The Wapshot Scandal is witty, sad, whimsical, outrageous, fan-tastic, rich in its flow of comic invention. As a novel, it is episodic, relaxed, modestly proportioned but generous in implication, precisely styled. Plainly, here is a writer with little patience for the closed point of view or the closed structure of the well-made novel. He works within an open form giving him greater opportunities for improvisation, relevance beyond mere reporting, and easy accommodation to the eccentric or the grotesque in human character and conduct. This freedom allows him to write about *almost* everything that falls within the scope of his observation, imagination, and talent. His effects are unpredictable. A situation may begin on a level of commonplace realism and then turn aside into a region of pure comedy, as on the two occasions when Miss Honora Wapshot disables a modern steamship, leaving it helpless and adrift, by plugging in her old-fashioned curling iron, or of nightmare such as Coverly Wapshot experiences in the old house haunted by his father's ghost. Fragments of myth and manifestations of the supernatural turn up in the most unexpected places. These matters are interesting in themselves as qualities of vision or devices of technique, but they do not explain Mr. Cheever's special power as a writer. That comes from the broader human significance achieved in his work by joining two forces usually not found together: an upward thrust of joy in man's fruitfulness, the promise of his continuity, and a sense of moral structure in the universe. His people are all veterans of the ancient conflict between "the head and the groin." In their efforts to define themselves, to communicate with one another, to find some road back into a past of innocence and promise, to face the future, they stand or fall simply because they are human, as vulnerable to the blunders,

absurdities, lusts, and cruelties of mankind as they are capable of goodness and compassion and brave commitment to life's portion of "some delight and some dismay." In John Cheever we confront a moralist. The characters in *The Wapshot Scandal* inhabit a wholly secular world, but to their creator the seven capital sins are still as real as they are deadly.

Like a navigator in offshore waters, Mr. Cheever takes three bearings on the chart of man's social and moral behavior. The first of these is St. Botolphs, an old Massachusetts river port giving the impression of permanence in the midst of change and providing a viable image of America's rural and maritime past. Here *The Wapshot Scandal* opens on Christmas Eve as carol singers are preparing to set out through falling snow that hides the dinginess of the old and the garishness of the new, and here it ends a year later with the Christmas dinner Miss Honora Wapshot had arranged, before her death, for eight inmates of the local asylum for the blind. Home of the Wapshots for generations, the town is also the setting for *The Wapshot Chronicle*. St. Botolphs is not an earthly paradise. As Mr. Cheever makes clear, it has its share of dishonesty, lewdness, drunkenness, and violent death. But within the traditional pattern of its life the worth and dignity of man are still possible. For this reason Mr. Cheever's first novel is a celebration, not of nostalgia for a lost and innocent past, but of those things that he finds continuing and meaningful in the human community: a sense of place, family ties, mortal love, the charms of memory, the lessons of the past.

Towering over that novel stands the lusty, almost legendary figure of old

292

Leander Wapshot. Descendant of men who had sailed around the world in the great days of the clipper ships, fought in their country's wars, and made love to girls they found in foreign ports or on the beaches of the Pacific islands, he has been reduced to ferrying a battered old launch to an amusement park across the bay and living on Cousin Honora Wapshot's charity. In his zest for life he is the guardian of tribal rituals and masculine skills. Because he believed that "love, death and fornication extracted from the rich green soup of life were no better than half-truths," he has, instead, taught his sons Moses and Coverly "to fell a tree, pluck and dress a chicken, sow, cultivate and harvest, catch a fish, save money, countersink a nail, make cider with a hand press, clean a gun, sail a boat." This knowledge leaves the boys poorly prepared for the world of status and competition in which they must live after they leave St. Botolphs to seek their fortunes. In them old Leander's sap of life flows to a slower pulse, but they take with them nonetheless a share of their father's belief that "the unobserved ceremoniousness of his life was a gesture or sacrament toward the excellence and continuousness of things." And they are the inheritors of a testament of living which is all that he, dying, has to give them:

Fear tastes like a rusty knife and do not let her into your home. Courage tastes like blood. Stand up straight. Admire the world. Relish the love of a gentle woman. Trust in the Lord.

In *The Wapshot Scandal* Leander's place has been taken by old Miss Honora Wapshot, a lesser figure but an indominatable woman marked by the same eccentricities that distinguish the older members of the Wapshot clan. For years she has ruled and bullied her family because she controls the purse strings. But she is capable of great kindness as well as arrogance, and after Moses and Coverly marry and father sons she settles a trust fund on both; her sense of family continuity and tradition is as strong as Leander's, but different. Miss Honora's world falls apart because she has never recognized the legality of paying income taxes in spite of the fact that her income is between seventy and a hundred thousand dollars a year. The uncle from whom she inherited her fortune had told her never to give money to the government and she has no intention of doing so. When the law finally catches up with her, in the person of an agent of the Internal Revenue Service, she flees to Europe with the money that the tax bureau claims. The agent follows her to Rome and there, in a final gesture, she gives away all she possesses, to nuns, clerks, musicians, pimps, salesmen, an American novelist, thieves, servants, and a dispossessed marquesa, while the revenue agent stands helplessly by and the voices of thousands call down blessings on their benefactress. "Money was filth and this was her ablution." Returned to St. Botolphs to await her trial, she hides herself in her great, empty house, drinks whiskey to keep up her spirits, and slowly starves herself to death.

Moses Wapshot works for "a shady brokerage firm" and he and his lovely wife Melissa live in Proxmire Manor, a smart, standardized community that is the second of Mr. Cheever's bearings. This is the world of suburbia, of the commuter's train, the station wagon, the mortgaged house, the country club,

293

the baby-sitter, the PTA, the cocktail parties and the Sunday golf. Like similar communities along the railroad line, it seems "to have eliminated, through adroit social pressures, the thorny side of life." Under the protective covering of gracious living, however, its citizens are haunted by specters of insecurity and guilt. This is the case with Gertrude Lockhart. Her downfall begins when the septic tank freezes and she finds herself in bed with the only workman she can hire to clear the clogged drains. She breaks a fingernail when she tries to open a package of bacon wrapped in a transparent wrapper. Then she turns up the thermostat and the furnace goes off. The electric washer breaks down, flooding the kitchen, and she waits three weeks for a repairman. The electric stove also goes and she is forced to cook on an electric plate. Meanwhile she drinks more and more while her promiscuous behavior becomes a neighborhood scandal. When the oil-burner breaks down again she goes into the garage and kills herself.

Gertrude Lockhart stands only on the edge of the action in *The Wapshot Scandal* but her story helps to illuminate the downward path followed by Moses and Melissa; Mr. Cheever seems to suggest that in a certain segment of our society morality is as much a part of some pattern of obsolescence as household appliances that break down and machines that wear out. Moses is the clever brother, touched by that early promise of success which often carries with it the seeds of failure. His story is quickly told, for it is contained in the memos, varying little from day to day, that Melissa finds in a table drawer: "12 noon 3 martinis. 3:20 1 pickmeup. 5:36 to 6:40 3 bourbons on train. 4

bourbons before dinner. 1 pint moselle. 2 whiskies after." Melissa's story is more complicated. Perhaps it begins with a neighbor's declaration that Gertrude Lockhart is a slut. At any rate her feelings of boredom and undefined desire lead to her infatuation with Emile Cranmer, a nineteen-year-old grocery delivery boy. Before long she is taking him on excursions to Nantucket and New York. Emile is by turn ardent and sulky, but always hungry. At the end of the novel the two are in Rome, where Melissa dubs English sound tracks into Italian films. Living with her youthful lover, she cultivates a girlish manner and dyes her hair. We catch our last glimpse of her in a Supra-Marketto Americano, and Mr. Cheever tells us "it is Ophelia she most resembles, gathering her fantastic garland not of crowflowers, nettles and long purples, but of salt, pepper, Bab-o, Kleenex, frozen codfish balls, lamb patties, hamburger, bread, butter, dressing, an American comic book for her son and for herself a bunch of carnations." Meanwhile she is chanting television commercials: "Winstons taste good like a cigarette should. Mr. Clean. Mr. Clean."

Mr. Cheever's third bearing takes us into the world of science and the nuclear age. Coverly Wapshot and his wife Betsey live in Talifer, a missile research and development center so secret that its name does not appear on any map and is never mentioned in public print. If *acedia*, or spiritual sloth, infects the citizens of Proxmire Manor, the people of Talifer are kept from normal human relationships by the shibboleth of security. No one visits; no one tries to be friendly. Betsey, her attention distracted momentarily from the television program she is watching,

294

sees a neighbor fall to his death while trying to remove a second-story storm window. She turns back to her program. "She had not wanted to do anything that would call attention to herself, that would involve giving testimony or answering questions." In this atmosphere tempers grow taut; Coverly and a neighbor come to blows over a garbage can. Betsey, a Southern girl with a desire for neighborliness, gives a party to which no one comes. Most of Talifer—offices, laboratories, missiles—is underground, beneath an abandoned farm that is a relic of the past and of a different way of life. Coverly, who has been trained as a taper, was through an error made by one of the computation machines, assigned to public relations when he was transferred to Talifer, and now the mistake is irrevokable. Sometimes he wanders over the old farm; it is there that a mysterious archer dressed in red shoots at him with an arrow. To pass the time he also runs the poems of John Keats through the computer to determine the word and frequency count. The result comes out as a machine-made poem: "Silence blendeth grief's awakened fall/The golden realms of death take all/Love's bitterness exceeds its grace/ That bestial scar on the angelic face/ Marks heaven with gall."

The presiding genius of Talifer is Dr. Lemuel Cameron, a man of vast scientific knowledge but a cultural and moral barbarian. Like Jove, he is the hurler of thunderbolts across the sky, but also like Jove, he is the victim of his own passions. His frequent trips to Italy are not to supply a missile for the Vatican but to sleep with a tart named Luciana. ("Oh, the wind and the rain and to hold in one's arms a willing love.") Dr. Cameron is scientifically

trained, intellectually arrogant, privately brutal, sexually obsessed. Ironically, the case against him and the threat he presents to all men of good will is voiced during a Congressional inquiry by an old man who is soon to die:

"We possess Promethean powers but don't we lack the awe, the humility, that primitive man brought to the sacred fire? Isn't it a time for uncommon awe, supreme humility? If I should have to make some final statement, and I shall very soon for I am nearing the end of my journey, it would be in the nature of a thanksgiving for stout-hearted friends, lovely women, blue skies, the bread and wine of life. Please don't destroy the earth, Dr. Cameron. . . . Oh, please, please don't destroy the earth."

The suggestion of myth, here casually presented, runs through *The Wapshot Scandal*, giving the novel a density and a breadth of implication it would otherwise lack. The search of Telemachus for the father, the descent into hell, Jove and his all too mortal loves—these are all identifiable, not presented directly but by hints of allusion and association that suggest the depth of human experience as well as its richness and variety. The most obvious use of this legendary material is also the most meaningful. The central office of the chain store where Emile Cranmer is employed has planned as a promotion scheme the distribution of one thousand Easter eggs on the lawns of St. Botolphs. All the eggs will contain a gift certificate, but five will be good for a three-week, all-expense vacation in London, Paris, Madrid, Venice, or Rome. Given the job of hiding the eggs, Emile is surprised by a sleepless housewife and before long he is pursued by women in nightclothes and hair-curlers. Ignoring their eager appeals, he dumps all of his eggs but one golden one. That, awarding its possessor a trip to Rome, he puts on Melissa's lawn. The apple of Eris, now changed to a golden egg, leads to an adulterous relationship less catastrophic but no less real than the love of Paris and Helen. This episode is more than simple foolery; it retells the ancient fable of man's surrender to the enchantress of his dreams.

In spite of the comic vision that enlivens and enriches much of *The Wapshot Scandal* the final impression of the novel would be one of sadness and despair if it were not for the account of the Christmas dinner at which Coverly the awkward, good-hearted innocent and Moses the alcoholic are hosts, according to Miss Honora's wish before her death, to eight guests from the home for the blind. These people, Coverly reflects, are likely to "know most about the raw material of human kindness":

A blow had been leveled at their sight, but this seemed not to be an infirmity but a heightened insight, as if aboriginal man had been blinded and this was some part of an ancient,

human condition; and they brought into the parlor with them the mysteries of the night. They seemed to be advocates for those in pain, for the taste of misery as fulsome as rapture, for the losers, the goner, the flops, for those who dream in terms of missed things—planes, trains, boats and opportunities—who see on waking the empty tarmac, the empty waiting room, the water in the empty slip, rank as Love's Tunnel when the ship is sailed; for all those who fear death.

On this note of compassion and faith the novel ends. Mr. Cheever does not blink at the violence and chaos of human existence. He accepts it and in the process he makes of its sad truths and little joys and great terrors a gift of the imagination. And as in *The Wapshot Chronicle* old Leander has the final say, for the narrator quotes a sentence found in Leander's wallet after his death: "Let us consider that the soul of man is immortal, able to endure every sort of good and every sort of evil." This is very much what Mr. Cheever has been saying all along in this novel which leavens his somber picture of human folly and failure with a comic vision capable of seeing also those consoling virtues that make life bearable.

Dayton Kohler

WHEN THE LEGENDS DIE

Author: Hal Borland (1900-   )
Publisher: J. B. Lippincott Company (Philadelphia and New York). 288 pp. $4.50
Type of work: Novel
Time: 1910-1940
Locale: Colorado, the Southwest, and New York

The story of a Ute boy who after a career as a big-time rodeo star realizes that he must return to the vital legends of his people in order to live on

Principal characters:

TOM BLACK BULL, as the reservation chaplain names him; BEAR'S FRIEND, as he calls himself; and KILLER TOM or DEVIL TOM, as the press categorizes him, an Indian who returns to the old way in order to preserve Ute ways

GEORGE BLACK BULL, his father who escapes white law only to be killed in an avalanche

BESSIE BLACK BULL, the resourceful widow who raises her son after the dream

BLUE ELK, an old Ute go-between who returns young Tom to "civilization" by trickery

JIM THATCHER, the friendly and loyal store owner who saves Tom's cub

RED DILLON, the gambling drunkard who trains the young Indian boy as a rodeo rider

MEO, a Mexican rider who runs the Dillon outfit and befriends Tom

BENNY GRAYBACK, the emancipated Indian who tries unsuccessfully to persuade the young Ute that reservation ways are best

MARY REDMOND, the competent nurse who tries again to convert Killer Tom

DR. FERGUSON, the surgeon who mends the broken rider's body and sees the deeper hurt

"Then he went out into the evening and up the slope a little way to a big rock where he could see Horse Mountain and Bald Mountain and the whole tumbled range of mountains. He sat there and watched the shadows darken into the valleys, and when the sun had set he whispered the chant to the evening. It was an old chant, a very old one, and he sang it not to the evening but to himself, to be sure he had not forgotten the words, to be sure he would never again forget." Tom Black Bull has returned from a pilgrimage of evil accommodation to ways forged against his inner will, and Bear's Friend speaks from the depths of ancient memories and tribal history. The new journey must soon begin, that of acting as a missionary to his own people, of calling upon them to remember the old ways. But the Ute brave must first sing all the old songs, especially the morning song in the chill ablutionary mountain waters, and prepare himself for his great task. This is the way the novel ends, the answer Hal Borland has his protagonist bring to the existentialist climate of today. With Jungian vision he sets out

297

to retrace tribal ways, to keep alive racial memory. "When the legends die, the dreams end. When the dreams end, there is no more greatness." On this great theme is this novel founded, only occasionally to falter.

Of the four parts of the novel, the poetic first and last are strongest. In "Bessie" the Ute family of three, escaping from the alien world of reservation justice, dwindles to one. In "The School" that one, Tom, learns all there is to know of treachery and vindictiveness, blandly from the whites and covertly from his own people. "The Arena" tells not only of the rodeo where he is the master of the methods learned but also of the place where he fights down his conscience. Finally, in "The Mountains," he stalks his own childhood as Bear's Friend and as Black Bull he tries to kill the last grizzly of the Rockies (perhaps his own cub of so many years ago). The hatred dying out of him, hatred in which he had killed ten rodeo horses in savage fury at his self-betrayal, he drops the sight of his rifle and fixes on his future, not among the alien corn but in the maize of his ancestors.

George Black Bull, in 1910, responded to the call of the wilderness and illegally hunted the open ranges of southern Colorado. Forced to return to the reservation or a lumber camp, he chose the latter for his family so that he might save up money to go back to the mountains. After Frank No Deer robbed him three times of the money which would have paid off contractual debts to the company store, George killed him and escaped to the mountains where Bessie and young Tom joined him. There he set up a lodge in the old way, but there, too, he met the ancient death by an avalanche of snow while hunting. Bessie took up his hand-crafted weapons, remembered all the ways of survival, and passed these skills and knowledge along to her son, who later amazed his school teachers especially with his artistic adroitness in basket weaving. After her death the boy, who had been allowed to choose his own name of Bear's Friend by identifying himself with this ancient symbolic animal order and saving an orphaned cub, returned to the village remembered from annual excursions with Bessie. Jim Thatcher, the storekeeper only too glad to receive the fine baskets of mother or son, saved the twelve-year-old's cub and prevented Blue Elk from capturing the breech-clouted "savage." Nonetheless, Blue Elk, who would have betrayed Tom's father and attempted to extort money from his mother for supposed protection, trails the boy to his lodge, prevails on him to return to the reservation on the pretext of bringing back the legends, and sells Bear's Friend into the bondage of civilization. From there on Benny Grayback takes over, persuades the boy to give up the cub and the old ways, but betrays his confidence as did Blue Elk. Tom runs away, but he eventually comes to understand the greatest treachery—the stealing of his tools and weapons, the burning of his lodge, the destruction of his values are only stages—is within himself as it is within all Utes who have managed to live under such servile conditions.

There is little wonder that his energies and hatreds lead him to accept Red Dillon's blandishments of fame and fortune through "throwing" bronco rides in small Southwestern rodeos. Red merely extends the system Tom has already learned: get yours before you're got. Meo, however, with the instinctive wisdom of his Mexican origins, mocks his young friend with the taunt that like a little bean he wants to make a big rumble. Tom Black Bull from that moment refuses to cheat in his riding and becomes Demon Tom who rides horses to their death, pitting his own savage retribution against malicious brute force. Red Dillon sees the justice of his protégé's actions, even though he loses his control over what he thought would be a fortune. Tom, remaining loyal to both Red and Meo, pays for the former's illness and death and observes the latter's buying his quiet end with money "liberated" from the drunken Dillon. Then he burns the ranch house and barns as a ritual sacrifice to that phase of his life which taught him self-reliance through cruelty. He works the big rodeos, buys expensive clothes and cars, and follows his fortunes to Madison Square Garden. In this section the novel becomes melodrama and journal-ism, an attempt to describe the final ride of the renowned, even infamous, Ute horse killer, a description presented in ritualistic terms. As he witnesses Tom's recovery from his many wounds and breaks, his physician, Dr. Ferguson, recognizes the smoldering independent nature behind the taciturn, even boorish, Indian and gives him a chance to walk but never ride again. Constantly returning to the nightmare world of his rise and fall, Mary Redmond, his nurse, almost persuades him to become domesticated. But he sees her finally as Blue Elk, Benny, Red, and all the others who had robbed him of his identity, and by an effort of will born of his final frustrations, he walks and then rides—on a domesticated sheepherder nag. In the quiet of the mountain meadows his hatreds resolve and at last he sees them as self-destroying. This is true revelation, the return of the native to the ancient wisdom.

William Tillson

WILLIAM FAULKNER
The Yoknapatawpha Country

Author: Cleanth Brooks (1906-   )
Publisher: The Yale University Press (New Haven). 500 pp. $7.50
Type of work: Literary criticism

A distinguished critic surveys the art of William Faulkner as it is revealed in the setting, characters, manners, and morals of the life presented in the novelist's imaginary Yoknapatawpha County

When William Faulkner's first books appeared, the reviewers, even the hostile ones, were quick to note the richly varied texture of his style, his daring but often baffling experiments in form, the effects of apocalyptic terror or grotesque humor sharply realized in the stories he told. What they failed to see at the time was the strong sense of place distinguishing his fiction, giving it unity and design. Faulkner's roots were deeply regional from the beginning, and in a period when most of his contemporaries were off to the Left Bank or the bullfights in Spain he stayed at home to take a single Mississippi county as his measure of the world. Everything he found there he set down with passion and fury, in prose that he made the equivalent in language of the landscapes and seasons he described: "opaque, slow, violent, shaping and creating the life of man in its own implacable image." His vision one of social ruin and moral decay, he seized upon a place and its people with boldness of imagination that showed him to be anything but a local colorist or a Southern realist in the naturalistic tradition. The result was that critics, identifying his themes of violence and horror with the larger pattern of his work, tagged him as a later-day Poe or another Ambrose Bierce, a craftsman whose literary stock in trade was a deliberate and callous aesthetic of shock.

This line of approach served its purposes of plausibility and convenience. Among other things it accounted for Miss Emily Grierson's dingy frame house where a man's skeleton lay moldering in the dusty bridal bed, the holocaust that ended Sutpen's great and impossible dream of founding a plantation dynasty, the atmosphere of doom hanging over families like the Sartorises and Compsons. Somehow these matters seemed all the more impressive because they were set against a Mississippi countryside whose solidity and fidelity to the familiar world in all lights and weathers were brought vividly to life with every reality of sight and sound—the town of Jefferson, built on a square mile of land a Chickasaw chief deeded to Jason Lycurgus Compson in exchange for a racing mare in 1822; Colonel John Sartoris' railroad line; the rutted, dusty roads, back-country store, and dilapidated plantation house near Frenchman's Bend; eroded pine hills with

weathered farmhouses and sparse corn patches set among the trees; bottom-land fields with stunted cotton growing to the dooryards of Negro cabins; and beyond the remnant of the wilderness where the men of Jefferson went to enact the yearly ritual of the hunt.

Actually, Faulkner was writing about two Mississippis. Like those novelists who make the greatest and most serious claims on our attention, he was reporting one world to establish the truth of fact and creating another to reveal some truth of the imagination. For the author is also the *auctor*, "he who adds." Within, and sometimes against, the factuality of things as they are he builds a local reality of his own, a society reduced in scale and meaningfully displayed, for which the real world provides a frame of geographical, historical, social, or moral reference; and if he is skillful enough, his image of life rearranged and filled with meaning may challenge the actual world in validity and dramatic vigor. Faulkner inhabited two such worlds. One was the very real Lafayette County to be found on any map of Mississippi. As a citizen of Oxford, the county seat, this was the place where he "belonged." The other was his legendary Yoknapatawpha County, its geography and people an imaginary construct of man in time and place, its county seat, Jefferson, the center of a moral universe. This is the fictional world he created out of private vision and need, and he was, as he subscribed himself, its "sole owner & proprietor." The best of his novels and short stories have this mythical country for background, a tract of 2,400 square miles lying between the Tallahatchie and Yoknapatawpha rivers in northern Mississippi. There his imagination was completely at home, and the region, painstakingly mapped and landmarked, is as real in every physical and social detail as Trollope's Barset or Hardy's Wessex. At the same time, no place in American fiction has been presented in more somber aspects of history and doom.

Faulkner, who belonged to a generation conditioned by the violence of war, found its counterpart in the life of his own region, which for years had been living with the effects of violence inherited from the frontier situation, the institution of chattel slavery, and the devastation of fratricidal conflict. Scenes and images of horror haunt our minds after we put his books aside: Popeye's violation of Temple Drake and Red's murder in *Sanctuary*, Benjy's idiocy and Quentin Compson's suicide in *The Sound and the Fury*, the history of violence ending only with the burning of Sutpen's Hundred in *Absalom, Absalom!*, and the weak-minded Snopes who fell in love with a cow in *The Hamlet*. There is implied violence even in the social cleavages of his region, among gone-to-seed descendants of the Sartoris and Compson families; the landless, grasping Snopeses who rose from bushwhacking and storekeeping to become the bankers and politicians in the new South; farmers from the hill country and poor-white sharecroppers; and Negroes living in tension with the "race which for two hundred years had held them in bondage and from which for another hundred years not even a bloody civil war would set them free." No other writer has given us so many instances of murder, suicide, rape, incest, miscegenation, and idiocy, for the signs of decay are in Faulkner's people as well as in the surroundings and circumstances of their lives.

Anyone who has read Faulkner carefully, however, will discover that the violence of his milieu is only part of his subject, never its final effect. Specifically, his subject is the destruction of the old order in the South and the further corruption of the descendants of that order by a ruthless and competitive industrial society. As a Southern writer he was committed to the historical predicament of his region; as a serious writer he explored its social and moral implications. Because he chose to present his findings in parallels of history and myth, not in social tracts thinly disguised as fiction, he often misled those critics who read him carelessly or naïvely. The writer we read today is a figure quite different from the earlier conception of Faulkner as the heir of the Gothic tradition, for he stands in the succession of those older novelists—Hawthorne, Melville, James—who reflected in fable and symbol man's haunted inner world of thought and feeling. His writing is ancestral in its troubled musings on the condition of man under the burden of history with its accumulated heritage of enmity, hatred, greed, and guilt, and it is prophetic because he gives us glimpses of the future taking shape under the impact of the past upon the present. Faulkner's Yoknapatawpha setting is more than the microcosm of the South that some have called it. It is a compass point on the geography of human fate.

There are many ways into the Yoknapatawpha world, but the course taken by Cleanth Brooks is the most recent and the best if we are interested in what Faulkner actually *wrote*. (Many critics, preferring their own notions of what he *intended* to say, are

301

not.) Mr. Brooks' method is so simple as to be revolutionary, a method all the more remarkable because in the past he has brought to the survey of any literary work the techniques of analysis and interpretation rather inaptly called the New Criticism. In his discussion of the thirteen novels making up the Yoknapatawpha chronicle he goes on the assumption that Faulkner knew what he was about, that each novel is a self-contained unit in which the novelist's meanings are clearly apparent in his strategy with theme, character, and form. (The novel *is*; only the critic explains.) As a study of Faulkner's powerful, complicated, and often ambiguous art, this book, the first part of a two-volume work, is both an excellent guide and a corrective to the unique and formidible bulk of Faulkner criticism. This is as it should be if we are to see Faulkner once more in proper perspective. During the last fifteen years of his life the novelist and his books were subjected to the most intense and varied scrutiny ever given to a living writer. Almost everything that literary history, criticism, philosophy, psychology, sociology, and anthropology have taught us in the past was employed in the process. The result was a mass of critical writing that is for the most part misleading or irrelevant. How hard it is to see Faulkner plain is shown in the opening chapters of Mr. Brooks' study, where we see him hacking his way through the undergrowth of Faulknerian criticism in an effort to clear away misconception and error. His chief indictment is against the sociologists and the symbol-seekers: those who discuss Faulkner as if his work represents "a surreptitious commerce between sociological-historical fact and fictional meaning" and those who re-gard the Faulkner novel "as a sort of grab bag out of which particular symbols can be drawn" with no regard for the larger context of theme or drama of human relationships within the book itself. The need to refute the false or expose the ridiculous is in a way unfortunate, for it causes Mr. Brooks to retrace much ground already familiar to those who have read Faulkner with close attention to the texts.

The task to which Mr. Brooks set himself is indicated by the ample proportions of his book. The introductory chapters are concerned with the position of the provincial writer, with interesting parallels drawn between Faulkner's Mississippi, Frost's New England, Hardy's Wessex, Yeats' Ireland, and Dylan Thomas' Wales; the place of the plain people—yeoman farmers, sharecroppers, and white trash —in Faulkner's fiction; and the poetry of nature that infuses so much of his work. From these Mr. Brooks turns to the novels themselves. Here his method of organization is indicated in his chapter titles: "The Community and the Pariah" (*Light in August*), "The Old Order" (*The Unvanquished*), "The Waste Land" (*Sartoris*), "Discovery of Evil" (*Sanctuary* and *Requiem for a Nun*), "Odyssey of the Bundrens" (*As I Lay Dying*), "Faulkner's Savage Arcadia" (*The Hamlet*), "Passion, Marriage, and Bourgeois Respectability" (*The Town*), "Faulkner's Revenger's Tragedy" (*The Mansion*), "The Story of the McCaslins" (*Go Down, Moses*), "The Community in Action" (*Intruder in the Dust*), "History and the Sense of the Tragic" (*Absalom, Absalom!*), "Man, Time and Eternity" (*The Sound and the Fury*), and "The World of William Faulkner" (*The Reivers*). Then comes a gener-

302

ous section of notes ranging from matters of disputed interpretation to the exact chronology of several of the novels and a full explanation, reduced to bookkeeping entries, of Ratliff's complicated transaction with Flem Snopes following the sale of a sewing machine to Mink Snopes. Another section gives the genealogical tables of the Compson, McCaslin, Stevens, Sartoris, Sutpen, and Snopes families. One index is devoted to the characters appearing in all of Faulkner's novels and short stories, another to the book at hand. At the end Faulkner's map of Yoknapatawpha County is reproduced from *Absalom, Absalom!* as an aid in locating the events with which the novels deal. Here, in other words, is something for everybody, from the reader coming to Faulkner for the first time to the scholar whose chief interests are criticism and research.

Mr. Brooks' purpose in this book, as he states, was "to determine and evaluate the meaning of the work in the fullness of its depth and amplitude." His proposed second volume, he announces, will "concentrate on Faulkner's development as an artist—his beginnings, the forging of his style, and the working out of the special fictional techniques associated with his name."

Surveying the Yoknapatawpha novels, Mr. Brooks finds that they rest on the idea of the community—its traditions, social groupings, and morality as represented by those descended from "the Anglo-Saxon, the pioneer, the tall man, roaring with Protestant scripture and boiled whiskey." This conception of the community is wide enough to take in the farmers of Frenchman's Bend, the townspeople of Jefferson, the lawless Gowries, and the shiftless poor whites, as distinguished from the

plantation aristocracy and the Negroes. In Mr. Brooks' view, Faulkner saw the community joined by a "common tradition and a common community of feeling" because it is "at once the field for man's action and the norm by which his action is judged and regulated." For this reason Mr. Brooks begins his discussion of the Yoknapatawpha novels with *Light in August,* the novel in which every major character is an exile or an outcast from community feeling and action. Joe Christmas is separated because of his inability to define or vindicate himself as a man, Joanna Burden by her carpetbagging background, Doc Hines by his fanaticism, Percy Grimm by murderous choice, Hightower by his immersion in martial fantasy. Even Lena Tower is outside the community because she is a wanderer, a sojourner. Having stated his case, Mr. Brooks then discusses the other novels and relates them on a variety of levels to his original premise of the community image on which Faulkner's novels rest. Along the way he uncovers fresh relevances and insights that open new avenues of investigation or appreciation in the reading of Faulkner. Here are some samples:

Of *Light in August:* ". . . the mode is that of comedy. To say so in the light of some of the terrible episodes may seem perverse. But Faulkner's comedy is frequently a makeweight to the terrible. The tender-minded reader may feel that Faulkner frequently uses a savage humor, but his is never a cynical and nihilistic humor. Its function is to maintain sanity and human perspective in a scene of brutality and horror."

Of *As I Lay Dying:* "Man's capacity to spend himself in a cause is always a remarkable thing and nowhere more so than when it springs from an unlikely soil and when it is not aware that it is remarkable."

Of The Hamlet: "In almost any other writer the symbolic tableau on which the curtain descends would be much too pat . . . but Faulkner keeps our attention upon the body of his world—its sights, smells, and sounds, the gestures and postures, the quality of the folk community which is so far removed from our own that it seems simple to the point of fabulousness, and yet which is in its essence so thoroughly and humanly ourselves that we continue to believe in it and find ourselves reflected in it."

Of The Mansion (surprisingly): "The novel is concerned even more than most Faulkner novels with the notion of honor."

Mr. Brooks' study is not without its flaws. For one thing, he tends to oversimplify, so that we miss in his discussions that effect of unresolved complication which we find in Faulkner's fiction. Although he tends to discredit parallels, he is not above drawing one of his own when he invokes the conception of romantic love described in Denis de Rougemont's Love in the Western World in order to explain Gavin Stevens as "a countrified descendant of Sir Tristan." Again, he makes a good case when he says that Absalom, Absalom! is Faulkner's best novel, but many readers will not agree with his choice, even though they may accept his argument that Sutpen represents that strange kind of American innocence which puts its trust in "rationality—an overweening confidence that plans work out, that life is simpler than it is."

But these qualifications do not add up to much against a book in which Mr. Brooks has given us so much that is lucid, insighted, and spoken with sense both common and critical. His summing up is worth noting:

Taken together, the Yoknapatawpha novels and stories create for us an amazingly rich and intricate world, and one that embodies its own principles of order. The human society there depicted shows the influence of the physical land and the climate. Even the town dwellers of Jefferson have not broken their ties with the land. Moreover, the society of Jefferson and Yoknapatawpha has its location in time as well as space. It bears a special and significant relation to history. It has a sort of collective memory. Because it does, it can see itself in a dramatic role. It embodies a style of life. Most of all, this society is bound together by unspoken assumptions—that is to say, it is a true community. Its members are related to each other not merely by function but by common loves, hates, and fears. The fact that it is provincial does not prevent its serving as an excellent mirror of the perennial triumphs and defeats of the human spirit. Nor does that fact insulate it from the great world outside. The special problems of modern man, on occasion, make their appearance within it, and their modernity is the more sharply defined by being set off against the concrete particularity of its old-fashioned order.

There are few who would disagree with this judgment or with Mr. Brooks' final statement that "Faulkner's work speaks ultimately of the possibilities and capacities of the human spirit for finding and embodying good."

Dayton Kohler

304